English Literature:

1800 TO 1900
Second Edition

Arthur H. Bell, Ph.D., and Bernard D. N. Grebanier, Ph.D.

BARRON'S

All inquiries should be addressed to:
Barron's Educational Series, Inc.
250 Wireless Boulevard
Hauppauge, New York 11788

Library of Congress Catalog Card No. 94-13989
International Standard Book No. 0-8120-1678-5

Library of Congress Cataloging-in-Publication Data

Bell, Arthur H. (Arthur Henry), 1946–
    English literature : 1800 to 1900 / by Arthur H. Bell and Bernard D. N.
Grebanier. – 2nd ed.
        p.   cm. – (College review series)
    Includes index.
    ISBN 0-8120-1678-5
    1. English literature—19th century—Examinations—Study guides.
2. English literature—19th century—Outlines, syllabi, etc.
I. Grebanier, Bernard D. N., 1903 –   . II. Title. III. Series.
PR451.B45   1994   94-13989
820.9'008—dc20   CIP

Printed in United States of America
4567 9770 987654321

PREFACE

The nineteenth century was, for most of its decades, the century of Queen Victoria. But little in the literature of the century seems "Victorian," in our perhaps unjust use of the term. For here is a century of almost constant innovation, experimentation, and reformulation. Beginning with the Romantic revolution in taste and manners at the beginning of the century, significant cultural changes can be observed year by year not only in the life of England but in the lives of its authors. Although the literature of the nineteenth century often seems optimistic in contrast to twentieth century literature, there are the seeds of a dark tone and spirit in the so-called demonic poems of Coleridge (including "Kubla Khan" and "Christabel"), the expressions of loss and despair in Tennyson, and the brutal ironies at the center of Hardy's novels and poetry. The literary richness of the nineteenth century also included an ever-increasing number of women writers such as Christina Rossetti, Elizabeth Barrett Browning, and the Brontë sisters. Philosophy, biology, history, and theology joined forces (or, just as often, locked horns) in social debates surrounding such works as Darwin's *Origin of the Species* and Newman's *Idea of a University*.

The serpentine path of literary events and personalities in the nineteenth century is fascinating and almost dizzying in its rises, falls, and sudden turns. As in the volumes treating other periods of English literature, we have endeavored here to focus on the particular whenever possible and to avoid generalizations about periods, beliefs, and tendencies. Reading the works discussed here inevitably would undo such generalizations. The English writers of the nineteenth century were above all individualists, often to the point of eccentricity. As a group they defy summarization.

Readers should note that this edition has been revised considerably, not only in content but by the addition of new features. For example, Review Questions appear at the end of each part as an aid to study, Works at a Glance appear at the beginning of each part, and a Chronology appears at the front of the volume.

The best preparation, of course, is to read as widely as possible in the literature of this exciting and often perplexing century. To that end, we have identified for each author the major works that have stood the test of time into our century. We have also touched upon the highlights of the life stories of these authors, some of whom lived at a level of intensity unmatched even in their writing.

San Francisco, California   *Arthur H. Bell*
March 1994   *University of San Francisco*

From
PREFACE TO THE FIRST EDITION

For the understanding and appreciation of so rich a literature as England's some idea of the history of that literature is necessary. Only when a given work is apprehended in correct perspective can its maximum of meaning be extracted. And that perspective involves an acquaintance with the temper and tendencies of the times as well as a conception of the position the work occupies in literary tradition. It is these needs which the present study undertakes to supply. In addition, the author feels that some basic information of the historical events of the time must be in the possession of the sincere student—and this too is herein provided. Moreover the summaries of major works found in these pages should smooth the road for the reader who goes directly to the work itself. Naturally, the most extensive consideration is accorded to the most important writers. The careers of Wordsworth, Coleridge, Byron, Shelley, Keats, Tennyson, and Browning, for instance, are given more particular attention than those of writers like Cowper, William Morris, or Francis Thompson.

In short, [this series] is intended to act as a reliable and sufficiently complete guide to reading the major as well as the minor writers who have made English Literature. The information which anthologies too often omit it proposes to make available.

Naturally, a history of literature can justify itself only to the extent that it succeeds in inviting its readers to study and enjoy the literature described. Nothing said in this volume can be a substitute for the actual reading of English poetry and prose. The author has little sympathy with that company of "scholars" which is familiar with literature by date and title only. On the other hand, he hopes that the student of English Literature will find in this book much of the assistance required for sound reading, as well as enough pregnant suggestion to encourage the formation of individual judgment and opinion. The only way to develop literary taste is to read the best that has been written, and to know what to look for in what is read. Above all, it is hoped that these ensuing pages will make quite clear which writings, amidst the bewildering variety of English Literature, are essential to read.

The author wishes to express his profound gratitude to Professor Vincent F. Hopper of New York University for going through every line of the manuscript before it was published, and for making many valuable suggestions.

The author wishes also to thank Mr. Seymour Reiter, late on the staff of Yale University and Athens College, for inspiring assistance and criticisms in the reading of proof.

Brooklyn, New York   *Bernard D. N. Grebanier*
October 15, 1948   *Brooklyn College*

CONTENTS

Part 1
PRE-ROMANTICISM AND ROMANTICISM

Part 2
THE VICTORIAN AGE

Part 3
LATE CENTURY EXPERIMENTATION

CHRONOLOGY OF ENGLISH HISTORICAL

ENGLISH HISTORICAL EVENTS

Nelson's victory at Trafalgar 1805

War of 1812 1812

Napoleon's defeat at Waterloo 1815

Death of George III; George IV crowned 1820

Combination Wage Laws 1825

Catholic Emancipation 1829

William IV crowned 1830

First Reform Act 1832

Beginning of Queen Victoria's reign 1837

Irish revolt 1848

Great Exhibition 1851

Death of Blake 1827

Adonais 1821

Keats's Odes 1819

Vanity Fair 1847

Death of Wordsworth 1850

Childe Harold's Pilgrimage 1812

Prometheus Unbound 1818

Sartor Resartus 1833

In Memoriam 1849–50

Preface to Lyrical Ballads 1800

Kubla Khan 1816

Castle Dangerous (Scott's Last Novel) 1831

David Copperfield 1849

ENGLISH LITERARY EVENTS

AND LITERARY EVENTS

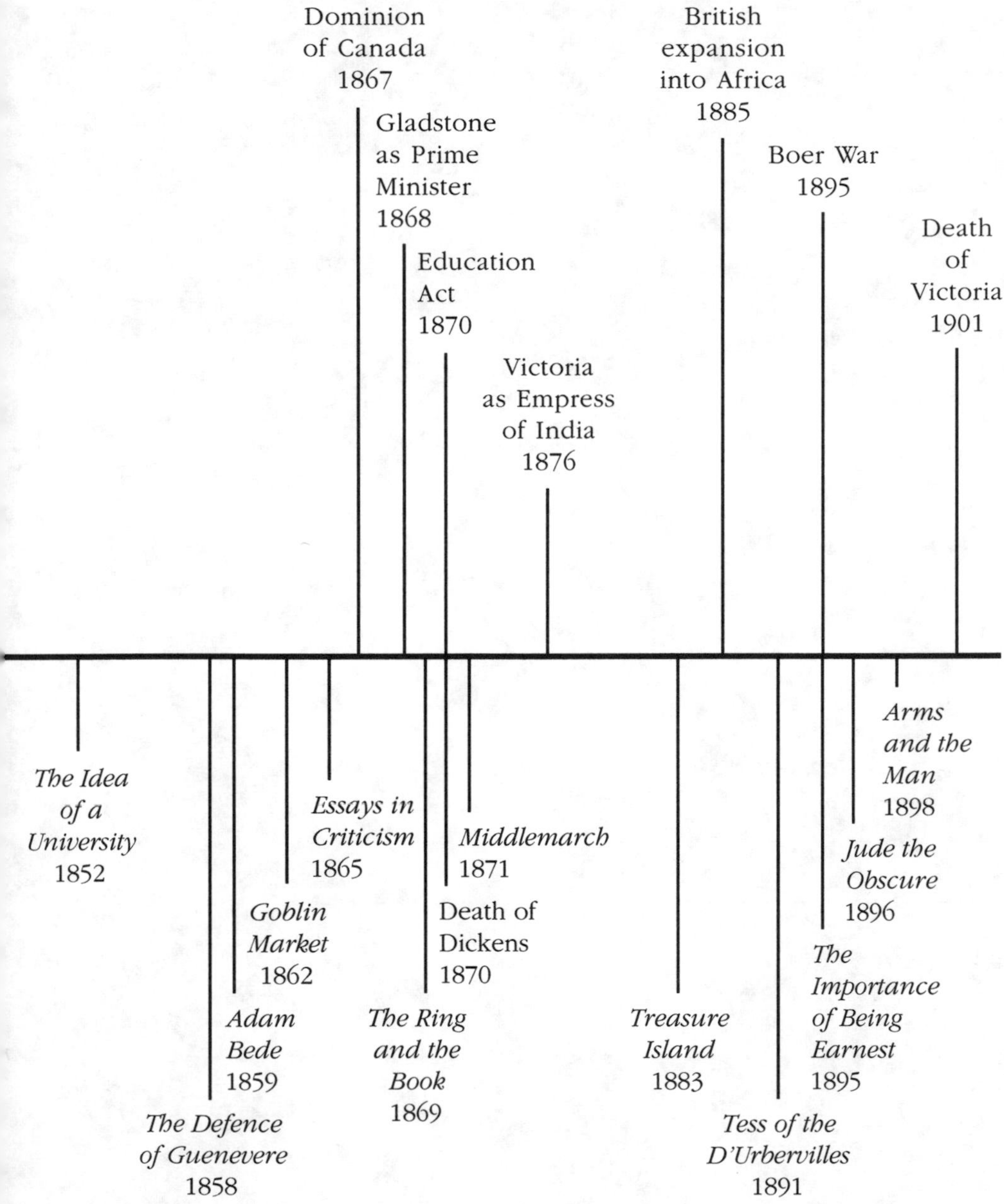

Dominion
of Canada
1867

British
expansion
into Africa
1885

Gladstone
as Prime
Minister
1868

Boer War
1895

Education
Act
1870

Death
of
Victoria
1901

Victoria
as Empress
of India
1876

*The Idea
of a
University*
1852

*Arms
and the
Man*
1898

*Essays in
Criticism*
1865

Middlemarch
1871

*Jude the
Obscure*
1896

*Goblin
Market*
1862

Death of
Dickens
1870

*The
Importance
of Being
Earnest*

*Adam
Bede*
1859

*The Ring
and the
Book*
1869

*Treasure
Island*
1883

*The Importance
of Being
Earnest*
1895

*The Defence
of Guenevere*
1858

*Tess of the
D'Urbervilles*
1891

Part *1*

PRE-ROMANTICISM AND ROMANTICISM

WORKS AT A GLANCE*

James Thomson

1726	*Winter*	1736	*Liberty*
1727	*Summer*	1740	*Alfred*
1728	*Spring*		"Rule, Britannia!"
1730	*Autumn*	1748	*The Castle of Indolence*
	The Seasons		

Thomas Gray

1742	"Ode on the Spring"	1751	"Elegy Written in a Country
1743	"Hymn to Adversity"		Churchyard"
1747	"Ode on a Distant Prospect	1753	*Six Poems*
	of Eton College"	1757	"The Progress of Poesy"
1748	"Ode on the Death of a		"The Bard"
	Favorite Cat, Drowned in a	1761	"The Fatal Sisters"
	Tub of Goldfishes"		"The Descent of Odin"

William Collins

1742	*Persian Eclogues*	1749	"Ode Occasioned by the
1746	*Odes on Several Descriptive*		Death of Mr. Thomson"
	and Allegorical Subjects		"Ode on the Popular
	"Ode to Evening"		Superstitions of the
	"Ode Written in the		Highlands of Scotland"
	Beginning of the Year 1746"	1757	*Oriental Eclogues*

William Cowper

1779	*Olney Hymns*	1785	*The Task*
	"Walking with God"	1798	"On the Receipt of My
	"Light Shining Out of		Mother's Picture"
	Darkness"	1799	"The Castaway"
	"Joy and Peace in Believing"	1804	"Yardley Oak"
	"Praise for the Fountain		
	Opened"		
1782	*Table Talk, Conversation,*		
	and Retirement		
	"The Diverting History of		
	John Gilpin"		

Thomas Chatterton

| 1763 | "Elinoure and Juga" | 1777 | *Rowley Poems* |

*Dates refer to date of publication unless otherwise noted.

James Macpherson

1769	*Fragments of Ancient Poetry Collected in the Highlands of Scotland*	1761	*Fingal, an Ancient Epic*
		1763	*Temora, an Epic Poem*
		1773	*The Poems of Ossian*

Edward Young

1725–1728	*Love of Fame*	1759	*Conjectures on Original Composition*
1742–1745	*Night Thoughts on Life, Death and Immortality*		

Thomas Percy

1765	*Reliques of Ancient English Poetry*

Mark Akenside

1744	*The Pleasures of Imagination*

Joseph Warton

1744	*The Enthusiast*
1756	*Essay on the Genius and Writings of Pope*

Thomas Warton

1747	*The Pleasures of Melancholy*	1774–1781	*History of English Poetry*
1754	*Observations on the Fairy Queen*		

George Crabbe

1775	*Inebriety*	1785	*The Newspaper*
1780	*The Candidate*	1810	*The Borough*
1781	*The Library*	1812	*Tales in Verse*
1783	*The Village*	1819	*Tales of the Hall*

Robert Burns

1784	"Highland Mary"	1785	"Epistle to John Lapraik"
	"To a Mountain Daisy"		"The Jolly Beggars"
	"The Cotter's Saturday Night"	1786	"To a Mouse"
	"The Holy Fair"	1787	"Green Grow the Rashes"
	"Address to the Deil"	1789	"Holy Willie's Prayer"

---

*Dates refer to date of publication unless otherwise noted.

Robert Burns *(continued)*

1789	"John Anderson, My Jo, John"	1792	"Ae Fond Kiss"
1790	"Willie Brewed a Peck o' Maut"	1794	"Scots, Wha Hae"
		1795	"A Man's a Man for A' That"
1791	"Tam o' Shanter"	1796	"A Red, Red Rose"

William Blake

1783	*Poetical Sketches*	1794	*The Book of Urizen*
	"Mad Song"		*Songs of Experience*
	"To the Muses"		"The Tiger"
	"How Sweet I Roamed"		"The Clod and the Pebble"
	"My Silks and Fine Array"		"A Poison Tree"
1789	*Songs of Innocence*	1795	*The Book of Los*
	"The Lamb"	1801–1803	*Auguries of Innocence*
	"The Little Black Boy"	1804	*The Four Zoas*
	The Book of Thel	1804–1809	*Milton*
1793	*The Mariage of Heaven and Hell*	1804–1820	*Jerusalem*
	America: A Prophecy	1822	*The Ghost of Abel*
1794	*Europe*		

Mary Wollstonecraft

1786	*Thoughts on the Education of Daughters*	1790	*Vindication of the Rights of Women*
1788	*Mary, a Fiction: Original Stories from Real Life*		

Ann Radcliffe

1794	*The Mysteries of Udolpho*	1797	*The Italian*

Robert Southey

1794	*Wat Tyler*	1805	*Madon*
1796	*Joan of Arc*	1810	*The Curse of Kehama*
1798	"The Battle of Blenheim"	1814	*Don Roderick*
1801	*Thalaba*	1823	"Cataract of Lodore"

William Wordsworth

1793	*An Evening Walk*	1798	"Expostulation and Reply"
	Descriptive Sketches		"The Tables Turned"
1798	*The Lyrical Ballads*		"Lines Composed a Few Miles Above Tintern Abbey"
	"We Are Seven"		
	"Lines Written in Early Spring"		

*Dates refer to date of publication unless otherwise noted.

William Wordsworth (continued)

1800	Preface to *The Lyrical Ballads*	1807	"Stepping Westward"
	"Lucy" poems		"The Solitary Reaper"
	"Michael"		"Yarrow Unvisited"
1802	"Composed by the Seaside		"Ode to Duty"
	near Calais, August 1802"		"Resolution and
	"It Is a Beauteous Evening,		Independence"
	Calm and Free"		"My Heart Leaps Up"
	"Near Dover, September 1802"		"Ode on Intimations of
	"On the Extinction of the		Immortality from Recollec-
	Venetian Republic"		tions of Early Childhood"
	"To Toussaint L'Ouverture"		"Thought of a Briton on
	"Composed upon Westminster		the Subjugation of
	Bridge, September 3, 1802"		Switzerland"
	"Written in London, 1802"	1814	*The Excursion*
1803	"Yew Trees"		"Yarrow Visited"
1804	"She Was a Phantom of	1825	"To a Sky-Lark"
	Delight"	1831	"The Trosachs"
1807	*Poems in Two Volumes*	1842	*The Borderers*
	"At the Grave of Burns"	1850	*The Prelude*

Samuel Taylor Coleridge

1794	"To a Young Ass, Its	1802	"Dejection: an Ode"
	Mother Chained to	1813	*Remorse*
	It near a Log"	1817	*Biographia Literaria*
	The Fall of Robespierre		*Zapolya*
	(with Southey)	1825	*Aids to Reflection*
1796	*Poems*		"Work Without Hope"
	"Lewti, or the Circas-	1840	*Confessions of an*
	sian Love–Chant"		*Inquiring Spirit*
	"Religious Musings"	1895	*Anima Poetae*
	"France"		
1797	"Kubla Khan"		
1797, 1800	"Christabel"		
1798	*Lyrical Ballads*		
	"The Rime of the		
	Ancient Mariner"		
	"Frost at Midnight"		

Sir Walter Scott

1802–1803	*Minstrelsy of the*	1810	*The Lady of the Lake*
	Scottish Border	1811	*The Vision of Don Roderick*
1805	*The Lay of the Last*	1813	*Rokeby*
	Minstrel		*The Bride of Triermain*
1808	*Marmion*	1814	*Waverly*

*Dates refer to date of publication unless otherwise noted.

Sir Walter Scott *(continued)*

1815	*The Lord of the Isles*	1820	*The Monastery*
1816	*The Antiquary*		*Ivanhoe*
1817	*Old Mortality*	1821	*Kennilworth*
	Harold the Dauntless	1823	*Quentin Durward*
1819	*The Bride of*	1825	*The Talisman*
	Lammermoor	1831	*Castle Dangerous*
1820	*The Abbot*		

George Gordon, Lord Byron

1806	*Fugitive Pieces*	1817	*The Lament of Tasso*
1808	*English Bards and Scotch Reviewers*		"So We'll Go No More A-Roving"
1812	*Childe Harold's Pilgrimage, Cantos I and II*	1818	*Childe Harold's Pilgrimage, Canto IV*
	"Maid of Athens"		*Beppo*
1813	*The Giaour*	1819	*Mazeppa*
	The Bride of Abydos		*Marino Faliero*
1814	*The Corsair*		*Sardanapalus*
	Lara		*Cain*
	The Siege of Corinth	1819–1824	*Don Juan*
1815	"She Walks in Beauty"	1821	*The Two Foscari*
	"The Destruction of Sennacherib"		*The Deformed Transformed*
1816	*Childe Harold's Pilgrimage, Canto III*		*Heaven and Earth*
	The Prisoner of Chillon		"To Thomas Moore"
	Manfred	1822	*Werner*
	"Sonnet on Chillon"	1824	"On This Day I Complete My Thirty-sixth Year"
	"When We Two Parted"		
	"Stanzas for Music"		

Percy Bysshe Shelley

1810	*The Necessity of Atheism*	1817	*Prince Athanase*
	Zastrozzi		*Rosalind and Helen*
1811	*Poetic Essay on the Existing State of Things*		*The Revolt of Islam*
			"Ozymandias"
	St. Irvyne	1818	*Julian and Maddalo*
1813	*Queen Mab*		"Lines Written Among the Euganean Hills"
1816	*Alastor, or The Spirit of Solitude*		"Stanzas Written in Dejection Near Naples"
	"Hymn to Intellectual Beauty"		

---

*Dates refer to date of publication unless otherwise noted.

Percy Bysshe Shelley *(continued)*

1819	"Ode to the West Wind"		1821	"Epipsychidion"
	"The Indian Serenade"			"Hellas"
	"Love's Philosophy"			"Adonais"
	"Peter Bell the Third"			"Time"
	"The Mask of Anarchy"			"A Lament"
	Prometheus Unbound			"Mutability"
	The Cenci			*A Defense of Poetry*
1820	"The Sensitive Plant"		1822	"A Dirge"
	"The Cloud"			"To Jane with a Guitar"
	"To a Skylark"			"When the Lamp Is
1821	"To Night"			Shattered"
	"Music When Soft Voices			"The Triumph of Life"
	Die"			*Charles the First*
	"One Word Is Too Often			
	Profaned"			

John Keats

1812	"Imitation of Spenser"		1819	"The Eve of St. Mark"
1816	"On First Looking into			"La Belle Dame Sans Merci"
	Chapman's Homer"			"Ode on a Grecian Urn"
	"On the Grasshopper and			"Ode on Melancholy"
	the Cricket"		1820	*Lamia*
	"To My Brothers"			*Isabella*
1817	*Poems*			*The Eve of St. Agnes and*
	"I Stood Tiptoe upon a			*Other Poems*
	Little Hill"			"To Autumn"
	"To One Who Has Been Long			"Lamia"
	in City Pent"			"Ode to a Nightingale"
	"Sleep and Poetry"			"Isabella"
	"On Seeing the Elgin Marbles"			"Fancy"
1818	*Endymion*			"Hyperion"
	"Robin Hood"			"Ode to Psyche"
	"Lines on the Mermaid Tavern"			"Bright Star, Would I Were
1819	"The Eve of St. Agnes"			Steadfast as Thou Art"

Walter Savage Landor

1802	"One Year Ago"		1847	*Hellenics*
	"Yes, I Write Verses"		1853	*Imaginary Conversations*
	"To Youth"			*of Greeks and Romans*
	"To Age"			
1806	"Rose Aylmer"			
1824–1846	*Imaginary Conversations*			
	of Literary Men and			
	Statesmen			

*Dates refer to date of publication unless otherwise noted.

Thomas Moore

1807–1835	*Irish Melodies*	1817	*Lallah Rookh*
	"Believe Me If All These	1827	*The Epicurean*
	Endearing Young	1825	Biography of Sheridan
	Charms"	1830	Biography of Byron
	" 'Tis the Last Rose of		
	Summer"		
	"The Harp The Once		
	Through Tara's Halls"		
	"Oh Breath Not		
	His Name!"		

Leigh Hunt

1816	*The Story of the Rimini*	1847	*Men, Women and Books*
1834	"About Ben Adam"	1848	*The Town*
1838	"Jennie Kissed Me"	1850	*Autobiography*
1846	*Stories from the Italian Poets*	1851	*Table Talk*

Thomas Hood

1826	*Whims and Oddities*	1843	*Whimsicalities*
1830	*The Comic Annual*		"The Bridge of Sighs"
1839	*Up the Rhine*		"The Song of the Shirt"

Charles Lamb

1798	*Rosamund Gray*	1820–1833	"A Dissertation on
1802	*John Woodvil*		Roast Pig"
1806	*Mr. H*		"Old China"
1807	*Tales from Shakespeare*		"Poor Relations"
	(with Mary Lamb)		"The Convalescent"
1808	*Specimens of English*		"In Praise of Chimney
	Dramatic Poets		Sweepers"
	Contemporary with		"A Chapter on Ears"
	Shakespeare		"That You Must Love Me
1820–1833	*Essays of Elia*		and Love My Dog"
	Last Essays of Elia		"That We Should Rise
	"Christ's Hospital, Five		with the Lark"
	and Thirty Years Ago"		"That We Should Lie
	"Dream Children: a		Down with the
	Reverie"		Lamb"

William Hazlitt

1804	*An Essay on the Principles*	1816	"On Gusto"
	of Human Action	1817	*The Characters of*
1807	*Reply to the Essay on*		*Shakespeare's Plays*
	Population by the		*The Round Table*
	Reverend T. R. Malthus	1818	*The English Poets*

*Dates refer to date of publication unless otherwise noted.

William Hazlitt (continued)

1819	*The English Comic Writers*	1824	*Sketches of the Principal Picture Galleries in England*
	Political Essays		
1820	*The Dramatic Literature of the Age of Elizabeth*	1826	*Notes of a Journey Through France and Italy*
1821	*A View of the English Stage*		*The Plain Speaker*
	"On Reading Old Books"	1828–1830	*Life of Napoleon Bonaparte*
1821–1822	*Table Talk*	1830	*Life of Titian*
1822	"The Fight"	1836	*Sketches and Essays*
1823	"My First Acquaintance with Poets"	1850	*Winterslow*
	Liber Amoris		

Thomas De Quincey

1821	*The Confessions of an English Opium Eater*	1845	*Suspira de Profundis*
		1847	*Joan of Arc*
1823	"On the Knocking at the Gate in *Macbeth*"	1848	*The Literature of Knowledge and the Literature of Power*
1827	*Murder Considered as One of the Fine Arts*	1849	*The English Mail Coach*
1838	Biographical Sketches of Shakespeare, Milton, Pope, Wordsworth, Coleridge, Southey, Lamb, Lessing, the Caesars		

William Godwin

1793	*Caleb Williams*	1799	*St. Leon*

William Beckford

1786	*The History of the Caliph Vathek*

Maria Edgeworth

1800	*Castle Rackrent*	1804	*Popular Tales*
1801	*Early Lessons*	1812	*The Absentee*
	Moral Tales	1817	*Ormond*
	Belinda		

*Dates refer to date of publication unless otherwise noted.

Jane Austen

1811	*Sense and Sensibility*	1816	*Emma*
1813	*Pride and Prejudice*	1818	*Northanger Abbey*
1814	*Mansfield Park*		*Persuasion*

Mary Wollstonecraft Shelley

1818	*Frankenstein*	1826	*The Last Man*
1823	*Valperga*		

*Dates refer to date of publication unless otherwise noted.

1
REVOLT AGAINST CLASSICISM

As has been pointed out, the eighteenth century was a century of Neoclassical conformity. The Neoclassicists wrote most of their poems in heroic couplets, made their center of interest London, were preeminently satirists, had little patience with individual deviations from the dictates of common sense, and placed good manners on a higher level than personal emotion. Perfection of form, for which the ancient world supplied the models, was for them an insurance of clarity of idea; and clarity of idea they far preferred to any exercise of the imagination. They considered it catastrophic to be unable to live in London, and had little interest in the countryside unless it could be tamed, laid out in walks, and civilized with statuary.

NEW VIEWS OF EMOTION AND NATURE

We have now to consider a number of writers who were contemporary with the Neoclassicists, but who are better dealt with in a class by themselves. These writers were, consciously or unconsciously, making a crack in the mold of classical conformity. They were not writers of major talents—were all, indeed, inferior to the leading writers of the eighteenth century (Pope, Swift, Addison and Steele, Johnson, Boswell, Goldsmith, and Sheridan). But they were preparing the way for a new mode of literary composition.

The complete break with classicism is not achieved until the end of the century when, in the poetry of Burns and Blake, we find romanticism unadulterated. Then, in 1798, Wordsworth and Coleridge more or less officially inaugurate the Romantic movement with the publication of *Lyrical Ballads*, a volume containing works by each of them.

The leading writers of the eighteenth century exhibit the characteristic rational approach to life that was the fashion of the time; to the emotions they accorded an inferior place. But there were other men in the eighteenth century who were already reacting against the frigid atmosphere of eighteenth century common sense. John Wesley, for instance, the founder of Methodism, was winning adherents in the very heart of the Age of Reason. He taught that emotion was the only road to understanding God. At meetings of the early Methodists there were orgies of hysteria, crying, and groaning, all of which were thought by Wesley's followers to bring them nearer to God.

This new evangelicalism was soon in the air, and even some Anglican preachers began to rebel against the rationalism that had invaded the Christian religion. It was by members of the latter group that the poet William Cowper was powerfully influenced.

Although the official Neoclassical writers were children of the metropolis and loathed the country, certain writers who were their contemporaries began to celebrate the pleasures of the countryside. James Thomson in *The Seasons* (1726–1730) was the first to make the aspects of nature his subject. Soon other poets began to follow his lead, notably Gray in his *Elegy*, Collins in his *Ode to Evening*, and Cowper in *The Task*. By the time we come to Blake and Burns, the countryside becomes the accepted locale for poetry.

These pre-Romantic writers also began to turn away from Neoclassical restrictions and conformity. They began to take an interest in simple, rather than cultivated, people (as in Gray's *Elegy*, Cowper's *The Task*). They began also to experiment with other forms than the heroic couplet, to rediscover blank verse and the Spenserian stanza. They began to look elsewhere than to ancient Greece and Rome for inspiration. They developed an interest in ancient Celtic and Teutonic folklore, and with this interest a zest for the primitive and barbaric. This anticlassicism led by easy stages to a rediscovery of medieval architecture, and the "Gothic pile" began to be a setting for their stories and poetic meditations.

The quiet and unsensational revolt against classicism by midcentury fell in with the new Rousseauistic philosophy that was in the air. Jean Jacques Rousseau (1712–1778), citizen of Geneva, despite his lack of logic and unending inconsistencies, turned out to be the most influential French philosopher of his time. He held that civilization and all social institutions were responsible for corrupting mankind. Man by nature was benevolent. Civilization had made him evil, and only in a state of nature would he ever find happiness again. The "natural man" began to be held as nature's nobleman, and presently it was fashionable to think of the simple peasant on his farm as far superior to the most educated man in the metropolis. Some of this nonsense survives in our own century. But by the early nineteenth century it was considered truth too evident to need proof.

JAMES THOMSON (1700–1748)

Thomson is a very uneven poet. In his own age his vogue as the man who had rediscovered a sympathy for the beauties of nature was almost unparalleled. Yet in all other respects he was a complacent Neoclassicist.

He was born in Roxburghshire, Scotland, and spent his boyhood on the wild Scottish border. It was there that his mind was filled with those impressions he later recorded in *The Seasons*. He came in 1725 to London with the purpose of trying his fortunes as a writer. The next year the publication of his *Winter* made him famous at once. His success encouraged him to compose *Summer* (1727) and *Spring* (1728). When *Autumn* was completed, he published the four poems as *The Seasons* (1730).

Thomson was a very amiable man, who made friends easily, and was generally well-liked. He accepted a post as tutor to a young nobleman, and thus was able to travel on the Continent. The impressions of his travels are recorded in a long, tedious poem, *Liberty* (1736). He was also the author of a number of dull Neoclassical tragedies. The best-known of his poems is of course his patriotic "Rule, Britannia!" (1740) with its often-quoted refrain:

> *Rule, Britannia, rule the waves;*
> *Britons never will be slaves.*

These verses were originally part of a masque called *Alfred*.

Thomson's last years were spent in rather luxurious retirement at Richmond. There he worked, when laziness did not overpower him, on his final literary undertaking, *The Castle of Indolence* (1748). Of his works only the first and the last, *The Seasons* and *The Castle of Indolence*, are important.

The Seasons is important for two reasons: the descriptions of nature and the use of blank verse. When Thomson is composing at his best, he is an excellent depicter of landscape and weather. In such passages his use of concrete language is at happy variance with the generalized diction of the Neoclassicists. Milton was the great influence on Thomson, and from Milton he took his blank verse, the use of which was a welcome departure from the omnipresent heroic couplet. But the Latinisms that are so perfectly in accord with Milton's temperament, intellect, and subject are curiously out of place in Thomson's description of landscape. Some of Thomson's phrases seem absurd to us today. When he speaks of "the conscious heifer," the "fond sequacious herd," or tells how the cattle "ruminate in the contiguous shade" he seems inordinately pompous. From the Neoclassicists, also, he too often caught the trick of generalized language, as when he prefers to speak of birds as "the plumy race," or sheep as "the bleating kind." In addition, *The Seasons* is defaced by many typically Neoclassical didactic digressions. Nevertheless, Thomson was a pioneer who was cutting out the path in which Wordsworth later was to walk.

The Castle of Indolence suffers from the same imperfections, and owns the same excellences. It has an additional importance. His use of the Spenserian stanza in it, and his incorporating the magic and Gothic atmosphere that he admired in *The Faerie Queene* were not greatly appreciated at the time. But *The Castle of Indolence* brought the attention of poets and readers to the wonderful potentialities of the Spenserian stanza and art, and did much to augment growing interest in the medieval.

THOMAS GRAY (1716–1771)

Gray lived the live of a scholar. He studied at Eton, where he became a close friend of Horace Walpole, went to Cambridge, and while still a student made a tour of Italy and France with young Walpole (1739–1741). Throughout her life he was deeply attached to his mother. His letters from the Continent to her demonstrate a sensitiveness to the beauties of wild mountain scenery that were not to have been expected from a contemporary of Addison.

On his return to England he spent two years with his mother at the village of Stoke Poges. There he wrote his first important poems: "Ode on the Spring," "Hymn to Adversity," and "Ode on a Distant Prospect of Eton College," with its celebrated lines:

> *Yet ah! why should they know their fate,*
> *Since sorrow never comes too late,*
> *And happiness too swiftly flies?*
> *Thought would destroy their paradise.*
> *No more; where ignorance is bliss,*
> *'Tis folly to be wise.*

Later in 1742 he returned to Cambridge, to carry on his studies in literature and history at Pembroke College.

Thereafter Gray left his books at Cambridge only when he wanted to consult others at the British Museum in London. After ten years of literary labors he published a volume, *Six Poems* (1753). Four years later he was offered the post of Poet Laureate, which he declined. In 1768 he was made Professor of History and Modern Languages at Cambridge. He never married, and seemed to find his chief emotional outlet in a wonderful series of letters to his friends. In some severe critical opinion Gray's letters are not only among the choicest in our language, but they are the best things he ever wrote. After an uneventful life he was buried by his request by his mother's side in the churchyard of Stoke Poges. His final resting place is thought to have been the site he had described in his "Elegy."

The bulk of Gray's poetry is one of the slenderest ever bequeathed by a celebrated poet. Poetry was his recreation; by profession he was a scholar, and it is for that reason that his letters give us a far closer view of his mind, temperament and opinions. His letters reveal him to have been a man of unlimited curiosity and cultivated judgment. Though some of his poetry makes him a leading pre-Romantic poet, his correspondence reveals him to have been essentially a Neoclassicist in temperament, with a critical but avid enthusiasm for learning. Even his verse shows the strenuous discipline of the scholar. No Neoclassical poet could have taken more care to polish his verse. The "Elegy" is said to have taken seven years to finish, and if that is so the chief objection that could be made to the poem is that it gives too much evidence of long labor. In some respects Gray's letters were more important than his poetry for opening up new vistas to the coming Romanticists. His correspondence is full of his lively interest in medievalism, folklore, nature, and Gothic architecture, and is a charming revelation of his own character.

After his volume of 1753, Gray began his studies for the composition of two elaborate Pindaric Odes, "The Progress of Poesy" and "The Bard," both published by his friend Walpole on a private printing press (1757). Gray's researches during this part of his life became significant to later poets. "The Bard" pioneers in three respects: The poem is set in wild mountain scenery, it is concerned with old Celtic lore, and it is laid in the Middle Ages. Gray's later odes reproduced the wild scenery, but went to an even more remote past and another culture for inspiration. "The Fatal Sisters" (1761) and "The Descent of Odin" (1761) are inspired by Icelandic legend. Besides all this gravely serious poetic composition, mention should be made of a delightful piece of light verse that Gray had written as a result of an experience at a friend's house, "Ode on the Death of a Favorite Cat, Drowned in a Tub of Goldfishes" (1748).

Of course the most celebrated of his poems, "The Elegy Written in a Country Churchyard," a favorite with schoolteachers all over the English-speaking world. Samuel Johnson, who liked no other of Grays poems, praised this one highly. Actually very little of the poem is original. Some of its best known phrases were commonplace among a group of minor poets whom we now describe as forming the "Graveyard School." These men and women, under a misapprehension of Milton's meaning in "Il Penseroso," devoted themselves to writing on melancholy subjects, such as death, night, solitude, and the grave. The chief poems in the "Graveyard School" were: "To the Nightingale" and "A Nocturnal Reverie" by Lady Winchelsea (1661–1720); "Night Thoughts on Life, Death and Immortality" by Edward Young (1683–1765); "The Grave" by Robert Blair (1699–1746); "Retirement" by Thomas Warton the Elder (1688–1745); "The Pleasures of Melancholy" by Thomas Warton the Younger (1728–1790); "Ode to Solitude" by Joseph Warton (1722–1800); and "A Night-Piece on Death" by Thomas Parnell (1679–1718). To this should be added Collins' beautiful "Ode to Evening," which will be considered later.

Gray's "Elegy" is more a summation of the whole "Graveyard School" than original work. Nevertheless, it would be idle to deny the historical importance of the "Elegy." Its sincere and deep feeling for common humanity strikes a chord beyond the range of Pope and his school or the "Graveyard School," and predicts the Age of Wordsworth. Moreover, the music in many stanzas of the "Elegy" is quiet and beautiful. But it is not possible honestly to agree with the popular verdict that the "Elegy" is a great poem. It contains some of the worst examples of Neoclassical abstractions, against which Wordsworth was to protest with vigor. The stanzas are defaced by the appearance of such empty figures as Knowledge, Penury, Memory, Honor, Flattery, Forgetfulness, Contemplation, Luxury, and Pride. These abstractions give the mind no image on which to dwell.

The poem begins with some of its best music:

> *The curfew tolls the knell of parting day,*
> *The lowing herd wind slowly o'er the lea*

The poet stands in the country churchyard thinking of the simple warm lives the "rude forefathers" of the village once led. Their "short and simple annals" need not provoke a smile. For even the most proud must come to such an end:

> *The paths of glory lead but to the grave.*

These simple folk have no elaborate tombs, yet who knows what undeveloped talents many of them may have owned?

> *Full many a gem of purest ray serene*
> *The dark unfathomed caves of ocean bear:*
> *Full many a flower is born to blush unseen*
> *And waste its sweetness on the desert air.*

Some of these men might have become great patriots or poets, had opportunity been theirs. But if their glories were unrealized, their sins were also not great. The poet concludes with a reflection that when he himself dies, few will know anything of his life as he lived it. And when he dies, he too will be satisfied with a simple epitaph telling the reader that he looks to God for understanding of the life he lived.

"The Bard" is a curious mixture of Romanticism and Neoclassicism. Its subject and setting are highly romantic. As King Edward I of England makes his way through the mountains of Wales during his bloody conquest of that country, he meets an old bard with hair and beard streaming in the wind. The bard bids the conqueror stop and listen to the curse that he is about to pronounce upon the monarch's line. The bard foretells disaster to Edward, his son and grandson, and their families. Then he foretells the eventual triumph of the Celts when a Welshman shall ascend the English throne (Henry VII, a Tudor). Then will follow the glorious age of Elizabethan poetry. The great work of Spenser, Shakespeare, and Milton are promised. With this vision the bard ceases, and, in the last line of the poem, plunges into the foaming torrent.

This wild mountain scenery, the Celtic bard, and the Celtic heroes mentioned, the roaring stream and blustering winds, the medieval setting, are all romantic. But the form of the poem is severely classical. Indeed, "The Bard" is the best example in English of the Pindaric ode. (A *Pindaric ode* is a lyrical poem of lofty mood written in groups of three stanzas: a strophe, an antistrophe, and an epode. The strophe and antistrophe are in the same meter and follow the same rhyme scheme. The epode is free. The form is imitated from the odes of the Greek poet Pindar.) "The Bard" is written in the form of three groups of the Pindaric strophe, antistrophe, and epode, and is therefore highly symmetrical. Part one gives the situation; part two is concerned with the curse; and part three deals with the eventual triumph of the Celtic line.

"The Bard," however, is not a good poem. It suffers from Neoclassical abstractions, and today the romantic effects that seemed startling to Gray's contemporaries, seem largely absurd. There is something silly about the picture of an old man standing with his beard streaming in the wind, and succeeding in making a whole army stop while he curses their king. Its severe form did not win for "The Bard" the approval of Samuel Johnson. He dismissed it with the remark: "To select a singular effect and swell it to a giant's bulk by fabulous appendages of spectres and predictions, has little difficulty."

WILLIAM COLLINS (1721–1759)

Like Gray, Collins wrote very little poetry. Unlike him, however, Collins was not much admired by his contemporaries. Nevertheless, although his poetry suffers from the abstractions and "poetic diction" of his age, Collins possessed qualities that his times could hardly appreciate. He was a profound admirer of Milton and Shakespeare and was perhaps the first eighteenth century poet able to capture some of the delicacy and free fancifulness of Elizabethan poets.

He was born in Sussex, educated at Oxford, and came to London in 1744. While at the University he published a volume of *Persian Eclogues* (1742), which he later reissued as *Oriental Eclogues* (1757). Ill health disabled him from carrying out the literary plans he had formed. His *Odes on Several Descriptive and Allegorical Subjects* (1746) won no attention, and in an access of wrath he burned most of the edition. His last publication was the "Ode Occasioned by the Death of Mr. Thomson" (1749). His "Ode on the Popular Superstitions of the Highlands of Scotland," written the same year, remained unpublished till long after his death. Shortly after penning his last poem, Collins began to be the prey of a disease that drove him to extreme melancholia, which ended in violent insanity. He was confined for a time in an asylum. The last years of his short life were spent in retirement; during them he had brief periods of intellectual balance alternated with longer periods of mental blankness.

IMPORTANCE

Collins was one of the most original poets of his day, but his qualities are difficult to define. In the midst of very bad Neoclassical language, we find a sensitive feeling for landscape and a highly imaginative talent for depicting the more sombre aspects of nature. In his "Ode to Evening" (1746) there is a kind of emotional intoxication which sounds in advance the kind of music that Keats was to make. The "Ode Written in the Beginning of the Year 1746" also shows his exquisite sense for subtle music. Both are indebted above all to Milton's *Il Penseroso* for their best traits.

WILLIAM COWPER (1731–1800)

In some respects Cowper was the most influential of the pre-Romantic poets. He did much to direct public taste towards the paths that nineteenth century writers were to take. The fact that the best nineteenth century poets excelled him has somewhat diminished his stature. That is a pity, for Cowper is a delightful poet. And his letters are among the best in English literature.

Cowper's father was a clergyman who had little understanding of his son. Cowper became utterly dependent on his mother as a child, and lost her when he was but six. Late in life he confessed that not a day passed in which he did not think of her. His "On the Receipt of My Mother's Picture" (1798), written at the close of his own life, gives one a very good idea of how deep his affection for her was. His boyhood at Westminster School was very unhappy because of the bullying of his classmates. He studied law and entered the profession in 1754. For a time certain unimportant government posts provided him with a livelihood and gave him time to write charming light verse and to make the most of his friendship with his two female cousins, Theodora and Harriet—the latter of whom is the celebrated Lady Hesketh of his letters. His mid-twenties were his only cheerful years.

He was preparing himself for examination before the House of Lords for a more advanced government position. As the time approached, his fear of failing drove him to the extremes of melancholia, during which he attempted to take his life, and lapsed into insanity. He was in an asylum for a year, and was brought back to sanity. During this dark year Cowper had convinced himself that he had committed the unpardonable sin for which the tortures of Hell would be his lot in eternity. He was never to be quite free of the anguish of that conviction. But he found some peace as a result of his conversion to the new evangelicalism in the Established Church.

He left the asylum to retire to Huntington, a village not far from Cambridge. His purpose was to escape the temptations that London offered for a frivolous life. At Huntington he became a friend of the Unwins, and went to live with them. Mrs. Unwin, who was much older than himself, became his second mother, and soon he was entirely dependent on her care. On the death of her husband she moved to the village of Olney, largely to be near the evangelist, the Reverend John Newton. Cowper moved to Olney with her in 1786, and there wrote his best work. He seems to have planned marrying her, but a temporary relapse into insanity in 1773 made matrimony seem unwise to him. He has recorded his indebtedness to her in his moving poem "To Mary." It was because of her influence that he began to write poetry again, and it was she who nursed him back to health during his frequent attacks of mental disorganization. In her old age she became paralyzed, and Cowper then watched over her with such anxiety that the intellectual chaos of his last years may be attributed to his concern over her final illness.

In 1782 Cowper published the writings he had created to please Mrs. Unwin—*Table Talk, Conversation, and Retirement.* In the verses in this volume, of which the poem "Retirement" is the best, one can see how much Cowper had fallen under the spell of Milton. Cowper's blank verse, the form in which he is most at home, reproduces the cadences and vocabulary of Milton. "Retirement" tells us how Cowper escaped from London because of his need for "divine communion." It is similar to the theme that Wordsworth was to treat in "The Excursion."

Newton's narrow theology was responsible for increasing the morbidity inherent in Cowper's make-up, and in adding to his fits of hopeless depression. Some of his despair can be read in the *Olney Hymns* (1779), which he wrote in collaboration with Newton. A great number of these hymns have been appropriated by the Church for its services. The best known of these are "Walking with God," "Light Shining Out of Darkness," "Joy and Peace in Believing," and "Praise for the Fountain Opened."

Cowper fought valiantly against depression and frequently gave way to his love of fun. In one of these happier moods he wrote "The Diverting History of John Gilpin" (1782), a rollicking poem in ballad style, which immediately won him fame.

The most important occurrence in Cowper's life as a poet was the coming of a charming woman, Lady Austen, to Olney. It was she who had told him the tale of John Gilpin. And it was because of her that he undertook his most important work. One day she urged him to write another poem in blank verse. He asked her for a subject. "Write upon this sofa," she suggested. And thus he began his best poem. Once he had made some progress, ideas came crowding on him until he had a whole volume, which he playfully gave the title of *The Task* (1785). Its purpose was to prove the superiority of "rural ease and leisure" for living a life of virtue to London life. Cowper was, therefore, the first eighteenth century poet to relish country life for its own sake. Even though his purposes were chiefly moral, his keen eye and delicate humor give the poem sprightliness and vividness.

It is, of course, a highly autobiographical work. His device is to take us with him on a tour of country life and scenery. Many of his passages give a foretaste of the kind of poetry Wordsworth was to write, and he was far more interested in natural description than Wordsworth was to be. As a poet

Cowper never rises into ecstasy, but *The Task* is full of warmth, sweetness, and good humor. It is highly unclassical in the intimate revelation it makes of its author.

Cowper's last years were devoted to a translation of Homer, an attempt to do more justice to the Greek original than had been attempted in the Pope translations. One of his finest pieces was left unfinished at the time of his death, "Yardley Oak." It was published in 1804. These last-named original works (*The Task* and "Yardley Oak") show Cowper at his best and most cheerful. But there are some poems in which we may read his spiritual torture. "The Castaway" (1799) was written one year before his death and shows the agony from which he never fully escaped. In it he compares his mental state to that of a drowning man whom no one is by to save.

His letters, completely candid in all of the author's moods, show every side of his character.

THOMAS CHATTERTON (1752–1770)

IMPORTANCE

Despite the brevity of his life, "the marvelous boy," as Wordsworth called Chatterton, wrote verse of considerable historical importance. His *Rowley Poems* are a significant instance of the rebirth of interest in the Middle Ages as well as the first thoroughly successful attempt in the eighteenth century to imitate the free lyricism of the Elizabethans. Chatterton's poems did much to influence Blake and Coleridge. But his unhappy life itself became in some respects even more important to the Romantic poets. He was to figure to the nineteenth century poets as a symbol for the neglect and misprizing that society accords poets. His death by his own hand in his seventeenth year seemed to them an indictment of a callous age.

Chatterton was born in Bristol very near the Church of St. Mary Redcliffe, which had been built in the fifteenth century. That church became his intellectual godmother. Poverty had reduced the Chatterton home to squalor, and the boy sought the refuge of beauty within St. Mary's old walls. He attended a charity school for seven years, where he was taught very little. But at night, when other boys were asleep, he was pouring over *The Faerie Queene,* the Elizabethan lyricists, Chaucer, and Lydgate, in the attic of the Chatterton home. He also took a fancy to dictionaries of early English.

This love for the antique had been inspired by the sight of some illuminated manuscripts that had been recovered upon the breaking open of some old chests in St. Mary's loft. When he was eleven he appeared at school with an amazing poem. "Elinoure and Juga," written on old parchment, and told a schoolmate that it was a medieval literary relic. His hoax was highly successful, and so he tried it on his teacher, who was deeply impressed. From then on Chatterton began to discover astounding quantities of "literary remains," which he himself manufactured at night in his garret.

He began to create a whole fifteenth century world of his own imagining around the historical personage of William Cannynge, who had been Lord Mayor of Bristol then. In his inventions Chatterton was aided by the inscriptions on tombs and his dictionary. These poems he professed to be the productions of one Thomas Rowley, a monk who was a poet (of Chatterton's own creation). The solid citizens of Bristol were flattered to discover that their families could be traced to these "rediscovered" Rowley poems. Chatterton was able at a surprising rate to produce "historical documents" glorifying them and Bristol.

In 1767 the boy entered an attorney's office, and began to send copies of the poems to Horace Walpole and to the publisher Dodsley in London. Walpole was something of a medievalist, but was thoroughly taken in at first by "Rowley." His friend Gray, however, knew better, pointed out the inconsistencies, and then Walpole decided to be furious with Chatterton for having deceived him. His correspondence with Chatterton is brutal and insensitive. Instead of seeing the boy's genius, Walpole was aware only of dealing with an impostor.

Chatterton decided to come to London to try his luck as a writer. He had already developed a double personality. As Thomas Rowley, he was half-medieval, half-Elizabethan. But as Thomas Chatterton he wrote heroic couplets, pastorals and odes in the true Neoclassical manner. In London he worked feverishly, but was unsuccessful in procuring any pay from the publishers. Those gentlemen had no desire to print the works of Rowley. The poor boy starved for a few months, and then rather than return home defeated, he took a dose of arsenic.

Even a casual reader today would know that the *Rowley Poems* could not have been written in the fifteenth century. Chatterton was far more familiar with Spenser than with Chaucer. The music of his verse is entirely Elizabethan, fresh and free. The diction that he manufactured under the illusion that he was recreating Chaucerian English, is a strange hodgepodge of words that were never so spelled at any time in their history. But Chatterton's contemporaries were so unfamiliar with their own literary history that the authenticity of the Rowley poems was debated for a long time. In Thomas Warton's *History of English Poetry* they were included in his discussion of fifteenth century poetry. Although unthanked for his gift, Chatterton's real contribution to English literature was his teaching English how to sing again.

JAMES MACPHERSON (1736–1796)

Macpherson was the center of another storm concerned with the authenticity of the poems he published as "translations." In Edinburgh the vogue for rediscovering ancient Celtic lore had enlisted the enthusiasm of many scholars. In 1759 a young Highland schoolmaster, James Macpherson, showed the dramatist John Home some copies he had made of Gaelic poems that he had taken down from the recitation of natives in the north of Scotland. Excited over them, Home sent them to Dr. Blair at the University of Edinburgh. Blair and Home then urged Macpherson to translate his collection, and in 1760 Blair issued them in *Fragments of Ancient Poetry Collected in the Highlands of Scotland.* The volume became a sensational success. It satisfied the popular ideas as to what primitive poetry should sound like—it was wild, heroic, and strange.

No one was more impressed with these poems than Gray, who little realized that his own researches and poems had done much to create the fashion for Celtic primitivism. Macpherson was given a grant so that he might tour the Highlands to recover what he could of ancient poetry. In 1761 Macpherson published *Fingal, an Ancient Epic*, and two years later *Temora, an Epic Poem.* Blair was delighted, and innocently pointed out that *Fingal* satisfied Aristotelian laws for an epic poem. It is strange that the poem's classic conformity should not have made him suspicious. Macpherson claimed that the epics he published were the product of an ancient bard, Ossian; in 1773 he reissued them as *The Poems of Ossian.*

By that year the battle over their authenticity was raging furiously. Sounder scholars were able to prove that the hero Finn was not Scottish but Irish historically, and lived not in the first century but in the third. More astute critics might have observed astonishing resemblances between Ossian's language and that of the Bible and Milton. In our day, moreover, we are amused at the prevalence in the poems of stormy seas, roaring winds, aged rocks, and thick mists, all of which were in the new (pre-Romantic) vogue. Samuel Johnson, at any rate, was convinced that the poems were actually Macpherson's own and did not think much of their quality. He was, of course, quite right. When Johnson demanded to see the original manuscripts from which the translations were supposed to have been made, Macpherson was very evasive.

The truth would seem to be that Macpherson built on a few authentic Gaelic fragments works of his own fabrication. What he wrote was perfectly calculated to satisfy the expectations of an uninformed public that had far more enthusiasm for, than knowledge about, primitive times. Towards the end of his career, he was emboldened by his successes to hint that the poems were his own and that the doubt still in people's minds was a compliment to his own genius. At any rate, he was so well thought of that on his death he was buried in Westminster Abbey.

IMPORTANCE

Macpherson's poems have little merit but were of overwhelming importance to world literature. No other author did so much as Macpherson to hasten the Romantic movement in western Europe. Blake never outgrew Macpherson's influence; and *The Poems of Ossian* was the favorite book of Napoleon and Chateaubriand. In Goethe's early novel, *The Sorrows of Young Werther*, the hero's whole life is involved with the book. *The Poems of Ossian* seemed to their century wonderfully new and powerful, however thin and shallow they are to us.

MINOR PRE-ROMANTIC WRITERS

Edward Young (1683–1765)

Edward Young was the most popular poet of the "Graveyard School." His best-known work is *Night Thoughts on Life, Death and Immortality*, issued in nine parts between 1742 and 1745. It is written in uninspired but not undignified blank verse and was intended to uphold the reasonableness of the Christian religion. From it comes the famous line, "Procrastination is the thief of time." Though much admired in its own time, *Night Thoughts* makes dull reading today because its pretentious philosophizing seems quite pedestrian. Young is also the author of *Love of Fame* (1725–1728), a collection of satires in heroic couplets; and *Conjectures on Original Composition* (1759), a prose piece suggesting the superiority of personal inspiration to imitation of the Greeks.

Thomas Percy (1729–1811)

Thomas Percy, the Bishop of Dromore, compiled one of the most important books ever published in England. In 1765 he issued his *Reliques of Ancient English Poetry,* a collection of old English and Scottish ballads and songs. Though some poems he included have since proved to be more modern than he thought, the *Reliques* is the first important collection of authentic balladry published in England. Most of the ballads that are now well-known were first published in that collection. With his book begins the first sincere scholarship on the old ballads. The popularity of the *Reliques* had much to do with the eventual breakdown of the prestige of Neoclassical poetry.

Mark Akenside (1721–1770)

Mark Akenside studied both theology and medicine, and practiced the latter. His *The Pleasures of Imagination* (1744) is pompous and clumsy but nevertheless historically important. Its blank verse is devoted to an exposition of the idea of the "scale of being" with which Pope deals in his *Essay on Man*.

Joseph Warton (1722–1800) and
Thomas Warton (1728–1790)

Joseph Warton and Thomas Warton the Younger were sons of Thomas Warton, Professor of Poetry at Oxford (1688–1745). Thomas Warton the Elder's verse has little quality but imitates Milton, Spenser, and Chaucer, and thereby served as an early model for pre-Romantic poetry when his volume was published in 1748. He also influenced the work of his sons, who were friends and schoolfellows of Collins. Joseph Warton's *The Enthusiast* (1744) and Thomas Warton's *The Pleasures of Melancholy* are both written in Miltonic blank verse, are in the "Graveyard" mood, and foster the vogue of wild nature and Gothic ruins. Joseph Warton's most important book is his *Essay on the Genius and Writings of Pope* (1756; 1782) in which he dethroned Pope from his position of being considered the greatest of English poets. He placed him below Spenser. Thomas Warton in his *Observations on the Fairy Queen* (1754) and in his *History of English Poetry* (1774–1781) proved his wide acquaintance with older English poetry, particularly that of the Middle Ages.

George Crabbe (1754–1832)

George Crabbe was widely admired in his own time, though his reputation was eclipsed by the greater poets who came after him. His literary position is paradoxical. In some respects he is the last of Pope's imitators, in others he is a forerunner of Wordsworth. He always wrote in the heroic couplet of Pope's school and had no sympathy with the attitudes of the pre-Romantic poets. But he was singularly free from the sham elegance of the later Neoclassicists and possessed a quite Romantic interest in simple human beings. His poetry is never inspired but always admirably honest and close to the truths of human experience. It is in this last respect that he is close to Wordsworth.

After writing several unsuccessful works, *Inebriety* (1775), *The Candidate* (1780), and *The Library* (1781), Crabbe discovered the true bent of his abilities as a result of his disgust with Goldsmith's "The Deserted Village." He had been born and raised in a wretched little seacoast town in Suffolk, and knew well the brutality and squalor that poverty breeds. He was angered at the ideal happiness pictured in Goldsmith's poem, and it was to give a true picture of the facts of village life as he knew them that Crabbe wrote his long poem, *The Village* (1783).

As might have been expected, Samuel Johnson was delighted with it, and even revised some of the lines for Crabbe. The book became a great success, and Crabbe followed up his popularity with *The Newspaper* (1785). Though Crabbe wrote a great deal thereafter, he destroyed most of his work, including three novels. After many years, he began publishing again: *The Borough* (1810), *Tales In Verse* (1812), and *Tales of the Hall* (1819). All these books were widely read.

IMPORTANCE

Crabbe was perhaps the first poet to see the country realistically; he was a knowing psychologist in his depiction of human conduct; he was among the earliest writers to recognize the power of environment; and his poems were important contributions to the development of English fiction. Among his great admirers have been men as dissimilar as Burke, Johnson, Wordsworth, Byron and Lamb.

The two poets whom we have now to consider, Robert Burns and William Blake, are generally classed among the pre-Romantic writers only because it has become customary to think of the Romantic Movement as being ushered in by the publication of the *Lyrical Ballads* of Wordsworth and Coleridge in 1798. Actually, however, the classification is quite inaccurate in the case of Burns and Blake. Both were thoroughly Romantic in their work, Blake incorrigibly so. It is true that Wordsworth exerted a powerful influence upon his contemporaries, and Blake exerted none. But Burns was widely read and admired. The career of these two men was coincidental with the intensification of revolutionary thought in France and the outbreak of the Revolution itself. And their work shows the powerful influence of those stirring times.

ROBERT BURNS (1759–1796)

For a long time gossip did much to obscure the facts of Burns's biography. He was falsely described as debauched, a drunkard and a philanderer—largely because his strong republicanism was best attacked by slandering the man. He was also bitingly satirical at the expense of religious cant and pretentious piety, and those who felt the lash of his mockery were naturally anxious to invalidate his opinions. It is true that he drank a great deal, but it was a vice of his times, and he seems to have contracted the habit in excess only after his introduction into high society. It is also true that he was fond of the girls, but that fact did not keep him from being a thoroughly devoted husband once he was married.

From his earliest days Burns knew only too well the extreme poverty of the Scottish peasant. He was born in a clay cottage of two rooms at Alloway on January 25, 1759. His father was an old man already worn out by hard work. Robert was the eldest of seven children. They all labored hard at the soil. But they never succeeded in making a decent living out of any farm. They moved from place to place, devoting all their strength to their toil, with little yield for their labors. It was in the midst of this cheerless gloom that somewhat before his sixteenth year Burns "committed," as he says, "the sin of rhyme." Burns had only three years of schooling but was a feverish reader in English literature, and had taught himself to speak French fluently. His affinity was from the very beginning with his own people, and he became an enthusiastic collector of Scottish folk songs. Indeed, most of his best poetry is not more than wonderful adaptation and imitation of crude lyrics made by forgotten Scottish singers.

He began as a rhymer of these folk pieces, became well-known in the towns near which he lived, and was satisfied at first with just local fame. Indeed, he was nearing thirty before he had ever traveled more than ten miles from his home. But at last he decided that he had had enough of farm labor. In 1786 he published the first edition of his poems at the little town of Kilmarnock, near his home. His reason for publishing them was to raise enough money to make a trip to Jamaica. But the volume was caught up in a wave of excitement, and he decided to try his luck with a larger edition that would circulate in the capital city. He went, therefore, to Edinburgh, where the poems were reissued in another edition.

He was lionized at once. "The Athens of the North" was in the grip of a Rousseauistic enthusiasm for the natural man. Burns seemed to be the living personification of that Romantic ideal. He was greeted by the Edinburgh critics as a marvelous case of untaught genius, a child of nature. But after a while society tired of pampering their peasant-genius, and Burns realized that there was no future for him in Edinburgh. In 1788 he married Jean Armour, who had already borne him a child, and he and his wife moved to a little farm. Very soon this venture proved plainly hopeless.

Through friends he procured the post of exciseman, and he made Dumfries his headquarters. From there he traveled every week several hundred miles. Burns was an outspoken advocate of the French Revolution; this fact and his love of drink alienated his neighbors.

Still very poor, he declined in health and the terrible labors of his youth began to take their toll. When he died at the age of thirty-seven, his enemies did all they could to exaggerate his weaknesses and obscure his genius.

Burns believed in the Rousseauistic doctrine that the heart was the best guide to truth. He despised narrow religiosity and smug self-righteousness. Such poems as "The Holy Fair," "Address to the Deil" (Devil), "Holy Willie's Prayer," and "Address to the Unco Guid" must have horrified the strict Calvinists of his country. But their anger was only an inducement to further insults from him. "Holy Willie's Prayer" is a fine piece of caustic satire at the expense of the religious hypocrite who loves the idea of Hell for others. This poem so alarmed the churchmen that they are said to have held three meetings over it. The "Address to the Unco Guid" states in its opening his objections to such folk:

> *O ye wha are sae guid yoursel,*
> *Sae pious and sae holy,*
> *Ye've naught to do but mark and tell*
> *Your neebour's fauts and folly!*

Burns is today admired mostly for his many beautiful songs. They vary from affectionate lightheartedness (as in "My Nanie, O" and "Green Grow the Rashes") to the hilarity of the drinking song (as in "Willie Brew'd a Peck o' Maut"); from the tender sadness of some love songs (as in "Ae Fond Kiss" and "Highland Mary") to fervent patriotism ("Scots, Wha Hae"). Some of his songs have a wonderful simple dignity ("John Anderson, My Jo, John"); some are touchingly pathetic ("The Bank o' Doon"); some have a burning passion ("A Red, Red Rose"); and some have a manly confidence in the future of the republican ideal ("A Man's a Man for A' That").

The soil which Burns knew so well was never distant from his thoughts. In "To a Mouse" he apologizes to a field mouse for having destroyed the little creature's home while digging the soil; in it he reflects half-humorously:

> *The best-laid schemes o' mice an' men*
> *Gang aft agley*

In "To a Mountain Daisy" he expresses similar chagrin for having uprooted the flower with his plough.

Burns considered his rollicking narrative poem, "Tam o' Shanter," to be his best. It is indeed a wonderful mixture of laughter and terror. It is a tale of the nightmarish experiences of Tam, who had drunk a little too much, on a wild ride through the night. "The Jolly Beggars," also devoted to the celebration of drink, is a zestful pagan work cast in a form of a cantata, part satirical, part serious.

One of Burns's most endearing works is his autobiographical "Epistle to John Lapraik," in which he ridicules the Neoclassical epistle by addressing a homespun one himself to Lapraik, a poet of the folk. In it he tells us of himself:

> *I am nae poet, in a sense;*
> *But just a rhymer like by chance,*
> *An' hae to learning nae pretence;*
> > *Yet, what the matter?*
> *Whene'er my Muse does on me glance,*
> > *I jingle at her.*

The stanza quoted above is a form Burns often employs, and has come to be known as the "Burns Stanza."

Burns's most ambitious poem is "The Cotter's Saturday Night" written in Spenserian stanzas. It is a work of uneven quality. At its best it gives us a very warm and dignified picture of the home-life of the simple farmer;

Burns's own father is thought to have sat for the portrait of the Cotter him-self. But the poem is defaced by some sentimentality as well as occasional outbursts of Neoclassical rhetoric.

For in Burns's poetry there is another side that has been forgotten. His brief period of being lionized in Edinburgh seems to have had the unfortu-nate effect on him of making him self-conscious of his lack of elegance in style. Despite his jeers at "Pope and Steele," Burns was sometimes tempted to try his hand at Neoclassical polish. When he did, he failed miserably. Those poems and passages which fail are always written in straight English. It is only when he is writing in the Scottish dialect that Burns is writing at his best. "The Cotter's Saturday Night" is very interesting from this point of view; the passages in Scottish dialect are all good; those in English are all bad. It is per-haps the greatest factor in the gradual diminution of Burns's reputation that his reader must master the Scottish dialect before reading the best poems.

Nevertheless, his immortality seems assured. Such manly measures as:

> *A man's a man for a' that ...*
> *The honest man, though e'er sae poor*
> *Is king o' men for a' that*

such stirring lines as:

> *Till a' the seas gang dry, my dear,*
> *And the rocks melt wi' the sun*

and such poignant verses as:

> *And my fause lover staw my rose,*
> *But ah! he left the thorn wi' me*

will not soon be forgotten.

WILLIAM BLAKE (1757–1827)

Background

No poet of the eighteenth century who wrote before the publication of the *Lyrical Ballads* of Wordsworth and Coleridge broke so completely with Neoclassicism as did William Blake. Had he achieved anything of the fame of Burns, he might have ushered in the Romantic movement himself, for his principles were at variance with everything the Age of Reason approved. His life, however, was uneventful, and his mystical turn of thought alienated a possible audience. It was not till the middle of the nineteenth century that Blake was rediscovered. Until then his poetical works were completely ignored. In our own time he has figured more and more as a poet equal to the best of the Romantics.

All but three years of Blake's life were spent in London. There is little to record in his biography. He was born on November 28, 1757, the son of a hosier. From boyhood days he had visions, and these continued throughout his life. When he was four, he saw God "put his head to the window." A few years later he met the prophet Ezekiel under a tree in the fields outside the city. A year later he saw a tree filled with angels. After trying to beat these visions out of their son, his parents were forced to acknowledge his sincerity. He was taught at home; though his parents had little to teach him, he learned much from the fields. Moreover, in his household there was exciting talk over the writings of the mystic Swedenborg, and the precise descriptions of Heaven to be found in the latter's works.

Blake was an artist at the age of ten and a poet at twelve. His poetry at no time in his life was more important to him than his engravings and paintings. He is one of England's greatest artists, and his designs for *The Book of Job* and Blair's *The Grave* are among the most amazing pieces of illustration ever made. He issued nearly all of his own poems in volumes designed, illustrated, and handcolored by himself.

He married when he was twenty-five a woman who could neither read nor write, Katherine Boucher, with whom he lived in great happiness. At various times Blake was very popular for his illustrations, until he tired of the fickleness of public favor. He lived most of his life neglected and very poor, but quite content. He was engaged on a wonderful series of pictures for *The Divine Comedy* when he died.

When still a boy, Blake found himself at home among the Elizabethans. His earliest poems (far more precocious even than Chatterton's), begun in his twelfth year, are limpid and fresh, like the songs of the Elizabethans. These were published by his friends in 1783 as *Poetical Sketches*. Many of them are lovely—notably the "Mad Song," "To the Muses," and the two songs "How Sweet I Roamed" and "My Silks and Fine Array." Unlike Burns, Blake never was in danger of following Neoclassical precept. His voice is as unaffected as though the school of Pope had never existed.

The volumes that followed were all devoted to a poetical exposition of Blake's beliefs. In them we find Blake's hatred for eighteenth century common sense and conformity. To this poet frenzy, imagination, and excess are the only roads to wisdom. Energy, he believed, is the fountain of life. He urged men to live in extremes. To him the evil principle in the world is Reason, for it puts shackles on man. Like Rousseau, Blake was hostile to human institutions, and looked upon man's primitive state as the purest.

Early Poems

The *Songs of Innocence* (1789) is a wonderful series of poems showing the soul complete in itself, uncorrupted by experience. These, among his most perfect poems, have the clarity of a sun-lit spring. The language has the simplicity of a child's vocabulary, and is perfect for conveying the innocence of the spirit, of which Blake was writing. These poems were composed, as Blake tells us in the *Introduction*, with:

> *A rural pen,*
> *And I stained the water clear*

In "The Lamb," in which the wooly animal represents innocence, the little lamb is told that it was made by God:

> *He is called by thy name,*
> *For he calls himself a Lamb.*
>
> *He is meek, and he is mild;*
> *He became a little child*

In "The Little Black Boy," the mother of the little black child tells him how white men and black men will be equal before God, and the boy concludes:

> *And thus I say to little English boy,*
> *When I from black, and he from white cloud free,*
> *. . . I'll shade him from the heat, till he can bear*
> *To lean in joy upon our father's knee.*

In *The Book of Thel* (1789), Blake deals with the soul "standing on the threshold of experience" in fear of the destiny which all mortals must undergo.

The *Songs of Experience* (1794) show the soul already exposed to evil, and knowing too well cruelty and death. This collection contains some of Blake's most startling imagery, a series of marvelous lyrics sung from the disillusionment of Hell. Here "The Tiger" becomes the symbol of evil, or experience. This evil is beautiful in its own dread province:

> *Tiger! tiger! burning bright*
> *In the forest of the night,*
> *What immortal hand or eye*
> *Could frame thy fearful symmetry? . . .*
>
> *And what shoulder, and what art,*
> *Could twist the sinews of thy heart? . . .*
> *. . . Did he smile his work to see?*
> *Did he who made the lamb make thee?*

In "The Clod and the Pebble" we read of two kinds of love, that of the downtrodden which knows how to build "a Heaven in Hell's despair," and that of the proud which can only build "a Hell in Heaven's despite." In "A Poison Tree" a man kept secret his anger against his enemy until it grew into a bright fruit tree, from which the foe stole an apple:

> *In the morning, glad, I see*
> *My foe outstretched beneath the tree.*

Thus, anger unexpressed, festers the soul.

Prophetic Books

The Marriage of Heaven and Hell (circa 1793) sings of innocence and experience, good and evil, united as they are in life because "Man has no body distinct from his soul." The *Proverbs of Hell* from this book are astounding in their imagination:

> *No bird soars too high if he soars with his own wings.*
>
> *The cistern contains: the fountain overflows.*
>
> *Sooner murder an infant in its cradle than nurse unacted desires.*

The books that Blake wrote thereafter, his so-called "prophetic books," present a certain impenetrability to the unmystical reader. Up to this point in his career Blake is not too difficult to understand. And even in *America* (1793), *Europe* (1794), *The Book of Urizen* (1794), *The Book of Los* (1795), *Milton* (1804–1809), *Jerusalem* (1804–1820), and *The Ghost of Abel* (1822) there are marvelous flashes of images illuminating profound truths. But for these books Blake manufactured an elaborate mythology that is often too obscure to follow. It is curious how in these "prophetic" works there is none of that masterful simplicity of line which ennobles his engravings. Scholarship has done much to elucidate the prophetic books, but it is unlikely that they will ever be as widely read as *Poetical Sketches, Songs of Innocence* and *Songs of Experience*.

Although Blake's early and simpler works, such as the *Songs of Innocence and Experience*, are understandably most familiar to today's readers, Blake himself considered his most important work to be these lengthy prophetic poems. They occupied the great majority of his time as both poet and illustrator. *The Marriage of Heaven and Hell,* composed between 1790 and 1793, is a satire that mocks not only the works of the Swedish mystic Emanuel Swedenborg but the whole system of moral and religious oppression that attempts to restrain what Blake viewed as man's natural energies. In this work, the Angels of Hell turn out to speak the truth, many Proverbs of Hell are indeed true ("A fool sees not the same tree that a wise man sees").

America: A Prophecy (1793) contains Blake's vision of the American revolution as not only a historical event, but a theological, psychological, and even sexual event as well. In spite of oppression by the Guardian Prince of Albion (England), the revolutionary spirit of Orc (centered in the American revolutionaries) lights the fire that, in Blake's view, eventually turns into the conflagration of the French Revolution.

The Four Zoas, an epic of 3,600 lines, tells the story of the fall of what Blake terms the "eternal man" and his eventual restoration and salvation. The title of this work stems from the four beasts described in *Revelation*, chapter 4. Blake interprets these beasts as psychological faculties of man; disharmony among these faculties leads to man's corruption and fall.

Although students of Blake continue to find a wealth of literary and philosophical riches in such prophetic works, these poems remain difficult reading at best. Alexander Gilchrist, an early biographer of Blake, admitted that he could only let his eyes "wander hopeless and disspirited up and down the pages" of many of the prophetic works.

Among his later works there are some wonderful lines in *Auguries of Innocence* (1801–1803):

> *To see the world in a grain of sand,*
> *And heaven in a wild flower;*
> *Hold infinity in the palm of your hand,*
> *And eternity in an hour.*

IMPORTANCE

The poetry of Blake is still being evaluated. He has exerted a great influence on recent writers. His incomparable gift of expressing the profoundest ideas in the simplest of language makes him almost unique among the great poets. He was an uncompromising rebel against all kinds of conformity, and the spiritual intensity of his work has never been surpassed.

MARY WOLLSTONECRAFT (1759–1797)

The mother of the writer Mary Shelley, Mary Wollstonecraft is the author of *A Vindication of the Rights of Women*, a pioneering text of 1792 that exposed and decried the injustices suffered by women in the patriarchal and increasingly industrial society of pre-Victorian England. Wollstonecraft's short life was filled with experiences that contributed to her acute observation, considered at that time a radical opinion, that women were an oppressed class. Women, Wollstonecraft concluded, were unable to rise to the social, political, and personal stature of men because of the limits imposed upon them by the preestablished social roles of society.

Wollstonecraft's childhood was marked by her father's violence, from which she often defended her hapless mother. As a young woman she was employed as a companion and then a governess in two wealthy families, during which time she became familiar with the life of the British upper class, giving her the firsthand experience she later used when she poured scorn upon the wealthy classes for their oppression of the poor in her *Vindication of the Rights of Women* (1792). With her two sisters and lifelong friend Fanny Blood, Wollstonecraft founded a girls' school near London, an effort that failed after the death of Blood but helped produce Wollstonecraft's first book, *Thoughts on the Education of Daughters* (1786). Her first novel, *Mary, a Fiction* was published in 1788, along with a volume of short stories, *Original Stories from Real Life*, illustrated by William Blake.

While living in Paris to observe the Revolution, Wollstonecraft fell in love with an American expatriate named Gilbert Imlay. Imlay was in fact a criminal, notorious for his infidelities to women, and their rocky relationship ended after two failed suicide attempts by Wollstonecraft. In a deep depression, Wollstonecraft continued to write and soon renewed an old relationship with William Godwin. The two were married despite their radical views on the topic of matrimony. Although they lived together, Godwin kept his own work space and they led fairly separate social lives. Wollstonecraft became pregnant and died of infection after giving birth to her daughter Mary. The following year Godwin published a frank and touching biography of his wife's life, *Memoirs of the author of "A Vindication of the Rights of Women."*

IMPORTANCE

Perhaps because of what her age saw as a scandalous life, or perhaps because of the same vastly limiting social roles that continued to oppress women well into the twentieth century, Wollstonecraft's work has often been overlooked. Only in the last few decades have readers and critics recognized the essential worth of her philosophic and social contributions to gender equality.

THE GOTHIC NOVEL

A pre-Romantic genre not to be overlooked, the Gothic novel exerted a significant influence on the English Romantic poets. Gothic, originally an architectural term referring to the medieval, postromanesque style, signifies in literature a move away from classical convention. The Gothic novel is both primitive and natural, often as extravagant in its plots as it is barbaric in its unexpected horrors and supernatural occurrences. The genre is generally characterized by its mystery, horror, magic, and chivalry, and although the traditional Gothic setting is a castle or a villa, the term *Gothic novel* applies more to the style of writing and the atmosphere created by the text.

Horace Walpole was one of the first Gothic writers, and his *Castle of Otranto* (1764) is usually named among the earliest novels of the genre. In this work, set in a medieval castle, Walpole establishes the classic Gothic atmosphere, complete with phantoms, trapdoors, a labyrinthian basement. His highly emotional, sometimes exaggerated style is also typically Gothic.

William Beckford's *Vathek, an Arabian Tale* (1786) added touches of eroticism and orientalism to the Gothic genre.

Ann Radcliffe (1764–1823)

One of the most influential and most-read Gothic romance writers was Ann Radcliffe. Her most notable novels include *The Mysteries of Udolpho* (1794) and *The Italian* (1797), which is perhaps her best work. Her characters are often quite two-dimensional, and appear to the modern reader as types, clearly marked as good or evil. Radcliffe's strength lies in her ability to weave intricate plot structures that, though sometimes improbable, serve to create and maintain suspense throughout the novel. Radcliffe's work was read by several Romantic poets, and she undoubtedly influenced Coleridge, Keats, Byron, and Shelley, as well as later writers of Gothic romance such as the Brontë sisters and Mary Shelley.

Not her most popular novel at the time, *The Italian* is today viewed as one of the most successful examples of Gothic romance. Set in the dark monasteries and gloomy dungeons typical of medieval Europe at the time of the Inquisition, the novel's plot is on the surface familiar, almost banal. It begins as a love story, telling of a blossoming romance between Ellena di Rosalba and Vincentio di Vivaldi. Vivaldi's mother does not wish to see the couple marry, and summons her adviser, the monk Schedoni, to ask his counsel. Schedoni, the villian, is certainly the most compelling character of the novel, and his evil and mysterious nature holds the reader's attention. Schedoni plots against the life of Ellena, but the scheming monk is discovered to be Count Ferando di Bruno, wanted for a variety of crimes, who has disguised himself within the Dominican order. After this revelation, and the subsequent suicide of the monk, Vincentio and Ellena are free from evil and able to pursue their love. The novel lacks the overt supernatural element present in *Udolpho* and other Gothic texts, but the overall tone suggests the demonic and ghostly. Radcliffe adds suspense to her work through expert pacing and a good dose of realism in her descriptions. The main theme of the novel is inhumanity, represented by the terrors of the Inquisition and essentially embodied in the villain Schedoni. Radcliffe's imaginative narrative is an obvious contributor to the beginnings of the romantic movement, particularly the Romantic interest in the nature and origins of evil.

Characteristics of the Genre

Although the characteristics of the Gothic novel differ somewhat from author to author, the following traits were generally associated with this genre in the period:

1. The setting is an old, grand, and often decaying castle or villa.
2. The protagonists, often female, are beset by perverted designs on their physical safety and virtue.
3. Mysterious phenomena occur, sometimes apparently supernatural.

4. One or more deeply evil antagonists are usually skilled at deception and black magic.
5. Suspense is sustained as perplexing circumstances conspire against the hero or heroine.
6. Eventually a natural explanation of apparently supernatural phenomena is revealed, with inevitable punishment for the wicked and reward (often in the form of marriage) for the virtuous.

Many writers of the nineteenth and twentieth centuries are loosely associated with the Gothic style. Dickens, for example, incorporates many elements of the Gothic in *Great Expectations*, and the short stories of Edgar Allen Poe ("The Black Cat," "The Cask of Amontillado"), often classed as fantastic, are also Gothic in theme and style. Other writers from the American South, such as William Faulkner, Tennessee Williams, and most recently Anne Rice have written clearly Gothic works.

2
THE ROMANTIC MOVEMENT, FIRST GENERATION

REVOLUTIONARY THOUGHT

During the evolution of the factory system, the merchant class became more and more significant in English national life. Cities multiplied in population, labor and life were cheap, and the industrialists developed a philosophy of individualism that would justify their enterprise without involving obligations to society. The Romantic writers were enemies of the idea of injustice, but they knew little about actual social conditions; they themselves did not come from the ranks of wage earners, since the latter had little opportunity to educate their children. But the Romantic writers were powerfully affected by the theories developed in France establishing the principles of Liberty, Fraternity and Equality. Before social abuses could be cured, these principles had to be established. The Victorian writers, later in the century, would be interested in the application of these principles. In the meantime, the Romantic writers did much to foster them.

Liberal forces in England had the immediate problem of fighting for universal suffrage. During the French Revolution, young English radicals were full of sympathy for the Revolution. With the triumph of reaction after the fall of Napoleon in 1815, the issues raised by the Revolution were still of paramount importance. The Tories were in power in the government from 1783 to 1830 with the exception of one brief interval. The lines between the liberal and the conservative were sharply drawn. Paine, Godwin, Burns, and Blake were strong partisans of republicanism. The first generation of Romantic poets (Wordsworth, Coleridge, and Southey) all were vigorous friends of revolution in their youth. Wordsworth first awoke intellectually in France during the crucial years of 1791 to 1792; Southey and Coleridge in 1794 were forming plans for a free society to be begun across the Atlantic. As the Revolution changed its course, however, under the leadership of Napoleon, all three lost heart. By the time the *Lyrical Ballads* appeared in 1798, Wordsworth and Coleridge (as well as Southey) were well on the way to becoming conservatives.

Among the second generation of Romantic poets, Shelley alone refused to surrender his optimism for revolutionary ideas. Keats felt that political matters had nothing to do with poetry, and Byron's political philosophy was purely negative. Scott, whose career bridges both generations, was frankly feudal in his politics. The second generation of Romantic poets, indeed, wrote in an atmosphere of complete skepticism over the possibility of emancipating society.

In Germany a whole literature had developed with despair of the world as its dominant tone. In Goethe's youthful novel, *The Sorrows of Young Werther*, we find a typical hero of the period, a highly sensitive man crushed by the cruelty of life. In another German work of the same epoch, Schiller's *The Robbers*, we find the same despair producing another type of hero, the strong man of stormy nature who refuses to succumb to the cruelty of society, and wages unending war against it. In the poetry of Shelley and Keats we find frequent symptoms of the Werther temperament; the heroes of Byron's poems are all first cousins to the hero of *The Robbers*. The first type, the Werther, has come to be called "the victim of the *Weltschmerz* (world sorrow)"; the second, the Robber, is known as the "Titan."

In the field of pure philosophy, the English Romantic Movement also felt the influence of German speculation. Kant (1724–1804) provided the philosophic foundation for Romanticism in his *Critique of Pure Reason* (1781), in which he denied the power of reason to discover ultimate reality. Kant established a school of philosophy that developed the idea that man's intuitive life is his truer one. This school of thought did much to influence the theories of Coleridge, who gave the English Romantic Movement much of its fundamental philosophic doctrine.

IDEAS OF THE FIRST GENERATION OF ROMANTICS

The Romantic Movement eventually exhibited traits diametrically opposed to those of Neoclassicism. Romantics typically revolt against the authority of reason and pay tribute to their senses, their emotions, and, most important of all, their imagination. In consequence, they willingly expose themselves to the lure of Nature, where these things most can be satisfied. All over Europe the writings of Rousseau, the great discoverer of Nature as teacher and nurse, had enormous prestige. In England, particularly, where the romantic temperament is at home and where the literature before Dryden had been essentially romantic in cast, the rediscovery of Nature became almost universal. The Romantics prefer to live in the country rather than the city (with the exception of Charles Lamb), and turn to Nature for their best inspiration. They become interested in simple folk and country people rather than the frequenters of salons. They find wonderful virtues in the farmer and peasant, a wisdom beyond what books can teach. The Romantics are also more concerned with the past than with the present, and with far-off lands than with their own. They are violent individualists and cultivate self-expression to the limit. They are interested in developing a multiplicity of verse techniques, convinced that the form must suit their meaning. They will not, like the Neoclassicists, pour their thought into the mold of one accepted form.

Wordsworth, Coleridge, and Southey went to live in the mountain districts of the north of England, in the famous Lake Country—for which reason they have been called the "Lake poets." Hazlitt and DeQuincey were on intimate terms with them, as was Lamb despite his preference for living in London. Of these men Southey was for a time the most widely admired, though he has few readers any longer.

The first generation of English Romantic poets (Blake, Wordsworth, Coleridge, and others) were raised in the philosophical traditions of the eighteenth century. Particularly influential was the pervasive empiricism of John Locke. Each in his own way, these first Romantic poets struggled against Locke's assumption that physical things alone are "real" and that we know this reality through the interaction of sensations, which imprint thoughts upon the blank slate *(tabula rasa)* of our minds. For Blake, this philosophy seemed to condemn human beings to the roles of victims, who are acted upon by their environments but exert no shaping influence over that environment. For Wordsworth (like Kant in many ways), human beings carried shaping powers of perception and imagination with them from their birth; the reality they fashioned was as much a product of those inner powers as of external sensation. For Coleridge (as for Hegel in some ways), mankind's inner faculties were fashioned in such a way as to participate in and fulfill the stimuli of the natural world. What human beings bring to the natural world, in Coleridge's view, makes possible a marriage of inner and outer worlds—and the creation of "reality" itself.

ROBERT SOUTHEY (1774–1843)

Southey started out as a burning radical. He was expelled from Westminster School for writing an essay that displeased the authorities and had trouble gaining admission to Oxford. Soon he became acquainted with Coleridge, then a student at Cambridge, and together they formed a scheme to start a new communal society in America. There they would put into practice all the libertarian ideas they had gleaned from their readings in the French revolutionary philosophers. The society was to be called *Pantisocracy,* a society in which all should be equal. Their plans stipulated for each young man to be equipped with a wife and to have a certain small sum with which to start out. As preparation for the experiment, Southey satisfied the first stipulation by marrying Edith Fricker, to whose sister Coleridge became engaged. Unhappily for his republican ardor, Southey at this time came into an inheritance. The idealistic scheme and the revolutionary philosophy were both presently given up. After a trip to Spain, made possible by the small annuity granted him, Southey devoted himself to poetry. He settled at Keswick for the rest of his life. In 1813 he was made Poet Laureate. Wordsworth, who succeeded him, wrote the inscription that is on his monument in Crosthwaite Churchyard.

Southey was a tireless writer, and pursued his work partly because of his love of writing, partly because of the need to support his family. He won respect and admiration quite beyond the merit of his poetic gifts. He was a kinder man and a better friend than either Wordsworth or Coleridge, and his letters are far more engaging now for us than his poetry. When very young he wrote *Wat Tyler* (1794) and *Joan of Arc* (1796), both full of inflammatory revolutionary sentiments. Once he settled down to conservatism and his vast output of writing, he proposed for himself the ambitious design of "exhibiting all the more important and poetical forms of mythology," making each mythology the basis of another poem. The result was a series of epics: *Thalaba* (1801), set in Arabia; *Madoc* (1805), set in Mexico; *The Curse of Kehama* (1810), set in India; and *Don Roderick* (1814), set in Spain. These long poems were written with great facility, and exhibit the more obvious aspects of Romanticism, such as the interest in distant times and places; but they lack any profound poetic quality. Southey was also the author of a number of ballads, of which the most celebrated is "The Battle of Blenheim." One of his poems is best known for Lewis Carroll's burlesque of it: "Father William." Southey's "Cataract of Lodore" has been admired for its attempt to reproduce a waterfall in verse.

After his fortieth year Southey's writings were mostly in prose. His biography of Nelson is the best of these. On the whole, Southey's importance is rather historical than literary.

WILLIAM WORDSWORTH (1770–1850)

Wordsworth was born in the Lake District of Cumberland, so intimately bound up with his name, at Cockermouth, on April 7, 1770. William was the second of three boys. Their one sister, Dorothy, born the year after him, spent the major part of her life in devoted service to him. The children had lost both parents when they were all still young. William was sent to Hawkshead School, and later to St. John's College, Cambridge, which he entered in 1787. With a college friend, Robert Jones, he made a tour on foot through France, Switzerland and Northern Italy. Out of this vacation he drew material that helped to launch his career as a poet. He took his B.A. in January 1791 and went to London for some months.

In November 1791, Wordsworth decided to go to France to learn the language. He chose a time when the Revolution in France seemed to be pursuing a moderate course; most Whigs and Tories in England were by no means hostile to what was going on in France. Wordsworth visited Paris and left for Orleans, in which latter vicinity he remained until October 1792. It was at

Orleans that his first great experiences occurred through his close relationship with Michel Beaupuy and Annette Vallon.

Beaupuy, an army officer enthusiastically devoted to the cause of the Revolution, was a disciple of Rousseau. From him Wordsworth discovered the philosophy of the great Genevan. The teachings of Rousseau were to be one of the most important elements in Wordsworth's own thinking.

Annette Vallon was a girl of good family. Wordsworth fell in love with her. After many clandestine meetings she found herself with child by him.

It is characteristic of Wordsworth that just before Annette's child was born, he left Orleans for Paris en route to England, apparently to procure his guardians' consent to a marriage with her. Once back in England, however, he allowed his sister Dorothy to be his spokesman. She failed to get their guardians' consent. And by degrees Wordsworth gave up any idea of marrying Annette. It should be added, lest anyone imagine Annette's life to have been ruined by her experience with Wordsworth, that she seems to have fared well and to have been well esteemed in her community.

Wordsworth's brief experience in France powerfully affected the rest of his life. Not only did he remain impressed with Beaupuy's teachings, even after he turned against the Revolution, but his experience with Annette seems to have left a scar on his heart that never healed. Though the world never heard of Wordsworth's French daughter until our own century, we find Wordsworth recurring again and again to the theme of a woman abandoned with her child by her lover.

In London he became part of a revolutionary group surrounding Godwin; in common with these young radicals, when England declared war against France in 1793, Wordsworth hoped to see a French victory. In the same year he published his first two volumes. *An Evening Walk* and *Descriptive Sketches*, both written in rhymed couplets. These early works show the influence of the Graveyard School. *An Evening Walk* has many interesting descriptive details, and shows Wordsworth's religious skepticism at this time of his life. *Descriptive Sketches* is the record of his Alpine journey with Jones, and reveals his strong Revolutionary enthusiasms. It was during this period also that he penned a heated reply to a sermon of Bishop Watson on *The Wisdom of God in Having Made Both Rich and Poor*; but he never published it.

A legacy of nine hundred pounds that fell to him in January 1795 enabled Wordsworth at last to devote his life to poetry. A friend offered him a home at Racedown, and Dorothy came to keep house for him. A woman of genius herself, who preferred to lay down her talents at the altar of her brother's, she taught William to find peace and comfort in Nature. It was at this time that Wordsworth came to know Samuel Taylor Coleridge, a young poet of the highest gifts. Coleridge was tremendously impressed with his new friend and confessed that he felt quite inferior to Wordsworth. It is not on record that Wordsworth ever attempted to disagree with him in his feeling that way.

Coleridge decided that they must live near each other, so that the Wordsworths moved to Alfoxden, a few miles from Coleridge's home at Nether Stowey. They saw one another daily. William, Dorothy and Coleridge would walk miles over the hills together talking over wonderful literary projects. The two men decided to publish a volume of poems jointly. Each was to approach poetry from a slightly different point of view. Wordsworth would take humble topics and make them seem magical; Coleridge would deal with the supernatural and make it seem real.

Lyrical Ballads

The book that resulted from the relationship described above was *Lyrical Ballads*, published in September 1798, and it has since been described as the volume that formally inaugurated the Romantic Movement. It contained some of Wordsworth's finest poems, such as "We Are Seven," "Lines Written in Early Spring," "Expostulation and Reply," "The Tables Turned" and "Lines Composed a Few Miles Above Tintern Abbey;" and Coleridge's masterpiece, "The Rime of the Ancient Mariner."

The friendship between Wordsworth and Coleridge was at first highly fruitful to them and to English literature. Coleridge was an undisciplined genius of fiery imagination and enormous reading; Wordsworth was reserved, strong, and self-disciplined. Coleridge gave Wordsworth new perspectives; Wordsworth was able for a time to teach Coleridge how important steady work is. Dorothy, to whom Coleridge was strongly attracted, was an important link in their relationships.

"We Are Seven" shows the poet interviewing an eight-year-old girl. She persists in saying that she is one of seven children even though a brother and sister lie buried in the churchyard. This child will not accept death as an important fact, and feels that it has not broken the family group.

"Lines Written in Early Spring" is a meditation in the midst of a sunny landscape on how mankind has perverted Nature's plan for harmony and peace.

"Expostulation and Reply" finds the poet sitting in quiet meditation in the country. His friend Matthew asks why he is wasting his time idling instead of reading. The poet answers that he is not idle, but is listening to the voice of nature:

> *The eye,—it cannot choose but see;*
> *We cannot bid the ear be still;*
> *Our bodies feel, where'er they be,*
> *Against or with our will.*
>
> *Nor less I deem that there are powers*
> *Which of themselves our minds impress;*
> *That we can feed this mind of ours*
> *In a wise passiveness.*

"The Tables Turned" returns to the same subject. In it the poet dismisses science and art as holding only "barren leaves." He bids his friend come forth and drink of nature:

> *One impulse from a vernal wood*
> *May teach you more of man,*
> *Of moral evil and of good,*
> *Than all the sages can.*

"Lines Composed a Few Miles above Tintern Abbey" contains some of Wordsworth's greatest lines. The poet finds himself after a lapse of five years on the banks of the River Wye in the company of his sister. As he looks over the lovely quiet landscape he reflects that the scene has often recurred to him when he was far distant from it; and as he used to recreate it in his mind's eye, he felt that the feelings it inspired ennobled even his smallest daily acts. To these feelings he has owed a sublime gift of learning how to listen to the voice of Nature. In this blessed mood, when we lose consciousness of our animal nature,

> *. . . we are laid asleep*
> *In body, and become a living soul;*
> *While with an eye made quiet by the power*
> *Of harmony, and the deep power of joy,*
> *We see into the life of things.*

He now considers that this renewed acquaintance with the scene will be food for the spirit in future years. When first he came among these hills he was mad with passion for Nature, but "more like a man flying from something that he dreads," than one seeking the object of his love. That time of dizzy rapture is gone, but has given place to a better feeling:

> *For I have learned*
> *To look on Nature, not as in the hour*
> *Of thoughtless youth; but hearing oftentimes*
> *The still, sad music of humanity*

In this mature mood he has developed:

> *. . . a sense sublime*
> *Of something far more deeply interfused,*
> *Whose dwelling is the light of setting suns,*
> *And the round ocean and the living air,*
> *And the blue sky, and in the mind of man;*
> *A motion and a spirit, that impels*
> *All thinking things, all objects of all thought,*
> *And rolls through all things.*

The poem concludes with a prayer that Nature, who "never did betray the heart that loved her," will also teach his sister to mature in the same way.

The "Lines Composed a Few Miles above Tintern Abbey" is for a number of reasons the most important of Wordsworth's poems in the 1798 volume. It is written in blank verse, a medium in which Wordsworth is often at his best. (The rhymes in his rhymed verse are never distinguished by any beauty of their own.) The poem shows to perfection that quiet meditative music of which Wordsworth could be on occasion supreme master. It also shows the essentially philosophical cast of his poetry; Wordsworth describes Nature very little; he is a great nature poet in the sense that his philosophy accords Nature the highest place as teacher and nurse. "Tintern Abbey" also contains several ideas that recur in Wordsworth's best poems: the fact that powerful impressions of natural scenery remain with one as a comfort throughout life; his belief in Nature as the great teacher; and his sense of having developed from a passionate lover of Nature to a quiet thoughtful student of her.

Preface to *Lyrical Ballads*

Lyrical Ballads was bitterly attacked in the more conservative periodicals. Nevertheless, it sold well enough to call for a second printing in 1800. The 1800 edition contains some important new poems, and an epoch-making "Preface" that Wordsworth wrote for it.

This "Preface" is one of the most important critical documents in our literature. In it the public is informed as to the poetic practice Wordsworth and Coleridge had been adopting. The "Preface," eminently Rousseauistic in its principles throughout, effectively routed the prestige of Neoclassical poetic theory.

The "Preface" to the *Lyrical Ballads* informs us that both poets believed that the situations of poetry should be taken from common life, and that they should be related in "language really used by men." The incidents related in the poem have been colored by the poet's imagination, with the result that commonplace happenings take on a quality of magic. These incidents were also selected because they exhibit the fundamental laws by which Nature operates. Since humble people and country life best illustrate these laws, humble people and the country have been chosen as the subject matter of the poems. Men living close to Nature derive their very language from her, and their discourse is by habit honest and eloquent. All poetry, the "Preface" avers, must have a purpose. "All good poetry is the spontaneous overflow of powerful feelings." But the poet must reflect long over his material. The strong emotions that poetry records are inevitably "emotion recollected in tranquillity."

The "Preface" points out that the poems of both poets, unlike those of the Neoclassicists, derive their power from the emotions they record; it is the emotion which gives meaning to the situation dealt with. The language of the poet should not be abstract, and Wordsworth scorns so-called "poetic diction." Between poetry and prose the difference is not very great, although the Neoclassicists had insisted otherwise. It is the figure of speech which makes poetry, not elegance of vocabulary. A poet is a man more sensitive and enthusiastic than other men. He can speak to other men because he knows more about human nature. He never forgets that the purpose of true poetry is the recording of truth. But this truth must be expressed in a manner that will excite the pleasure to be expected of metrical composition. It is this pleasure that is the cause for the poet's not writing in prose.

"Lucy" Poems and "Michael"

Among the new poems in the 1800 edition which exemplify these theories at their best are the five poems known as the "Lucy" poems, and "Michael."

The first Lucy poem, "Strange Fits of Passion Have I Known," tells of the lover's sudden terror at the thought that life would be unendurable if Lucy were dead; the second, "She Dwelt among the Untrodden Ways," informs us that Lucy has died. To him she was precious even though she had been:

> *A violet by a mossy stone*
> *Half-hidden from the eye!*
> *—Fair as a star, when only one*
> *Is shining in the sky.*

The third poem of this series shows the lover in a foreign land dreaming of Lucy as she sat by an English fireside; it opens:

> *I traveled among unknown men*

The fourth:

> *Three years she grew in sun and shower*

shows Nature deciding to take Lucy to herself and rearing her as a child of nature. The fifth:

> *A slumber did my spirit seal*

is a reflection of how Lucy is now one with rocks, stones and trees in Nature. The "Lucy" poems have been much admired for their perfect simplicity and directness of language.

"Michael" was Wordsworth's attempt to show that a pastoral poem need not be the artificial thing that tradition has made it. Written in blank verse with some of his most eloquent simplicity, the story Wordsworth tells is a humble one, very grave and very moving, a story that is truly of the soil. Old Michael is a shepherd at Grasmere, who lives a frugal simple life, but is warmly attached to his land. His wife is a capable housewife, who shares the responsibility of making a full life. Their whole existence is concentrated on their hopes for their son Luke. All their labors are aimed at handing on the land to him free of debt. But Luke goes to the city and eventually comes to a bad end. The old shepherd and his wife die, and the sheepfold that Michael had begun building with Luke for the boy's future use is never finished.

Late in 1798 William, Dorothy, and Coleridge went to Germany. It was there that the "Lucy" poems were written. On their return to England the Wordsworths made their residence in their native Lake Country on Grasmere Lake; there they found an abandoned inn which they called Dove Cottage. For the rest of his life Wordsworth remained in this vicinity. Coleridge lived near them too on his return, and their companionship continued. The years between 1800 and 1807 were the most productive in Wordsworth's career. In 1802 the payment with interest of a debt long overdue to the Wordsworths made it possible for William to marry his childhood friend Mary Hutchinson. Coleridge wrote his "Dejection, an Ode" as a wedding present, one of the strangest wedding presents ever made.

Short Lyrics

In August 1803, only a few days after Mrs. Wordsworth had given birth to their first son, William, his sister and Coleridge set out for a tour of Scotland. After two weeks, Coleridge decided to go on alone on foot. This separation was the beginning of a cooling of feeling on Coleridge's part. On this trip, however, William stored a host of impressions that inspired some of his loveliest poems: "At The Grave of Burns," "Stepping Westward," "The Solitary Reaper," and "Yarrow Unvisited." For Dorothy the trip resulted in her gathering material for her vivid *Recollections of a Tour Made In Scotland* (which was not published until 1874).

"At The Grave of Burns" is written in the Burns stanza. It is a tribute to Burns's genius, a regretful realization that Wordsworth and he could have been friends had they met, and a prayer that God would take Burns's spirit into His embrace.

"Stepping Westward" is a charming poem on the encounter of the poet and his sister with two women, one of whom asks, courteously, "What, are you stepping westward?" The question and the voice that asked it somehow reminded him of human sweetness.

"The Solitary Reaper," one of the best of Wordsworth's poems, is a reflection on a Highland lass he had passed as she was reaping and singing in the fields. Her voice reminds him of the nightingale singing in far-off Arabia, or of the thrilling summons of spring of the cuckoo bird singing "among the farthest Hebrides."

> *Will no one tell me what she sings? . . .*
> *Perhaps the plaintive numbers flow*
> *For old, unhappy, far-off things,*
> *And battles long ago.*
> *Or is it some more humble lay,*
> *Familiar matter of today?*
> *Some natural sorrow, loss, or pain,*
> *That has been, and may be again?*

The poem concludes with the observation that the music of this experience remained in the poet's heart long after the event was over.

"Yarrow Unvisited" tells how the poet, because he has never visited the banks of Yarrow, has come to think of the river as an ideal associated with all that is happy and full of delight. He will refrain from visiting it for some time so that he may know that there is always a bonny spot still to be seen.

Coleridge left for Malta in 1804. When he returned two years later all real friendship between the two poets was ended. The actual break, which soon followed, more or less marks the end of the great poetic creativeness of both men.

The death of Wordsworth's brother John in 1805 made a profound impression upon the poet, and his thoughts began to turn more and more towards formal Christianity. Eventually Wordsworth ended by attending church. As for his politics, these were some time before altered because of his disillusionment over Napoleon's career. The older he grew, the more conservative Wordsworth became. For a number of years he sought a government post, and in 1813 he was appointed Distributor of Stamps in Westmoreland County. From this office, which had few duties, he derived a good income.

In 1819 the Wordsworths moved to Rydal Mount, where he remained until his death in 1850. During the last thirty years of his life Wordsworth was a staunch conservative, an enemy of Parliamentary reform, universal suffrage, Catholic Emancipation, and the freedom of the press. He had little sympathy for the new generation of Romantic poets, Byron, Shelley, and Keats, who owed so much to his precedent, and all of whom he long outlived. During this last period of his life Wordsworth continued to write but with diminishing power, although to the very end he could write many excellent isolated lines. Upon Southey's death he was appointed Poet Laureate in 1843. He died on April 23, 1850, and was buried in Grasmere Churchyard. In Westminster Abbey a monument was erected to him.

IMPORTANCE

To be fair to Wordsworth it is necessary to dissociate his unattractive personality from his work. It is also necessary to discount perhaps as much as ninety percent of his work. It is on the basis of the remaining ten percent that Matthew Arnold placed him below only Shakespeare and Milton. If this judgment is extreme, it is nonetheless true that Wordsworth's best poems deserve a very high place in critical regard, and that they are among the crowning achievements of the Romantic Movement.

The Prelude

Among Wordsworth's most interesting works is a long autobiographical poem for which he wrote some of his best passages, *The Prelude*. This work was actually composed between 1799 and 1805. As first completed it was a fairly faithful record of his intellectual and emotional experiences. Even the Vallon experience was included, although in a disguised form. But although the poem was completed in 1805 Wordsworth did not publish it. He continued to revise it through the years; and as his orthodoxy hardened, he modified the poem to tone down and in some cases eradicate his youthful radicalism and pantheism. When it was finally printed in 1850, although there were magnificent passages, *The Prelude* was distinctly less than an honest account of his intellectual and emotional development.

The development which the poem records consisted, as Wordsworth saw it, of three stages. As a child he had been a wild thoughtless animal, unconsciously imbibing the wonders of Nature. Then came young manhood when Nature was a passion loved for her colors and form. As he approached thirty this appetite passed, and he learned to listen to Nature for the deep wisdom she could teach. (These three stages must be kept in mind when one reads many of his shorter poems, such as "Tintern Abbey," "Expostulation and Reply," the "Lucy" poems and "Michael.")

The Prelude contains many fine sections: the descriptions of his experiences as a boy rowing a boat on the lake amid the silent hills of Northumberland, the thrilling times when there was ice skating; his friendship and conversations with Beaupuy; the effect of these experiences on his mind, and more. *The Prelude* contains some of Wordsworth's finest blank verse.

Later Poems

There are a number of other works of Wordsworth's worthy of notice. *The Borderers* is his only drama, written in blank verse, and expresses Wordsworth's rejection by 1796 of Godwin's teachings; it was not published until 1842. *The Excursion* (1814) is a long, rather stuffy philosophical poem on the relationship of man to Nature. It was intended to be a second part of a longer work to be called *The Recluse;* of this projected work *The Prelude* was to have been the first part. *The River Duddon* (1820) is a collection of thirty-four sonnets constituting a kind of poetical geography of the river; it has few inspiring passages. *The Ecclesiastical Sonnets* (1822) consist of 102 (later augmented to 132), which form a sequence on the history and dogma of the Church of England; of these only the sonnets called "Mutability" and "Inside of Kings College Chapel" have quality.

There are a number of individual poems of Wordsworth that must be mentioned. "Lucy Gray" (1800) is a ballad written in Wordsworth's simplest style, done with much ease and imagination. The "Ode to Duty" (1807) expresses the poet's conviction of the omnipresence of good in the universe. "Resolution and Independence" (1807) is a poem telling of the encounter of the poet with a poor gatherer of leeches; this simple man, decrepit in body but firm in mind has given the poet many hours of faith and comfort because of his simple words; Lewis Carroll's burlesque of this poem, "The White Knight's Song," however, makes it difficult now to take Wordsworth's original seriously. One tiny poem is a gem, "My Heart Leaps Up," in which the poet acknowledges all that he owes as an adult to the impressions of his childhood. "Yew Trees" (1803) is a remarkable passage in blank verse describing in very Miltonic phraseology a number of trees that have stood in silent dignity for many centuries. "She Was a Phantom of Delight" (1804) is a tribute to a beautiful womanly woman. "I Wandered Lonely as a Cloud" recounts how the sight of a field of daffodils has afforded endless comfort in after years to the poet. "Yarrow Visited" (1814) is a tribute to the River Yarrow when at last seen. "To a Sky-Lark" (1825) finds the "ethereal minstrel" a symbol of "the wise who soar but never roam" far from their own dwellings.

The most ambitious of these poems is the "Ode on Intimations of Immortatity from Recollections of Early Childhood" composed between 1802 and 1806. In it Wordsworth notes that although his eyes behold the beauty of nature, his heart no longer can feel the rapture it used to know in such scenes:

> *The pansy at my feet*
> *Doth the same tale repeat:*
> *Whither is fled the visionary gleam?*
> *Where is it now, the glory and the dream?*

The poet then reflects that our birth into this world is but "a forgetting" of another existence the soul knew. For we come into this world:

> *Not in entire forgetfulness,*
> *And not in utter nakedness,*
> *But trailing clouds of glory do we come*
> *From God, who is our home*

As we get older we lose more and more of this heavenly glory, for this life is like a pleasant prisonhouse for the soul. The little child is already busy imitating in his play the affairs of grown men and women. Why is he so anxious to take upon his young years the heavy burdens of earthly life, thus quickly forsaking those truths which he will seek all his life in vain to find again? The poem concludes with the reflection that luckily we never quite lose the sense of that eternity from which we came:

> *Thanks to the human heart by which we live,*
> *Thanks to its tenderness, its joys, and fears,*
> *To me the meanest flower that blows can give*
> *Thoughts that do often lie too deep for tears.*

Sonnets

Wordsworth's sonnets, a variation in form of the "Italian sonnet," are among the best of his shorter poems. Several of these express profound patriotism. "Composed by the Seaside near Calais, August 1802" is inspired by the evening star, which the poet feels might be his country's emblem; he is fearful for his dear fatherland because he is among her enemies. "It Is a Beauteous Evening, Calm and Free" (1802) was written on the beach near Calais when Wordsworth once went there to meet his French daughter; the evening has a holy calm, and the child walking by his side partakes in her nature of divinity too:

> *Thou liest in Abraham's bosom all the year,...*
> *God being with thee when we know it not*

In "Near Dover, September 1802" the poet looks across the straits towards the coast of France, and shudders to think how close the evil going on there is to England; God's decree is that by the soul only shall the nations be great and free. "On the Extinction of the Venetian Republic" is a reflection on the passing away of the glory of Venice. "To Toussaint L'Ouverture" is addressed to the Negro revolutionary leader fighting for the independence of Haiti, and promising him that though he falls he will never be forgotten because of "man's unconquerable mind." "Composed upon Westminster Bridge, September 3, 1802," the best of the sonnets, finds the poet looking over the city of London at early morning; he surveys the panorama of the city in a deep calm:

> *Dear God! the very houses seem asleep;*
> *And all that mighty heart is lying still!*

"Written in London, 1802" is a lament for the respect that wealth can command and for the prevalence of avarice and lechery; the homely beauty of household living is a thing of the past, "London 1802" has a stirring opening:

> *Milton! thou shouldst be living at this hour:*
> *England hath need of thee*

for she has fallen a prey to selfishness; Milton's spirit is needed to remind Englishmen of freedom and virtue; Milton with his "voice whose sound was like the sea" lived a life of simple and cheerful godliness. "The World is Too Much with Us" (1806) deplores the fact that men have given up their natural heritage, and are out of tune with the best in nature; the poet feels he would rather be:

> *A pagan suckled in a creed outworn;*
> *So might I, standing on this pleasant lea...*
> *. . . Hear old Tritan blow his wreathed horn.*

"Thought of a Briton on the Subjugation of Switzerland" (1807) avers that Liberty loved the sea and the mountains; the tyrant Napoleon came to rout

Liberty and has driven her from her Alpine hold; since she has been forced to flee the mountains, let her voice at least still be heard on the ocean. "The Trosachs" (1831) celebrates a mountain-pass in the Highlands, made famous by Scott's *Lady of the Lake*:

> *Life is but a tale of morning grass withered*
> *at eve.*

SAMUEL TAYLOR COLERIDGE (1772–1834)

IMPORTANCE

The failure of Coleridge to create even a small portion of the great poetry that his genius had endowed him to write, constitutes one of the most tragic histories of wasted gifts on record. His poetic talents were of the highest, but he has left us only a handful of great poems. Wordsworth and he both outlived by many years the period of their inspiration; unlike Wordsworth, Coleridge wrote few verses in his later years. His rich intellect was not dormant, however, and after he had given up the poetic vein, he wrote some important literary criticism.

Coleridge was born in Devonshire, the thirteenth child of the rector of Ottery St. Mary's. While still a very young boy he became a bookworm like his father. *The Arabian Nights* with its marvelous world of magic, color, and mystery made a profound impression on his youthful mind. Temperamentally Coleridge was prone to live in a realm of his own imagining, and the great Oriental classic only deepened this tendency. The death of his father, to whom he had been very dear, ended, before he was ten, his happy wanderings over the Devonshire countryside. He was sent to school at Christ's Hospital in London, a charity school. There he met as a fellow student Charles Lamb, who remained, except for a brief interval of misunderstanding, his close friend for the rest of his days.

The year in which Wordsworth left that university, Coleridge was admitted to Cambridge, as a sizar at Jesus College. He was miserably poor there. In 1792 he won a medal for a Greek ode on the slave trade; the next year he was granted a scholarship. He was already an omnivorous reader, and in poetry had fallen under the spell of Chatterton, Macpherson, and a minor poet, Bowles. He had already, too, formed the habit of taking opium to relieve any kind of physical pain. His debts were mounting, and he was growing restless. Suddenly in November 1793 he left the university, and in a few days had enlisted in the Light Dragoons under the absurd alias of Silas Tomkyn Comberbacke. It is characteristic of Coleridge that, hating war and dreading even mounting a horse, he should have joined the cavalry. Luckily, his brother procured his release, and he returned to Cambridge.

In the summer of 1794 on a visit to Oxford he made the acquaintance of young Robert Southey. Both boys were fervent republicans, disgusted with the conservatism of England. They hit upon a scheme for establishing a colony to be lived by the most ideal of Rousseauistic standards in America, on the banks of the Susquehanna. Their new society was to be called *Pantisocracy* (a society in which everyone would be equal to everyone else). Southey enlisted his mother and his sweetheart Edith Fricker as his first disciples. Edith's sister Mary, married to Southey's friend Robert Lovell, was ready to go too. But the experiment would require money. Southey and Coleridge decided that would be easy: all they had to do was a little lecturing to raise funds. In the meantime their plans required each man to be married; since the Fricker girls seemed to be closely involved in Pantisocracy's future, Coleridge thought it not inadvisable to become engaged to one of the three still available sisters, the eldest, Sara Fricker. Coleridge's great hopes for reforming the world can be read in a silly poem he wrote at this time, "To a Young Ass, Its Mother Chained to It near a Log" (1794). He tells the starved-looking beast:

> *I hail thee* Brother—*spite of the fools scorn!*
> *And fain would take thee with me, in the Dell*
> *Where high-souled Pantisocracy shall dwell*

Their financial aims failing, Coleridge and Southey collaborated on a play, *The Fall of Robespierre* (1794), which netted them nothing.

Before a year was out both young revolutionaries had married their fiancées. Before another had passed, Coleridge was so pressed with the financial responsibilities of his household that he ceased dreaming of Pantisocracy. Southey, for similar reasons, had already lost interest.

In 1796 Coleridge published a volume, *Poems,* and another the next year. These prove that he had not yet found himself, though everywhere there is abundant evidence of genius. The poem "Lewti, or the Circassian Love-Chaunt," for instance, is truly beautiful; "Religious Musings" has many fine lines. The poem called "France" shows that by this time Coleridge had become disillusioned in the French Revolution, though he had not given up the cause of freedom.

His feverish intellect was never at rest. He was forever outlining in his mind vast literary projects; but before any one of them was committed to paper, he was busy planning the next one. The fact that he was writing so little tortured his peace; he tried to escape his conscience by editing a newspaper, *The Watchman* (1796), which died after ten issues, and by occasionally preaching as a Unitarian, and indulging in his favorite avenue of escape from work—talk.

"The Rime of the Ancient Mariner"

In 1797, while he was living at Nether Stowey, he came to know William and Dorothy Wordsworth, with both of whom he was soon close friends.

They removed to Alfoxden to be near him, and the three would take long walks every day, vastly enriching one another in ideas and inspiration. It was during these walks that they planned publishing the *Lyrical Ballads* (1798) in which appeared Coleridge's great poem, "The Ancient Mariner."

Now he had indeed found himself, and within the space of a few months he had composed not only "The Ancient Mariner," but also the incomparable "fragment" "Kubla Khan" and the wonderful first part of "Christabel." That Coleridge's genius at last came to flowering is certainly partly owing to the example of regular work that Wordsworth could hold up to him, as well as to Wordsworth's command of simple direct expression. His own earlier manner was somewhat too involved. But Wordsworth owed him just as much. Coleridge's marvelous imagination showered sparks upon Wordsworth, and began the period of the latter's greatest composition. At this time Coleridge also met the young William Hazlitt; that meeting has been made immortal by Hazlitt's brilliant essay, "First Acquaintance with Poets."

"The Ancient Mariner," which was greeted by a critic as "the strangest story of cock and bull that we ever saw on paper" when it appeared in *Lyrical Ballads* (1798), is one of the greatest achievements in our poetry. It was originally to have been a collaboration between Wordsworth and Coleridge. They had talked over the contents of the poem together, and began its composition. But Wordsworth was able to contribute only two unimpressive lines:

> *And listened like a three years' child;*
> *The Mariner had his will.*

Coleridge wrote the poem at amazing speed; his imagination was at a fever heat.

He had greatly admired Percy's *Reliques*, and from it imitated the old ballad stanza. Nowhere is his superb power to make the supernatural seem real better exemplified. And throughout the poem the simple direct diction, painting shapes of sea and sky with amazing boldness, shows perfectly with what power the language of the average man can be employed.

The story is of an ancient mariner who detains a wedding guest, and holds him with "his glittering eye" while he tells a tale. In clear bold strokes the mariner speaks of the ship on which he had once sailed south, and how it made its way in good wind to the equator. A storm came up and the ship was driven toward the South Pole. They sailed to seas where ice "as green as emerald" sent forth "a dismal sheen," and there were no signs of life about:

> *The ice was here, the ice was there,*
> *The ice was all around:*
> *It cracked and growled, and roared and howled,*
> *Like noises in a swound!*

Suddenly a huge seabird, an albatross, came through the fog, and the sailors welcomed the sight of this living thing with joy. The bird ate their food, and followed the ship. Almost at once the ship was able to break through the ice, a strong south wind sprang up, and the ship made its way north. The bird kept them company for nine days. Then, for no reason at all, the mariner took his crossbow and shot the albatross. His fellow sailors cried out against him for having killed the bird that made the breeze blow. But when the fog began to clear and the sun to shine, the sailors approved his deed, for, they now said, the albatross had brought the fog and mist. Thus, by their condoning the mariner, they shared in his crime. In a marvelous series of stanzas the poet recounts how the ship suddenly entered the Pacific Ocean:

> *The fair breeze blew, the white foam flew,*
> *The furrow followed free;*
> *We were the first that ever burst*
> *Into that silent sea.*

> *Down dropt the breeze, the sails dropt down,*
> *'Twas sad as sad could be;*
> *And we did speak only to break*
> *The silence of the sea!*

> *All in a hot and copper sky,*
> *The bloody Sun, at noon,*
> *Right above the mast did stand,*
> *No bigger than the Moon.*

> *Day after day, day after day,*
> *We stuck, nor breath nor motion;*
> *As idle as a painted ship*
> *Upon a painted ocean.*

The very boards of the ship began to shrink. There was

> *Water, water, everywhere,*
> *Nor any drop to drink.*

The sea was covered with slimy things, and at night the water seemed to be aflame. The mariners, parched for lack of water, could not speak; but in their looks they blamed the mariner, and they hung the albatross around his neck as though it were a cross. After a long weary time, they beheld "a something" on the horizon:

> *At first it seemed a little speck*
> *And then it seemed a mist*

As it came nearer, it took on the shape of a ship veering crazily toward them. The mariner bit his arm, sucked his blood, and cried, "A sail!" But now they were all stricken with horror. How could a ship sail without a breeze or tide? The sun was on the horizon, and as the scudding ship came between them and the sun, the sun's rays shone through the sides of that bark! As the specter-ship neared, they beheld only two passengers: Death and a Woman:

> *Her lips were red, her looks were free,*
> *Her locks were yellow as gold:*
> *Her skin was as white as leprosy,*
> *The Night-mare Life-in-Death was she*

Death and Life-in-Death were playing dice for the ship's crew, and she won the life of the mariner; and as she whistled thrice:

> *The Sun's rim dips; the stars rush out:*
> *At one stride comes the dark;*
> *With far-heard whisper, o'er the sea,*
> *Off shot the spectre-bark.*

The moon rose, and one by one the mariner's shipmates dropped down dead. Everyone of their souls passed by him like the whizz of his crossbow. He was all alone with the dead now. As he looked upon the rotting sea, he hated the slimy things crawling in it. For seven days and nights he dwelt in this horror. And then the eighth night when the moon rose and cast a light like April frost upon the sea, he watched the water snakes playing in the water; some saint took pity on him then, for they suddenly seemed so beautiful to him that:

> *A spring of love gushed from my heart,*
> *And I blessed them unaware.*

That moment he could pray for the first time again, and the albatross fell from his neck into the sea. He was able to sleep. When he awoke, it was raining, and a wind arose once more. The sailors, their bodies directed by a group of angelic spirits, stood up and began to direct the ship on its way. The ship went with supernatural speed north, and the mariner awoke from his trance to behold that the ship was approaching his native land. Turning his eyes back to the deck, he saw that the dead sailors were all lying prone again, and that above each dead man stood an angelic spirit. Soon he heard the plash of oars, and the Pilot's boat appeared; in it were the Pilot, his boy, and a holy Hermit. As their little boat came up to the ship, the ship suddenly sank. They saved the mariner. The sight of the man they had rescued terrified the Pilot and drove his boy out of his mind. The mariner pleaded with the Hermit to shrive him of his sin, and told him his tale. His penance ever since has been to tell all who need to hear, his experience. And so he goes from place to place finding the men to whom he must teach the lesson that:

> *He prayeth best, who loveth best*
> *All things both great and small;*
> *For the dear God who loveth us,*
> *He made and loveth all.*

The mariner, his tale told, goes his way. The wedding guest turns away from the wedding feast:

> *A sadder and a wiser man,*
> *He rose the morrow morn.*

"Kubla Khan"

If Coleridge had written nothing more than "The Ancient Mariner," he would still have to be counted one of our great poets, for there is nothing like it in English literature. But the fragment "Kubla Khan" (1797) is just as unique in its own way. Coleridge's own account of the circumstances under which it was composed informs us that he had fallen asleep while reading in an Elizabethan travel book, Purchas's *Pilgrimage*, about the Khan Kubla and his palace. Coleridge had taken a slight dose of that drug to which he was so fatally addicted, and under its influence he composed some three hundred lines of poetry in his dream. He awakened and started eagerly to write down the lines he could remember. In the midst of this feverish writing, he was interrupted "by a person on business from Porlock," who kept him an hour. After getting rid of the intruder, Coleridge found to his dismay that the rest of the poem was gone from his memory.

That gentleman from Porlock (a creditor, of course!) has been roundly cursed by posterity. But the truth is that the lines with which Coleridge finished off this fragment make it quite complete, and it stands as one of the most magical poems in our language; its music is exquisite; and the Miltonic passages that became transformed into something entirely Coleridge's own in his dream are among the most haunting ever written. The opening lines speak of Kubla Khan's "stately pleasure-dome" near the river Alph, which for five miles "meandering with a mazy motion," sometimes ran underground, and then burst forth into a powerful geyser:

> *Amidst whose swift, half-intermitted burst*
> *Huge fragments vaulted like rebounding hail.*

The pleasure-dome was reflected on the waves; and it had wonderful caves of ice. There is now a break in the poem, and the poet remembers a vision he had of an Abyssinian maid playing on her dulcimer. If, he says, he could only revive her music within himself, he would rebuild that pleasure-dome and the caves of ice in words so real that:

> *. . . all who heard should see them there,*
> *And all should cry, Beware! Beware!*
> *His flashing eyes, his floating hair!*
> *Weave a circle round him thrice,*
> *And close your eyes with holy dread,*
> *For he on honey-dew hath fed,*
> *And drunk the milk of Paradise.*

"Kubla Khan" is, in fact, two visions of the creative imagination. Coleridge was deeply attracted to each of these creative worlds, but could not reconcile them into one. This famous poem, therefore, remains a fragment.

The first realm of imaginative endeavor is that of the pagan creator, Kubla. He fashions a pleasure ground nurtured by Imagination (the river Alph). As pleasing as these structures and landscapes are, however, Coleridge observes that their source of life, the river of Imagination, leads ultimately to "sunless seas." After a break in the poem, he turns abruptly to the second approach to artistic creation—the song of an Abyssinian maiden, representing the Christian (or Miltonic) creator. Coleridge expresses deep yearning to imitate this form of imaginative creation, but ends this poetic fragment with the depressed thought that the Christian community would reject him, his art, and, by implication, his opium-addicted life style.

"Christabel"

"Christabel" is another uncompleted work of the poet. The first part was written in 1797, the second in 1800, and Coleridge was unable to conclude it because it had got out of hand. Only the first part is equal to his best; but that is remarkable for its evocation of the eerie and the mysterious. The meter of the poem is particularly interesting: as in Anglo-Saxon poetry, Coleridge has four accents in every line, but admits any number of weak syllables:

> She máketh ánswer tó the clóck
> Foúr for the quárters, and twélve for the hoúr

Part One opens on a chill April night when the full moon is barely hidden by a thin grey cloud. The lovely lady Christabel goes a furlong out of her castle into the woods to pray for her lover-knight. She kneels under an oak tree but rises in fear as she hears a moan. It cannot be the wind for there is not wind enough to twirl the last red leaf on the topmost twig. She looks at the other side of the broad oak and there she sees a beautiful lady dressed in silken white, with gems glittering wildly in her hair. The lady identifies herself as Geraldine, and says that she had been captured by five warriors and left temporarily under the tree. She asks Christabel to help her flee, and Christabel promises her the aid of her father's knights. They go back quickly to the castle, where Christabel's father, Sir Leoline, is asleep. They cross the moat, and are about to enter the vast gate through a little door, when Geraldine sinks to the ground. Christabel does not know that Geraldine is a witch, and a witch cannot enter the home of the innocent by herself. So, unsuspecting, Christabel lifts Geraldine over the threshold. After that Geraldine walks easily across the courtyard. They pass the sleeping mastiff, who moans in her sleep. As they pass through the hall, a dying brand in the hearth leaps into flame as Geraldine approaches. They come to Christabel's chamber, where Geraldine asks about Christabel's mother. Informed that Christabel's mother died giving birth to her, Geraldine expresses the wish that the mother were there. Suddenly Geraldine gazes into space and cries:

> *Off wandering mother! Peak and pine!*
> *I have power to bid thee flee.*

Christabel, not understanding that her mother's spirit had come to aid her, believes her new friend distracted by her experiences. They make ready for bed now. Geraldine pretends that she must pray while Christabel undresses. As Christabel lies in bed, she leans over to look at Geraldine, and Coleridge masterfully evokes terror in the passage describing what she sees:

> *Beneath the lamp the lady bowed,*
> *And slowly rolled her eyes around;*
> *Then drawing in her breath aloud,*
> *Like one that shuddered, she unbound*
> *The cincture from beneath her breast:*
> *Her silken robe, and inner vest,*
> *Dropt to her feet, and full in view,*
> *Behold! her bosom and half her side—*
> *A sight to dream of, not to tell!*
> *O shield her, shield sweet Christabel!*

Part One ends with an incantation by Geraldine as she lies beside her victim.

After this promising beginning, Part Two is very disappointing, and turns out to be an uninteresting tale of knightly adventure, which was just as well not finished.

Other Poetry

In 1799 Coleridge was granted a small annuity by the Wedgwood family, and it enabled him to accompany William and Dorothy Wordsworth on a trip to Germany. It was there that he came into contact with what was to be the paramount influence of his later life, the philosophical writings of that country. On his return to England later than the Wordsworths, he moved with his family to Keswick, near the Wordsworths' home at Grasmere.

In 1800 he issued his translation of portions of the drama *Wallenstein*, a trilogy by the great German poet Schiller, which Coleridge Englished into excellent blank verse. He now spent much time in London, lecturing and writing for periodicals. His poetic powers were already waning. In 1803 he accompanied William and Dorothy on an intended tour of Scotland, but Coleridge and the Wordsworths did not get on very well. After two weeks, they allotted Coleridge six out of the thirty-five pounds they had in a common purse, kept the jaunting cart, and allowed Coleridge, who had been suffering great pain from rheumatism, to go on his way by foot. The great friendship was approaching its end.

The next year he went to Malta as a secretary in the diplomatic service. There he became more deeply involved than ever in his researches into German philosophy. The more he read, the less he wrote; reading became his favorite drug. In 1802 he had already sung an epitaph to his poetic powers in "Dejection: an Ode." This poem was originally written, curiously enough, as a present for Wordsworth on his approaching marriage. When it was printed later, however, because of the break in their friendship Coleridge substituted Otway's for William's name in the seventh stanza, and the phrase, "Dear Lady!" in the eighth stanza.

This powerful poem begins with a description of the signs in the heaven foretelling storm and rain. If only when the wind will blow, it could startle into life his dull pain! For now as he gazes at star and moon:

> *I see them all so excellently fair,*
> *I see, not feel, how beautiful they are!*

He knows he can no longer win from outward things a "passion" and a "life." There was a time, he ruefully reflects, when misfortune could not touch him, but became instead the stuff out of which he could make dreams of happiness. But now he knows that his greatest gift, his imagination, is withering. He turns from his own sad thoughts to consider the wonderful poetic creations of his friend, and to wish all happiness and joy to that friend.

He returned to England and made the acquaintance of De Quincey. He tried lecturing again. In 1809 he began to publish *The Friend*, a magazine devoted to philosophy and politics. Although it ran for only eight months it was very influential in beginning the popularizing in England of German philosophy.

Haunted by the loss of his poetic faculties, he spent the rest of his life lecturing, talking, and writing chiefly prose. All his great poetic writing was behind him.

Besides the poems we have already discussed or mentioned only one other deserves to be classed among his best, "Frost at Midnight" (1798). This is his meditation by the side of his sleeping child, Hartley (who was born in 1796); it expresses his hope that the boy will grow up amidst the beauty of the Lake Country and thus learn to hear the voice of God moving in all nature around him. There are tenderness and sweetness in the cadences of this blank verse.

Prose Works

However we may deplore his writing no more poetry of quality, the scholarly labors of Coleridge's later life were not wasted efforts. He taught England that there were great treasures to be explored in German literature and philosophy. And, most important of all, he gave the Romantic Movement its philosophy in his greatest prose work, the *Biographia Literaria* (1817). This book, which is a combination of autobiography, literary criticism, and philosophy, contains some basic ideas on the superiority of the imagination to mere logic. It also contains an extended criticism of Wordsworth's poetry, its shortcomings, its too frequent prosiness, which Coleridge sees clearly. *Biographia Literaria* includes some valuable considerations of the philosophy of Kant, Fichte, and Schelling as well.

Biographia Literaria is at once a storehouse of brilliant critical insights (including definitions of fancy, imagination, symbol, allegory, and other concepts) and a wasteland of some of Coleridge's worst writing, including many pages plagiarized (though translated) directly from German authors. Coleridge undertook this prose work as his own version of an autobiography like that achieved by Wordsworth in *The Prelude*. Coleridge focuses less on his life experiences, however, than on his intellectual development and judgments. The work, unfinished as are so many of Coleridge's projects, remains a partially built cathedral in many ways—grand in design and occasional detail, but flawed and incomplete in workmanship.

As a critic of Shakespeare, Coleridge has never been surpassed for his profound judgment, despite the fact that more recent Shakespearean scholarship has invalidated a certain amount of what he said. Nevertheless his opinions, collected as *Essays and Lectures*, very often demonstrate that he hazarded guesses that later scholarship has proved; and his insight into some of the *dramatis personae* has all the brilliance of a great imagination and the understanding of a great poet.

Coleridge wrote two plays, *Remorse* (published in 1813) and *Zapolya* (1817), both tragedies influenced by Shakespeare. His *Aids to Reflection* (1825) is an attempt to apply the tenets of the German Kantian philosophy to Christianity. His *Anima Poetae* (published in 1895), a treasury of scattered thoughts from his notebooks, and his *Confessions of an Inquiring Spirit* (1840) are full of challenging reflections. His *Letters* are a record of the varying fortunes of his life and genius.

In 1825 he wrote a pathetic poem, "Work Without Hope." In it he sees, while all the world is waking in the new springtime, that he alone of all God's creatures is "the sole unbusy thing." Once he knew the founts of inspiration. But for him they are dried now:

> *Work without Hope draws nectar in a sieve,*
> *And Hope without an object cannot live.*

What killed that great poetic gift? The reasons are not single. He never learned to discipline himself to regular work; he needed to have paper and pen at hand when inspiration came, or it was forever lost. Moreover, he became too used to escaping work by reading other men's books. The opium habit, which he was never able to overcome, helped paralyze his will. The subtleties of German metaphysics became another drug in which he could forget himself. It is also possible that the hardness in Wordsworth's character did much to destroy his self-confidence, for Wordsworth returned none of his warmth, and exchanged little of the admiration he willingly accepted from Coleridge. It was in Coleridge's nature to depreciate himself because of his reverence for Wordsworth's genius; but there is some evidence that Wordsworth discouraged his friend from further poetic composition after the second edition of *Lyrical Ballads* (1800).

Coleridge's last efforts were those of a great teacher. About him clustered the new generation of writers to listen to his unending and inspiring monologues.

SIR WALTER SCOTT (1771–1832)

In his own time Scott was widely admired as a narrator of tales in verse. It was by his own decision that he gave up that career; he was convinced that Byron was far his superior, and, without being asked, gracefully yielded place to the younger man. Now Scott's poetry is not much read outside of his native Scotland. He turned from stories in verse to the novel.

As a novelist he won an international reputation second to none. Oddly enough, his novels too have diminished in importance with time. The reason for the decline of Scott's reputation is not far to seek. Of all the concerns of the Romantic writers none is perhaps more superficial than their love of the glamorous past. It is this aspect of the Romantic Movement that Scott particularly exemplified in his works; and that may be the chief reason why his works were so popular. But now, despite a certain vigor, he seems deficient in the more profound imagination of such poets as Wordsworth, Coleridge, Shelley, and Keats; and as a novelist he seems to have failed to equal the wit, realism, or deep humanity of novelists like Jane Austen, Emily Brontë, Dickens, Thackeray, or Meredith.

It is indeed a pity that Scott's muse has been neglected. He is the author of some excellent verse, and much of his poetry has an admirable ease and manliness.

He was born in Edinburgh, the son of an attorney of good family, on August 15, 1771. He studied law, was admitted to the bar, and held a number of legal offices. But he was still a boy when his love of literature became evident. At the age of twelve he was already collecting old ballads. At school he fell under the spell of Spenser and Macpherson. From Spenser in particular he learned a love for the world of romance peopled by knights, ladies, giants and dragons. A lameness contracted through a childhood disease did not keep him from making many tours of the Highlands and the Cheviot Hills, which his fancy populated with Scotland's romantic past.

He married the daughter of a French émigré in 1797, and in 1804 moved from Lasswade (near Edinburgh) to Ashestiel in Selkirkshire. The popularity of his poetry enabled him to build at Abbotsford a castle in imitation of the medieval style. It is with that estate that his name is particularly associated. He surrounded himself with all the trappings of feudal life, and enjoyed living like a medieval baron. He was essentially an aristocrat, deeply attached to his native country and its heroic legendry.

Among his first literary labors were the translating into English of German ballads and *Götz von Berlichingen*, a wildly romantic play by Goethe. Scott next published his own collection of ballads, *Minstrelsy of the Scottish Border* (1802–1803) in three volumes; this work contains very interesting critical forewords and digressions as well as some of Scott's own imitations of the ancient ballads.

He was thirty-four before he chose to appear as an original poet. *The Lay of the Last Minstrel* (1805), somewhat inspired by Coleridge's "Christabel," won him immediate fame. Scott based it upon an old legend, and wrote it in a style that combines Neoclassical finish with early Romantic supernaturalism; the basic plot is the effort and success of Cranstoun in winning the hand of Margaret of Branksome Hall. Of the lyrical passages in *The Lay of the Last Minstrel*, the one which is now best known is Harold's song to Rosabelle, beginning:

> *O listen, listen, ladies gay!*
> *No haughty feat of arms I tell;*
> *Soft is the note, and sad the lay,*
> *That mourns the lovely Rosabelle.*

Marmion (1808) is better constructed, and has some lively descriptive passages, notably the view of Edinburgh from Blackford Hill, and the battle of Flodden Field. The story reaches its climax in that fatal battle, where Marmion is slain. *The Lady of the Lake* (1810) was even more popular, and made Lake Katrine in the Trossachs a new resort for tourists; the story has much of the more obvious Romantic claptrap: a king travelling in humble guise and handsomely giving up his beloved to his rival, a refined heroine, and a glamorous villain. One song of this work is celebrated:

> *Soldier, rest! thy warfare o'er,*
> *Sleep the sleep that knows not breaking:*
> *Dream of battle-fields no more,*
> *Days of danger, nights of waking.*

The Vision of Don Roderick (1811) is rather carelessly written in uninspired Spenserian stanzas; it did not make much of an impression on the public. *Rokeby* (1812) is a tale of the English Civil War; it contains some of his best songs; particularly admired has been Edmund's song:

> *O, Brignall banks are wild and fair,*
> *And Greta woods are green,*
> *And you may gather garlands there,*
> *Would grace a summer queen.*

The Bride of Triermain (1813) is a charming love story laid in Arthurian times, a tale of magic in which Merlin the Magician appears. *The Lord of the*

Isles (1815) is a tale of gallant adventure and war such as Scott was to write so often in the Waverley novels; *The Battle of Bannockbourn* from this work is well known. *Harold the Dauntless* (1817) was the last of Scott's long narrative poems, and is easily the weakest of them. By this time he found himself completely drawn to novel writing.

These tales in verse did much to complete the victory of the Romantic Movement among the general public. The average reader was tired of Pope's imitators, but not yet ready to accept the innovations of Wordsworth and Coleridge. Scott's verse was easy to read, had a free swinging rhythm, and demanded no subtlety in understanding. When a greater poet appeared to continue in this tradition, he found an audience prepared for him. Between 1812 and 1814 Byron issued a series of verse tales that were enormously popular, and Scott decided to surrender the field uncontested.

He had, in the meantime, become a secret partner in a publishing firm headed by the Ballantyne Brothers. His expensive tastes at Abbotsford required his finding a new source of income. In 1814, therefore, he issued his first novel, *Waverley*, anonymously. It was the first of a long series of novels written by him, and read and admired all over the world. His authorship was soon recognized, and he gave up his anonymity.

Despite his vast success, the Ballantynes failed. Scott, who need not have undertaken any of the financial responsibility, nevertheless himself undertook to pay off with his future novels and writings the entire debt, £117,000. The rest of his life was spent in untiring labor to discharge the amount. Besides his many novels, he wrote a nine-volume biography of Napoleon, a history of Scotland, and edited the works of Dryden and Swift. The pressure of so much work took a serious toll of his health, but even on his bed of pain he continued to dictate. The shadow of that debt haunted him until his death. His sense of honor has justly evoked the profoundest admiration for him as a man. By the time of his death he had paid off half the sum, and the sale of his copyrights discharged the rest.

In a later section we shall consider Scott's novels. But here it should be pointed out that his love of poetry never died. Some of the best pages of his novels are those that contain songs. In *The Heart of Midlothian*, for instance, occurs one of his best:

> *Proud Maisie is in the wood,*
> *Walking so early;*
> *Sweet Robin sits on the bush,*
> *Singing so rarely.*

3
THE ROMANTIC MOVEMENT, SECOND GENERATION

The next generation of Romantic poets grew up in a world that was still shuddering at how nearly successful Napoleon had been. The French Revolution was everywhere pronounced to have failed to establish its principles, and Europe was in the grip of extreme political reaction. There was little left for the imagination of the young revolutionaries other than to take refuge in despair. The typical hero of the day was either a frustrated over-sensitive victim of the *Weltschmerz* ("World-sorrow"), such as Goethe's young Werther; or the rebellious "Titan" warring antisocially against the rest of humanity, such as Schiller's Robber. The first generation of Romantic poets—Southey, Wordsworth, and Coleridge, all ardent revolutionaries in their youth—had all retreated into conservatism and were proud to be known as bulwarks of convention and respectability. The second generation of Romantics rebelled more fiercely than their predecessors. Their passion and fervor are more intense. Byron, Shelley, and Keats all died young, as though they had consumed themselves in their own fire.

GEORGE GORDON, LORD BYRON (1788–1824)

Even at this date it is not entirely possible to dissociate the interest we feel in Byron's biography from that which we take in his work. This confusion already existed in his own time, for to his contemporaries he seemed like the very incarnation of the Romantic hero—Werther and The Robber and Rousseau's child of nature combined in one. No lover of English literature today would fail to give Shelley and Keats a higher place as poets; but in their generation they were largely unknown, while Byron was read all over Europe. Many Europeans still think of him as a better poet than he actually was, if only because he exerted so powerful an effect on the literature of France, Germany, Italy, and Russia. Luckily for his reputation, Byron has translated well into other languages; he employed a racy, not deeply poetical style that loses little in transference to another language.

He came of a line that was proverbially wicked. His father was an adventurer who had eloped with the Lord Chamberlain's wife, quickly run through her fortune, and lost her after she bore him a daughter, Augusta. He returned to Scotland to court an heiress, and married her when his daughter was fifteen months old. Of this union George, our poet, was born on January 22, 1788, in London. Byron's father dissipated this second fortune very quickly and died in France, an exile from his creditors, when George was three.

Byron was thus left unhappily to the tutelage of his mother, an hysterical, ill-tempered woman. As it was, he was born lame and therefore, with his fierce pride, certain to carry an abnormal sensitiveness through life. But his mother ruined whatever seeds of normal living were in him: she would alternate fits of effusive affection over him with violent seizures of insane anger during which she would call him a "lame brat," revile his father, and throw anything at hand at the boy. He grew to despise her, and when he was sent to school at Harrow in 1801, he was ready to be revenged upon the world. His grand-uncle's death, three years earlier, had brought him the inheritance of the title of Lord Byron.

At school, because of his lameness, he made a point of excelling in athletics, especially at boxing and at cricket. But he also was already an avid reader. In 1805 he entered Trinity College, Cambridge, and saw to it that he became notorious for a flamboyant life. He engaged a professional boxer to teach him the sport. His extravagance was legendary, and his pointed wit widely admired. He published his first volume, *Fugitive Pieces*, in 1806 with the aid of his friend Hobhouse. This was revised and reissued the next year as *Hours of Idleness*.

Byron's first volume possessed little merit, being hardly more than a collection of stilted imitations of the pre-Romantic poets. The preface written for the 1807 edition was, however, insufferable. In it his young lordship announced to the world: "It is highly improbable from my situation and pursuits hereafter that I should ever obtrude myself a second time upon the public." It was throughout Byron's life a favorite pose that he wrote poetry only because he was physically disabled from leading a more active life; but this condescension of the youthful nobleman to poetry incensed some of the critics. The *Edinburgh Review* treated him to some elaborate sarcasm, and urged him to hold fast to his resolution to write no more.

Byron was infuriated, and answered with a trenchant satire, *English Bards and Scotch Reviewers* (1808). As has been noted, he was the master of cutting wit and malicious repartee—trained to them by his early skirmishes with his mother; it is not strange that Pope was his favorite poet, and had he lived in the Age of Queen Anne, he would certainly have been a threat to Pope's preeminence. This satire exhibits a turn of mind that the philosophy of Romanticism gave Byron little opportunity to employ. Only in *Don Juan*, perhaps, did he again feel equally free to indulge his talent for ridicule. Usually his letters and his conversation formed the outlet for that gift. In *English Bards and Scotch Reviewers* he had a veritable holiday, striking out not only against his critics, but against all poets and authors towards whom he bore a grudge. After this book, the critics were more than a little afraid of Byron's anger and found it in their discretion to admire his work.

In 1808 Byron also took his M.A. and assumed his seat in the House of Lords, where he made a brief stir by his radical opinions. He was twenty-one and already felt himself doomed. At Newstead Abbey, the Byrons' ancestral home, where he had spent much time reveling in morbid thoughts among the Gothic ruins, he had been jilted in love, and had concluded that all women were light and false. He found deep satisfaction, too, in dwelling on the bad line from which he was descended.

A career in the House of Lords was not tempting, so he set out on his travels in the company of his friend Hobhouse in the summer of 1809. He chose an unconventional and highly romantic itinerary. Instead of seeking Paris and classic Rome, he went through Portugal, Spain, the Mediterranean, Turkey, Albania, Asia Minor, the Troad, and Greece. He visited peoples Englishmen hardly knew and was treated as though he were an important plenipotentiary. He returned to England after two years, strong of body, his mind excited over what he had seen and experienced in Greece and the East. He began to record his impressions in poetry. In 1812 the first two cantos of *Childe Harold's Pilgrimage* were published, and he became famous overnight. (Canto III was published in 1816, and Canto IV in 1818.)

Childe Harold's Pilgrimage

Childe Harold, the first great poem in Spenserian stanzas since *The Faerie Queene*, is a kind of inspired poetical travelbook. The third and fourth cantos are superior to the first two in imagery and diction; but throughout there is an ease, a raciness always characteristic of Byron. For although Byron is not frequently profoundly poetic, he is never dull. It is not hard to explain *Childe Harold's* immediate success. It is full of descriptions of nature, and of the enthusiasm and melancholy that were already established aspects of Romanticism. All three elements, for instance, may be read in this one quotation:

> *Roll on, thou deep and dark blue ocean, roll!*
> *Ten thousand fleets sweep over thee in vain;*
> *Man marks the earth with ruin,—his control*
> *Stops with the shore.*

This time the *Edinburgh Review* said: "Lord Byron, we think, must be allowed to take precedence of all his distinguished contemporaries."

Among the best passages of the poem is the long one on the battle of Waterloo in Canto III. But Canto III is throughout the most admired portion of *Childe Harold*. It opens with an address to the child Ada whom Lady Byron had borne him. Is her face like her mother's? (He had not seen the little girl since her fifth week of life.) The poet is "once more upon the waters" that carry him away from England. It is years (his "youth's summer") since he sang last of Harold. Now he is changed, though he still can feed on Time's "bitter fruits." In the eighth stanza he turns to his hero. Harold had drunk the dregs of life and found them wormwood. Feeling colder towards life, Harold mixed among men, but could find only in Nature any relief from his painful thoughts:

> *Where rose the mountains, there to him were friends;*
> *Where rolled the ocean, thereon was his home;*
> *Where a blue sky, and glowing clime, extends,*
> *He had the passion and the power to roam.*

But among men Harold "became a thing restless and worn." Self-exiled, he began to travel again, less gloomy in thoughts but less hopeful in heart. At Waterloo he stands "on an Empire's dust." This Waterloo is "the grave of France," for here the enemies of liberty banded together to tear to pieces the eagle of freedom. The conquest over Napoleon, though it has made one despot fall, has given power to the other kings. In the twenty-first stanza the poet begins to paint the background of the great battle. In "Belgium's capital" there was feasting and revelry by "fair women and brave men." The music was making all merry when suddenly there was a deep sound "like a rising knell." The dancers would not hear it:

> *On with the dance! let joy be unconfined.*

But the cannon's roar was nearer. The Duke of Brunswick heard its tone and knew that death was near. He rushed into the field and fell in the fight. After that there was much hurrying, weeping, sudden parting, clattering of cars, forming of the ranks of war. Before the morning star rose the battles were formed. After a night devoted to proud beauty, "rider and horse,—friend,—foe" lay together "in one red burial." Napoleon, who was defeated on that day, was the greatest and not the worst of men. His spirit was a mixture of mighty and petty objectives. Had he been less extreme, he might still have been on his throne. Even now the world trembles at Napoleon's name, now that he is no more than the "jest of fame." This strain leads to melancholy thoughts. That man who ascends the mountains will find "the loftiest peaks most wrapped in clouds and snow." The man who subdues mankind must look down on mankind's hate. Harold leaves his melancholy reflections to think of Nature. He passes abandoned castles once consecrated to power. The old barons performed many an unrecorded deed of prowess, and participated in many a keen contest looking down on the Rhine. In stanza fifty the poet addresses that river, and reflects on the thousand battles that have taken place on its banks, the carnage washed away by the tide. Harold continues his journey. His days of passion are over but he counts on the trust of "one fond breast." He has learned to love children too. By the crags of Drachenfels overhanging the Rhine he sends a song to the one who loves him purely, wishing she were with him. He passes by Coblentz. In the fifty-ninth stanza he takes leave of the Rhine, and makes for the Alps. He is drawn to Lake Leman (known to us as Lake Geneva). "There is too much of man here" as he gazes into the mirror of the lake. He flies from mankind but does not hate it. Not all are fit to toil among men. It is better to be alone and love earth only for its own sake. He lives not in himself, and says:

> *I become*
> *Portion of that around me; and to me*
> *High mountains are a feeling, but the hum*
> *Of human cities torture.*

Are not the mountains, waves and skies a part of him and his soul? In the seventy-sixth stanza the poet is led to think of Rousseau, who is associated with Geneva, Rousseau, "the apostle of affliction" who knew "how to make madness beautiful." The poet thinks also of Rousseau's heroine Julie (from *The New Eloisa*) and of her lover who received from her every morn a memorable kiss. Rousseau was ever warring with imaginary foes; nevertheless this very madness was part of his inspired genius. Clarens is visited by Harold, a town sacred to Rousseau's lovers. Everywhere the atmosphere breeds memories of Rousseau. And everywhere there is beauty.

> *. . . here the Rhone*
> *Hath spread himself a couch, the Alps have reared a throne.*

Stanza one hundred and five, passing through Lausanne and Ferney, brings up memories of Gibbon and Voltaire. In stanza one hundred and ten he is in Italy. Here he pauses to say: "I have not loved the world, nor the world me." He has not flattered the world's rank breath nor bowed to its idolatries. Yet he still believes that there is truth and virtue and goodness. He closes with an apostrophe to his daughter Ada. Though parted from him through bitter conditions she will understand him some day. She has in her his blood too, though more tempered. From across the seas and mountains he sends her his blessings.

IMPORTANCE

A special interest attaches to *Childe Harold* for the reason that in it we have the first "Byronic hero," the first of a long series who reappear in works including *The Giaour* (1813), *The Bride of Abydos* (1813), *The Corsair* (1814), *Lara* (1814), and *The Siege of Corinth* (1814). (The dates will show with what feverish rapidity Byron was writing.) This Byronic hero has always the same traits: he is a man disgusted with civilized society, satiated with pleasure, who lives with extreme pride which wilfully suppresses all his tender feelings, though deep in his heart is pure love for a gentle woman; deeper yet lies festering a sorrow that he disdains ever to reveal, but which, it is hinted, is connected with some unforgivable sin committed in youth. That Byron placed these stories in the Orient, could only insure their success in that age. *The*

Giaour takes place in the chambers of the Caliph Hassan; *The Bride of Abydos* deals with a Pasha and a pirate; *The Corsair* has a Sultan and another pirate; *Lara* is a sequel to *The Corsair*. The public seized upon these romantic Eastern tales with delight; it was precisely what they had been waiting for. No one was more impressed than Sir Walter Scott, who because of them gave up writing narrative poetry himself.

In 1812, while the furor over *Childe Harold* was raging, Byron decided to make his first speech in the House of Lords. He made it in defense of the weavers, who, having destroyed the power looms that had thrown them out of employment, were about to be punished by a bill before the Lords that would make such acts a capital offense. Byron's defense, the unpopular side, was so stirring that he was labeled a dangerous radical. Although he remained a friend of revolutionary causes, aiding the Italians against their Austrian oppressors, and later giving his life for Greek independence, Byron's political views were chiefly negative. He once summed up his beliefs by saying: "I have simplified my politics with an utter detestation of all existing governments."

His literary and political success made him the lion of London society. Byron was dangerously handsome, all the more irresistible to women because of his slight limp, his pride, his fame, and his caustic tongue. Although he did not mind the reputation of philanderer which he began to have, the truth would seem to be that most of the women with whom he had affairs were the aggressors in the case. Somehow or other in the midst of a mad whirl of parties and love affairs, he managed to write a great deal—between "dressing and undressing," as he put it. But he did not like his life and began to think that marriage alone could save him.

The only girl he could admire in the fast London society in which he moved was a well-educated girl from the country, Miss Annabella Milbanke. But he was unsuited to marriage, and she was too much of a moralizing woman to help him. They were married on January 2, 1815, and they were hardly settled in the carriage after the ceremony when he began to torture her. He knew he had been foolish to marry, and he let loose on his poor wife all his talent for mockery and sarcasm. She bore him a daughter at the end of a year, and a few weeks later left him forever. Somehow their separation became the occasion for airing all the malice against him which his pride and wit had evoked, and his name became a byword for dissoluteness.

Verse Dramas and Other Narrative Poems

Enraged that his wife would not return to him, he left England forever on April 25, 1816. He managed to convince himself that his wife had treated him shamefully, and he never forgave her. In Switzerland he met Shelley, and spent the summer with him, Mary Shelley, and her stepsister Jane Clairmont, with whom he had an affair. Here he wrote the third canto of *Childe Harold, The Prisoner of Chillon,* and part of his finest poetic drama, *Manfred.* It was during these days that Mary Shelley also composed her celebrated novel *Frankenstein,* written to amuse Shelley and Byron during their evenings together.

The Prisoner of Chillon, written in rhymed lines somewhat resembling Coleridge's "Christabel" meter for the most part, is an indictment of political tyranny. It tells the story of Bonnivard, imprisoned by the Duke of Savoy because he had championed the cause of freedom and the Republic of Geneva against the tyrant. He and his six brothers were chained by the leg to pillars in the dungeon of Chillon. Bonnivard, the speaker in the poem, tells how he watched them die one by one. They had chained him and two of his brothers so that they could not see one another. The younger brother who resembled their mother, was especially dear to him because of his pride; the other brother, a warrior at heart, had already died in spirit in his chains. The older brother dies, and then the younger. Now Bonnivard is the only one left. He walks up and down his cell, having broken his chain, and sometimes looks out through the bars of his prison on the mountains and the water of Lake Leman. At last his captors set him free, but he does not care to go. His dungeon has become his home and he is loath to leave it.

The "Sonnet on Chillon" (1816), a companion piece, is a tribute to "a man worthy of the best age of ancient freedom." It praises Bonnivard, and reflects that the place of his imprisonment has become an altar of liberty. For liberty is "brightest in dungeons."

Manfred, begun in Switzerland in 1816, was published in June 1817. One reviewer greeted it with wild enthusiasm as proof that "to no poet was there ever given so awful a revelation of the passions of the human soul," and concluded that no living poet has ever achieved "such complete, such perfect triumph." Obviously, the critics were anxious to avoid feeling the smart of Byron's rod a second time.

Despite the resemblances between *Manfred* and the plays on *Faust* written by Marlowe and Goethe, Byron had never read either. Goethe himself felt there was a resemblance but thought that nevertheless *Manfred* was a highly original work. Manfred, the hero of the play, is another Byronic hero of unbroken will, living in morose apartness in the silences of the Alps. Like his literary relatives, Lara, the Corsair, and the others, he nurtures in his bosom the secret of some terrible youthful crime. He is desirous of wresting the secrets of the Universe from the spirit world, and summons seven spirits to come and grant him self-forgetfulness. This boon the spirits cannot bestow, nor will they reveal the secrets of death. Manfred longs for death himself, and attempts suicide. But a chamois hunter seizes him just as he is about to jump from a cliff. In a valley of the Alps Manfred now calls forth the spirit of the waters, a witch who knows Manfred's past. To her Manfred confesses that there was one woman in the world, who resembles Manfred himself, to whom he had felt close. But he had only ruined her life and has since been a prey to his own despair. The witch is willing to offer Manfred all he desires in the way of self-oblivion on condition that he surrender his individuality and obey her. In sight of his goal, Manfred renounces what he has been seeking because he will not bow his will to anyone. In the end on his deathbed Manfred is as always alone, thinking of the wonders of Nature and the great events of the past. An abbot arrives in futile hope of converting him. The spirits come for Manfred now that his hour has struck, but Manfred defies them too, declaring they have no power over him. As he dies, he denies that it is the evil spirits that have brought about his end and his strong will makes the spirits vanish. So perishes this lonely soul.

Though the blank verse of *Manfred* is racy, any attempt to present it on the stage would be foolhardy. Indeed, it is interesting to note that the major poets, many of them, in the nineteenth century, wrote poetic dramas without any thought of their adaptability to the stage. The taste of the public as reflected in successful contemporary drama on the boards was at an all-time low. The poets were therefore content to write "closet dramas," that is, dramas to be read rather than acted. Wordsworth wrote *The Borderers;* and Byron *Manfred* and *Cain;* Shelley *Prometheus Unbound* and *The Cenci;* Browning, Tennyson and Swinburne wrote many plays. Of these only *The Cenci* has proved actable.

After his summer in Switzerland with the Shelleys, Byron went to Venice, where Jane Clairmont bore him a daughter, Allegra. The friendship with Shelley proved very important to Byron. Shelley's high-minded revolutionary optimism had nothing in common with Byron's pose of cynicism, and Byron caught some of Shelley's passionate hope for humanity of the future.

In 1819 Byron settled down to a kind of semipermanent relationship with the Countess Guiccioli (with the consent of her husband). She was a bore and an unimaginative shrew, but Byron did not break with her for the rest of his life. He lived at Pisa, Genoa, or Venice during these years, and was visited by Shelley, Tom Moore, Leigh Hunt, and other English friends. During this time he wrote most of what constitutes his large output of poetry. Among his longer works are *The Lament of Tasso* (1817), *Beppo* (1818), *Marino Faliero* (1819), *Sardanapalus* (1819) and *Cain* (1819).

The Lament of Tasso is an eloquent soliloquy put in the mouth of the great Italian poet, and dealing with his love for Leonora D'Este. *Beppo* is a half-dramatic, half-humorous narrative based on some of Byron's experiences in Venice; it is a kind of forerunner of his last great work, *Don Juan,* and is an earlier experiment with ottava rima (*ottava rima* is a stanza of eight iambic pentameter lines rhyming *abababcc*). *Marino Faliero, Sardanapalus* and *Cain* are all poetic dramas. In addition to these, Byron's other plays are *The Two Foscari* (1821), *Werner* (1822), and two fragments, *The Deformed Transformed* (1821), and *Heaven and Earth* (1821). *Marino Faliero* is based on the story of a conspiracy in Venice; *Sardanapalus,* more autobiographical, and with some powerful passages indicting war, tells of the voluptuous King of

Syria, his triumph over the Medes and Chaldeans, and of his eventual defeat and suicide. *Cain* is one of Byron's most powerful works. Its hero is the first murderer, a true Byronic lost soul who refuses to worship a Divinity who permits the existence of evil and death for His own creations. The play is much indebted to Milton's portrait of Satan, or rather to the interpretation the Romantics gave to Milton's Satan as a noble defier of God.

Don Juan

Although Byron's "dark" works such as *Childe Harold* and *Manfred* caught the imagination of his day, it is for his satiric and comic gifts that he is most remembered today. The well-spring of Byron's lighter side is *Don Juan*, a mock-heroic epic begun in 1818 and left unfinished at Byron's death. It tells the hilarious and often sentimental story of a naive Don Juan set upon by many women. Just as important as the ostensible characters in the poem is the character of the narrator himself, a version of Byron. This host and commentator—at once wry, cynical, tearful, outraged, and sly—reveals Byron's brilliant wit in verbal pyrotechnics.

The poem follows Don Juan's course from his early romantic experimentation with Julia through other affairs in England and abroad. In the process, Byron verbally visits some of his favorite places; comments on wars, fashions, wine, food, and entertainment; takes clever potshots at his fellow poets; and, in general, has his say on virtually any topic that interests him.

Typical of the comic art of this poem is the stanza on Don Juan's early infatuation with Julia:

> *He thought about himself, and the whole earth,*
> *Of man the wonderful, and of the stars,*
> *And how the deuce they ever could have birth;*
> *And then he thought of earthquakes, and of wars,*
> *How many miles the moon might have in girth,*
> *Of air-balloons, and of the many bars*
> *To perfect knowledge of the boundless skies—*
> *And then he thought of Donna Julia's eyes.*

In this work above all others he managed to bring together the best qualities of his genius. Even though unfinished, it is a work of considerable length, and written mostly in ottava rima. It does not contain a dull page. The sixteen completed cantos reveal Byron characteristically. The tone constantly changes from the heroic to the romantic, from the romantic to the satiric. Byron's love of Pope can clearly be understood here, yet the spontaneous hero of the poem is also a relative of the heroes of *Werther* and *The Robbers*—in short a true Byronic hero. The poem rises to heights of poetic inspiration, and then as though Byron scorned you for having taken him seriously, he maliciously buffoons, often at his own expense. The following passages from the third canto will reveal these intended contradictions:

> *The isles of Greece, the isles of Greece!*
> *Where burning Sappho loved and sung,*
> *Where grew the arts of war and peace,*
> *Where Delos rose, and Phoebus sprung!*
> *Eternal summer gilds them yet,*
> *But all, except their sun, is set . . .*

> *Thus sung, or would, or could, or should have sung,*
> *The modern Greek, in tolerable verse;*
> *If not like Orpheus quite, when Greece was young,*
> *Yet in these times he might have done much worse:*
> *His strain displayed some feeling, right or wrong;*
> *And feeling, in a poet, is the source*
> *Of others' feeling; but they are such liars,*
> *And take all colors like the hands of dyers.*

The *Dedication* of *Don Juan* is to Southey, and is full of insults at Southey's expense, as well as at Wordsworth's and Coleridge's—largely because of the Lake Poets' apostasy from radicalism. Perhaps the cruelest blow is at Coleridge's "explaining metaphysics to the nation." "I wish," says Byron, "he would explain his explanation."

The third Canto of *Don Juan* has been much admired. It is full of Byron's devotion to the past of Greece and to the cause of Greek independence to which he soon after devoted his life. He blushes at the fact that no Greek seems interested now in rescuing his fatherland from the Turk's tyranny. After an impassioned lyric to Greece, he turns to the consideration of fame. One of these stanzas is very moving:

> *But words are things, and a small drop of ink,*
> *Falling like dew, upon a thought, produces*
> *That which makes thousands, perhaps millions, think;*
> *'Tis strange, the shortest letter which man uses*
> *Instead of speech, may form a lasting link*
> *Of ages; to what straits old Time reduces*
> *Frail man, when paper—even a rag like this,*
> *Survives himself, his tomb, and all that's his.*

In this canto Byron lashes out once more at the Lake Poets, sneering at Southey's long dreary narratives—exclaiming that if Homer sometimes sleeps, "Wordsworth sometimes wakes"—and deploring the latter's seas of drivel, with special attention to

> *A drowsy frowzy poem called 'The Excursion'*
> *Writ in a manner which is my aversion.*

The fourth Canto returns to the celebrated story of Don Juan's ideal life on a little island with Haidee, who has saved his life after shipwreck. Their happiness is broken by the reappearance of her father Labro, the pirate. Don Juan is seized by the pirates and is taken aboard ship. Haidee loses her mind because of her grief at her lover's wounds. In this canto occurs the famous line:

Whom the gods love die young.

The movement for Greek independence took hold of Byron's fancy, and he decided to enact a personal part in it. At last had come his opportunity for a life of action to which he believed himself intended by nature. He converted all his possessions into money, and invested it in military equipment and pay for mercenaries. The Greeks had to be bribed to fight for their own liberty. He set out for Greece on July 14, 1823. The very hardships and deprivations of a soldier's life delighted him. But before he could participate in the great battle for which he was preparing, he was seized with a fever in the malarial swamps near Missolonghi. On April 19, 1824, a night of fierce thunder and torrents of rain, he died like a true Byronic hero. Today he is considered by the Greeks one of the greatest of their national heroes and it has been said that his example did much to shame the Greeks into putting up a good fight against their Turkish masters.

Mazeppa

Byron's longer works do not please as much as they used to. To our taste they seem too oratorical in style to be truly poetic. Of his longer narrative poems only *Mazeppa* (1819) is still read because of its romantic story. It is a tale of the chief of the Cossacks who joined the army of Charles XII of Sweden. The poem opens with a description of the flight of the royal leader after the battle of Pultowa. Mazeppa is with Charles, is complimented by his leader for his bravery, and asked to relate how he came to be so excellent a horseman. The bulk of the poem is Mazeppa's narrative. At the court of the gentle Casimir, the boy Mazeppa was a page. An avaricious and family-proud nobleman, Count Palatine, was married to a beautiful wife, Teresa, thirty years younger than himself. Mazeppa, falling in love with her, found his attentions welcomed. But one night he was caught in his love-making. To punish his page, the Count caused Mazeppa to be leashed to the back of a wild horse. The horse was whipped into action, and a wild ride began. Mazeppa broke some of his fetters and was able to sit up. But the hazard was too much and the boy fainted. When he awoke it was to find that the horse was swimming across a river. On the opposite bank they crossed a green meadow. The horse, exhausted, dropped dead. Mazeppa's legs and hands were still tied, and he lay there while a raven began to feast on the corpse of the horse. The boy fainted again. This time when he awoke he was in a hut and a Cossack girl was attending to him. He stayed with her family until he was well again. Mazeppa ends his story and bids goodnight to his comrades.

Short Lyrics

It is probable Byron will be longest read not for the narrative poems that made him famous but for his many lovely lyrics, among the simplest and most moving ever written in our language. They are unpretentious, romantic, and often full of sweet pathos. Among the best of these are: "When We Two Parted," "Maid of Athens," "She Walks in Beauty," "Stanzas for Music," "So We'll Go No More A-Roving," "To Thomas Moore," and "On This Day I Complete My Thirty-Sixth Year." The short narrative, "The Destruction of Sennacherib" is also one of his most effective pieces.

"When We Two Parted" is a song about a terminated love affair that ended "in silence and tears." Although she has forgotten him and deceived him, if they should meet again, he would greet her "with silence and tears."

"Maid of Athens" is a song before eternal parting. He asks her: "Give me back my heart." He knows that no matter where he will go, his heart and soul will be at Athens.

"She Walks in Beauty" has two magnificent opening lines:

> She walks in beauty, like the night
> Of cloudless climes and starry skies

One touch more of shadow or light would have ruined her perfect beauty, which eloquently expresses the purity of her heart and the innocence of her love.

"Stanzas for Music" is a perfect expression of the *Weltschmerz*. It is a lament for the fact that we outlive our ability to feel deeply. As we live we grow harder and are driven into guilt and excess:

> That heavy chill has frozen o'er the fountain
> of our tears,
> And though the eye may sparkle still, 'tis
> where the ice appears.

He would give anything if he could feel what he once felt and weep as he once wept.

"So We'll Go No More A-Roving" expresses the poet's desire to rest from his endless wandering:

> For the sword outwears its sheath,
> And the soul wears out the breast.

Love itself must rest too.

"To Thomas Moore" is a tribute to the Irish poet on Byron's leaving England. No matter how fortune may cross him, he will always manage to drink to Tom Moore.

"On This Day I Complete My Thirty-Sixth Year" is one of his last poems, and expresses an awareness that his days are numbered. Nothing is left him but despair and bitter memories, and the fire in his bosom is like a funeral pyre, burning only what is already dead. Still he has a better cause to fight than life has heretofore afforded him—the fight for Greek independence. He will be indifferent now to the lure of beautiful women. And if life holds nothing else, he at least can say to himself:

> Seek out—less often sought than found—
> A soldier's grave, for thee the best;
> Then look around, and choose thy ground,
> And take thy rest.

"The Destruction of Sennacherib" is based on the account in the second book of *Kings* in the Bible of the attack of the Assyrian King upon the Israelites. God sent the Angel of Death to overwhelm the enemies of His people, and the idols in the Temple of Baal lie shattered. For the might of the Israelite's enemies "hath melted like snow in the glance of the Lord."

PERCY BYSSHE SHELLEY (1792–1822)

If Wordsworth is heralded as the leading poet of the Romantic Movement, Shelley is certainly its most beloved poet. Like Spenser, he has been called "the poet's poet." No English poet has ever possessed a lyric genius so pure as his. His early death was perhaps the greatest catastrophe English poetry ever suffered, for he was a man not only of the highest idealism, but also of enormous intellectual breadth. It is likely that, had he lived, his genius might have matured into such magnificence and grandeur as we associate only with Milton. Yet in his own day, while Byron's name was on everyone's lips, Shelley's, if mentioned at all, was uttered only as a synonym for turpitude and moral degeneracy. It is ironical that Shelley was all his life one of the most intensely ethical men who ever lived, although unfortunately for his comfort he could not accept the code of morals that convention prescribes. It is strange that Byron should have been one of the few people who understood him. He never tired of saying about Shelley that he "was without exception the best and least selfish man I ever knew." The friendship between these two poets was odd enough in itself. Byron was flippant, deliberately malicious, and anxious to shock; Shelley was modest, sincere, tense, and never quite at home in the world.

Shelley was born at Field Place in Sussex, August 4, 1792, the son of a hidebound and wealthy country squire. The elder Shelley never understood his son and tried in vain to make the poet conform to his conservative politics and notions of respectability. In the end Shelley thought of his father as typifying all that he loathed in the world. His boyhood was spent in the companionship of his sisters until he was sent to Eton. At school he already showed his inability to adapt himself to the studies and sports that were traditional there. He much preferred to saunter in the country by himself, to sail pieces of paper down the brooks, or to indulge in dangerous experiments with his box of chemicals. At Eton he made the great discovery of his life, the *Political Justice* of William Godwin, a book long ago forgotten by the public. But it created a fire in Shelley's brain as he read Godwin's methodical account of the age of perfection that was sure to come in the millennium. He pictured himself already tilting with the loathed enemy, Intolerance. In a letter of 1811 to his friend Hogg, he exclaims: "Down with Bigotry! Down with Intolerance!"

Shelley entered University College, Oxford, in 1810, and made no attempt to fall in with the routine of academic life. His stay there was brief. Godwin's book had led him to the writings of the French skeptics, and under their influence he had published an original tract on *The Necessity of Atheism.* The authorities haled him in for an explanation, and he and his friend Hogg were expelled. Shelley's father now demanded that he break his friendship with Hogg (whom the elder Shelley vainly supposed responsible for his son's opinions). Shelley refused, and was forbidden to come home.

His sisters providing pocket money, Shelley took up residence in London. There he came to know Harriet Westbrook, who fell in love with him. She was only too willing to become a disciple, as his sisters had already become, and he enjoyed expounding to her Godwin's wonderful teachings. Shelley was already proving himself a brave knight in the cause of Justice. When an Irish journalist was imprisoned for an attack on the Minister of War, Shelley wrote his *Poetic Essay on the Existing State of Things* (1811). Soon after, when the writer Leigh Hunt was acquitted after his trial brought about by his exposé of the army, Shelley introduced himself in a letter that proposed forming a society to propagate freedom of speech. He also sent copies of *The Necessity of Atheism* to various clergymen. To his account of all these great deeds Harriet was an admiring listener. She began to represent that she too was being persecuted at home and at school. What could Shelley do but save her? They eloped to Scotland, and despite Shelley's objection to matrimony, he married her in August 1811 when she was sixteen and he nineteen.

Their first exploit was to deliver the Irish people from tyranny. They crossed the Irish Channel. From the balcony of their hotel together they showered down copies of various pamphlets printed at Shelley's own expense: *An Address to the Irish People, Proposals for an Association of Philanthropists,* and *Declaration of Rights.* Probably Shelley most enjoyed attaching copies of some of these to little balloons that they sent sailing over the city. The Irish people proving indifferent to their own salvation, the Shelleys left Ireland. Moreover, Godwin, who had been sent the tracts, thoroughly disapproved of any attempt to hasten the natural growth of perfectibility. Shelley manfully admitted his error.

Early Poems

He had already published, while at college, some verse and two extravagant Gothic prose romances, *Zastrozzi* (1810) and *St. Irvyne* (1811). In 1813 he finished his first important poem, *Queen Mab.* This work, though full of immaturities, and later despised by Shelley himself, was eventually used against the poet in court when he was suing for custody of his children. It shows the influence of the French philosophers and Godwin, and its poetic form is borrowed from Southey's *Thalaba*. It contains some of Shelley's leading ideas: his dislike of orthodox Christianity, his plea for religious tolerance, his hatred of kings and tyrants, and his belief in the perfectibility of man.

The plot of *Queen Mab* is quite simple. Ianthe lies asleep while her disembodied soul is carried to superterrestrial spheres by Queen Mab, Queen of the fairies. She is thus able to view in perspective past, present and future. She learns that the animating principle of life is Necessity, which extends throughout the Universe and governs every minute of time. Everything that occurs is predestined. All the evils from which mankind suffers must eventually disappear because evil corrupts itself.

Perhaps the most significant thing about *Queen Mab* is that it exhibits one fundamental characteristic of Shelley. Throughout his life he wrote because he was convinced that as a writer he could pave the way for a better society. Even in his shorter pieces, the social idea is the central one. It is true that Shelley is one of our very greatest nature poets, but it is too often overlooked that some of his most superb descriptions of nature are incidental to the political ideas of the poems. *Queen Mab* is therefore only the first ambitious poem of a long series of this kind. As interesing as the poem itself is the appendix of copious notes in which he states his case against governments and institutions.

After two years of a wandering life, Harriet began to tire of her husband's revolutionary ardor. More and more she began to wish for the respectable affluent life that the son of a wealthy squire might lead if he chose to be reasonable. In this new philosophy she was encouraged by her omnipresent sister, Eliza, whom Shelley began with some reason to regard as a serpent. In the meantime the young poet had become acquainted personally with Godwin, his great mentor. From the very beginning Godwin appealed to Shelley for aid because of his own lack of funds—a habit he never gave up for the rest of Shelley's life. The young man was only too glad to be at the service of his great master.

During his frequent calls Shelley had met at the Godwin home the philosopher's daughter, Mary. Her mother, who had died a few days after having given birth to her, had been the wonderfully courageous vindicator of women's rights, Mary Wollstonecraft. At once Shelley recognized a profound sympathy of ideas in Mary, and he felt that she was destined to be his mate. He was unwilling, however, to live adulterously, and he pointed out to Harriet that it was immoral for them to live together any longer since they no longer shared anything in common. They could remain friends, but their marriage had been a mistake. Harriet stoutly refused to terminate their marriage. Shelley, in despair, took a dose of laudanum, which luckily did not prove fatal. Then, with the courage of desperation, he eloped with Mary to the Continent, July 1814.

Two years later Harriet drowned herself. Thereafter Shelley's name became synonymous with that of scoundrel until the day of his death. He himself never recovered from a sense of responsibility for her death, and a sense of guilt clouded the rest of his days. Yet the truth is that Harriet had taken a lover while he was on the Continent, and may very well have committed suicide because as a conventional girl she could not face the prospect of bearing the illegitimate child with which she was pregnant at the time of her suicide. This aspect of her own life was never mentioned while the world was busy accusing Shelley as her murderer.

Mary and Shelley had had a brief visit in England again, spending a summer in Windsor Forest. There he composed his first masterpiece, the beautiful long poem *Alastor, or The Spirit of Solitude,* which was published in 1816. *Alastor* is one of the most amazing poems ever penned by a young man of twenty-three. Merely on the technical side, it is a miracle of rhythmic design, and its blank verse is among the noblest in our language. The title is a Greek word meaning "the avenging genius." The poem opens with a beautiful invocation to Nature and a statement of the poet's untiring search for Nature's essence—a passage that shows that Shelley knew the best of Wordsworth well. This introduction closes with an image that recurs throughout the poem, that of the Aeolian Harp (a stringed instrument suspended in a tree for the winds to sweep at will across its strings):

> *I wait thy breath, Great Parent, that my*
> > *strain*
> *May modulate with murmurs of the air,*
> *And motions of the forests and the sea* . . .

The poem then proceeds to tell of a solitary poet-wanderer, who visits ruins and waste places during his search for truth. He does not accept the proffered love of an Arabian girl. But in Cashmire he experiences a wonderful vision of a beautiful veiled maiden, with whom he dreams he is united. On waking he goes in search of this ideal, as far as the Caspian Sea, which he crosses by boat in a storm. The tide carries him into subterranean waters in the Caucasus. Through these caverns his bark passes into a canyon, past a whirlpool, and on to a quiet river that brings him to a lovely valley. Here he leaves his boat, pursuing still his dream. While proceeding on foot, he has a second vision—this time of a disembodied spirit beckoning to him. This second vision has become a reflection of himself—and like Narcissus, it is with himself now that he yearns for union. Weakened spiritually and physically, he comes to a mountain nook, and there lies down and dies. The poem concludes with a lament for the loss of this refined soul. The point Shelley makes in this beautiful work is that such "self-centered seclusion" as this poet chose can end only in ruin. "Those who love not their fellow-beings live unfruitful lives."

In 1816 Shelley, Mary, and Jane Clairmont went to Switzerland, where they met Byron, with whom all formed a close friendship. They came back to England in the fall, soon to be overwhelmed by double catastrophe. First occurred the suicide of Mary's sister Fanny, the daughter of her mother by an earlier attachment; and then came Harriet's suicide. The shock of these two tragedies did much to impair Shelley's health, but he was brought near the edge of collapse by a long and losing suit to procure custody of his two children. The courts decided that such a monster as he was unfit to be a father to Harriet's children. Perhaps it was for relief that he engaged on a project of ambitious writing this year. *Prince Athanase, Rosalind and Helen,* and *The Revolt of Islam* were written in 1817 during all these difficulties. The last mentioned is an ideological sequel to *Queen Mab,* and is written in Spenserian stanzas. The work proves that Shelley alone of his generation was not tempted to despair of the failure of the French Revolution. The story tells of the collapse of a revolution led by two high-minded revolutionists because the struggle had been brought about prematurely. Shelley concludes that even though the revolution has proved abortive, the effort has not been wasted for it has shown to the people an ideal of freedom that they will continue to seek and eventually find.

It seemed folly to live any longer in England. Therefore, in March 1818 Shelley left forever with Mary (whom he had by now legally married), Jane Clairmont, and the latter's child by Byron. For the rest of the four years remaining in Shelley's life he lived in Italy. The beauty of that country seemed calculated to bring his wonderful genius into magnificent blossoming, and it was there that he produced his greatest works. His household was always crowded with various people who counted upon his help for spiritual nourishment. But such time as was his to devote to himself, when he could free himself from the heavy depression with which Harriet's death has scarred his spirit, enabled him to study and write, and to enjoy the beauties of Italy. A visit to Byron in Venice in 1818 has been commemorated for us by the interesting narrative poem *Julian and Maddalo,* written in iambic pentameter couplets. In it we find impressive portraits of Shelley (Julian) and Byron (Maddalo). Here Shelley through the mask of Julian's name tells us of his mental anguish, as well as his inability to be silent in his hostility to tyranny. As the guest of Byron in the latter's villa in the Euganean Hills, Shelley began writing his masterpiece, *Prometheus Unbound.*

Lyrics, 1818–1819

It was at this time that he also composed his wonderful "Lines Written Among the Euganean Hills" (1818), in tetrameter couplets. The poem begins in sorrow and ends in hope, as it moves from the world of everyday reality to the world of the ideal. The opening lines are memorable:

> *Many a green isle needs must be*
> *In the deep wide sea of Misery,*
> *Or the mariner, worn and wan,*
> *Never more could voyage on.*

The end of life's dreary voyage always is death. But the poet reflects that the view of the sunrise over Venice that the Euganean Hills affords him is typical of the unexpected blessings life can offer. Venice now indeed is succumbing under the tyranny of Austria, but the visit of a great genius like Byron will immortalize Venice more than her conquerors can. It will take but one spark from the lamp of learning which tyranny is attempting to quench, and the whole earth may yet be enkindled. The poem concludes that:

> *Other flowering isles must be*
> *In the sea of Life and Agony.*

and, as the moon rises, he reflects that brotherhood will yet be on earth,

> *And the earth grow young again.*

"Stanzas Written in Dejection Near Naples" (1818) belongs to the same year. It is a very moving lyric in which the poet contrasts the splendors of the great Bay of Naples with his own tortured mind and failing health. As he looks on the beautiful scene:

> *Yet now despair itself is mild,*
> *Even as the winds and waters are;*
> *I could lie down like a tired child,*
> *And weep away the life of care*
> *Which I have borne and yet must bear.*

The next year, 1819, was a wonderful year for Shelley and for English poetry. In it he came into full control of his art. Within these amazing twelve months he composed some of his greatest lyrical poems, the "Ode to the West Wind," "The Indian Serenade," and "Love's Philosophy;" a bitter satire on such renegades from republicanism as he believed Wordsworth to be, "Peter Bell the Third;" his impassioned defense of republicanism, "The Mask of Anarchy;" the complete version of *Prometheus Unbound;* and the noblest poetic tragedy written since the days of the Elizabethans, *The Cenci,* the only tragedy by a great nineteenth century poet that has proved successful on the stage.

The "Ode to the West Wind," written in a modified form of *terza rima,* has been sometimes called the most inspired lyrical poem describing nature in our language. But to Shelley it was a revolutionary rather than a descriptive poem. It would be a mistake, because its magnificent lines have such sweep of spontaneity, to overlook the great artistry with which it has been written.

There is a brilliant symmetry of form here, equal in elegance to anything a classicist could contrive. The five fourteen-line stanzas each develop one aspect of the thought. In the first stanza Shelley describes the West Wind in the forest; in the second, in the sky; in the third, on the sea. In the fourth stanza he states the reason for the prayer that he must make, and in the fifth comes the prayer itself, containing the central meaning of the poem.

The idea for this piece came to him in a wood outside of Florence, and as the wind began to rise and gather fury, he suddenly saw the cycle of the seasons as a wonderful allegory on the hopes he entertained for mankind. In the forest he sees the leaves driven like ghosts before the wind. This same wind is charioting the seeds to their beds, where they will lie until Spring shall come and bid them bring life again to earth. In the sky the clouds, "angels of rain and lightning," are mustering their congregated might to pour forth rain and fire. On the sea the quiet waters are about to be churned into fury and "the sapless foliage of the ocean" to grow grey with fear. If he were a leaf, a cloud or a wave, and thus could feel the impulse of the wind, he would not need to make this prayer. Being a mortal chained to time he asks the wind to make him its Aeolian Harp:

> *Make me thy lyre, ev'n as the forest is:*
> *What if my leaves are falling like its own!*
> *The tumult of thy mighty harmonies*
>
> *Will take from both a deep, autumnal tone,*
> *Sweet though in sadness. Be thou, Spirit*
> > *fierce,*
> *My spirit! be thou me, impetuous one!*
>
> *Drive my dead thoughts over the universe,*
> *Like withered leaves, to quicken a new birth!*
> *And, by the incantation of this verse,*
>
> *Scatter, as from an unextinguished hearth*
> *Ashes and sparks, my words among mankind!*
> *Be through my lips to unawakened earth*
>
> *The trumpet of a prophecy! O wind,*
> *If Winter comes, can Spring be far behind?*

"The Indian Serenade" is a beautiful love lyric, placed in India. The lover begins:

> *I arise from dreams of thee*
> *In the first sweet sleep of night.*

He has come to her window while the nightingale sings. He asks to be taken to her heart and be revived by her kisses.

"Love's Philosophy" argues that since dreams mingle with the river, the river with the ocean, the winds with one another, since "nothing in the world is single," why should his sweetheart not mingle in one spirit with him?

Prometheus Unbound

Prometheus Unbound is generally considered to be Shelley's masterpiece. In it the splendor of his imagination may be read in almost every line. It forms a third in an ideological trilogy with *Queen Mab* and *The Revolt of Islam.* *Queen Mab* is an indictment of contemporary evil and a vision of the splendor to be; *The Revolt of Islam* is a picture of an abortive attempt to liberate mankind. *Prometheus Unbound* tells us how the liberation of man is to come about, and describes the fundamental laws by which the new order will exist.

A play by this title is known to have been written by Aeschylus, the first great Greek dramatist, but now is lost. Aeschylus' *Prometheus Bound,* however, exists. That play deals with the punishment of Prometheus by the Father of the Gods. Prometheus had been the benefactor of humanity in giving to man the secret of making fire and the knowledge of all the arts which fire makes possible. In this beneficence Prometheus angered Zeus, for with fire men began to rival the gods in power and wisdom. Zeus punished Prometheus by having him chained to a precipice in the Caucasus, where daily a vulture preys on his heart to torture him.

But Shelley's play, which opens at this point, after Prometheus has thus suffered for ages, is not, dramatically speaking, really a sequel to Aeschylus' *Prometheus Bound.* For it is not drama at all: Prometheus' release begins almost from the very opening passage. *Prometheus Unbound* is rather a superb poetic pageant.

Shelley rightly believed it to be his own best poetic creation. He told Trelawney: "If that is not durable poetry, tried by the severest test, I do not know what it is. It is a lofty subject not inadequately treated, and shall not perish with me." The first three acts were completed in Rome in the spring of 1819. The last act, the fourth, a magnificent choral epilogue, was an afterthought, and composed some months later at Florence.

In the story itself Shelley departs from the dénouement that Aeschylus is known to have employed in his lost play. In Aeschylus, as in the old myth, Prometheus is liberated when he reveals to Jupiter (Zeus) the disasters to be visited upon the Father of the Gods if he persists in his desire to wed Thetis. Thus, in the old legend, Prometheus does not continue to rebel against the gods. But Shelley's Prometheus is mankind's champion, who could never have compromised with the oppressor of humanity. In Shelley's dramatic poem it is Jupiter (Zeus) who capitulates, not Prometheus.

In *Prometheus Unbound,* many of the ideas in *Queen Mab* are restated, but with greater magnificence. Christ, however, is here sympathetically treated, not with the hostility of the earlier work. Kings and priests are still the chief authors of human ills, for they sponsor the great sicknesses which prey on human beings: hatred, revenge, hypocrisy, fear, convention, and organized religion. The apogee of human misery is to be found in the mental anguish of such preservers of humanity as Prometheus, or the grief of a Christ when He beholds how His good intentions have been perverted to evil ends. But evil, Shelley is convinced, is doomed. Its own death lies in itself. And the end of evil will be hastened by the practice of Shelley's cardinal virtues, which are Gentleness, Virtue, Wisdom, and Endurance—and, above all, Love.

In the first act Prometheus is willing enough to revoke the curse he has called down on Jupiter's head, but he is unwilling despite his dreadful torture to give up the secret that would secure Jupiter's reign of despotism. Prometheus will not interfere with the law which makes Evil fall through its own weakness. This Evil first came into the world when Jupiter became ruler. Yet it was Prometheus himself who first placed Jupiter in his position of power. Thus, Man has created his own Evil by putting up with kings and priests. When Jupiter falls, Evil falls with him.

Prometheus Unbound is the supreme expression in literature of the doctrine of the perfectibility of the human race. The new age will dawn when Man has learned to overcome hatred and revenge. Prometheus' torture and Jupiter's reign both end when Prometheus is suddenly able to give up all ideas of hatred and revenge against his oppressor, and can actually pity him for being an instrument of evil.

Various interpretations have been advanced as to the allegorical significance of the characters in the play. It is certain that Prometheus stands for Humanity, Jupiter for the Principle of Evil (as exemplified in the order of things today), Asia for Nature, and Demogorgon for the Primal Power of the world. Asia also probably represents Love and Beauty (as found ideally expressed in Nature); Hercules stands for Strength, Thetis for false ideals, Panthea for Faith, and Ione for Hope. The Furies are the various causes of suffering abroad in the world of man; and the Spirits who come to comfort Prometheus are the goodness in Man that will make for Man's happiness.

Mary Shelley's note to the play will be found helpful:

> He [Shelley] followed certain classical authorities in figuring Saturn as the good principle, Jupiter the usurping evil one, and Prometheus as the regenerator, who . . . used knowledge as a weapon to defeat evil, by leading mankind . . . to that [state] in which they are virtuous through wisdom. Jupiter punished the temerity of the Titan [Prometheus] by chaining him to a rock of Caucasus, and causing a vulture to devour his still-renewed heart. There was a prophecy afloat in heaven portending the fall of Jove [Jupiter], the secret of averting which was known only to Prometheus, and the god offered freedom from torture on condition of its being communicated to him. . . . This referred to the offspring of Thetis, who was destined to be greater than his father. . . . Shelley adapted the catastrophe of this story to his peculiar views. . . . Prometheus defies the power of his enemy, and endures centuries of torture; till the hour arrives when Jove, blind to the real event, but darkly guessing that some great good to himself will flow, espouses Thetis. At the moment, the Primal Power of the world drives him from his usurped throne, and Strength, in the person of Hercules, liberates Humanity, typified in Prometheus. . . . Asia . . . is the wife of Prometheus—she was . . . the same as Venus and Nature. When the benefactor of humanity is liberated, Nature resumes the beauty of her prime, and is united

to her husband. . . . In the Fourth Act, the Poet . . . idealizes the forms of creation. . . . Maternal Earth, the mighty parent, is superseded by the Spirit of the Earth, the guide of our planet through the realms of sky; while his fair and weaker companion and attendant, the Spirit of the Moon, receives bliss from the annihilation of Evil in the superior sphere.

Act I: The first act takes place in a ravine of icy rocks in the Indian Caucasus, with Prometheus bound to the precipice. Panthea and Ione are seated at his feet. It is night. As the scene advances the light of morning slowly breaks. Prometheus speaks of his torture; it is intense but he has found patience. For every hour brings nearer the end of Jupiter's reign. As he thinks of Jupiter's fall, he can even pity him, and would recall his curse on him. He asks the Mountains, Springs, the Air, and the Whirlwinds to repeat that curse. The Earth answers that they fear to utter it lest Jupiter torture them eternally. The Earth, Prometheus' mother, bids him call on one of the mighty Gods of Evil to speak what he wishes to hear. Prometheus now calls up the Phantasm of Jupiter to speak the old curse, and it obeys. Prometheus' old curse was a defiance of Jupiter:

Ay, do thy worst. Thou art omnipotent.
*   O'er all things but thyself I gave thee power,*
And my own will . . . .
Heap on thy soul, by virtue of this Curse
*   Ill deads, then be thou damned, beholding good . . . .*
*   An awful image of calm power*
*   Though now thou sittest, let the hour*
*   Come, when thou must appear to be*
*   That which thou art internally;*
And after many a false and fruitless crime
Scorn track thy lagging fall through boundless space and
*   time.*

Hearing these words, Prometheus repents having uttered them. "I wish no living thing to suffer pain." Mercury enters with the Three Furies. The Furies are enraptured at the thought of torturing him. Mercury announces new tortures to be visited upon Prometheus, but expresses his sympathy for the hero. He suggests that Prometheus reveal the secret he alone knows and pray to Jupiter to forgive him. Prometheus answers:

*   Evil Minds*
*   Change good to their own nature. I gave all*
*   He has; and in return he chains me here . . .*
*   Whilst my beloved race is trampled down*
*   By his thought-executing ministers: 'tis just:*
*   He who is evil can receive no good;*
*   And for a world bestowed, or a friend lost,*

> *He can feel hate, fear, or shame; not gratitude;*
> *He but requites me for his own misdeed.*

Prometheus avers he can never submit to the Oppressor. The Furies, joined by other Furies, come forth to begin their torture. They unfold a vision of the agony of Christ at the mockery of his teachings by Christians, and another vision of the corruption of the noble ends of the French Revolution. The Furies vanish. After they leave the atmosphere charged with despair over the fact that good may result in so much evil, a Chorus of Spirits sings a sweeter message: evil, they say, becomes in the long run the means of occasioning greater good. The Fourth Spirit's song is a wonderful expression of poetic idealism:

> *On a poet's lips I slept*
> *Dreaming like a love-adept*
> *In the sound his breathing kept;*
> *Nor seeks nor finds he mortal blisses,*
> *But feeds on the aëreal kisses*
> *Of shapes that haunt thought's wildernesses.*
> *He will watch from dawn to gloom*
> *The lake-reflected sun illume*
> *The yellow bees in the ivy-bloom,*
> *Nor heed nor see, what things they be;*
> *But from these create he can*
> *Forms more real than living man,*
> *Nurslings of immortality!*

The dawn is breaking now, and Asia "waits in that far Indian vale" for his delivery. Prometheus' night of agony is over.

Act II: The second act begins in that Indian vale where Asia waits in exile for the new day. Her sister Panthea comes to her from her recent vigil at Prometheus' feet. A mysterious spirit enters, crying, "Follow, follow, follow me." This spirit leads them on, purposing to take them to Demogorgon's Cave, where the great Change is to begin. The second scene of this act shows Asia and Panthea making their way through a forest. In the third scene they arrive on a pinnacle of rock in the mountains. From this point they can observe the beginning of the New Order. In the great fourth scene of the act, they arrive at the Cave of Demogorgon. Asia tells how it was Prometheus who gave strength and wisdom to the usurper Jupiter, on the provision that Man be left free. Instead Jupiter visited Man with every kind of affliction. Against Jupiter, the cause of man's sufferings, Prometheus once more becomes Man's Champion. He gave Man knowledge and Science. And it was for this goodness that Jupiter punished him. But now, Demogorgon says, the hour of liberation has arrived. Demogorgon mounts the chariot of the Spirit of the Hour and departs to do his work. In the fifth scene of the act occurs the emotional climax of the poem. A Voice in the Air sings a wonderful hymn to Intellectual Beauty:

> *Light of Life! thy lips enkindle*
> *With their love the breath between them.*

—this Intellectual Beauty that now resides in Asia (Nature). Asia answers in a song equally wonderful:

> *My soul is an enchanted boat,*
> *Which, like a sleeping swan, doth float*
> *Upon the silver waves of thy sweet singing.*

Act III: The third act opens with Jupiter celebrating his nuptials to Thetis. Jupiter expects that he can now subdue Man's soul and be at last truly omnipotent. While he is boasting, the Car of the Hour arrives, and Demogorgon at once bids him quit his throne and dwell with him "henceforth in darkness." Now there is no respite for Jupiter, and in his defeat he declares that Prometheus, to whom he has been so unjust. would never be so cruel to him. But Necessity cannot be thwarted, and Jupiter sinks down into darkness. In the second scene we have a beautiful interlude between Apollo and Ocean, who discuss Jupiter's fall. In the third scene Hercules comes to the pinnacle of the Caucusus, and unbinds Prometheus, and Asia is united to Prometheus at last. In the fourth scene Prometheus comes with Asia and her sisters to a cave in the forest; from this spot they will be able to hear the echoes of the regeneration of the world. The Earth is purged of all evil:

> *The painted veil, by those who were, called life,*
> *Which mimicked, as with colors idly spread,*
> *All men believed and hoped, is torn aside;*
> *The loathsome mask has fallen, the man remains*
> *Sceptreless, free, uncircumscribed, but man*
> *Equal, unclassed, tribeless, and nationless,*
> *Exempt from awe, worship, degree, the king*
> *Over himself; just, gentle, wise: but man*
> *Passionless?—no, yet free from guilt or pain.*

Thus ends the play as Shelley first planned it.

Act IV: The fourth act, added later, is a marvelous hymn of deliverance— Shelley's lyric genius at its greatest. It is like a wonderful symphony in which we seem to hear the music of the spheres. The Ghosts of the Dead Hours bear Time to its tomb in Eternity. A new series of Hours takes their places. Those Spirits which had consoled Prometheus during his tortures, now reappear and sing a song of deliverance. Ione and Panthea behold now a wonderful vision of the Moon Spirit and the Earth Spirit. Both have been revitalized, and sing to each other in love. Man has become like a sea reflecting Love. Demogorgon rises to address Spirits and Gods, and the Dead. This is the day in which the despotism of Heaven is over. Prometheus' Gentleness, Virtue, Wisdom, and Endurance will keep tyranny forever enchained. To suffer and forgive, to defy and to love—that is victory:

> *To defy Power which seems omnipotent;*
> *To love, and to bear; to hope till Hope creates*
> *From its own wreck the thing it contemplates;*
> *Neither to change, nor falter, nor repent;. . .*
> *This is alone Life, Joy, Empire, and Victory.*

The Cenci

The Cenci, though written in 1819 was not acted until 1886, when it made a favorable impression. It is considered the one acting play of quality until the closing years of the century. It shows the influence of Shakespeare, particularly the latter's greatest dramatic poem, *Macbeth.* The plot is taken from an exciting chapter in Italian Renaissance history, which historically took place during the last year of the sixteenth century. Count Francesco Cenci, a very wealthy and powerful noble, detests all his children with the exception of his daughter Beatrice, for whom he feels an incestuous attraction. To put an end to the monstrosities of her father's conduct, Beatrice enters into a plot with her stepmother and her brother to murder Count Francesco. They hire two assassins to do the deed. Their plot is uncovered after her father's death, and they are arrested and sentenced to execution. Although the public sympathizes with them, the Pope orders their execution. Despite certain excesses in the writing of this play, the tremendous passion which the poet has infused into the lines imparts a great power to this drama.

Later Poems

In the winter of 1819, the Shelleys moved to Pisa, where a circle of interesting friends surrounded them: Medwin, the Williamses, Byron, the adventurer Trelawney, Leigh Hunt with his wife and six children, and the Greek patriot Prince Mavrocordato. In 1820 Shelley wrote a series of wonderful poems: "The Sensitive Plant," "The Cloud," "To a Skylark;" and in 1821: "To Night," "Music When Soft Voices Die," "One Word Is Too Often Profaned," "Epipsychidion," the lyrical drama *Hellas,* and the most wonderful of all, "Adonais."

"The Sensitive Plant," written in tetrameter couplets, is a poem of delicate fancy; it concludes with an idea more fully developed in "Adonais," that life and death are both deceptions as we know them, for life is but a shadow of reality, and our death, therefore, is but the death of a shadow.

"The Cloud" is one of Shelley's greatest nature poems and is written with his most exquisite music. In the poem it is the cloud that speaks of its own history. The work is a good example of Shelley's constant ability to make wonderful poetry out of scientific fact, for "The Cloud" is a statement in high imaginative terms of what scientists call the "rain cycle." The poem is also highly typical of Shelley because of its imagery. No other poet has been so fond of the use of intangibles for the making of images to the extent that Shelley employs them. His favorite pictures are drawn from clouds, sunlight, sunrise, sunset, moonlight, hail, rain, thunder, snow, and lightning. Images from all these aspects of nature appear in "The Cloud." The Cloud tells us how she brings showers for the flowers, dew, and shade:

> When rocked to rest on their mother's breast,
> As she dances about the sun . . .

She brings the snows, the hail and the rain, and herself sleeps on the snow of the mountains as her white pillow. The sunrise leaps on her back, and at sunset she rests airily. The moonlight glimmers on the cloud's floor; and where the moonlight's feet may have broken a space, the stars peep through:

> And I laugh to see them whirl and flee
> Like a swarm of golden bees,
> When I widen the rent in my wind-built tent

Sometimes the Cloud hangs thick like a roof; sometimes she brings the rainbow.

> I am the daughter of earth and water
> And the nursling of the sky;
> I pass through the pores of the ocean and shores;
> I change but I cannot die

For, when a stainless sky seems to show the Cloud is dead, she laughs and starts to unbuild this monument to her passing.

"To A Skylark" from its first line insists that this melodious bird is pure spirit, and not of the earth:

> Hail to thee, blithe spirit!
> Bird thou never wert

It sings as it mounts higher and higher as though it were an "unbodied joy," and it can be heard when it is no longer seen, as moonlight can be felt in the dawn. The bird is like a poet singing beautifully in obscurity, like a lovelorn maiden in a high tower, like a glow-worm hidden in the dewy grass, like a rosebud hidden among its leaves. This joyous song is fresher than the rain, and more divine than any love song or triumphal hymn. What can be the cause of this pure joy? Surely the bird could never know mortals' sadness. It must know the truth about death, or how could it sing so purely? As for us mortals:

> We look before and after
>   And pine for what is not;
> Our sincerest laughter
>   With some pain is fraught;
> Our sweetest songs are those that tell
>   of saddest thought.

The poem concludes with a prayer to the bird to teach the poet the secret of its music so that the world be compelled to listen to him.

"To Night" is one of the most wonderful songs in our language, an invocation to the spirit of night written with a wonderful hushed music:

> *Swiftly walk o'er the western wave*
> *Spirit of night!*

"Music When Soft Voices Die" is another exquisite song which tells how memory survives the experience of music, fragrance, and idea. "One Word is Too Often Profaned" is a love song in which the poet offers the kind of love, the love of the spirit, which men have profaned by their misuse of the word.

"Epipsychidion," whose title means "a picture of the soul out of my soul," was addressed to Emilia Viviani. Shelley had met her late in 1820, after learning that her father had shut her up in a convent until she was ready to marry. Shelley felt it was his duty to rescue her. And when he saw how beautiful she was, he decided that she was a sister of his soul. "Epipsychidion" is a hymn of platonic love, in which Emilia is made to be the ideal soul personified; all his life he had hoped to meet this perfection. The poem concludes with a plea to her to fly with him to a place of refuge. Written in pentameter couplets, the poem has several wonderful passages, especially the passage beginning:

> *There was a Being whom my spirit oft*
> *Met on its visioned wanderings, far aloft*

It is a kind of ideal history of the soul. It is perhaps unimportant to remark that shortly after the composition of the poem, Emilia was commonplace enough to marry the man who had been selected for her, and Shelley lost all interest in her.

Hellas, a lyrical drama influenced by Aeschylus, was inspired by the Greek struggle for independence from their Turkish rulers. It tells the story of the fight at Salamis, and prophesies the eventual freedom of the Greeks. Though the play itself is not too good, the choruses are among Shelley's most inspired lyrics. Especially celebrated is a passage beginning:

> *The world's great age begins anew,*
> *The golden years return,*
> *The earth doth like a snake renew*
> *Her winter weeds outworn:*
> *Heaven smiles, and faiths and empires gleam,*
> *Like wrecks of a dissolving dream.*

"Adonais"

"Adonais" is one of Shelley's most important poems and takes its place beside Milton's "Lycidas" as being one of the two greatest elegies in our language. It is interesting that both "Lycidas" and "Adonais" are modeled on the ancient Greek pastoral elegy of the poet Moschus, "A Lament For Bion."

Shelley and his fellow poet Keats were not much more than acquaintances, although Shelley had financed the publication of one of Keats's volumes. Nor were they deeply impressed with the quality of each other's work. Shelley objected to Keats's unwillingness to incorporate ideas of intellectual depth in his work, and Keats disliked Shelley's conviction that poetry must be used as a vehicle for social improvement. But when Shelley heard that Keats was in very bad health, he invited him, with that generosity so typical of him, to come as his guest to Pisa. Keats was too proud to accept. Within a year Keats died. His friends were convinced that he had been slain by the harsh criticism his poetry had been subjected to, particularly that of an anonymous reviewer. There seems little reason now to take this view of Keats's death, but it is easy to see that with Shelley's sensitiveness to injustice it is an idea that must have appealed to him. He no sooner believed Keats killed by the critics than he convinced himself that Keats had been a very great poet. He wrote "Adonais" as an elegy on Keats, with the double purpose of paying tribute to the younger poet's memory and of castigating his critics. Like "Lycidas," therefore, "Adonais" departs in passages from its elegiac mood to indulge in fierce but wonderfully moving invective. But Shelley's art wonderfully fuses the pastoral and satirical elements into a splendid whole. It is doubtful whether the Spenserian stanza has ever been used with such radiant beauty as in this poem. Besides the magnificence of the imagery, the exalted beauty of Shelley's personifications, his noble exposition of Plato's view of the soul, and his characteristic magnanimity towards his fellow poets, he is particularly interesting in "Adonais" because of a stirring autobiographical passage, where he at last speaks out concerning his heavy sense of guilt over Harriet's death.

The poem opens with a lament for Adonais (Shelley's pastoral name for Keats). The poet asks Urania, the Muse of Heavenly Poetry, where she could have been when her favorite child died. She was in her own Paradise. He calls upon her to come and join with the poet in his lament for Adonais. He remembers how Milton died blind and lonely in an age he hated, yet how Milton went "unterrified into the gulf of death." Men of meaner ambitions dared not aspire so high:

> *And happier they their happiness who knew*
> *Whose tapers yet burn through that night of*
> > *time*
> *In which suns perished*

Adonais came to Rome to find death, and there his body lies as if in dewy sleep. Corruption waits to lead him to her palace. In the meantime, Adonais' dreams cling round his corpse. One of them, seeing a teardrop on his eyelashes, thinks it a tear, fondly imagines that Adonais still is alive.

> *Lost Angel of a ruined Paradise!*
> *She knew not 'twas her own.*

Other splendors come: Desires, Adorations, Wingèd Persuasions, Veiled Destinies, Glooms, Twilight Fantasies, Incarnations of hopes and fears, Sorrow, Sighs, and Pleasure blind with tears—all come to mourn over Keats in a pageantry like autumnal mist. Nature mourns too. The ground is wet with tears and the sun's eyes are dimmed. The ocean is unquiet, and the winds sob. Echo mourns Adonais, and Spring now is like an Autumn. The Nightingale and the Eagle both wail for Adonais's passing. Spring is here and all the Earth is awakening to Beauty. Adonais's corpse, touched by this reawakening, itself exhales a gentle perfume: "like incarnations of the stars." Adonais's soul cannot be dead:

> *Naught we know, dies. Shall that alone which*
> *knows* (the soul)
> *Be as a sword consumed before the sheath . . . ?*

But all that his friends knew of Adonais is gone. For Death is the universal law of earthly values:

> *As long as skies are blue and fields are*
> *green,*
> *Evening must usher night, night urge the*
> *morrow,*
> *Month follow month with woe, and year wait*
> *year to sorrow*

Urania is awakened in her Paradise, and begins her procession to Rome. She passes through cities made of stone and steel, with human hearts as hard; these wound the palms of her feet with their harsh thoughts and rend her form. But they cannot kill her, who is immortal; indeed her blood paves "with eternal flowers that undeserving way." In the death chamber Urania kisses Adonais, but it is Death that meets her caress. In Urania's mouth the poet now puts his assault on the critics who have killed Adonais. These are wolves and ravens, feeding on Death, and vultures who are true only to the conqueror. How they fled when Byron attacked them only once! After Urania's lament, Keats's friends come to mourn over him—Byron, Tom Moore, and Leigh Hunt, and others. Among these is one of lesser note, Shelley himself. He has been hunted over the world, pursued by his own thoughts, as though they were hounds. His head is shrouded, but when he makes bare his brow it is branded "like Cain's or Christ's." The poet now leaves the death chamber to attack the critic on his own account. That "nameless worm" could fail to feel the magic of Adonais's songs. But to the poet the greatest curse that can be visited upon this wretch is to be compelled to be himself, free every season to spill his poison. A worse fate no one could wish upon anyone. As for Adonais, we need not weep for him. He does not sleep, he has "awakened from the dream of life." It is we who still live who dwell in a world of phantoms. Adonais's spirit is now one with nature, and is "a portion of the loveliness which once he made more lovely." Death cannot obscure that brightness. Where his spirit has gone he is greeted by other poets who died too young, Chatterton, Sidney, Lucan, and many others whose names are not known on earth. The poet now moves to the Protestant Cemetery in Rome where Keats's remains are to lie. As the poet stands there he reflects that the one spirit moving through all things is deathless:

> *The One remains, the many change and pass;*
> *Heaven's light for ever shines, Earth's*
> *shadows fly;*
> *Life, like a dome of many-colored glass,*
> *Stains the white radiance of Eternity,*
> *Until Death tramples it to fragments.*

The fifty-fourth stanza adresses that all-sustaining Love "whose smile kindles the Universe," to shine upon the poet and burn up the last remnants of his mortality, for this Love moves in all beings, man and beast, and

> *Burns bright or dim, as each are mirrors of*
> *The fire for which all thirst*

The next stanza, the last, bears witness to the poet's feeling the breath of death upon him too. The lines in which he images the death that must soon come for him are almost terrifying to read because they are almost literally a description of what was actually to happen to him before another year was out:

> *my spirit's bark is driven*
> *Far from the shore, far from the trembling throng*
> *Whose sails were never to the tempest given;*
> *The massy earth and sphered skies are riven!*
> *I am borne darkly, fearfully, afar.*

On July 8, 1822, Shelley set out on a sailboat with his friend Williams for a trip to Leghorn. The boat was caught in a terrific storm, and ten days later their bodies were washed ashore. Byron, Trelawney, and Leigh Hunt were present on the beach at the cremation of the poet's remains. In the Protestant Cemetery at Rome, which he had described in "Adonais," his ashes and his heart, which would not burn, repose near the grave of Keats.

Other Lyrics

Among the poems of Shelley which have not yet been discussed are a number worthy of consideration: "Hymn to Intellectual Beauty," "Ozymandias," "Time," "Mutability," "A Lament," "A Dirge," "To Jane, with a Guitar," "When the Lamp Is Shattered," and "The Triumph of Life."

"Hymn to Intellectual Beauty" (1816), one of his earliest great poems, is a statement of the Platonic concept of Beauty, as incorporated into Shelley's own philosophy. Beauty is a quality to which all beautiful objects aspire. This beauty is a power unseen among us, but felt in all things, "and yet dearer for its mystery." The poet then asks why this ideal of beauty will not dwell among us since it alone lends meaning to what we perceive. Our life is but a dream, and the Platonic world of ideas is the only reality. Beauty will not dwell among us because if she did men would be immortal. As a boy the poet sought her in caves and ruins and starlit woods. Suddenly he felt the ecstasy of her presence. From that moment he vowed to dedicate his powers to her, since she alone can free the world from slavery. He pleads with Beauty not to forsake him since it is she who has taught the poet "to fear himself and love all humankind."

"Ozymandias" (1817) is a sonnet expressing the vanity of the works of man. In an ancient land there is a wreck of what was once a colossal monument, bearing the inscription:

> *"My name is Ozymandias, king of kings;*
> *Look on my works, ye Mighty, and despair!"*
> *Nothing beside remains.*

"Time" (1821) is a short poem comparing time to the unfathomable ocean that vomits up wrecks on the shore. Like the sea, time is treacherous. "Mutability" (1821) reflects on the impermanence of all things:

> *The flower that smiles today*
> *Tomorrow dies*

Virtue, Friendship and Love do not last even as long as we ourselves. Then, while we can, we should "make glad the day." "A Lament" (1821), addressed to the World, Life and Time, is a wonderful short poem asking when will return the glory of their youth. The answer is "no more—oh, never more." "A Dirge" (1822) is addressed to the wind, bidding it "wail for the world's wrong." "To Jane, with a Guitar" (1822) is addressed from Shakespeare's Ariel to Miranda, a very graceful poem on the story of *The Tempest,* and on the musical instrument. "When the Lamp is Shattered" (1822) is a beautiful lyric beginning:

> *When the lamp is shattered,*
> *The light in the dust lies dead*

In the same way when the spirit is silent the heart has no song to sing. Once hearts have mingled, love leaves its dwelling, and the abandoned one is left naked to the winds and the wintry sky. "The Triumph of Life" (1822) was never finished, but in its fragmentary form it is very impressive. Written in terza rima, it shows greatly the influence of Dante. It is a dream poem on life and death.

Mention should also be made of the drama *Charles the First* (1822), a fragment showing Shakespearean influence, in powerful blank verse; and also of Shelley's great prose work, *A Defense of Poetry* (1821), a brilliant and noble defense of his beloved art, showing how profoundly he was influenced by Plato's philosophy. Thomas Love Peacock had written in *The Four Ages of Poetry* (1820) his conviction that poetry was becoming extinct since its practice is a survival of barbaric times. Defending his profession with pride, Shelley says, among other things,

> Poetry thus makes immortal all that is best and most beautiful in the world; . . . redeems from decay the visitations of the divinity in man, . . . turns all things to loveliness . . . Poets are the unacknowledged legislators of the world.

IMPORTANCE

There are several recurring ideas in Shelley's poetry. The fundamental one is that love is the great regenerating influence, and through love alone will the world come into its maturity; this theme is basic to "Alastor," "Hymn to Intellectual Beauty," "The Sensitive Plant," *Prometheus Unbound*, and "Adonais," among other poems. This conception Shelley derived from Plato. Shelley's other great concern, learned from Godwin, was the future of mankind in a better society; *Queen Mab, The Revolt of Islam, Prometheus Unbound*, "Ode to the West Wind," "To a Skylark," and *Hellas* are concerned with this idea. But the greatness of Shelley is not only in the nobility and dignity of his ideas. His superb artistry, his glowing imagination, and his incomparable feeling for the most exquisite and impalpable aspects of nature place him in the very front rank of English poets. He is a far subtler poet than Wordsworth, and an incomparably greater musician. The quality of the ethereal lifts most of what he wrote into the highest poetic realm. It is doubtful whether any poet of so brief a life as Shelley's has left so large a quantity of great poetry.

JOHN KEATS (1795–1821)

John Keats, the apostle of Beauty, was born over his father's livery stable in London on October 29, 1795. At the age of seven he was sent with his younger brother George to school at Enfield. At the school he became a close friend of the headmaster's son, Charles Cowden Clarke. Keats quickly developed a reputation for his willingness to fight at any time of day or night with anyone. Though slight of physique, Keats's character was thoroughly virile. It is worthwhile mentioning this since his devotion to beauty and his very early death have made some people sentimentalize him into a delicate effeminate creature. Nothing could be further from the truth.

Early Poems

As a boy he was very little interested in books until his last year at school, when young Clarke encouraged him to read. But Keats was an extremist, and before very long he had read clean through the school library. Keats had lost his father when he was nine and his mother when he was fifteen. His guardians removed him from school in 1811 and apprenticed him to a surgeon in Edmonton. For the necessary five years he studied surgery, apparently without any objection, and passed his examinations. But during these years he often went to Enfield to see Clarke. On one of these expeditions Keats made his great discovery in the world of English literature, a volume of Spenser. He borrowed the book and read it enraptured. It was then that he knew that poetry would be important in his life. One of his first pieces is the "Imitation of Spenser" (1812), his first attempt in the Spenserian stanza, which he was later to employ masterfully in "The Eve of St. Agnes."

His guardians permitted him to go to London in 1815 to continue his medical studies in the hospitals. But though he worked hard at first in this profession, the claims of poetry became stronger and stronger. His friend Clarke had shown the critic Leigh Hunt some of Keats's verses, and on May 5, 1816, in Hunt's weekly periodical, *The Examiner,* appeared Keats's sonnet *To Solitude.* This proved a crucial event in the young man's life. He soon made the acquaintance of Hunt, who became a devoted friend, and by the fall of that year was in a circle of writers surrounding Hunt, who then enjoyed considerable popularity as a poet and a radical. Keats now had a license to set up as an apothecary, but he decided to devote himself to poetry. His guardians thought he had gone insane, but he answered quietly that he was sure of his abilities.

In the midst of the joy of self-discovery, Keats was nonetheless aware of all that he had yet to learn. In October 1816, Clarke introduced him to the works of Homer as translated by the Elizabethan Chapman. This was Keats's first important contact with the world of Greek culture—a world that was to enrich his imagination and excite him more than any other. This unforgettable experience has been recorded for us in his beautiful sonnet, "On First Looking into Chapman's Homer." In this sonnet the young poet speaks of having traveled much in the literature of the west, but having never known that other region which "deep-browed Homer ruled" as his domain. It was through Chapman that he first heard Homer "speak out loud and bold." That experience was like the excitement of an astronomer when he finds a new planet, or when the discoverer "Cortez" first stood "upon a peak in Darien," Panama, and was the first man to look upon the Pacific Ocean.

The beauty of this poem is somewhat impaired by the fact that Keats was ill-informed in history. It was Balboa, not Cortez, who discovered the Pacific. This defect in knowledge is unfortunately characteristic of Keats's poetry throughout. He will mistake the name of a famous fountain for that of a wine; he will constantly use words incorrectly. It was for these shortcomings that he was to be so bitterly attacked. It must be acknowledged that in a man who was an apostle of beauty, these errors are particularly vexing, and at first glance have the tendency to lend an air of pretentiousness to the poet's work. Such a judgment is both unjust and inaccurate, but Keats's contemporaries cannot entirely be blamed for making it on face value. What is to their discredit is that they missed the phenomenal innate artistry and inspiration of the young poet; they chose to ignore, moreover, Keats's own modest confession in his prefaces that he was well aware of his own limitations.

"On First Looking into Chapman's Homer" was first published by Leigh Hunt in December 1816. Within a few months Keats had decided that his life was to be devoted to poetry. At Hunt's he met Shelley, who financed the publication of Keats's first slender volume, which was entitled *Poems* (1817). The critics took no notice of it. He then began composition of his *Endymion,* which he declared would be "a trial of my powers of imagination and chiefly of my invention." When the poem appeared in 1818, it was brutally attacked even though Keats's preface admitted its inadequacies. The cruelty of the critics is all the more unpardonable when one considers that their abuse was leveled at Keats only because of their enmity to Hunt. They had given Hunt the doubtful honor of being founder of the "Cockney School" of poetry; and the *Edinburgh Magazine* said of Keats's *Endymion* that its hero was much more of a "young Cockney rhymster" than a Greek shepherd. Keats was attacked for his "loose, nerveless, versification and Cockney rhymes . . . . Mr. Hunt is a small poet, but he is a clever man. Mr. Keats is a still smaller poet, and he is only a boy of pretty abilities. . . . It is a better and wiser thing to be a starved apothecary than a starved poet; so back to the shop, Mr. John, back to plaster, pills, and ointment boxes."

The attack in the *Quarterly Review* was hardly less savage; the reviewer there dissected the first book of *Endymion,* and averred that he could read no further. For a long time Shelley, Byron, and Keats's other friends believed that the inhumanity of the critics was responsible for the early death of the poet. Nevertheless, Keats had a stronger character than is generally known. A short time after this hostility had been showered upon him, he was writing to his publisher: "I know nothing—I have read nothing—and I mean to follow Solomon's directions, 'get learning—get understanding.'" He was far more interested in self-development than in brooding over the wound inflicted by the critics. Hunt's influence had been priceless to him at the beginning, for it had led him to the treasures of English literature, and it had given him the encouragement of seeing his early sonnets in print. But Hunt was a mediocre poet himself, and Keats began to understand that he had more to learn than Hunt could teach him.

Endymion

Endymion is concerned with a quest for ideal beauty. The story is the classic one of the beautiful shepherd Endymion and the love for him of the Moon Goddess. The poem contains, among other things, a violent attack on royalty, and a hymn to nature. It suffers from a lack of connection in the episodes and a faulty structure. Keats himself soon accused it of "mawkishness." Nevertheless, its rhymed couplets are full of wonderful imagery and color. And the opening passage dealing with the permanence of beauty in nature and in poetry, will always be famous:

A thing of beauty is a joy forever:
Its loveliness increases; it will never
Pass into nothingness; but still will keep
A bower quiet for us, and a sleep
Full of sweet dreams, and health, and quiet
breathing.

Among the poems published in Keats's first volume, *Poems* (1817), are several worthy of mention: "I Stood Tiptoe upon a Little Hill," a charming piece of description; "To One Who Has Been Long in City Pent," a charming sonnet on the pleasures of the country; and "Sleep and Poetry," a more ambitious work, in couplets, defending the new trend in the Romantic school.

While working on *Endymion,* Keats had his first symptoms of tuberculosis, a disease that had decimated his family. He took a vacation to the English Lakes and to Scotland. When he returned to Hampstead, he met Fanny Brawne in the autumn of 1818 and fell violently in love with her. His passion was thwarted from the beginning. During this very period he learned that his beloved brother Tom was dying from the disease; he was being attacked by the critics; and he was totally occupied nursing his brother from August through December. Popular rumor has erroneously depicted Fanny Brawne as insensitive to the poet's affections. As a matter of fact, if Keats's love for her was blighted, it was certainly not her fault, for he knew that she completely returned his affections. What she could not understand was his failure to propose marriage; the poet never broached the subject because of his inability to support her as well as because of the doom hanging over his head as his disease advanced. He was convinced that he had no right to ask for her love, and the severe anguish this struggle cost him did much to enfeeble his health and to hasten his end.

Poems of 1819–1820

Only in poetry could he find peace from the tortures of love and disease. After his brother's death, in the few months between January and May 1819, he composed an amazing series of masterpieces: "The Eve of St. Agnes," "The Eve of St. Mark," "La Belle Dame Sans Merci," "Ode on a Grecian Urn," and "Ode on Melancholy." In July 1820 these appeared in his third volume, which was entitled, *Lamia, Isabella, The Eve of St. Agnes and Other Poems.* It is by reason of this volume that Keats has won his place among the immortals. Among the other works included in this volume are "To Autumn," "Lamia," "Ode to a Nightingale," "Isabella," "Fancy," "Hyperion," and "Ode to Psyche."

"The Eve of St. Agnes": This narrative poem is one of the most brilliant examples in English poetry of the use of the Spenserian stanza. The tale is based upon the legend that a maid who desired to see her true love in a dream on St. Agnes' Eve (January 20) could do so if she followed certain prescriptions, such as going supperless to bed. The setting is in the Middle Ages. That year St. Agnes' Eve was very cold:

> *St. Agnes' Eve—Ah, bitter chill it was!*
> *The owl, for all his feathers, was a-cold.*

In the chapel of the castle a holy man has been praying for the soul of sinners, and as he goes his way through the long corridors, we hear the sounds of revelry in the castle:

> *Music's golden tongue*
> *Flatter'd to tears this aged man and poor . . .*
> *The silver, snarling trumpets 'gan to chide.*

Amidst the gay throng at these festivities, Madeline moves unaware of what is going on about her. She is waiting for the night to come and for her wonderful dream. She has scarcely heard "the music yearning like a god in pain." Meanwhile, her lover, Porphyro, has come across the moors on the chance that he may see her. This exploit is full of danger to him, for he comes of an enemy house. He ventures in and luckily meets the one person in the household besides Madeline from whom he might expect kindness, old Angela. She is worried at seeing him there, and leads him to her own distant chamber to learn the reason for his appearance. When he inquires for Madeline, she tells him of the girl's going through the ritual connected with St. Agnes' Eve. The thought of "Madeline asleep in lap of legends old" gives him an idea:

> *Sudden a thought came like a full-blown rose,*
> *Flushing his brow, and in his pained heart*
> *Made purple riot: then doth he propose*

that Angela lead him to Madeline's chamber. When he convinces the old woman that his purposes are not wicked, she agrees. They go through many a dusty gallery until they reach a room "silken, hushed, and chaste." Madeline enters, her heart full of the magic of the evening. She kneels in the many-colored light of the stained glass "triple-arched" window, like a saint. Her prayers over, she retires to bed, her soul soon enfolded in sleep "as though a rose should shut and be a bud again." Porphyro tiptoes from the closet in which he has been hiding, and brings out the dainties that Angela has prepared:

> *Of candied apple, quince, and plum, and gourd;*
> *With jellies soother than the creamy curd,*
> *And lucent syrops, tinct with cinnamon;*
> *Manna and dates, in argosy transferred*
> *From Fez; and spiced dainties, every one,*
> *From silken Samarcand to cedared Lebanon.*

(This passage illustrates very well Keats's great power to appeal to the senses—a power that he was at great pains to cultivate, and which is his distinguishing quality as a poet.) Porphyro now takes up Madeline's lute and begins to sing an ancient Provençal ditty. She awakes from her dream of him, and as he kneels by her bedside in the moonlight, afraid to move lest he frighten her, she takes him for a ghost. She begins to weep at the thought that he is dead.

> *Beyond a mortal man impassioned far*
> *At these voluptuous accents, he arose,*
> *Ethereal, flushed, and like a throbbing star*
> *Seen mid the sapphire heaven's deep repose;*
> *Into her dream he melted, as the rose*
> *Blendeth its odor with the violet—*

But he is awakened from his reverie by the sound of the sleet beating against the window. He assures her that he is very much alive, that he wishes to wed her, and that she must elope with him. They glide like phantoms through the halls, past the drunken porter and the bloodhound. They open the locks, and are gone. This beautiful adaptation of *Romeo and Juliet* is one of the most perfect achievements of Keats.

"The Eve of St. Mark's": A fragment written in four-foot couplets like many of the old ballads, it was, unfortunately, never finished, but the passage Keats published is written in his best style.

"La Belle Dame Sans Merci": One of the great art ballads in our language, it is one of the poet's most brilliant successes. The opening stanza sets the tone of desolateness in the landscape:

> *Ah, what can ail thee, wretched wight,*
> *Alone and palely loitering?*
> *The sedge is withered from the lake,*
> *And no birds sing.*

This knight had met a beautiful lady with long hair and wild eyes. He placed her on his steed, fashioned garlands for her, and could think of nothing else but her all day long. She took him to her grotto and sighed him to sleep. They slept together on the moss, and in his dream he saw royal warriors who warned him that he was in thrall to La Belle Dame Sans Merci (the beautiful lady without pity). Their starved lips were a warning to him, for when he awoke, he found himself alone on the cold hill. And there he stays alone, unable to dream of anything but her. This beautiful ballad has been allegorically interpreted as the vain pursuit of ideal beauty.

"Ode on a Grecian Urn": A perfectly wrought series of stanzas on the idea already expressed in *Endymion* that "a thing of beauty is a joy forever," it is addressed to an ancient urn depicting a pastoral scene of youths pursuing maidens. There are pipes being played, and of these the poet reflects that since they pipe to the spirit, not to the "sensual ear":

> *Heard melodies are sweet, but those unheard*
> *Are sweeter*

The bold lover on the urn can never reach his girl to kiss her, but she will always be young and he will always love her. The trees on the urn will never shed their leaves. The lovers will never be satiated with their love. The urn is a pastoral poem in marble. When this generation is gone it will still remain to remind men that "Beauty is truth, truth beauty."

"Ode on Melancholy": The poet tells us that "when the melancholy fit shall fall," one should not seek forgetfulness through poison or seek understanding of the beetle or the owl. But one should observe the beauties of nature:

> *Then glut thy sorrow on a morning rose,*
> *Or on the rainbow of the salt sand-wave,*
> *Or on the wealth of globéd peonies*

or on the beauty of a mistress flashing with anger. Melancholy dwells with Beauty, and with Joy whose fingers are ever at his lips bidding farewell. Melancholy's shrine is in the very temple of delight, but only those who know how to taste the greatest joy can ever know what melancholy is.

"Lamia": This is perhaps the finest narrative poem Keats wrote. It has certain unevennesses, but contains some of his most radiant verse. It tells the story of a young Corinthian, Menippus Lycius, who met a beautiful lady, and was taken by her to her home. She entertained him and feasted him in a manner he had never known before, and averred that she would live with him and die with him. He remained with her until the philosopher Apollonius came to visit them, and found out that she was a lamia, or serpent-woman, and that all the richness of her furnishings were illusions. When she was thus discovered, she pleaded that Lycius be spared the truth, but Apollonius was adamant. Then she and all her appurtenances vanished. This long poem, showing a strong Miltonic influence, exemplifies the idea that beauty should not be subjected to scientific scrutiny. As Keats puts it, "Philosophy will clip an angel's wings."

"Ode to a Nightingale": This has been considered a serious challenge to the "Ode to the West Wind" as the greatest of English Romantic lyrical poems. We perceive here that the experience of beauty was so intense for Keats that it brought him near the point of swooning.

The opening lines set the mood:

> *My heart aches, and a drowsy numbness pains*
> *My sense, as though of hemlock I had drunk,*
> *Or emptied some dull opiate to the drains*
> *One minute past, and Lethe-wards had sunk.*

It is not that he envies the bird's happy lot, but that he is too happy in the bird's happiness. He wishes for a draught of heady wine that he might fade away with the bird into the dim forest, and quit the fever and the fret of man's world where everything lives but a day. He will fly to the bird on the wings of poetry. Now he is with the bird, and he sees the Queen Moon on her throne surrounded by her starry court. He smells the perfume of the flowers beneath him, and reflects that this would be the most wonderful of all times to die:

> *To cease upon the midnight with no pain,*
> *While thou art pouring forth thy soul abroad*
> *In such an ecstacy!*

The song of this bird is immortal. The song the poet hears is the same song that found a path

> *Through the sad heart of Ruth, when, sick for*
> *home,*
> *She stood in tears amid the alien corn*

It is the same song that has been heard in Fairylands forlorn. But the word *forlorn* is a bell that tolls the poet back to himself. His vision is shattered and he awakes from his dream. The bird's song is fainter and fainter, and now is lost in the next valley:

> *Was it a vision, or a waking dream?*
> *Fled is that music—do I wake or sleep?*

The "Ode to a Nightingale," perhaps the most ecstatic poem Keats ever wrote, is the triumph of his poetic objectives. He seems to do all that both painter and musician could do in making real the experiences of his imagination. One can feel the moonlight, smell the fragrance of the forest, drink the heady wine—with which the various stanzas deal. The inspiration of the poem never flags, and the only flaw in the poem is the poet's misconception concerning the fountain Hippocrene, sacred to the Muses, which he describes as a purple foaming wine. Even the stanzaic divisions are brilliantly managed; each stanza is a complete imaginative experience, and yet the flow between stanzas is perfect.

"To Autumn": This is Keats's finest nature poem. In it he wonderfully reproduces in words the colors, shapes and sounds of autumn. The poem shows to perfection his phenomenal ability so to stir the senses that even the salivary glands start functioning at his music. The first stanza appeals to all five senses:

> *Season of mist and mellow fruitfulness,*
> *Close bosom-friend of the maturing sun;*
> *Conspiring with him how to load and bless*
> *With fruit the vines that round the thatch-eaves run;*
>
> *To bend with apples the mossed cottage-trees,*
> *And fill all fruit with ripeness to the core;*
> *To swell the gourd, and plump the hazel shells*

> *With a sweet kernel; to set budding more,*
> *And still more, later flowers for the bees,*
> *Until they think warm days will never cease,*
> *For summer has o'er-brimmed their clammy cells.*

The poem then proceeds to describe the harvest, the late flowers, the cider being pressed, the heavy rosy clouds, the goats, the bleating lambs, the singing crickets and the whistling birds. The music of autumn is more beautiful to Keats than that of spring.

"Isabella": An incomplete work, it is a tragedy, first told by Boccaccio in his *Decameron,* of the maid whose lover was killed by her brothers; his head was presented to her, and buried in a pot from which the plant now known as basil first grew. Keats considered his poem weak, and it does suffer from an excess of sensuousness in detail. But its stanzas in *ottava rima* are well-managed, and there are many fine touches.

"Fancy" is a spontaneous poem, a tribute to the power of the imagination:

> *Ever let the Fancy roam,*
> *Pleasure never is at home*

"Hyperion": Another unfinished work, which only ill health prevented his completing, it contains some of his finest passages, and indicates that Keats was moving into planes of even higher eloquence than his work had heretofore shown. The scope of the intended poem was vast, and its blank verse is usually equal to the grandeur of the subject. The poem opens with Saturn, the Titan, overthrown by the younger generation of Gods under the leadership of Jove. Of the overthrown dynasty, shining Hyperion alone still sits sovereign in his orb of fire. Hyperion is infuriated at the possibility that Saturn's fate may be his too. He promises defeat to Jove, whom he warns that Saturn will be reseated on his throne. But the Sky reminds Hyperion that the seasons cannot be altered, and that Hyperion must follow Saturn to the Earth. The Sky promises in Hyperion's absence to take charge of the sun and the seasons. The fragment concludes with Hyperion's departure.

"Ode to Psyche": Not one of Keats's best odes, it is interesting because of the variety of its verse. The poet here speaks of himself as a priest of Psyche (the soul). Once he saw two creatures in a love tryst, wingéd Cupid and Psyche. Since he is her priest he will create all that delight, all that thought can win "to let the warm love in."

Other Works

Keats had collaborated with his friend Brown on a tragedy *Otho the Great* (published 1848), a work far too melodramatic. From this and *Hyperion* Keats had hoped to earn some money, but was bitterly disappointed. On February 3, 1820, he coughed up a drop of blood, and recognized it as his death warrant. He spent a year battling against his fate. Half of this year he sat staring at Fanny, as she walked in the garden, through the windows of her mother's house, where he had rooms. In September he sailed for Italy with little hope of recovery. In the company of the young painter Joseph Severn, he went to Rome. There he died on February 23, 1821, and was buried in the Protestant Cemetery. His stone bears the epitaph he had written for himself: "Here lies one whose name was writ in water."

IMPORTANCE

Time has proved that epitaph to have been the product of needless despair. No poet of his generation has more greatly influenced the course of English poetry than Keats. A whole movement (the Pre-Raphaelite) acknowledged him to be its master; and the poetry of Tennyson, Browning, Swinburne, and many twentieth century poets shows the powerful impress of Keats's works. His death at the age of twenty-six was one of the great deprivations that English literature has suffered.

Keats's ideals in poetry were completely dissimilar to those of Shelley. He felt that political doctrine should not be expressed in poetry. Poetry to Keats was a fine art that should make the depiction of beauty an end in itself. The kind of beauty to which he responded was not the ethereal aspects of nature that give Shelley's poetry so haunting a quality. For Keats it was beauty of line, color, shape, odor, and taste that was enthralling; and this beauty was for him the only source of joy. And that joy was rendered all the more poignant by the knowledge that all things on earth have but a brief span of life. The very impermanence of mortal things made him fasten all the more intensely on beauty as the only rewarding experience. The preception of beauty to Keats was so enrapturing that we often find him speaking of it as being close to pain in the intensity of feeling it evoked.

A number of other poems of quality must be discussed: "To My Brothers" (1816), "On the Grasshopper and the Cricket" (1816), "On Seeing the Elgin Marbles" (1817), "Robin Hood" (1818), "Lines on the Mermaid Tavern" (1818), and "Bright Star, Would I Were Steadfast as Thou Art" (1820).

"To My Brothers" was written on Tom's birthday, in hopes that the poet and his brothers would spend many years together. "On The Grasshopper and the Cricket" was written in competition with Leigh Hunt, both poets having agreed to write on the same subject. "The poetry of earth is never dead," and the grasshopper's song belongs to summer as does the cricket's to winter. In winter the cricket's song to one half-drowsy is much like the grasshopper's "among some grassy hills." "On Seeing the Elgin Marbles" records how overwhelming an experience it was for Keats when he first beheld the friezes of the Parthenon which had been brought back to England by the expedition of Lord Elgin. These are "a shadow of a magnitude," which make him feel like "a sick eagle looking at the sky." "Robin Hood" is a spirited reflection on the past days of the merry bandit, and ends with a song to Robin Hood and his band. "Lines on the Mermaid Tavern" asks the

> *Souls of poets dead and gone,*
> *What Elysium have ye known,*
> *Happy field or mossy cavern,*
> *Choicer than the Mermaid Tavern?*

These dead Elizabethans must in their Elysium be pledging one another's health with divine wine, just as in the old days. "Bright Star, Would I Were Steadfast as Thou Art," Keats's most moving sonnet, was written on a fly-leaf of a volume of Shakespeare while Keats was waiting on the deck of the ship that was to take him from England forever. As he sees the evening star rising he wishes he could be so steadfast and unchanging. But better that that he would wish to be lying on his fair love's breast, to live there forever "or else swoon to death."

Keats's Letters

T. S. Eliot regarded Keats's letters as "the most notable and the most important ever written by any English poet." This high praise does not spring from their artfulness; to the contrary, Keats achieves in his letters an appealing artlessness, even to the point of frequent misspellings, jokes, and trivial asides. In these letters (as in Wordsworth's *Prelude*) we observe the rapid growth of a brilliant talent as Keats reflects upon his reading, day-to-day thoughts, friendships, love relations, and poetic efforts.

The letters contain his profound and unpretentious musings about "negative capability" (the ability to withhold judgment, even in the midst of crisis), the relative merits of Wordsworth (poet of "the human heart") versus more intellectual poets, the role of life experiences in forming the human soul, and the Mansion of Many Apartments, an extended analogy by which Keats describes his own development as poet.

WALTER SAVAGE LANDOR (1775–1864)

The long span of Walter Savage Landor's life covers a period of enormous change in the history of English literature. He was born in Wordsworth's generation; had most of his adult life before him when Keats, Shelley, and Byron came to their early deaths; and lived long enough to witness the growth of the poetic talents of the great Victorian poets, Tennyson, Browning, Arnold, and Swinburne. In short, his career traverses the decline of Neoclassicism, the growth of Romanticism, and the triumph of Victorianism. By literary temperament his sympathies were classical. His politics were close enough to those of Shelley's generation, but he was essentially a man of letters in his interests. As a man of letters he was devoted to the clarity and neatness so dear to eighteenth century writers, though there is warmth suffusing what he had to say. His works partake of a happy combination of the classic and romantic, and possess a mellowness and refinement all their own.

Landor was the son of a well-known physician, was born at Warwick, and was educated at Rugby and at Trinity College, Cambridge. While still a student he was a violent partisan of republicanism. Always the victim of a fierce temper, Landor was suspended from Cambridge for shooting into a neighbor's window. His radical views in politics alienated his father. For a time the young man lived in Wales, busy with his books and writing poetry. It is characteristic of Landor that throughout his life, although he was involved in one series of emotional complications after another, he thought of himself as a retired scholar and bookworm. Actually he was a man of great animal spirits, a lover of children and pets, and an enthusiast in gardens. Somewhat contradictory to these strains of sweetness and generosity in his character was his delight in forever going to the law to engage in a suit against someone or other.

His father's death in 1805 made Landor master of a large fortune, and he was thereafter free to live as he pleased. In 1808 he enlisted in Spain as a volunteer in the rebellion against Napoleon. When he returned to England he bought Llanthony Abbey, and married a woman to whom he was ill-suited. His marriage to her was an interminable series of wranglings and quarrels. In 1814 he went to live in Italy, where he resided at Como, Pisa, and chiefly in a villa at Fiesole, which had been the scene of Boccaccio's *Decameron*. Twenty years later he visited England, but decided, because of a suit for libel, to return to Italy. There he became a close friend of the Brownings. He died in Italy, nearly ninety years of age, in 1864.

Landor's works exhibit considerable range and variety. In 1793 he published a volume of poems, some in Latin, some in English. In 1798 appeared *Gebir,* an Oriental tale on the Moorish invasion in Spain; this work, though exhibiting all the extravagance of spirit common to early Romanticism, is very elegant in style. In 1812 he published *Count Julian*, a poetic tragedy. At about this time he also translated *Gebir* into Latin, wrote a volume of Latin verse, and published a treatise on the use of Latin in modern literary composition. Up to this time Landor had not yet revealed his best talents, though his love of the ancient classical world was truly in evidence.

Prose Works

It was between 1824 and 1846 that he issued five volumes of his *Imaginary Conversations of Literary Men and Statesmen,* his prose masterpiece, the blossoming of his profound reading in the past. These, together with the *Imaginary Conversations of Greeks and Romans* (1853), comprise some one hundred fifty fragments of historical drama—a series of subtle psychological dialogues between fascinating historical persons. They are a kind of forerunner of Browning's dramatic monologues in verse. Landor takes a couple of dramatic and historically important characters in each of these *Conversations* and gives them such dialogue as makes them reveal with great vividness themselves and their times. Unlike a dramatist, however, he is not interested in individualizing their talk, nor does he care about being faithful to the letter of history. On the contrary, the characters are the mouthpieces for Landor's own interpretations of the past. The *Conversations* maintain a high level of intellectual excitement and tense drama. The range and variety of Landor's subjects are amazing. In his historical gallery, among others, we find Plato and Diogenes, Achilles and Helen, Aesop and Rhodope, Caesar and Lucullus, Henry VIII and Anne Boleyn, Rousseau and Malesherbes, John of Gaunt and the Duchess of Kent, Dante and Beatrice, Fra Filippo and the Pope, Queen Elizabeth and Cecil, Marcus Tullius Cicero and his brother Quinctus. Of these pieces perhaps the most ambitious is a series of five dialogues between Petrarch and Boccaccio, entitled *The Pentameron.*

These prose dialogues give Landor a high place among English stylists. In them are to be found noble eloquence and sensitiveness, which are always admirable and are frequently inspired.

Poetry

In 1847 appeared his *Hellenics,* a translation into English of verses which he had originally written in Latin. These capture perfectly the authentic classic spirit, not as the Neoclassicists practiced it, but as the ancients did. They are unique in our literature. The *Iphigenia and Agamemnon* in this collection achieves a simple nobility foreign to the school of Pope. Agamemnon's daughter, of whom the priest Calchas had told her death alone could propitiate Diana so that the ships assembled at Aulis might sail at last for Troy, is the leading figure in this intense drama of fifty-eight lines. The girl, Iphigenia, seeks to turn aside her fate by pleading with her father that the priest might not have heard the oracle correctly, and begging that her father's love save her from the knife. But the great general, though shaken, is firm in his resolve. The pale maiden:

> *Looked up and saw*
> *The fillet of the priest and calm cold eyes.*
> *Then turned she where her parent stood and cried,*
> *"O Father! grieve no more: the ships can sail."*

Landor is the author of many wonderful little poems, all marked by the same happy combination of restrained feeling and exquisite form. Of these the best known are: "Rose Aylmer," a love lyric celebrating a girl's graces and consecrating "a night of memories and of sighs" to her; "One Year Ago," in which the poet reflects sadly that a year ago his step was light, his brow serene, but that in that year the hot days of youth have fled with love; "Yes, I Write Verses," in which the poet reflects with chagrin that he cannot dance or jump over fences with the sprightliness of young men, and observes with a shudder the giddiness of the younger generation; "To Youth," in which he asks where youth has fled, and finds that only in his sleep is it still with him; "To Age," in which he greets old age with thanks for having sharpened his intelligence and having taught him to overcome fear and hope. Landor's eulogy "To Robert Browning," compares the new poet to Chaucer for his inquiring eye, manly utterance, and varied tongue; at a time when Browning had practically no audience as yet, Landor was able to recognize the younger man's greatness. The most celebrated of Landor's poems is the wonderful epigram he wrote as introduction to a volume entitled *The Last Fruit off an Old Tree*:

> *I strove with none, for none was worth my strife.*
> *Nature I loved, and, next to Nature, Art;*
> *I warmed both hands before the fire of Life;*
> *It sinks, and I am ready to depart.*

MINOR ROMANTIC POETS

In addition to the poets already discussed, mention should be made of several minor poets, all of them able and still read: Thomas Moore, Leigh Hunt and Thomas Hood.

Thomas Moore (1779–1852)

Moore, Ireland's most popular poet, was born in Dublin, took his degree at Trinity College in his native city, and spent some time in Bermuda as a government official. His first series of *Irish Melodies* (1807) was enormously successful in both Ireland and England, and he continued to issue more volumes in the same manner until 1835. These poems are unblushingly emotional, lyrical, and simple to read and understand. Moore was master of the sentimental love phrase, and it is likely that his lyrics will be admired for a long time. For many of these poems Moore composed the tune to which they are still sung. Everyone knows "Believe Me If All These Endearing Young Charms" and "'Tis the Last Rose of Summer." Besides such facile love-poems, Moore is the author of many patriotic verses dear to the hearts of his countrymen. Of these, the best-known are: "The Harp That Once Through Tara's Halls" and "Oh Breathe Not His Name!" (on the Irish patriot Robert Emmet). For a long time Moore's Oriental tale in verse, *Lalla Rookh* (1817), written in a style made popular by his friend Byron (and earlier, though in Scottish setting, by his friend Scott), was read all over the English-speaking world.

Moore was a man of greater literary talent than the reader of these pieces might guess. There is considerable variety in his work. His translations into

English verse of the poems of Anacreon and Anacreon's school, issued in 1800, are manly and stirring. His novel, *The Epicurean* (1827) is interesting; and his biographies of Sheridan (1825) and Byron (1830) are still invaluable. He also edited the *Works,* the *Letters,* and the *Journal* of Byron, between 1830 and 1835, and these remain among the chief editions of his friend's writings.

Leigh Hunt (1784–1859)

James Henry Leigh Hunt, better known as Leigh Hunt, was very much in the public eye when Byron, Shelley, and Keats embarked upon their careers. He was born in Middlesex, and educated at Christ's Hospital. While still a youth he entered upon a journalistic career. In 1808, with his brother John he established a widely admired liberal weekly, *The Examiner.* In 1809 he married Marianne Kent, who bore him a large family that kept him turning out thousands of words for its support for the rest of his life. An article criticizing the Prince Regent (later crowned George IV), and calling him a fat "Adonis of fifty" resulted in Hunt's being thrown into prison for two years (1813–1815). But he continued to edit his journal, though in jail, and his prison came to be a kind of court of honor to the young radicals. There Byron, Moore, Lamb, and many others came to pay him their respects.

Hunt was one of the few people then alive in England who recognized the genius of Shelley and Keats, and he published several pieces of their early work. He was a man of generosity and charm, but unfortunately was convinced that he himself was a major poet. Among sentimental ladies his poetry had indeed a considerable vogue. Of the far too many pieces he wrote, the most ambitious was *The Story of Rimini* (1816), a tale dealing with the love of Paolo and Francesca, the celebrated lovers in Dante. Today the lack of taste and bad judgment exhibited on every page is truly amazing, but in Hunt's day his verse was considered by some an important contribution towards introducing a colloquial style in poetry. It was for such efforts that Hunt was dubbed the leader of the "Cockney School of Poetry." It should be remembered that his poetry inspired two fine poems, Keats's *Endymion* and Shelley's *Julian and Maddalo,* so far as their familiar style is concerned. Today, Hunt is better remembered for several shorter poems, chiefly "Abou Ben Adhem" (1834), which countless children had to memorize, and the graceful "Jennie Kissed Me" (1838).

Of his prose works, the most interesting is his *Autobiography* (1850), an important document on his contemporaries. He was the author of many other prose pieces, including *Stories from Italian Poets* (1846), *Men, Women and Books* (1847), *The Town* (1848) and *Table Talk* (1851).

Thomas Hood (1799–1845)

Thomas Hood was a man of considerable talent, but his life is a record of suffering, bitter disappointment, and an unsuccessful struggle against poverty. Ironically, it is for his light verse that he is still best remembered.

He was born in London, the son of an impoverished bookseller. The first volume to bring him to the attention of the public was a collection of humorous pieces, *Whims and Oddities* (1826). He worked this vein again in *The Comic Annual* (1830), *Up the Rhine* (1839), and *Whimsicalities* (1843). During his later years he edited a magazine of humor, *Hood's Magazine*. It is a paradox that this life-long victim of poverty should have clung to the career of humorist; all the pieces he wrote in this strain had little to do with his own deep feeling and lofty humanitarian ideals. It was only on occasion that he allowed himself the relief of penning something deeply felt. Of such poems there are two which are likely to outlive everything else he wrote, "The Bridge of Sighs" and "The Song of the Shirt," both powerful and sincere songs of the people. "The Bridge of Sighs" deals with a young girl who has committed suicide because of her inability to cope with society. Hood asks us to leave to her Savior the judging of her sins:

> *Take her up tenderly,*
> *Lift her with care;*
> *Fashioned so slenderly,*
> *Young, and so fair!*

"The Song of the Shirt" is the song of a woman working over sewing in a factory. The line *"Work—work—work!"* which opens many of the stanzas is well-known. This woman finds it would be better to be a slave among the Turks than a Christian doing such labors without respite.

4
ROMANTIC PROSE

The leading Romantic prose writers—Lamb, Hazlitt, and De Quincey—were all good friends of the Lake Poets and have indeed left us fascinating records of their relations with them. Like the poets, their approach to literature is on the imaginative side. Nothing could be further from the strong, clear light that emanates from the prose of Swift than the colorful allusive light and shadow that play about the prose of Lamb and De Quincey. In the styles of these Romantics, English prose is carried back to the highly individualistic and imagination-stirring traditions of the seventeenth century, when writers like Sir Thomas Browne and Jeremy Taylor wrote a prose very close in its cadence and imagery to poetry.

CHARLES LAMB (1775–1834)

IMPORTANCE

Probably no English writer has been so universally loved and admired as Charles Lamb. There may be critics who do not like his essays, but one has not heard of them. Lamb is the perfect familiar essayist. With some fitness called "The English Montaigne," he makes clearer than any other essayist the title of the familiar essay to be described, as it has been, as "the prose lyric." The revelation of personality is one of the great charms of the familiar essay, and in the art of self-revelation no essayist has approached Lamb in charm and lovableness. The paradox is that although the *Essays of Elia* are the reflection of a sunny temperament, very few men have lived a life more tragic or more heroic than Lamb.

Lamb was born the son of John Lamb, clerk to a lawyer of the Inner Temple, where the Lambs also lived, in London. His father's employer allowed the boy to roam through his books, and also used his influence to gain Lamb admission at Christ's Hospital, the "free school" in London, intended for the brighter children of poor people. There he met Coleridge, who became his life-long friend. Unlike his friend, Lamb was unable to go to the University. His formal education was terminated at the age of fifteen, when his family's financial needs required his taking a position as a clerk at South Sea House, where his brother was already employed. After a few months he procured a better position at East India House, and there he worked for thirty-three years (1792–1825). At the age of fifty he was retired on a good pension. The last nine years of his life were spent in comfortable leisure.

That vast erudition, that unerring taste for the best things in literature, that quick eye to discover the rare and unknown in books—those were talents that Lamb acquired without the benefit of schooling. It is amazing to consider that he could have made himself master of so much learning during those few hours when he was not enslaved to his accounts at East India House. But it is even more astounding to remember that he contrived to have a rich life under circumstances that would have destroyed most people. There was a strain of insanity in his family. When he was twenty he himself was a victim of the only attack of the disease he had in his lifetime, when he spent six weeks in a madhouse. Shortly after this experience, on his return one day from the office, he found that his sister Mary in a seizure of insanity had killed their mother and wounded their father. Convinced that if she were confined in an asylum she would become completely insane, Lamb undertook full responsibility for her for the rest of his life.

This sacrifice made marriage impossible for him. Mary Lamb had many returns of her insane fits, but her brother's tender care lengthened her periods of intellectual sanity. They learned to recognize the symptoms, and Charles was able to hurry her off to an asylum in time for treatment. The curiosity of neighbors made them move constantly from one home to another. Nevertheless, Lamb would probably have been amazed at the idea that he had anything other than a wonderful life. His reading and original composition were a source of unfailing spiritual courage to him. There is no note of complaint against his fate in his essays. Nor were his days destitute of many rewards. Except during attacks of her disease, Mary was a marvelous companion to her brother, shared all his interests, loved his favorite books, and collaborated with him on some of his work. Their home was the gathering-place of the best men of their time: Southey, Wordsworth, Coleridge, Hazlitt, De Quincey, Godwin, and Leigh Hunt, among others. The hearth of the Lambs was a favorite resort of these men even before Lamb had any reputation as a writer himself.

Lamb was a lover of the past. He also delighted in the rarities rather than in the great familiar things of literature. He read Sterne rather than Richardson, Smollett rather than Fielding. His best-loved books were Burton's *Anatomy of Melancholy* and Sir Thomas Browne's *Religio Medici;* it is from these two writers that he learned much of the whimsical and subtle cadence of his own prose. Lamb rediscovered Shakespeare's fellow dramatists, whose work had fallen into neglect during the eighteenth century. The scholarship that has since accumulated on Marlowe, Beaumont and Fletcher, Webster, and their fellows could never have been inspired if Lamb had not pointed to his contemporaries this forgotten treasure-house of dramatic poetry. In 1808 he published *Specimens of English Dramatic Poets Contemporary with Shakespeare,* an anthology of great scenes from Elizabethan drama, accompanied by sensitive and enthusiastic commentary.

Early Works

Lamb did not at once discover his own true gifts. His first work was as a poet; for an early volume of Coleridge's poetry (1796) he wrote four indifferent sonnets. His next attempt was a prose romance, *Rosamund Gray,* which has little merit. In 1802 he wrote a tragedy on an Elizabethan model, *John Woodvil,* but for very good reasons it has never been produced. He wrote a farce, *Mr. H.,* which was hissed off the stage at its first appearance (1806), and Lamb himself hissed louder than anyone. The next year was published his *Tales from Shakespeare* (1807), written in collaboration with his sister, and, as the title page observes, "designed for the use of young persons."

Essays

Lamb was forty-five before he discovered that his true medium was the essay. In 1820 he began to publish a series of essays under the pseudonym of "Elia," in the *London Magazine.* He collected twenty-five of them in 1823 as *The Essays of Elia.* Ten years later appeared the *Last Essays of Elia.* It is because of these two volumes and the volumes of his incomparable letters that Lamb occupies his unique position as a master of English prose. The *Letters* are themselves second only to the *Essays of Elia* among the great essays of the nineteenth century.

Few writers, in prose or verse, have so completely woven the tapestry of their lives into their literary composition. In his essays we see his childhood, his days at school, his hours at East India House, his daily life with Mary (who is called Bridget in the essays), his hopes, his reveries, his enthusiasms among books, his prejudices, his friends, his love of fun and jokes. All these, which went to make up his personality, are displayed before us in a highly original style, a style entirely personal, in a prose that is a wonderful mixture of thoughtfulness and quaintness, deep feeling and extravagance.

Alone among the Romantics, Lamb had little taste for the country. He loved London, but not as the Neoclassicists had loved the city. He loved it for its sights and sounds, which for him were much more stirring to the imagination than all the beauties of the countryside. He said of his native city that he would not exchange her "dirtiest drab-frequented alley and her lowest bowing tradesman" for the mountains of the Lake District "and the Parson into the bargain."

The level maintained in the *Essays of Elia is* very high, and though it is possible here to describe only the best-known essays, there are many others of equal merit.

"Christ's Hospital, Five and Thirty Years Ago": A delightful reminiscence of Lamb's days at school, it reveals the lot of a "charity boy" in all its poignancy, especially in wintertime "shivering at cold windows of print shops to extract a little amusement." Lamb here speaks of himself with great frankness as "L." He remembers his teachers and fellow students with affection and tolerance. There is a memorable apostrophe to Coleridge,

> logician, metaphysician, bard! . . . How have I seen the casual passer through the Cloisters stand still entranced with admiration . . . to hear thee unfold in thy deep and sweet intonations, the mysteries of Jamblichus or Plotinus . . . or reciting Homer in his Greek, or Pindar—while the walls of the old Grey Friars re-echoed to the accents of the inspired charity-boy.

"Dream Children: a Reverie": Lamb daydreams about the family he might have had. Out of his fancy he conjures his two dream children, John and Alice, and to them he recounts their family's imagined history. But as his account to these creatures of his fancy ends, the children's faces grow dim, and without speech they seem to say that they are not the offspring of Lamb and his sweetheart Alice W. "We are not of Alice, nor of thee, nor are we children at all. . . . We are nothing; less than nothing, and dreams. We are only what might have been."

"A Dissertation upon Roast Pig": Lamb in his merriest vein offers a witty fanciful account of the origin of roast pork as a food, through a lucky accident that occurred long ago in China. Ho-ti is a swineherd who leaves his cottage under the supervision of his son Bo-bo, an idiot of a boy. Carelessly Bo-bo, who is fond of playing with fire, allows the whole house to ignite. Soon it is a pile of ashes. In the midst of his lamentations "an odor assailed his nostrils, unlike any scent which he had before experienced!" He discovers that the delicious smell comes from the carcass of one of the pigs which has been burned to death. Bending over to examine it, he burns one of his fingers, naturally puts his finger in his mouth to alleviate the pain— and thus makes the great discovery. Burnt pig is incomparably delicious. Naturally when Ho-ti returns he abuses his son, and is scandalized to hear the boy recommending the burnt pig. He too scorches his finger, applies his finger to his mouth, and is enchanted with the taste. Father and son agree not to let their neighbors in on their great discovery. But the vicinity is disturbed to find that Ho-ti's cottage is forever burning down and to discover that the father is now very tolerant of his son. Spies watch them, and their arson is noted. At the trial, the judge and jury handle the carcass of a pig as evidence, burn their fingers, taste the evidence, and find the prisoners not guilty. For a while after this there is a wave of arson over the countryside. Then a genius appears who discovers it is not necessary to burn down a house in order to roast a pig. The essay concludes with some appetite-provoking reminiscences on the part of the author concerning various ways he has known roast pork to have been served.

"Old China": The essay begins with the author's admission of his partiality for old china. He is examining and describing a recent purchase of old china, when his cousin Bridget (actually his sister Mary) comments with some bitterness on how much less pleasure is involved these days in their little luxuries. They had much more fun out of life when they were too poor to indulge themselves often. There is no longer the delight in the orchestra seats at the theater that there used to be in the narrow uncomfortable places in the gallery where once they were compelled to sit. Where has fled the wonderful pleasure of debating whether Lamb should purchase a badly needed suit or an old edition of Beaumont and Fletcher? There was a delight, when they were poor, in indulging the extravagance of fruit and vegetables when they were not in season. Now that they can afford such treats, the experience loses its meaning. These days, Bridget complains, "We never do make much of ourselves. None but the poor can do it . . . persons as we were, just above poverty." Listening to all this, Lamb reflects wistfully that they are no longer so young as they were, and therefore it is well that they have a better income, since more money gives them a "supplementary youth." It is right for them to ride instead of walking, to "live better and lie softer." But if he could be young again with her and once more be crowding with her up the inconvenient gallery staircases, he would be willing to give up more wealth in exchange than Croesus ever had.

"Poor Relations": In his most flippant manner Lamb says a poor relation:

> is the most irrelevant thing in nature—a piece of impertinent correspondency—an odious approximation—a haunting conscience—a preposterous shadow . . . a perpetually recurring mortification—a drain on your purse . . . a drawback upon success—a rebuke to your rising—a stain in your blood . . . a fly in your ointment.

You can tell the poor relation by his knock—too familiar, and yet not familiar enough. Your friends, as he "just happens" to drop in precisely at dinner time, do not know how to treat him. His conduct is as humble as that of a servant, and yet far too familiar. He brings up anecdotes of the days when the family was not so prosperous. When he goes, you dismiss his chair with relief into a corner. But the female poor relation is deadlier than the male. She insists upon being helped at dinner "*after* the gentleman," and calls the servant "*sir*." Lamb remembers a fellow student at Christ's Hospital, a boy of much promise, who went on to Oxford; but the boy's father, a cringing, scraping housepainter, decided to take up his abode at Oxford too; in despair over his inability to be quit of his father's shadow, the scholar joined the regiment bound for Portugal, and was among the first to die before the walls of St. Sebastian. Lamb next reminisces on a man who used to dine at the Lambs' table, and the author recalls that a particular pudding was always served on the days he came. This guest had been a schoolfellow of Lamb's father. One fatal day, Lamb's aunt tried to press another helping of the pudding on their guest: "Do take another slice . . . for you do not get pudding every day." The guest maintained silence but later in the evening the old gentleman said to the aunt, "Woman, you are superannuated." He did not long survive that evening. He was a poor relation.

"The Convalescent": This is a delightful piece on the pleasures of being a recuperating invalid. The sick man is a monarch in his bed. Everything in the establishment is subject to his comfort. In bed "he changes sides oftener than a politician." He can indulge in the luxury of self-pity, revel in the delights of making an inventory of every ache and pain—and is encouraged to do so. He is spared knowledge of the vexations or annoyances of the household or the larger outside world. But as health returns to him, he is pampered less and cut down in stature. No longer are inquiries made after him, no longer is a severe hush maintained around the house. The essay concludes with Lamb's address to the editor. Now that his sickroom is dwindling to its actual size in importance, he is ready to take up once more his profession of essayist.

"In Praise of Chimney Sweepers": This essay is a testimony to Lamb's affection for them. Ever since he was a child he enjoyed watching them at their profession. He hopes that the reader will give any chimney sweeper he chances to meet a penny—or better yet twopence. And if the weather be severe, let it be sixpence. By imperceptible degrees Lamb is soon talking about the drink which is the delight of chimney sweepers, sassafras tea. Next he considers the fact that though other folk can annoy him by impudence on the street, the good-humored insolence of chimney-sweeps is easy to forgive. He remembers slipping once on the ice, and how a chimney-sweep stood laughing at him, convulsed with merriment. It was like a painting by Hogarth. He also takes pleasure in the boys' sparkling white teeth in the frame of their black faces. His friend, Jen White, used to give an annual party for chimney sweepers, where the host behaved as though he were entertaining the aristocracy, and discussed the rarity of the beer, and the quality of the sausages, as though he were speaking of wines and delicate meats. There was much drinking at these gatherings. But White is now dead and these parties are no more.

"A Chapter on Ears": The author confesss his insensitivity to music. He has no ear. Not that he lacks the appendages for hearing, but that opera drives him almost to distraction. The audience at an Oratorio makes him feel that he is at some theatre in Hades. But concertos are the worst of all because Lamb finds himself wandering off during their performance. The author then speaks of an organist friend who, because of his performances on his favorite instrument, makes every day a Sunday. While having to listen to the attacks of the music of Haydn, Mozart, Beethoven and Bach, Lamb finds it a great help to believe in the power of music if he can have a good draught of beer while he is forced to listen.

Among the *Last Essays of Elia* is a collection of short essays grouped under the general heading of *Popular Fallacies*. In these the author undertakes to show the error of popular thinking as exhibited in certain well-known maxims. Each of these essays is written with great whimsicality.

"That You Must Love Me and Love My Dog": Here Lamb reflects on the unhappiness of having to accept certain appendages to the people one loves. Attractive girls have lost suitors because of their brothers or viper sisters; attractive men have lost friends because of cousins, wives, or annoying children.

"That We Should Rise with the Lark": This is a protest at rising too early in the day; those who do so have no benefit of their dreams. For the early hours of the morning should be spent in bed rehearsing "the sadder nocturnal tragedies," or dragging "into daylight a struggling and half-vanishing nightmare." These are spiritual communications. And since death is for himself not too far distant, it is well, thinks the author, that he should become acquainted with the world of dreams, and "contract politic alliances with shadows. It is good to have friends at court."

"That We Should Lie Down with the Lamb": A companion piece protests against early retiring. Going to bed early is well enough for a sheep, since he has nothing better to do. But every experience is more delightful by candlelight. Daylight may furnish the crude images for poetry, but it is only at night that the creative process can work well. At the end the author feels that he would like to compose something "about the Solar System—Betty bring the candles."

WILLIAM HAZLITT (1778–1830)

If Lamb is the most lovable of English essayists, Hazlitt is the most admirable. Lamb deliberately cultivated his prejudices as much as his preferences; part of his charm is the extent to which he circumscribed his interests. Hazlitt is England's leading essayist because of the scope of his interests and the breadth of his knowledge.

He was born the son of a Unitarian minister in Kent at Maidstone on April 10, 1778. The Unitarians were then the most radical of Protestants. Because of the elder Hazlitt's interest in the affairs of the United States, the family moved to Massachusetts in 1783. But since there was no permanent post in the church available there, they returned to England in 1786, to live in Shropshire.

From earliest childhood Hazlitt was used to the atmosphere of intellectual radicalism. Throughout his life he was never disillusioned in the principles of the French Revolution. It was perhaps for him a misfortune that England was rigidly Tory during his day, for his maladjustment to society seems to have been intensified by his resentment over that fact. He was only a boy when he was writing to the newspapers in indignant protest against political conservatism. His first work, *An Essay on the Principles of Human Action* (1804), was written to prove that man is by nature benevolent. From the same point of view he composed a *Reply to the Essay on Population by the Reverend T. R. Malthus* (1807), a strong defense of the rights of the poor.

Although the rights of men and the principles of liberty were the banner under which Hazlitt always fought, he was capable of expressing powerful hatred against those he disliked—and they seemed to be more numerous than those he loved. His attack was leveled alike at Tories, the world of fashion, the aristocracy, the Roman Catholic Church, and the Established English Church. Among the poets who came in for his abuse were Byron, Shelley, Scott, and even his friend Coleridge. Too often his adverse criticism of writers was based on unfair or irrelevant political considerations.

In 1798, after deciding not to finish his course at a theological seminary, he met Coleridge. This was one of the greatest experiences in his life, and he has told us about it in one of his best essays, "My First Acquaintance with Poets" (1823). The friendship of Coleridge was, in his own words, a light that shone into his soul.

For some ten years Hazlitt worked hard at art, hoping to achieve the success that his brother John already had as a painter. In 1802 he went to Paris to study. Eventually he decided that his abilities were not great enough to justify a career in painting. But the time he had spent studying was not wasted. Hazlitt is the author of some important art criticism; and in all his essays there is a constant awareness of line and color that must have been the fruit of his years as art student.

He married Sarah Stoddard in 1808, and they lived for some time at Winterslow near Salisbury. No side of Hazlitt's character is more unattractive than that which is revealed by his relations with women. There was a great deal of the Bohemian in his nature. He separated from his wife and later had a half-insane love affair with Sarah Walker; it is amazing that Hazlitt should have been willing to expose before the public without any sense of shame the history of that unfortunate relationship in his *Liber Amoris* (1823), where one may read how much he was the disciple of Rousseau in his frank exhibition of intimate suffering and folly. In 1824 he married again, a Mrs. Bridgewater, from whom he was soon separated. His *Notes of a Journey Through France and Italy* (1826) is the story of his life with her.

Critical Essays

None of these books bears any importance when measured with Hazlitt's major writings. He was equally at home in politics, economics, philosophy, the fine arts, literature, or observation on daily life. And the criticism and lectures he composed are amazing in their range and variety. Perhaps the process of self-discovery began with a series of dramatic criticisms he wrote for the *Morning Chronicle*. There followed four important collections of criticism: *The Characters of Shakespeare's Plays* (1817), a fluent series of notes intended to expound and popularize Shakespeare's works; *The English Poets*

(1818), a review of major English writers from the Romantic, anticlassical point of view; *The English Comic Writers* (1819), a series of lectures elaborating Hazlitt's enthusiasms, and his veneration and love for Chaucer; and *The Dramatic Literature of the Age of Elizabeth* (1820), on Shakespeare's contemporaries. Coleridge and Lamb are the authors of important criticism, but it is fragmentary in character; these books make Hazlitt the most important of the Romantic critics. He supplemented them by *A View of the English Stage* (1821), a collection of his dramatic reviews.

But he never lost interest in politics. In 1819 appeared a collection of *Political Essays;* this was followed by his *Life of Napoleon Bonaparte* (1828–1830). The four volumes of the latter work are the fruit of perhaps more ambitious labors than any of Hazlitt's undertakings, and he considered it his major achievement. He admired Napoleon as the annihilator of kingship and the destroyer of conservative tradition.

His art criticism will be found scattered through his book on France and Italy. He collaborated with the painter Haydon on articles for the *Encyclopedia Britannica;* Hazlitt also wrote *Sketches of the Principal Picture Galleries in England* (1824), and the *Life of Titian* (1830). His volumes of essays are full of references to painting, and some of his best essays are *On the Pleasure of Painting* and *On Hogarth's Marriage à la Mode.*

Familiar Essays

However, it is for his familiar essays that Hazlitt is now read. Most of these were originally written for various periodicals, including Hunt's *Examiner* and the *London Magazine.* They were later collected in book form under the titles of *The Round Table* (1817), *Table Talk* (1821–1822), and *The Plain Speaker* (1826). After his death two volumes in the same style were collected by his son: *Sketches and Essays* (1839) and *Winterslow* (1850).

These five volumes establish Hazlitt as England's leading essayist. In versatility alone Hazlitt has never been equalled among essayists. He has an essay "On Gusto," and that quality permeates all that he wrote. Indeed, it may be that Hazlitt's true self was revealed only in his writing. Certainly it is kinder to think so, for he was universally disliked by even the most charitable of his contemporaries. But to his writings he brought a wonderful enthusiasm, generosity and zest for ideas. There is a fine sense of large horizons and clean air in Hazlitt's writings, and he never wrote a dull page in his life. He is always the Romantic, whether he is looking at life or at literature.

As a critic he is frankly impressionistic. His crticism is a record of his adventures among books. Such criticism can be the best or the worst in the world, and unlike more objective criticism, its value depends entirely upon the quality of the critic. The stature of Hazlitt's mind and the depth of his taste make his criticism second to none in the century.

In addition to the essays mentioned, Hazlitt's best include: "Of Persons One Would Wish to Have Seen," "On Disagreeable People," "On Taste," "On

Familiar Style," "On Reading Old Books," "On Reading New Books," "On Going a Journey," and "The Fight." The last-named is particularly interesting as being one of the few instances in which a literary man has taken pugilism as a subject; the essay is an account of a prize fight which Hazlitt witnessed. "On Familiar Style" is an essay on the informal essay; Hazlitt observes that it is a highly difficult style to cultivate because of the precision and ease that it requires; an elaborate showy style is much easier to come by. In "On Going a Journey," one of Hazlitt's most delightful pieces, the author speaks of the pleasures of traveling in the country alone; conversation is to be avoided on such trips; the great advantage of solitary traveling is that we can shed all the circumstances of our everyday life; indeed, Hazlitt concludes, if he could be allowed another life at home afterwards, he would like to spend one whole life traveling abroad alone.

THOMAS DE QUINCEY (1785–1859)

Thomas De Quincey, the most extreme Romantic stylist of the Romantics, was born on August 17, 1785, at Manchester, the son of a wealthy merchant. De Quincey's father was living abroad because of tuberculosis, and the son never knew him until he came home to die. At that time he first became acquainted with his elder brother William, who had been on the continent with their father. William proved a tyrant at whose hands Thomas went through every kind of humiliation and suffering. Both boys were well taught by a clergyman. When De Quincey entered the grammar school of Bath, he was considered a genius in Latin and Greek.

In 1798, De Quincey was felled by a blow intended by the master for another student. The injury to his head required medical attention for a long time. While convalescing, he immersed himself in Milton and the Italian epic poets. The summer of 1800 he spent in making a tour of Ireland with a friend. Back in England, he was sent to the Manchester Grammar School. He found that institution so intolerable that he ran away during his second year there. He spent that summer walking through Wales with an allowance of a guinea a week. De Quincey had been left a considerable fortune, but its disposal was in the hands of guardians.

He was tired of living according to their whim, so he went to London at the age of seventeen, and spent a winter there in the worst kind of poverty. He would roam the streets by day and sleep at night on the floor of a bare room. His only friends were a young streetwalker whom he had met on his rounds of London, and a ten-year-old servant girl. It was during this terrible winter that he incurred a severe disease in the intestines, to deaden the pain he later began taking opium. His friends at last rescued him, and he went home. On the stipulation that he go to Oxford, his guardians allowed him a hundred pounds a year.

He entered Worcester College in 1803, making only one friend, a German. But he was reading voluminously in English literature. He wrote a letter of admiration to Wordsworth, and this began a long allegiance to the Lake Poet. In 1804, he paid a brief visit to London, and there took his first dose of opium.

Three years later he met Coleridge, whose financial difficulties of the moment he relieved by an anonymous gift. With the Coleridges he visited Wordsworth. The latter was just about to leave Grasmere, and suggested that De Quincey take over the cottage. In 1809 he established himself there. In 1816 he married the daughter of a farmer in the neighborhood.

By 1813 he was a confirmed slave of the opium-eating habit because of the pain he would otherwise have had to endure. He was forever increasing the amount he consumed, and in consequence was a victim of intermittent mental depression. He had learned, however, to control the habit to the extent that he would not suffer from an overdose. His fortune was now all spent, and he was compelled to turn to writing. He began *The Confessions of an English Opium Eater* (1821) for the *London Magazine.* This work won instant recognition; his success determined him to write professionally for the periodicals. For the next four years he wrote chiefly for the *London Magazine* (which had published many of Lamb's essays) and *The Quarterly Magazine.* In 1826 he began to write for *Blackwood's Magazine,* one of the leading Scottish publications, issued at Edinburgh.

De Quincey's circle of friends was small. During his frequent visits to London he saw much of Lamb, Hazlitt and Hood. He moved in 1830 to Edinburgh, and there won the friendship of Carlyle. For the rest of his life he was oppressed by financial difficulties, and was perpetually crossed by dunning from landlords, tradesmen and publishers. Nevertheless, his study and writing continued. He lived in a chaotic confusion of books and papers, and at one time had four book-cluttered residences. His wife died in 1887. De Quincey then took a cottage at Lasswade, a suburb of Edinburgh. He spent the last ten years of his life preparing a collected edition of his works and finished the last volume just before his death in 1859.

There is great variety in De Quincey's work. David Masson classifies his writings under three heads: Descriptive, Biographical, and Historical; Speculative, Didactic and Critical; Imaginative Writings and Prose Poetry. The first category includes the following of his works: *Confessions of an English Opium Eater;* his *Autobiography;* and his biographical sketches of *Shakespeare, Milton, Pope, Wordsworth, Coleridge, Southey, Lamb, Lessing,* and the *Caesars.* The second group includes his pieces on *Rhetoric, Style,* the *Theory of Greek Tragedy,* and *Kant.* The third group, the most important, includes: parts of the *Confessions of an English Opium Eater,* the *Suspiria de Profundis, The English Mail Coach, Murder Considered as One of the Fine Arts, Joan of Arc, The Spanish Military Nun,* and *Early Memorials of Grasmere.*

IMPORTANCE

Everywhere in De Quincey's work can be read an enthusiasm for knowledge as an end in itself and a love of delicate distinction in thought. No English writer has been less of the propagandist than De Quincey; he has little to say about ethics or morals. The charge of triviality has been leveled against some of his work, and he sometimes comes dangerously near pedantry. There is an air about him of detachment, which makes one feel that he never quite belonged to the human species. At his best, however, the wonderful music of his prose with its marked rhythms, and the splendor of his imagery exhibit Romantic prose at his best. He is capable of amazing flashes of inspiration, notably exhibited in his brilliant criticism, "On the Knocking at the Gate in *Macbeth*."

Critical Works

"On the Knocking at the Gate in *Macbeth*" takes as its point of departure the furious knocking that is heard by the audience immediately after the murder of Duncan. For years De Quincey had pondered on the terrible solemnity caused by Shakespeare's stage direction at that moment of the drama. Analysis finally revealed to the critic that there was a deep-seated wisdom in Shakespeare's judgment. Macbeth and Lady Macbeth have fashioned for themselves an artificial world in which they could commit the murder—a world in which love and human warmth do not exist. The knocking at the gate is a call from another world than that of their fabrication; and we are brought back by it to realization of all the human values involved in Duncan's murder.

Another important discussion of De Quincey's is on *The Literature of Knowledge and the Literature of Power,* in which he makes a very important definition. The word *literature* might be held to include everything that is printed in book form. But in all this vast printed matter, two kinds are discernible. There is a *literature of knowledge;* the purpose of this literature is to instruct. There is also a *literature of power;* the purpose of this literature is to move. The first kind appeals to our rational understanding. The literature of power makes its appeal through a sense of pleasure to our human sympathies, and to our experience.

Autobiography

The best-known of De Quincey's work is his autobiographical *The Confessions of an English Opium Eater* (1821) which was enlarged in a second edition of 1856. There is nothing sensational about the contents of the book, and very little of it deals with his taking of opium. It is a full autobiography emphasizing his childhood experiences and impressions, and carries the author into his mid-thirties. There is great frankness about himself in his description of the beginnings and progress of the opium habit. There is also much of his characteristic digressing from the subject at hand and some unexpected joking. Certain passages are amazing in their brilliance. There is an air of great dignity throughout the whole book. Not the least interesting portions are those which deal with his illustrious friends.

De Quincey is at his most characteristic in the sequel to the *Confessions*, a work that he called *Suspiria de Profundis—Sighs from the Depths*. This book was originally a series of three pieces, begun in 1845 and written for *Blackwood's Magazine*. When the book appeared, there were only six "visions" of many more intended. This work carries De Quincey from 1819, where the *Confessions* ended, down to 1845. It is here that he records for us the dreams he had while under the influence of opium. The work is considered to be the best example of De Quincey's prose style, with all its most admirable traits in evidence.

The best-known of the dreams is the last, *Levana and Our Ladies of Sorrow*. In this piece De Quincey tells us of the three goddesses he saw in his visions, the three ladies who presided over the various kinds of sorrow. The eldest of the three is Our Lady of Tears. "She it is that night and day raves and moans, calling for vanished faces . . . her eyes are sweet and subtle, wild and sleepy by turns. . . . She could go abroad upon the winds, when she heard the sobbing of litanies or the thundering of organs, and when she beheld the mustering of summer clouds." She visits beggar and king. She "glides a ghostly intruder into the chambers of sleepless man, sleepless women, sleepless children." The second sister is Our Lady of Sighs. "She never scales the clouds . . . and her eyes, if they were ever seen, would be neither sweet nor subtle . . . they would be found filled with perishing dreams, and with wrecks of forgotten delirium. But she raises not her eyes . . . for ever fastens on the dust. She weeps not. She groans not. . . . Our Lady of Sighs never clamors, never defies . . . hers is the meekness that belongs to the hopeless." Her children are the "houseless vagrants of every clime." The third sister is Our Lady of Darkness. "This younger sister moves with incalculable motions, bounding, and with a tiger's leaps. . . . Though coming rarely amongst men, she storms all doors at which she is permitted to enter at all." Her children are those few "in whom a profound nature has been upheaved by central convulsions; in whom the heart trembles and the brain rocks, under conspiracies of tempests from without and tempests from within." In his Oxford days De Quincey saw these three goddesses in his opium dreams. And by signs he understood that Our Lady of Tears, having taught the boy to yearn for the grave, confided his care now to Our Lady of Sighs, whom she bade season him for the youngest sister. And to the youngest sister she commanded, "Take him from her . . . suffer not woman or her tenderness to sit near him in his darkness . . . scorch the fountains of tears: curse him as only thou canst curse. . . . And so shall our commission be accomplished which from God we had—to plague his heart until we had unfolded the capacities of the spirit."

Other Works

Murder Considered as One of the Fine Arts (1827; 1839; 1854) is one of De Quincey's more successful excursions into humor. It was inspired by a series of carefully thought-out murders committed in 1811 by a man named Wilkins. The satire is extravagant, sometimes ghastly, but always entertaining.

De Quincey's *Joan of Arc* (1847) is a biography of the soldier-saint, highly romantic, and with many brilliant passages.

One of the most admirable of De Quincey's many volumes is *The English Mail Coach* (1849). It contains one of his best-known pieces, the "dream-fugue," known as "The Vision of Sudden Death." Here his prose is closest to poetry, and the musical element in it most insistent.

THE NOVEL DURING THE ROMANTIC ERA

As we have seen, the novel began as an important literary form during the Neoclassical Age. During the early Romantic movement at the close of the eighteenth century, and during the nineteenth century, it gradually developed into a leading vehicle of literary expression.

The teachings of the French Revolutionary philosophers, particularly Rousseau, inspired a number of minor novels among the radicals of the last decade of the eighteenth century. Of these, the most talked-of were: Robert Bage's pictures of the Rousseauistic natural man at home and in London society, *Man as He Is* (1792) and *Hermsprong, or Man as He Is Not* (1796); Thomas Holcroft's attacks on contemporary social institutions, with views of a better society, *Anna St. Ives* (1792) and *Hugh Trevor* (1794); and Mrs. Inchbald's Rousseauistic idealizations of the power of Nature, *A Simple Story* (1791) and *Nature and Art* (1796). In this school, but quite superior to these productions, belongs a novel by the philosopher William Godwin.

William Godwin (1756–1836)

Godwin's *Caleb Williams, or Things as They Are* (1793) was written to exemplify in story form some of the principles the author had recently advocated in his celebrated *Political Justice*. The book is full of interest even today because of the admirable way in which Godwin maintains suspense. It has been called the first detective novel. There are several powerful chapters describing vividly the appalling conditions prevalent in English prisons, and there are stirring indictments of the whole English penal system. A man named Hawkins and his son are allowed to hang for the murder of the oppressive Tyrrel, though they are innocent. This part of the book is an argument against capital punishment. Tyrrel, and the actual murderer, Falkland, because they are both men of position and wealth, are able to commit crimes against humanity in perfect security. Caleb Williams, on the other hand, a son of the poor, though blameless, is forced to endure the law's persecution until he is almost at the point of suicide. Emily Melville, too, comes to her death because of Tyrrel's unpunished brutality.

But the reader will be most fascinated in the character of Falkland, who is a kind of fallen angel. A man of great goodness and principle, he has befriended young Williams and made him his secretary. Spurred on by powerful reasons, he murders the monster Tyrrel. But then, because of his pride in his reputation, he stands by while the innocent Hawkinses pay for his act. Insatiable curiosity provokes Caleb Williams to investigate until he discovers Falkland's secret. Circumstances thus force Falkland himself to become a monster of persecution, who hounds Williams remorselessly, until at last Williams has no way out but to accuse publicly his erstwhile benefactor, whom he has loved.

Godwin is also the author of *St. Leon* (1799), a much inferior novel, promulgating other revolutionary ideas, but debased by sentimentality.

William Beckford (1759–1844)

Somewhat harder to classify is an admirable novel by the wealthiest man in England of his day, William Beckford, which he entitled *The History of the Caliph Vathek* (1786), and first wrote in French. It would seem to belong to the "Gothic school" of Walpole and Radcliffe but actually preceded them by a number of years. It is a strange, but fascinating, mixture of Oriental tale and tale of horror. It shows that the author was powerfully affected by *Paradise Lost,* for the demon Eblis is obviously modeled on Milton's Satan. Though composed in a fine, direct and forceful style, it abounds in color and fantasy that are highly romantic—a kind of foretaste of the Byronic flavor.

Maria Edgeworth (1767–1849)

The novels of Maria Edgeworth are interesting for showing the transition from eighteenth century to nineteenth century ideas on the novel. Some of her stories are frankly didactic—*Early Lessons* (1801), *Moral Tales* (1801), and *Popular Tales* (1804). These were addressed to young people. Edgeworth came from an enormously large family herself (she had twenty brothers and sisters); and a powerful family feeling permeates these books. But her important work is a series of lively novels, free of moral preaching, in which she follows in the path set by Burney as a painter of contemporary manners. Nevertheless she avers that her purpose is to combat the frivolity of her times. She lived for a long time in Ireland, and is at her best when using that country as her locale. The best of these novels of manners is *Castle Rackrent* (1800), *Belinda* (1801), *The Absentee* (1812), and *Ormond* (1817).

Castle Rackrent is told through the personality of an old Irish servant, Thady Quirk, through whose eyes we view the fortunes of the family she has long served. There are wonderful flashes of humor, intended and unintended by the simple old soul, as we watch the disintegration of a once proud family. *The Absentee* is also laid partly in Ireland, and is an effective picture of the evils attendant upon absentee landlordism. We see the young master of an Irish estate ruining himself and his tenantry while he tries to keep up with London society.

The importance of Maria Edgeworth's novels of social life is her introduction of the lower classes into comic fiction. It was from her that Walter Scott took the idea of going to the people of his own country for authentic background in his novels of local Scottish life. And the incomparable Jane Austen confessed her own profound admiration for Edgeworth's novels.

The major novelists of the Romantic Period are, of course, these two—Sir Walter Scott and Jane Austen.

Sir Walter Scott (1771–1832)

We have already traced the successful career of poet from which Sir Walter Scott turned to become the most popular European novelist of his times. His first novel, issued anonymously, was called *Waverley* (1814). Beginning with that book and ending with *Castle Dangerous* (1831), a matter of seventeen years, Scott produced twenty-seven books dealing with historical settings that span seven centuries. We have already noted his taste for feudal manners and how he tried to establish at Abbotsford a baronial life on the medieval pattern. The whole chivalric setting never ceased to charm or delight him. In his historical novels (popularly called "The Waverley Novels") this love of the glamorous past is everywhere evident. The best of these are *The Antiquary* (1816), which takes place in the late eighteenth century; *Old Mortality* (1817), during the time of James II and the Glorious Revolution; *Rob Roy* (1818), during the reign of George I; *The Heart of Midlothian* (1818), in the age of Queen Anne; *The Bride of Lammermoor* (1819), which provided the story for Donizetti's perennial opera, in the late seventeenth century; *The Abbot* (1820) and *The Monastery* (1820), which deal with the fortunes of Mary Stuart; *Ivanhoe* (1820), which takes place in the time of Richard I, nicknamed "the Lion-Hearted"; *Kenilworth* (1821), at the court of Queen Elizabeth; *The Fortunes of Nigel* (1822), in the times of the first Stuart, James I; *Peveril of the Peak* (1822), in the time of Charles II; *Quentin Durward* (1823), in France during the reign of Louis XI; and *The Talisman* (1825), of which the central character is Richard the Lion-Hearted.

IMPORTANCE

The speed with which these books were written, and we have listed only the best of them, inevitably resulted in a debasing of the literary quality. Scott was writing feverishly to make enough money to discharge the enormous debt he had assumed when the publishing house of which he was silent partner failed. There is much unevenness about these novels. Some pages have power and eloquence, others are dull or stilted. Scott's greatest defect, a serious one in a novelist, is a superficiality in portraying the human character. He is very successful in shedding the light of glamor over his novels through the pomp and pageantry of history, setting, and costume. But a modern reader is likely to feel about many of these novels a lack of depth and reality in the persons of the story. Scott's canvases are crowded and are often exciting, but are painted on the surface. His international reputation was based on the love of the romantic past which the Romantic movement was fostering all over Europe. But as an historical novelist he has been excelled by a number of his followers. He paved the way for some of the best works of Dickens and Thackeray, but the former's *Tale of Two Cities* and the latter's *Vanity Fair* and *Henry Esmond* are much better novels than any Scott produced.

Actually Scott was at his best not when dealing with the important persons and aristocrats who crowd his pages, but with the few simple characters taken from the humble ranks of Scottish life.

Kenilworth: The story opens when Queen Elizabeth is still a young woman, at an inn a few miles from Oxford. Giles Gosling, host of the inn, is visited by his nephew, Michael Lambourne, after an absence of many years. Inquiring after old friends, Michael discovers that Tony Foster is now married and has been converted to the popular Protestant faith. He also learns that there is a mysterious beautiful woman known to be at Foster's mansion house, even though it is common knowledge that she is rarely seen in public. Having drunk too much, Michael wagers that he can compel Foster to introduce him to the mysterious lady. Another guest at the inn, Tressilian, accompanies him. When they arrive next morning, Foster is plainly unhappy at seeing Michael, whom he leads into another room. Left alone, Tressilian, is accosted by a beautiful young lady of eighteen. It is she, Amy Robsart, whom Tressilian has been searching for, for she is his fiancée. He deplores her dwelling in what is for her a prison, and informs her that her father is extremely ill. She promises to come home as soon as she wins permission to leave this place. Tressilian is dumbfounded at this answer; but as he moves toward her she screams, Michael and Foster reappear, and he leaves in anger. On his way he meets Varney, master of horse to the Earl of Leicester, upon whom he draws his sword. Suspecting him of evil intent upon Amy, Tressilian is prevented from killing Varney only by Michael's arrival. Tressilian now determines to win the Queen's intercession. He does not know that Amy is already secretly married to the Earl of Leicester. Tressilian goes to the Queen's court at Greenwich, through the help of Lord Sussex. There he is the witness to Sir Walter Ralegh's winning Elizabeth's favor by the famous cloak-spreading incident. When the Queen hears Tressilian's complaint through Sussex, she calls for Varney, and the Earl of Leicester. Varney pretends that he is Amy's husband. Elizabeth now orders him to appear with Amy at Leicester's estate, Kenilworth, for the festivities. In the meantime Amy is anxious to take on publicly her position as Leicester's wife. She had agreed to secrecy only because the Earl had insisted it was necessary for reasons of court politics. Despite Varney's attempt to restrain her, she makes her way to Kenilworth. There a gorgeous pageantry is being enacted to entertain the Queen. Chance finds Tressilian lodged in the same room with some strolling players, among whom is Amy in disguise. She forbids him to reveal her identity. Elizabeth asks to see Varney's wife, but Varney responds that she was too ill to attend. Encouraged by Varney to believe that the stars augur well for Leicester's marriage to Elizabeth, the Earl attempts to make love to the Queen in the garden. Elizabeth answers, "Were I, as others, free to seek my own happiness, then indeed—but it cannot be." Walking now by herself, the Queen comes upon Amy, who reveals that she is not Varney's wife, without saying more about her marriage to Leicester beyond the fact that the Earl may be consulted for the truth. Indignant, the Queen brings Amy to confront Leicester before other courtiers. But Amy's speech is so disconnected that she is believed mad, and placed in custody. Leicester now asks his wife to pretend she is married to Varney. She angrily refuses and pleads with him to tell the truth to the Queen. But Varney now convinces Leicester that Amy is in love with Tressilian. Leicester therefore says nothing when Elizabeth hands Amy over to Varney. Varney removes her from the court with the object of doing away with her. Tressilian and Leicester fight a duel, and the arrival of a lost letter reveals to Leicester that his wife has been faithful. He now reveals all to Elizabeth, who is enraged at the deception and the personal indignity to herself. She issues an order for Varney's arrest, and demands that Amy be brought back. Amy is now confined again in a chamber of Foster's home, for Foster is an underling of Varney's. Varney has taken away the supports of a trap door outside the chamber door, so that if Amy takes one step out of the room she will fall into a deep abyss. Foster, however, in pity, warns her to stay in the room until Leicester comes for her. Varney pretends he is Leicester by imitating the latter's whistle, the old signal between Amy and the Earl. She opens her door, the trap door opens, and she falls. Too late, the Queen's envoys break in. Foster cannot be found, but Varney commits suicide. Years later Foster's skeleton is discovered in the secret chamber where he had been piling up gold. Leicester stays away from the court for a while, but is later recalled to the Queen's favor. Tressilian goes with Ralegh to Virginia.

The plot of this novel is typical of the kind of events that make up a Scott story. *The Heart of Midlothian* is the most admired of the Scottish novels.

The Heart of Midlothian is a euphemism by which the people refer to the sombre prison of Tolbooth, in Edinburgh. At the time of our story, there are two inmates expecting death—Captain John Porteous, once Captain of the Guard, and the lovely girl, Effie Deans. Porteous had fired on a mob that had been unruly during an execution; Effie has been accused of the murder of her illegitimate child. A temporary stay of execution arrives for Porteous. The people who hate him attack the prison and carry him off. The mob is led by an outlaw, George Robertson, disguised as a woman. Robertson's purpose was actually to rescue Effie, for he was her lover, but his plan fails. Porteous is brought by the mob to the place of execution and is hanged. A young minister, Reuben Butler, has been forced by the mob to officiate at Porteous's last moments. Butler was always devoted to Effie's family, who had done much to help him with his career at the university. He knew the family to be a pious one; indeed, he had always hoped to marry Effie's elder half-sister, Jeannie. Effie's father, David Deans, is now well-to-do, but grief-stricken at the catastrophic results of his daughter's love for the outlaw. Butler brings a message to Jeannie confided in his care by a stranger. Jeannie is summoned by this message to a meeting in moonlight with Robertson, the outlaw. The outlaw tells Jeannie that if she will swear in court that Effie had admitted being with child before its birth, Effie could be cleared of the charge of murdering the child to conceal her parentage. But Effie had never made such an admission, and Jeannie is a girl of stern religious conscience who could not swear to an untruth even to save her own sister's life. The child's body has never been found, but Effie seems fated to die. Just before Effie's trial, Jeannie comes to the prison to speak to her sister. Effie is happy to hear how untiringly her outlaw-lover is attempting to save her. But when she hears that there has been no trace of her baby, she faints. Now that she is sure of Robertson's continued love, Effie begs her sister to tell the untruth for which Robertson had asked, but Jeannie's conscience will not permit her to do so. The trial takes place next day; Jeannie will not tell the lie, and Effie is found guilty. But Jeannie hopes that if she goes to London she can win a pardon for her sister from the King. Jeannie says her farewells to Butler, who begs her to marry him. She answers that she cannot until the present emergency is over. Butler is able to give her a letter to a powerful noble, the Duke of Argyle. Jeannie is compelled to go to London on foot, and she travels without shoes. But in England she can no longer endure the looks of the people, and she buys a pair. In London she presents her letter to the Duke of Argyle. He arranges an audience with the Queen, who is impressed by Jeannie's unflagging courage and high moral standards. A few days later the King grants Effie pardon but banishes her for fourteen years from Scotland. The Duke of Argyle sends Jeannie back to Scotland in his carriage. At home she finds her father in better health, and learns that Effie has joined her outlaw-lover. Butler and Jeannie soon marry, and with the Duke of Argyle's patronage Butler is granted a parish. After a time Jeannie hears that the outlaw and Effie have been married, and that he is now living a respectable life. But their child was never found, for it was well-established that it had been stolen by gypsies. The former outlaw, under a new name, uses his talents so well that he becomes Sir George Staunton, widely respected in the community. Effie and Jeannie become close friends again.

Jane Austen (1775–1817)

IMPORTANCE

The novels of Jane Austen are among the most admired and best-loved in English. Every one of them is a delight to read. The author was the daughter of a clergyman in Hampshire, and wisely determined to write about the small affairs which she knew well from experience and her incomparable gift of satirical observation.

Her temperament was largely unsympathetic to the Romantic Movement. In many respects she is a belated Augustan. Though she writes about parish life, she has no interest in nature; like Addison, her attention was focussed on human nature. But in the depiction of that she is fascinated not by great waves of elevated emotion, not by passion or heroic experience, but by the trivia and petty details of everyday living. She is thus the first realist in the English novel—a lively graceful realist, with a calm but caustic understanding of human foibles. As one reads her novels, one gathers the impression that the most important thing in life for such communities as she knew was the business of providing husbands for marriageable daughters. Several of her novels were composed in a mood of conscious hostility to the Romantic view of the world.

When Austen was twenty-one she began to write *Sense and Sensibility,* a witty and subtly satiric attack on the sentimental traditions of love. Her heroine eventually finds happiness through the use of calm sense and level-headedness; her target, the heroine's sister, finds only misery and causes mischief to all who love her because she will have romantic rapture at any cost. *Northanger Abbey* is equally antiromantic, and was intended by its author as a burlesque on Radcliffe's school of Gothic terror novels.

But Jane Austen was very unlucky in her efforts to publish, and *Sense and Sensibility* was not published until fourteen years after its first composition, and then at her own expense. It was only then (1811) that a publisher was willing to take a chance on issuing her revision of a work also written many years earlier, and reentitled as *Pride and Prejudice. Northanger Abbey* had been accepted in 1803, her royalties being all of ten pounds, but for some obscure reason the publisher failed to issue the book, and it never saw the light of publication until 1818, a year after her death. *Mansfield Park* (1814) and *Emma* (1815) were published without much difficulty, and *Persuasion,* completed just before the author's death, was published in 1818. Those of her books that were issued in her lifetime were all published anonymously. She died without any idea of the great reputation that was to be hers.

When compared with the quiet real life of Jane Austen's novels, the world of Scott seems made of tinsel. She never raises her voice, never hurries her pace, but never drags a page. Her humor is omnipresent, not boisterous, but sharp and fundamental. Her admirers are legion and so fanatical in their devotion as almost to form a cult.

Pride and Prejudice, though many readers will prefer one or another of the Austen novels, is her best-known work. It opens with the excitement attendant upon a ball to be given at the Assembly Rooms. A rich young bachelor, Charles Bingley, is to attend with his friends, and the Bennet family is greatly exercised with curiosity over this newcomer to their neighborhood. The Bennets, with their five eligible daughters, are a prominent family at Longbourn. Mr. Bennet, a quiet though whimsical scholarly man, lives a mental life into which his handsome wife, a woman of petty interests and no knowledge, cannot penetrate, much to her exasperation. To Mrs. Bennet the ball is naturally a great occasion for her daughters' possibly meeting suitable young men. Mr. Bennet refuses to think of the marriage of his daughters as his chief concern in life, though his wife never ceases to compel his attention on that subject. Mr. Bingley at the ball proves to be a personable young man. He is accompanied by his two sisters, his brother-in-law Hurst, and a very handsome young man to whom great wealth is attributed by gossip, Fitzwilliam Darcy. But Darcy strikes the girls as insufferably arrogant. He refuses to dance with anyone but Bingley's sisters, and will not be introduced to any other girl present. Elizabeth, our heroine, overhears Darcy observing to Bingley his lack of interest in all the females present, and that there is only one good-looking girl at the ball, Jane Bennet, the oldest of the Bennet girls. As for Elizabeth, Darcy dismisses her as being merely tolerable to look at. Although not pleased with this estimate of herself, Elizabeth, loving merriment, tells the story about.

The Bingley household and the Bennets are soon on very cordial terms. Charles Bingley and Jane Bennet are plainly attracted to each other. Elizabeth, who is the second eldest, becomes a great favorite of Charles's sisters, but they can barely put up with Mrs. Bennet for being tedious and trivial. Elizabeth's sisters, Lydia and Kitty, are man-crazy and excessively giddy, while Mary is too plain to attract anyone. Apparently despite himself, Darcy becomes interested in Elizabeth. Their friendship is founded largely on their ability to be ironic with each other. On a visit to the Bingleys, Jane becomes the victim of a bad cold. Mrs. Bennet makes capital of the situation by seizing it as an excuse for a longer stay. Elizabeth has not yet forgotten her first impression of Darcy's arrogance. It is only strengthened when a handsome officer of the military, Wickham, informs her that although Darcy's father had left a will requiring Wickham's being provided for as the son of a trusty servant to the Darcy family, Darcy has refused to carry out his father's wishes.

The Reverend Mr. Collins now appears on a visit to the Bennets. He is conceited, tactless, and stupid. He comes to propose to Elizabeth for purely financial reasons. She is disgusted with his stilted memorized speech, and rejects him. After several more attempts, Collins gives up and marries Charlotte Lucas, an unimaginative girl who has been a friend of Elizabeth's.

Elizabeth goes to visit the couple at their new home. Darcy happens also to be visiting in that neighborhood. But Elizabeth likes him even less when she seems to have reason to think that he persuaded his friend Bingley to terminate his attentions to her sister Jane. She is overwhelmed when Darcy out of the clear sky announces that he is in love with her. He makes a very poor case of it by admitting that it was difficult for him to propose marriage to a girl of inferior family such as hers. She rejects his proposal with an honest account of her reasons. When Darcy leaves he sends her a letter in which his portraits of certain members of her family, though bitterly sketched, are only too justified. Darcy also explains in the letter that Wickham, far from being unfairly dealt with, is a scamp who has repaid kindness by outrage and immoral conduct.

Sometime later, Elizabeth finds herself visiting in the neighborhood of Darcy's home in Derbyshire. Because the master is not at home, she is willing to be shown the place. She is surprised to hear the enthusiasm of his housekeeper for Darcy. Then, Darcy appears on the scene. Elizabeth begins to think more kindly of Darcy. Suddenly word arrives that her sister Lydia has eloped with Wickham, and is living in sin with him in London. Darcy is deeply moved. Mr. Bennet goes to London to find his daughter. Mrs. Bennet's only concern is for the wedding clothes that Lydia will have to buy when Wickham is compelled to do right by her. The Bennets learn that someone has paid Wickham to marry the dowerless Lydia, and that Wickham is to join a regiment at Newcastle.

Lydia, a true daughter of her mother, now that she is married, begins to patronize her unmarried sisters, and avers that she may be able to get husbands for them. It turns out that Darcy had found the erring couple first, and had bribed Wickham into marrying Lydia by the gift of two thousand pounds and the purchase of Wickham's commission. Elizabeth alone knows this. She is therefore distressed when Mrs. Bennet treats Darcy very coldly. Darcy proposes to Elizabeth again, and this time, estimating him more justly, she accepts. Bingley and Jane are engaged to be married, and the novel concludes with Mr. Bennet's humorously anticipating suitors for Kitty and Mary.

Mary Wollstonecraft Shelley (1797–1851)

Mary Shelley, whose first novel *Frankenstein* (1818) remains one of the prose achievements of the Romantic period, was the daughter of Mary Wollstonecraft, author of *A Vindication of the Rights of Women*. Her father was the philosopher and political reformer William Godwin, a minor novelist whose work is now far overshadowed by that of his daughter. One of Godwin's apprentices to his radical philosophy was the poet Percy Bysshe Shelley, who first met the young Mary Wollstonecraft when she was sixteen. Mary soon began her liaison with Shelley, recently estranged from his wife Harriet, and in the summer of 1814, finding herself pregnant, escaped to Europe with her young lover.

Mary's life with Shelley was by no means easy, and their eight-year union ended in tragedy when Shelley drowned in the Gulf of Spezia, Italy, in 1822. Mary had four children by Shelley, only one of whom survived, and she lived out much of her life in poverty, relying on Shelley's father and her writings as her only means of support. Her youth, filled with travels and the hunger for glory extolled by her father and Shelley, stands in stark opposition to her widowhood, a time of great loneliness and self-doubt for Mary Shelley. She continued to write after Shelley's death, both as novelist— *Valperga* (1823) and *The Last Man* (1826) are among her best novels—and critic, and also made important contributions to her husband's texts, editing and prefacing them as well as adding important bibliographical notes to many of his poems.

In the spring of 1816 Mary Shelley travelled with Shelley and their friend Claire Clairmont to Geneva, where they spent a rather enchanted summer with the poet Byron and his personal physician, Doctor Polidori, at the Villa Diodati. In this undeniably Gothic setting, the five spent long nights telling stories, reading poetry, and letting their romantic imaginations run free. These six weeks, now recreated and somewhat fictionalized in Howard Brenton's play *Bloody Poetry* (1985) and in the Ken Russell film *Gothic* (1987), were, according to Mary Shelley, inspirational to her creation of *Frankenstein*, which was published anonymously in 1818.

Although in some ways an exemplary Gothic romance, *Frankenstein* possesses an element of what can best be labelled early science fiction; this distinguishes it both thematically and stylistically from its predecessors. The nineteen-year-old Mary Shelley had in fact written an archetypal Romantic novel. While encompassing and revitalizing themes found in the Bible and Milton, the text also treats several prominent motifs of Romanticism. The scientist Frankenstein, who only dehumanizes himself trying to create what is human, represents in the author's conception the destructive force of overzealous creative ambition. At the same time, the monster created by Frankenstein (who in a later confusion of the myth took on his creator's name), can be viewed as the Romantic preoccupation with alienation. The monster, totally separated from society by his nature, feels only isolation, and needs companionship that he will never attain. He becomes in a sense the example of a tragic Romantic hero, and his pleading for human sympathy, always thrown scornfully back in his face, leads him to a violent and horrible end.

REVIEW QUESTIONS

PRE-ROMANTICISM AND ROMANTICISM

Multiple Choice

1. _____ The revolt against Neoclassicism included all of the following EXCEPT
   a. a new interest in the importance of emotions
   b. preference for the country over the city
   c. renewed interest in Celtic and Teutonic literature
   d. emphasis on self-restraint and decorum

2. _____ *The Seasons* is important for its use of
   a. blank verse and nature descriptions
   b. rhymed couplets and city scenes
   c. music and illustrations
   d. the illustrations of William Blake

3. _____ In addition to his remarkable abilities as a poet, Blake was also
   a. a Liberal politician
   b. a novelist
   c. a military leader
   d. an engraver and illustrator

4. _____ Wordsworth's *The Prelude* is devoted primarily to
   a. his development as a poet
   b. British history from 1750 to 1830
   c. literary developments in Europe
   d. the day-to-day activities of Wordsworth's children

5. _____ The events of Byron's *Childe Harold* closely parallel
   a. the life of an historical English nobleman
   b. the events in Byron's own life
   c. the adventures of Don Juan
   d. the life of the German poet Goethe

6. _____ In his day, Shelley was
   a. more famous than his contemporary Byron
   b. popular with the general public
   c. associated with moral degeneracy by the general public
   d. the acknowledged leader of the Romantic Movement

7. _____ In *Prometheus Unbound*, Prometheus
   a. repents of his defiant curse against Jupiter
   b. vows undying hatred for Jupiter
   c. accepts the inevitability of Jupiter's dominance
   d. opposes the action of Demogorgon

8. _____ Keats wrote much of his most famous poetry
   a. in steady increments over a period of fifteen years
   b. in a matter of months
   c. while an expatriate in Italy
   d. in the last months of his life

9. _____ In "Ode on a Grecian Urn" the images described on the urn are primarily
   a. pastoral
   b. urban
   c. ominous
   d. martial
10. _____ Charles Lamb expressed his social and literary opinions mainly in
   a. novels
   b. poetry
   c. travel narratives
   d. essays

True or False

11. _____ The Romantic Movement began approximately twenty years after the first publications of Wordsworth and Coleridge.
12. _____ Chatterton was deeply influenced by the poetry of Spenser.
13. _____ William Blake's ideas are relatively simple compared to the complexity of his language.
14. _____ Romantic writers were influenced more profoundly by the American Revolution than by the French Revolution.
15. _____ *Lyrical Ballads* was an immediate literary success and established the fame of Wordsworth and Coleridge as major English poets.
16. _____ The "Preface" to the *Lyrical Ballads* emphasizes the importance of poetry by and for a highly educated elite.
17. _____ The typical Byronic hero is disgusted by the constraints and hypocrisy of ordinary society.
18. _____ Shelley exercised a considerable influence on the poetry of Coleridge.
19. _____ Mary Wollstonecraft won immediate fame with her novel *Frankenstein.*
20. _____ When they were involved in politics, the young Romantic poets and essayists were usually radicals.

Fill-in

21. Robert Burns is most closely associated with the national literature of _____.
22. To accompany *Songs of Innocence*, Blake wrote _____.
23. For Wordsworth, the strong feelings recorded by poetry are "emotions recollected in _____."
24. Coleridge's lengthy prose work treating his life and writings was titled _____.
25. One of Byron's political causes, and the one in which he lost his life, was the _____ struggle for independence.

26. "Intellectual Beauty" is an idea that appears in the poetry of
_____.

27. Sensuous imagery, as in "The Eve of St. Agnes," is typical of the poetry
of _____.

28. _____ began as a narrative poet but turned to the writing of
historical novels.

29. The novelist who wrote in the tradition of the comedy of manners and
was temperamentally close to Neoclassicism is _____.

30. _____ is the term Keats used to refer to the ability of an author to
identify with the thoughts and emotions of a wide variety of characters.

Matching

31. _____ William Blake
32. _____ Robert Burns
33. _____ Thomas Gray
34. _____ William Wordsworth
35. _____ Samuel Taylor Coleridge
36. _____ Percy Bysshe Shelley
37. _____ Lord Byron
38. _____ John Keats
39. _____ William Hazlitt
40. _____ Charles Lamb

a. "Dream Children"
b. "Elegy in a Country Churchyard"
c. "To Autumn"
d. "On Going a Journey"
e. "The Cotter's Saturday Night"
f. "The Tiger"
g. "Ode to the West Wind"
h. "Frost at Midnight"
i. "Resolution and Independence"
j. "She Walks in Beauty"

Answers

1. d	15. f	27. Keats
2. a	16. f	28. Sir Walter Scott
3. d	17. t	29. Jane Austen
4. a	18. f	30. Negative capability
5. b	19. f	31. f
6. c	20. t	32. e
7. b	21. Scotland	33. b
8. b	22. *Songs of*	34. i
9. a	*Experience*	35. h
10. d	23. tranquility	36. g
11. f	24. *Biographia*	37. j
12. t	*Literaria*	38. c
13. f	25. Greek	39. d
14. f	26. Shelley	40. a

Part 2

THE VICTORIAN AGE

WORKS AT A GLANCE*

Thomas Carlyle

1823	*The Life of Friedrich Schiller*	1834	*Sartor Resartus*
1824	translation of Goethe's	1837	*The French Revolution*
	Wilhelm Meister	1840	*Heroes and Hero*
1827	*German Romance*		*Worship*
	The State of German	1843	*Past and Present*
	Literature	1845	*Oliver Cromwell*
1828	*Essay on Burns*	1851	*Life of John Sterling*
1832	Essay on *Boswell's Life*	1858–1865	*Frederick the Great*
	of Johnson	1883	*Letters and Memorials*

Thomas Babington Macaulay

1842, 1848, 1855	*Lays of Ancient Rome*
1861	*History of England from the Accession of James II*

John Henry Newman

1833	"Lead Kindly, Light"	1863	*Lyra Apostolica*
1833–1842	*Tracts for the Times*	1864	*Apologia Pro Vita Sua*
1850	*The Present Position of*	1865	*The Dream of Gerontius*
	Catholics in England	1870	*Grammar of Assent*
1852	*The Idea of a University*		

John Ruskin

1843, 1846	*Modern Painters*	1858	*The Political Economy*
1849	*The Seven Lamps of*		*of Art*
	Architecture	1860	*Unto This Last*
1851–1853	*The Stones of Venice*	1862–1863	*Munera Pulveris*
1857–1859	*The Elements of*	1865	*Sesame and Lilies*
	Drawing	1866	*A Crown of Olives*
	The Elements of	1871–1874	*Fors Clavigera*
	Perspective	1885–1889	*Praeterita*

Alfred Tennyson

1827	*Poems by Two Brothers*		"The Palace of Art"
1830	*Poems, Chiefly Lyrical*		"The Lotos-Eaters"
1832	*Poems by Alfred Tennyson*		"Œnone"
	"The Lady of Shalott"	1837	"St. Agnes' Eve"

---

*Dates refer to date of publication unless otherwise noted.

Alfred Tennyson (continued)

1842	Poems	1877	Harold
	"Morte d'Arthur"	1878	"The Revenge"
	"Ulysses"	1880	Ballads and Poems
	"Locksley Hall"	1881	The Cup
	"Break, Break, Break"	1882	The Promise of May
1847	The Princess	1884	Beckett
1850	In Memoriam	1885	Tiresias
	"Milton"	1886	Locksley Hall Sixty Years
1854	"The Charge of the Light		After
	Brigade"	1889	Demeter
1855	Maud		"Crossing the Bar"
1864	Enoch Arden	1892	The Death of Œnone
1875	Queen Mary		The Foresters

Robert Browning

1833	Pauline	1855	"Fra Lippo Lippi"
1835	Paracelsus		"A Toccata of
1841–1846	Bells and Pomegranates		Galuppi's"
1841	Pippa Passes		"Childe Roland to the
1842	King Victor and		Dark Tower Came"
	King Charles		"The Statue and
	"Cavalier Tunes"		the Bust"
	"My Last Duchess"		"The Last Ride
	"Soliloquy of the		Together"
	Spanish Cloister"		"Andrea del Sarto"
1843	The Return of the		"In a Balcony"
	Druses		"Saul"
	A Blot on the 'Scutcheon		"Two in the
1844	Colombe's Birthday		Campagna"
1845	Dramatic Romances		"A Grammarian's
	and Lyrics		Funeral"
	"The Lost Leader"		"Memorabilia"
	"The Bishop Orders His		"Misconceptions"
	Tomb"		"One Word More"
	"Home Thoughts from	1864	Dramatis Personae
	Abroad"		"Abt Vogler"
	"How They Brought the		"Rabbi Ben Ezra"
	Good News from		"Caliban upon
	Ghent to Aix"		Setebos"
1846	Luria, A Soul's Tragedy		"Prospice"
1855	Men and Women	1869	The Ring and the
	"Love Among the Ruins"		Book
	"Evelyn Hope"	1879, 1880	Dramatic Idyls
	"Up at a Villa—Down	1883	Jocoseria
	at a City"	1884	Ferishtah's Fancies

*Dates refer to date of publication unless otherwise noted.

Robert Browning *(continued)*

1887	*Parleyings with Certain People of Importance*	1889	*Asolando*

Elizabeth Barrett Browning

1884	"The Cry of the Children"	1860	*Poems Before Congress*
1850	*Sonnets from the Portuguese*		"A Musical Instrument"
1851	*Casa Guidi Windows*		

Edward Fitzgerald

1859	*The Rubaiyát of Omar Khayyám*

Charles Darwin

1859	*Origin of the Species*

Thomas Henry Huxley

1863	*Evidences as to Man's Place in Nature*
1860s	"A Liberal Education and Where to Find It"
	"On a Piece of Chalk"
	"On the Physical Basis of Life"

Matthew Arnold

1849	*The Strayed Reveler and Other Poems*	1853	*Poems*
	"The Forsaken Merman"		"Prcfacc"
	"To a Friend"		"Philomela"
	"Shakespeare"		"Requiescat"
	"Quiet Work"		"Sohrab and Rustum"
	"Resignation"		"The Scholar Gypsy"
1852	*Empedocles on Etna and Other Poems*	1858	*Merope*
	"Lines Written in Kensington Gardens"	1861	*Popular Education in France*
	"To Marguerite"		*On Translating Homer*
	"A Summer Night"	1862	*Translating Homer: Last Words*
	"Self-Dependence"	1864	*A French Eton*
	"The Buried Life"	1865	*Essays in Criticism, First Series*

*Dates refer to date of publication unless otherwise noted.

Matthew Arnold (continued)

1865	"Preface"	1869	"Sweetness and Light"
	"The Function of Criticism at		"Hebraism and Hellenism"
	the Present Time"	1877	*Last Essays on Church and*
1867	*New Poems*		*Religion*
	"Thyrsis"	1879	*Mixed Essays*
	"Dover Beach"	1882	*Irish Essays and Others*
	"Growing Old"	1885	*Discourses in America*
	"The Austerity of Poetry"		"Democracy"
	"Rugby Chapel"		"Emerson"
	"The Last Word"		"Literature and Science"
1868	*Schools and Universities on*	1888	*Essays in Criticism,*
	the Continent		*Second Series*
1869	*Culture and Anarchy*		"The Study of Poetry"

Arthur Hugh Clough

1848	*The Bothis of Tober-na-*	1862	"Qui Laborat Orat"
	Vuolich		"Say Not the Struggle Nought
1849	*Amours de Voyage*		Availeth"
	Ambarvalia		"All Is Well"
1850	*Dipsychus*		"Life Is Struggle"
1862	*Poems*	1869	*Poems*
	"Qua Cursum Ventus"		*Prose Remains*

Frederick Marryatt

| 1834 | *Peter Simple, Jacob Faithful* | 1836 | *Midshipman Easy* |

Thomas Love Peacock

1806	*Palmyra*	1820	*The Four Ages of Poetry*
1810	*The Genius of the Thames*	1822	*Maid Marian*
1816	*Headlong Hall*	1829	*The Misfortunes of Elphin*
1817	*Melincourt*	1831	*Crotchet Castle*
1818	*Rhododaphne*	1860	*Gryll Grange*
	Nightmare Abbey		

William Harrison Ainsworth

1834	*Rookwood*	1841	*Old St. Paul's*
1839	*Jack Sheppard*	1843	*Windsor Castle*
1840	*The Tower of London*	1848	*The Lancashire Witches*

---

*Dates refer to date of publication unless otherwise noted.

Edward Bulwer-Lytton

1827	*Falkland*	1843	*The Last of the Barons*
1832	*Pelham*	1846	*Lucretia, or Children of the*
1830	*Paul Clifford*		*Night*
1832	*Eugene Aram*	1848	*Harold*
1834	*The Last Days of Pompeii*	1850	*The Caxtons*
1835	*Rienzi*	1853	*My Novel*
1842	*Zanoni*	1858	*Will He Do It?*

Benjamin Disraeli

1826	*Vivian Grey*	1844	*Coningsby*
1828	*Ixion in Heaven*	1845	*Sybil*
1831	*The Young Duke*	1847	*Tancred*
1832	*Contarini Fleming*	1870	*Lothair*
1833	*Alroy*	1880	*Endymion*
1837	*Venetia*		

Elizabeth Cleghorn Gaskell

1848	*Mary Barton*	1863	*Sylvia's Lovers*
1851–1853	*Cranford*	1864	*Cousin Phyllis*
1853	*Ruth*	1864–1866	*Wives and Daughters*
1855	*North and South*		(unfinished)
1857	*Life of Charlotte Bontë*		

Charles Kingsley

1848	*The Saint's Tragedy*	1857	*Two Years Ago*
	Yeast	1858	*Andromeda*
1850	*Alton Locke*	1863	*The Water Babies*
1853	*Hypatia*	1866	*Hereward the Wake*
1855	*Westward Ho!*		

Charlotte Brontë

1847	*Jane Eyre*	1853	*Villette*
1849	*Shirley*	1857	*The Professor*

Emily Brontë

1846	"Remembrance"	1848	*Wuthering Heights*
	"The Visionary"		
	"The Old Stoic"		
	"Last Lines"		

---

*Dates refer to date of publication unless otherwise noted.

Anne Brontë

1848	*Agnes Grey, The Tenant of Wildfell Hall*

Charles Dickens

1836, 1837	*Sketches by Boz*	1848	*Dombey and Son*
1836–1837	*The Posthumous Papers of the Pickwick Club*	1850	*David Copperfield*
		1853	*Bleak House*
1838	*Oliver Twist*	1854	*Hard Times*
1839	*Nicholas Nickleby*	1857	*Little Dorritt*
1840–1841	*The Old Curiosity Shop*	1859	*A Tale of Two Cities*
	Barnaby Rudge	1861	*Great Expectations*
1842	*American Notes*	1865	*Our Mutual Friend*
1843	*A Christmas Carol*	1879	*The Mystery of Edwin Drood*
1844	*Martin Chuzzlewit*		
1846	*Pictures from Italy*		

William Makepeace Thackeray

1836	*Flore et Zéphyr*	1853	*Henry Esmond*
1837–1838	*The Yellowplush Papers*		*The English Humorists of the 18th Century*
1844	*Barry Lyndon*		
1846–1847	*Tickletoby's Lectures on English History*	1855	*The Newcomes*
		1859	*The Virginians*
	Snobs of England	1860	*Roundabout Papers*
1847	*Punch's Prize Novelists*		*Lovel the Widower*
1848	*Vanity Fair*	1862	*The Adventures of Philip*
1850	*Pendennis*		

Charles Reade

1853	*Peg Woffington, Christine Johnstone*	1866	*Griffith Gaunt*
		1870	*Put Yourself in His Place*
1856	*It Is Never Too Late to Mend*	1871	*A Terrible Temptation*
1861	*The Cloister and the Hearth*	1879	*Drink*
1863	*Hard Cash*		

George Eliot (Mary Anne Evans)

1859	*Adam Bede*	1866	*Felix Holt*
1860	*The Mill on the Floss*	1873	*Middlemarch*
1861	*Silas Marner*	1876	*Daniel Deronda*
1863	*Romola*		

---

*Dates refer to date of publication unless otherwise noted.

Wilkie Collins

1860	*The Woman in White*	1868	*The Moonstone*
1866	*Armadale*		

George Borrow

1843	*The Bible in Spain*	1857	*The Romany Rye*
1851	*Lavengro*	1862	*Wild Wales*

Anthony Trollope

1855	*The Warden*	1861	*Framley Parsonage*
1857	*Barchester Towers*	1864	*The Small House at Allington*
1858	*Doctor Thorne*	1867	*The Last Chronicle of Barset*

---

*Dates refer to date of publication unless otherwise noted.

5
THE AUTHOR IN SOCIETY

Queen Victoria was monarch of England from 1887 to 1901, and it has been found convenient to group the writings produced during that long stretch of years as "Victorian." But the classification is perhaps too facile. To begin with, the Queen had very little to do with the best productions of her times. In an age that abounded in great literature and music, her own preferences were for second-rate authors and composers whose works are already forgotten. Moreover, no earlier period of English literature exhibits so vast a variety of traits, style, and ideas. It is absurd to pretend that the label "Victorian" communicates any idea common to the works of writers so different as Macaulay, Dickens, Emily Brontë, Tennyson, Browning, Rossetti, Arnold, Swinburne and Meredith.

The term "Victorian" itself is often used in a fashion that is misleading. Popularly it connotes bad taste, stuffy morals, and moral priggishness. These were attributes true enough of the Queen's private household and for that reason they are indeed "Victorian." But they are certainly not to be found among the ideas and beliefs of Browning, Rossetti, Arnold or Meredith, to mention only a few. Finally, although our own contemporaries are fond of thinking of themselves as reacting against "Victorianism," in the field of political theory the dogmas of the twentieth century are essentially only elaborations of principles laid down in the nineteenth.

POLITICAL AND SOCIAL DEVELOPMENTS

The concern with specific social problems is the most noticeable distinction between Victorian literature and the literature of the preceding centuries. The impulse is generally recognized to have started before Victoria came to the throne, with the First Reform Bill (1832). That act of Parliament recognized the economic dominance of the middle class by finally placing direct political power in its hands. The vote was thus extended to all members of this class. At this time the old concepts of "Whig" and "Tory" made way for "Liberal" and "Conservative." Liberals were anxious to see operating in full effect the principle that Adam Smith had laid down— the economic "law" of unlimited free competition in trade. They flattered themselves that the world, under their leadership, was becoming more and more attractive. In 1829 the Catholic Emancipation Act had been passed; in 1833 slavery was abolished;

in 1846 free trade became a national policy with the repeal of the Corn Laws; in 1845 Jews were made eligible for public office; and in 1872 the institution of voting by ballot was inaugurated. The Conservatives were as responsible as the Liberals for the passage of these acts; for a long time there was little difference between the two parties. Both were committed to the teaching of Utilitarianism, as promulgated by Bentham, that it was necessary to achieve the greatest good for the greatest number. Bentham's disciple was James Mill; and Mill's son, John Stuart Mill (1806–1873), became the most influential of Victorian Utilitarians. The last-mentioned taught that the only reason that can be adduced for limiting the rights of any individual in the community "is to prevent harm to others."

This philosophy of unrestricted individualism in economics vastly increased the holdings of the middle class as well as its material comforts. The British colonial empire expanded in Asia and Africa by conquest and colonization. There were many who could exclaim with the Roebuck whom Matthew Arnold made immortal by attacking, "I pray that our unrivalled happiness may last."

But there was a less attractive side to the picture which industrialists chose to overlook. The philosophy of noninterference by the government meant unrestricted hardship to the legions of workers who were dependent for their very existence upon their employers. Labor was cheap, the birth rate high, and slum conditions became increasingly worse. The earliest attempt of workingmen to combine for better living conditions met with ferocious opposition in Parliament. A law of 1825 fixed punishment at hard labor as the penalty for attempting any act inconsistent with the freedom of employers to make contracts. The Victorian Age, from a working-class point of view, is the record of a long struggle of wage earners to win recognition from the government. A People's Charter was drawn up in 1838, and began the so-called Chartist movement, which demanded universal manhood suffrage, the secret ballot, and abolition of property qualifications for members of Parliament. Universal manhood suffrage was perhaps inevitably the foundation of any further progress. Actually it was not until 1917 that the point was won in the Manhood Suffrage Bill. Before that act was passed, the decades were punctuated by a series of strikes and riots in urban centers. Though the Chartist movement was for a long time unsuccessful, it served the function of making the general public aware of the problems involved. By unceasing protest, small gains were realized. In 1847 a ten-hour work day was established. In 1842 women and children were forbidden employment in the mines. In 1867 and 1873 women and children were excluded from heavier agricultural work. By 1875 a series of public health acts had become law.

Meanwhile, Liberal and Conservative alike had no intention of impeding the solid profits of British industry. As long ago as 1798, Malthus (in his answer to Godwin) had given them the theory that justified governmental indifference. Malthus's *Essay on Population* had insisted that poverty, disease, and war are necessary to prevent the greater catastrophe of overpopulation; to coddle the people, it warned, was to upset natural law. Among the many idealists who arose to dispute this official view were some who dreamed of a return to manufacture by hand—an idea that appealed powerfully to certain important authors. One of the few who looked to the future instead of the past was Robert Owen (1771–1858), who originated the idea of cooperatives. He was convinced that the machine must be controlled for the benefit of the people who run it. His socialistic self-supporting communities made their experiments in Ireland, Scotland and the New World. Some succeeded at first; all eventually failed. But Owen's teachings have had important bearing on the history of trade unions, and various species of socialist theory.

Science took on a heretofore undreamt-of importance in the Victorian age. The whole world was brought closer together, first by the building of railroads, then by the telegraph, the telephone, the automobile, and the beginnings of travel by air. Everywhere machinery was revolutionized by the use of steam and electricity. Superficially scientists could claim that they were vastly improving the pleasures of living—though their inventions benefited as yet only the few.

THE VICTORIAN LITERARY RESPONSE

The growth of material well-being of the middle class and the development of scientific invention provoked violent reactions on the part of some writers. There were men then alive who felt that all this progress was suicidal to the soul. Carlyle was sick at the sight of the sordid lives led by men and women in the factories and he sought refuge from the tentacles of the machine by preaching the doctrine that human labor alone was sacred. An enemy of industrialization, he looked back to the Middle Ages to prove that consecration to humble labor had made great souls. John Ruskin was to a certain degree his disciple. Preeminently concerned with art, Ruskin concluded that only great spiritual values can make for great art; he denounced Utilitarianism as an apology for the evils of industrialized society. He too found in the Middle Ages a noble spiritual ideal which the modern world had lost.

In the Victorian Age this escape to the Middle Ages became a favorite resource for many who could not bear the ugliness of contemporary life. The Pre-Raphaelite Brotherhood, of which the leaders were Rossetti and Morris, frankly imitated medieval painters and poets in their own work. In the field of religion, John Henry Newman, leader of the Oxford Movement, found in the ritual of the medieval Church a beauty nourishing to the soul; he sought to annihilate the traditions of Puritanism that he felt had impoverished the English Church. In the end he was drawn to the Roman Catholic Church, of which he became a Cardinal. His own spiritual struggles mark the beginnings of a rebirth of Roman Catholicism and the conversion to that faith of thousands in England.

Perhaps most cataclysmic of all new ideas were those advanced in natural science. The theory of evolution, which for some time had been undermining the prestige of the idea that the universe had been created for man, was finally summed up in the writings of Charles Darwin. He was able to put before the public a mass of facts justifying the theory of organic evolution, in a manner that could no longer be ignored. The very foundations of religion began to rock, and the authority of the Bible was subjected to such doubts as the world had never known before. Many felt that the whole groundwork of ethics and morals was crumbling. The doubt and despair occasioned by the Darwinian theories can be read in a number of Victoran writers, notably in the poetry of Matthew Arnold. But Darwin's disciple, Thomas Huxley, went up and down the English-speaking world to acquaint the average man with what the Darwinian teachings actually were. Through his influence, agnosticism was understood to be by no means inconsistent with high ethics, and towards the close of the century Huxley's view became increasingly that of the English intellectual.

Towards these various currents of Victorian experience and thinking, we find individual writers adopting their own views, offering their own solutions.

Thomas Carlyle (1795–1881)

Thomas Carlyle's teachings proved to be among the most influential of his period. His style was no less original than his thought, and his battles against the materialism of the century were a challenge hard to ignore.

He was born in southern Scotland at Ecclefechan on December 4, 1795, the eldest of a large family. His father was first a stonemason and later a farmer, severely Protestant in his religious tenets. The boy's childhood was spent in an atmosphere of intense austerity but deep personal affection. Though very poor, his parents decided that his gifts entitled him to higher learning. They scrimped and saved to enable him to prepare for the church. In November 1809, young Thomas walked all the way to Edinburgh to enter the University there. Despite the fact that his fellow students soon looked up to him, he did not make a brilliant record as a student. He spent several years teaching, and then decided against the ministry. One of his closest friends during this time was Edward Irving, a young Scot with a large library. Among those books Carlyle read avidly, with the result that his faith in Calvinistic dogma began to waver. He lost his belief in his father's religion, but his interest in spiritual values became only stronger.

In 1819 he began to study German. In the poets and philosophers of Germany he found the basis for his own convictions. It was a literature still almost unknown in England, and Carlyle now spent some years in making translations of his favorites into English. In 1823 he wrote *The Life of Friedrich Schiller;* in 1824 he translated Goethe's most important novel, *Wilhelm Meister's Apprenticeship and Travels*; in 1827 he issued four volumes of *German Romance,* containing translations from various writers including Richter, Goethe, Tieck, Hoffmann, and others. In the same year he wrote a book on Richter and a treatise on the *State of German Literature.* There followed a series of essays on medieval German literature, on the life of Goethe, on Goethe's other works and on German playwrights; he also made various translations from Goethe's contemporaries. Beyond these his concern had thus far been limited to only two English writers. He wrote an *Essay on Burns* in 1828, and one on *Boswell's Life of Johnson* (1832).

In 1824 he came to London to try his fortunes there, and soon knew a number of writers. None of his friendships impressed him more than the one he formed with Coleridge. But Carlyle did not like London and decided to return to his native land where he felt he could continue his literary work without molestation. But he never found the tranquility he sought, for dyspepsia and insomnia were soon victimizing him, and he lived under their tyranny for the rest of his life.

In 1822 he had met Jane Welsh, a beautiful and brilliant girl with marked literary gifts. They began a correspondence that constitutes one of the most fascinating series of love letters ever written. It was four years before Jane Welsh consented to marry him. Their marriage in October 1826 began a strange and stimulating relationship. Their friends often misinterpreted the frequent frictions that arose between Carlyle and his wife. But they were deeply devoted to each other, and her death in 1866 had a shattering effect upon him. For the forty years of their life together, they were the center of a circle of remarkable friends.

They lived for their first year at Edinburgh, where they found their slender means inadequate. In 1828 they moved to a farm at Craigenputtock. The most crucial years of their lives were spent there. Carlyle now embarked upon his most important works, but since he was determined not to print them before they were perfected, his financial problems became increasingly serious. But his authoritative works on German literature were augmenting his reputation in England and on the Continent. By correspondence he was carrying on a friendship with Goethe. Most important of all his intellectual ties, however, was that which he developed with Ralph Waldo Emerson, a young American, who came to visit him at Craigenputtock. They were drawn towards the same philosophy, and the similarity of their ideas formed the basis of a life-long friendship, a friendship that was of the utmost significance to their respective careers.

The basis of Carlyle's great work is his profound disgust with the materialism of his age. His hostility to what he considered the soul-destroying forces abroad in the nineteenth century world made him into a prophet almost of Old Testament stature. His first important book, which some consider his greatest, is *Sartor Resartus*, which appeared in installments first in *Fraser's Magazine* in 1834. It was first published as a book in Boston in 1836, and two years later in England. It is essentially a great spiritual autobiography. Carlyle himself described the work to his brother as: "A very singular piece I assure you! It glances from Heaven to Earth and back again in a strange and satirical frenzy." The idea for the book, the title of which means "Tailor Retailored" was suggested to Carlyle by a passage in Swift's *Tale of a Tub:* Swift asks: "What is man himself but a microcoat" in a universe that is itself like a "large suit of clothes which invests everything."

In *Sartor Resartus* Carlyle pretends to be merely the commentator on and the expositor of the philosophy of a certain eccentric German professor, Diogenes Teufelsdröckh (Born of God, Dung for the Devil), who is a lecturer at the University of Weissnichtwo (Nobody-Knows-Where). The good professor is especially concerned with the philosophy of "clothes, their origin and influence." Under this guise, Carlyle is able to write a profound book on the difference between things as they seem and things as they actually are. Carlyle's reading in the German philosophers had confirmed his innate spiritual idealism. The book is a denial of corporal reality, and an exposition on the falsehood of the appearances of things. The shams of civilized life are the highly decorated though worn-at-the-hem robes with which the world conceals its soul. The divine principle, which is all that is of importance to man, is hidden from view, and Carlyle's book nobly tears aside the concealing garment. Those who deny God, who have no faith in spiritual values, give "the Everlasting No" to life; those who understand that through labor and spiritual courage life can take on deep meaning say "the Everlasting Yea." From man Carlyle carries the image of the clothes-sham to the larger meanings in the Universe itself. Time and space are the clothes which hide from us the true meaning of the Universe. At the end of the book there is a wonderful rhapsodic passage in which all Creation is understood as the robe behind which lies the divine spirit of God.

Fundamental to discovering the values of truth in life, according to Carlyle, is the understanding of the importance of Work. Happiness is not the highest good for man. Higher than happiness is union with God, the ability to say Yea to life, and resolve all life's contradictions. One must renounce life before it will offer its rewards. In the wonderful section called "Natural Supernaturalism" Professor Teufelsdröckh observes how little science has penetrated to the spiritual secrets of nature. We are all the slaves of custom, and all true thinking is an unceasing war against custom. Science, the friend of custom, seeks to negate the existence of the miraculous by pretending that mere labeling and repetition can make a miracle seem ordinary. He concludes with Shakespeare that we are indeed such stuff as dreams are made on.

The style in which Carlyle chose to write *Sartor Resartus* is one of the strangest and most original in English prose, and has come to be called "Carlylese." Superficially, Carlylese is an attempt to import into English the structure peculiar to German prose. There are very un-English inversions, strange coinings of words and stranger combinations, sudden tangents, and unexpected changes in tone. It is the last-mentioned trait that is the most important. Carlyle will be writing in a thumping, heavy-footed style, close to the earth, when suddenly, without warning, the passage will take on wings and soar to inspired poetic heights. The prose is now full of acid, then tender, now full of passion, now burlesque—everything by turns. It was deliberately forged by its author to shock the self-complacency of his public and compel close attention to what he had to say. Although *Sartor Resartus* is the most extreme instance of Carlylese, the same elements continue to be present in the rest of Carlyle's important books.

In the summer of 1834 the Carlyles moved to London where they lived in a charming house in Chelsea, which is now a Carlyle Museum. This was their home for the rest of their lives. Carlyle then embarked upon his most ambitious undertaking, *The French Revolution*. After endless study and work, he completed the first volume and gave his only copy of it to his friend John Stuart Mill to read. Through the stupidity of a maid, the manuscript was burned. Carlyle was at this time at the end of his financial resources, and desperate over the loss of time and energy. Nevertheless, Carlyle wrote a letter to Mill in which he was more concerned over his friend's feelings than his own cause for anguish. Sick at heart, he started all over again to write his book. By 1837 he had the three volumes that comprise the work completed. Happily, the book was a great success and put an end to his financial troubles.

Great enemy of Utilitarianism, Carlyle could not think of the world except in terms of individuals. Great movements and notable gains of humanity in progress were in his opinion never attributable to mass development, but to the work and inspiration of great individual leaders. Thus his *French Revolution* is really a series of wonderful individual portraits of the striking personalities connected with world-shaking events. It is the King, Marat, Mirabeau, Robespierre and the other persons of the drama, in whom Carlyle is particularly interested. He recreates with incomparable vividness the great scenes of the Revolution—the taking of the Bastille by the mob, Charlotte Corday's assassination of the tyrant Marat, the celebrated and agonizing Night of Spurs. In short, *The French Revolution* continues Carlyle's depiction of the world as a manifestation of the divinity in man as exhibited in the deeds of the leaders. His historical facts are not always entirely reliable. But the work is a literary masterpiece because of its vividness and wonderful series of paintings of great events.

Carlyle now turned his attack more directly to current social conditions. He loathed everything connected with the industrial system—particularly the horrors of the factory, the soul-destroying nature of machine labor, the dreadful conditions of the workers, and the worship of money by everyone. The *laissez-faire* policy of official economists—their "dismal science," as he called it—was destroying the spiritual life of Europe. But Carlyle came to the conclusion that the movement towards democracy was responsible for all this. Therefore, although he thought of himself as a radical, and was indeed one of the most radical thinkers of his generation, he opposed the Chartist movement. He wrote *Chartism* (1839) in profound sympathy with the wage-earning victims of the factory system; but he argued that only through great individual leaders of society would relief come. This doctrine was more fully elaborated in a series of lectures delivered in 1839, and collected the next year as *Heroes and Hero Worship* (1840). This book, one of his most challenging, takes as Hero poet (Dante, Shakespeare) and author (Rousseau, Johnson), great religionist (Luther) and great soldier (Cromwell), as well as ruler of governments (Napoleon). The essays in this volume center about men like Mohammed, Luther, Dante, Shakespeare, Rousseau, Samuel Johnson, Robert Burns, Cromwell, and Napoleon. These men have shaped the destiny of humanity, Carlyle avers. It is the record of their deeds which makes history. Not all of us can be great as these men were; it is the duty of such as are not great to find a hero to lead them. This same philosophy gives the basic concept of Carlyle's biographies of *Oliver Cromwell* (1845) and *Frederick the Great* (1858–1865). The one biography written in a thoroughly different strain is Carlyle's *Life of John Sterling* (1851), his tribute composed with affection to a dear friend.

He came to grips with politics in *Past and Present* (1843). Here he attacks the mediocrity and spiritual sterility that are, he feels, the offspring of industrialism and democracy. The solution, he decides, is a return to the values of medieval monasticism. He wishes to see a government strong enough to put an end to social injustices as well as social disorders. The ideal ruler for him is the benevolent despot.

IMPORTANCE

It must be admitted that twentieth century history has proved at terrible cost the danger and impracticality of Carlyle's conclusions. Many of his attacks against democracy are just enough, and his pleas for the distribution of profits and extended educational privileges are certainly advanced, but his conclusions are perhaps less than valid.

His importance to his times, however, cannot be underestimated. He awoke the conscience of Englishmen to the sordidness of the lives being led by the workers, and inspired the thinking of great writers like Ruskin, Elizabeth Barrett Browning, Rossetti, Morris, and many others. His conviction that honest hard work was the only solution for man's spiritual health—curiously a recapitulation of the message in the fourteenth century poem, *Piers Plowman*, was a healthy doctrine, a disturbing stone flung in the lake of middle-class complacency.

Carlyle's greatest weakness as a philosopher is that he actually had no system. He saw social ills in flashes of moral indignation. In the end he will be admired as an artist, the master of a brilliant original style, the coiner of memorable phrases, the man who could be both sublime and homely in the same sentence.

Carlyle's last years saw full recognition of his greatness. There were honors and rewards for him. Before his death he annotated his wife's wonderful letters; they were published under the title of *Letters and Memorials* (1883).

Thomas Babington Macaulay (1800–1859)

Macaulay was born in Leicestershire at Rothley Temple on October 25, 1800, the son of a well-known philanthropist who had fought for the abolition of the slave trade. At the age of four Thomas was already incredibly precocious; and for the rest of his life he possessed a phenomenal memory and a stock of information that provoked endless admiration. He attended Trinity College, Cambridge, and in 1826 was admitted to the bar. His essay on Milton, published in *The Edinburgh Review* (1825), gave him a reputation as a leading writer.

That early work marks an important turning point in English prose. Its smooth elegance and brilliant balancing of ideas reminds one of the best essay writing of the eighteenth century. But the temperament revealed is essentially a modern one. The structure of his prose is particularly admirable for its clarity. And the lucidity with which the topic sentence of each paragraph is logically developed, has made his style a model for students.

The piece on Milton indicated Macaulay's lively interest in politics. Thereafter, historian though he was, he always wrote from the standpoint of party politics. He never doubted that the Whigs and those earlier parties whose politics were conformable to Whig doctrine, had always been right.

He was not thirty when he was already known in London society for his brilliant conversation. In 1830 he won a seat in the House of Commons. The time was most opportune for his talents. He made himself well known in Parliament during the long debates on the Reform Bill for his eloquent speeches. After that he was recognized as a leader of his party. He had an important hand in the elaboration of the penal code for India, held several important cabinet positions, and kept his seat until 1847. Except for a brief return to Parliament, he then retired to private life so that he might work on his great history.

He never married, but was a frequent guest in the best society. His last years were spent more and more at the home of his sister Hannah, who was the wife of Sir Charles Trevelyan. It is thus that his nephew George, who wrote the most important of the biographies of Macaulay, came to know him well.

In 1842 Macaulay published his only volume of poems, *Lays of Ancient Rome*, a series of dramatic episodes from the ancient history of Rome, written with considerable facility in ballad style. These were for a long time very popular. Though facile and direct, these poems, however, have not stood the test of time, and seem now essentially commonplace. But the poem "Horatius" was memorized by generations of schoolboys.

In 1843 Macaulay issued a volume of thirty-six essays he had written by then—most of them critical. They were on all kinds of subjects, literary, historical and political. They were read with enthusiasm by the public.

Most of his attention during his last years was given to his *History of England from the Accession of James II*, its volumes issued in 1848, 1855, and the last after his death, in 1861. The five-volume work covers only a few years of English history, as far as the death of William III. He had intended, had he lived, to bring it down to his own time. No writer has reconstructed so brilliantly the life of the late seventeenth century in England. The pictures are clear and brilliant, the rhetoric stirring, sometimes to the point of the theatrical. Of course, history is presented with a strong bias of Whig politics and Protestant theology.

In 1857 Macaulay became Baron Macaulay of Rothley. Though so vastly admired in his own time—he was buried in Westminster Abbey—his reputation has steadily declined. The chief charge against him is superficiality. It is to be feared that Macaulay was far more interested in being witty and brilliant than in telling the strict truth. His writings are addicted to paradox and antithesis for dramatic effect. The world is black and white for him. The very clarity of his style, which is at the opposite pole from the tortured prose of Carlyle, has proved only too faithful a mirror of the lack of depth and subtlety of his thoughts.

The differences between Macaulay and Carlyle can be pointedly exhibited by a comparison of the essay each of them wrote upon James Boswell. Macaulay, who is largely responsible for a century of injustice to the character of Johnson's biographer, says (1831) in highly characteristic fashion:

> The 'Life of Johnson' is assuredly a great, a very great, work. Homer is not more decidely the first of dramatists, Demosthenes is not more decidedly the first of orators, than Boswell is the first of biographers. He has no second. He has distanced all his competitors so decidedly that it is not worthwhile to place them. Eclipse is first, and the rest nowhere.
>
> We are not sure that there is in the whole history of the human intellect so strange a phenomenon as this book. Many of the greatest men that ever lived have written biography. Boswell was one of the smallest men that ever lived, and he has beaten them all.

He goes on to prove to his own satisfaction that it is only because Boswell was contemptible enough to be used as a doormat that he could write so great a book on Johnson. By brilliantly selected examples he would seem to prove his point.

Carlyle, on the other hand, in his piece on Boswell from his *Essay on Johnson* (1832) remarks on all of Boswell's many shortcomings that they are "visible, palpable to the dullest. His good qualities again, belong not to the time he lived in." He spurns the idea that a contemptible soul could author so great a book:

> Boswell was a hunter after spiritual notabilities, . . . he loved such, and longed, and even crept and crawled to be near them; . . . he did all this, and could not help doing it, had an open sense, an open loving heart, which so few have: where excellence

existed he was compelled to acknowledge it; was drawn towards it, and . . . could not but walk with it—if not as superior, if not as equal, then as inferior and lackey, better so than not at all. . . . Boswell wrote a good book because he had a heart and an eye to discern wisdom.

No one reading these two judgments can fail to understand how essentially superficial and unjust Macaulay seems. The findings of recent scholarship have only proved how right Carlyle was.

John Henry Newman (1801–1890)

In the Victorian escape to the Middle Ages, no man exercised a greater influence than did John Henry Newman. He was a man who made some enemies, but his friends were legion. He became in his time the chief threat to the English Church in the eyes of some of its adherents, but even his bitterest foes could not question his integrity as his religious beliefs altered from extreme Protestantism to Roman Catholicism.

He was born in London on February 21, 1801, the son of a banker. As a boy he was already a confirmed bookworm. But it was not until 1816 that his reflections on religion began. In that year he was converted to a belief in God by a Calvinistic group that he had joined; naturally at this period he was strongly anti-Catholic. He entered Trinity College, Oxford, during the same year; but the failure of his father's bank compelled him to live a meager existence on the scholarships he won. He decided upon the career of a clergyman.

In 1822 he was elected Fellow of Oriel College, Oxford. In the midst of his religious reading, the narrow Calvinism he had absorbed began to be liberalized. But he never relaxed his habit of self-examination. His life as a clergyman began in 1824 when he became the curate of Saint Clements, Oxford. During the ensuing years he occupied various clerical posts in the town of Oxford until 1831 when he was appointed Preacher to the University. During this time of his life he was becoming more and more convinced that the rationalistic approach to religion, which the English Church of his time prided itself in, was a mistaken one.

In pursuit of a change for the sake of his health, physical as well as spiritual, he went on a tour of the Mediterranean with a friend. On the way to Marseilles in June 1833 his ship was becalmed, and he wrote the most famous of his poems, the hymn, "Lead, Kindly Light" (sometimes known as "The Pillar of the Cloud")—in which the fervency of his belief can be plainly read. It was during this year that he also composed most of the poems collected as *Lyra Apostolica* (published 1863).

On his return to England he joined and became the leader of the new Oxford Movement. In a series of pamphlets, *Tracts for the Times*, he leveled his criticism against the ritual and dogma of the English Church, and in his Sunday sermons explained more popularly his intention. These tracts and sermons drew many followers to read and hear him, and by 1839 his influence at Oxford was at its height. Because of his pamphlets, the movement came to be known as "Tractarian." What Newman was trying to do was to find a position midway between Roman Catholicism and Protestantism.

But Newman's revulsion against the bareness of ceremony and the lack of spiritual beauty in the service of the English Church was drawing him, without his being aware of it, slowly but surely to the Roman Catholic Church. More and more he attempted to show that many of the tenets of the Roman Church were not inconsistent with membership in the English Church. One of the *Tracts* that maintained this argument was condemned by the University. As a result Newman and a number of his followers retired in 1842 to Littlemore, where they led almost a monastic life. In 1843 Newman published anonymously a retraction of all that he had written against the Roman Catholic Church, and on October 9, 1845, he became a Roman Catholic. In 1846, he was ordained as a priest in the church of his adoption, and awarded a degree of Doctor of Divinity by the Pope. He joined the order of Oratorians, and settled at the establishment of the order near Birmingham at Egbaston. There he remained for more than thirty years as head of the institution.

A brilliant series of his sermons delivered in 1850 on *The Present Position of Catholics in England* received wide attention, and involved him in a libel suit for an attack on an ex-friar. He was fined £100 and ordered by the court to pay £14,000 for the costs of the trial. But Newman's followers were now so numerous that this immense sum was raised by popular subscription in England and America. In addition admirers purchased for him a property at Rednal, where he was eventually buried. In 1852, he was invited to become Rector of the new Catholic University at Dublin. He retained this position for four years, and delivered there some of his most famous lectures, those on *The Idea of a University*.

The most troublesome event of his life was his quarrel with Charles Kingsley, a clergyman with a considerable and justified reputation as a minor poet and able novelist. In January 1864 Kingsley began the attack in *Macmillan's Magazine*, by insinuating that Newman defended lying in the cause of truth. Newman wrote to Kingsley, and received a half-apology. But then Kingsley stirred up even greater contention by issuing a pamphlet, *What Then Does Dr. Newman Mean?* It was in answer to this pamphlet that Newman wrote his beautiful autobiography, *Apologia Pro Vita Sua*, issued in a series of pamphlets (1864). Newman's sincerity and personal integrity are plain in every line, and his autobiography banished much of the enmity he had incurred at the time of his conversion to Catholicism.

In 1865 appeared his exquisite religious poem, *The Dream of Gerontius*, a poetic dialogue on the adventure of the soul after it has left its earthly habitation on its journey from earth to purgatory. It is Newman's most ambitious poetical work, and contains brilliant lyrical passages.

In 1870 he wrote a sequel to his autobiography in the *Grammar of Assent*. He was made Honorary Fellow of Trinity College, Oxford, and by 1878 there were few men in England more universally respected. In 1879 the Roman

Catholic Church bestowed upon him the highest honor (with the exclusion of the Papacy) it can bestow upon any man; he was appointed Cardinal. During the last eleven years of his life he wrote very little, probably because of the duties attached to his position. He died August 11, 1890.

It is interesting to reflect that Newman should have had so extended an influence on English thought even though his writings were, with few exceptions, all of a religious character. Even in the English Church, which his convictions forced him to leave, his influence has been great. Because of the Oxford Movement the English Church has gradually incorporated more and more of the mystical beauty in its service that was banished with the birth of Protestantism in England. And because of Newman's prestige there was a considerable increase in the numbers of Englishmen converted to Roman Catholicism, parrticularly among literary people—a tendency that has not yet diminished.

IMPORTANCE

Outside of ecclesiastical matters Newman's influence was hardly less significant. An appreciation of the spiritual intensity of the Middle Ages and of the formal beauties of medieval worship that Newman so much admired, deepened, through the attention which Newman was calling to them, the current of medievalism that was being fed through other philosophies by men like Carlyle, Ruskin, Rossetti, and Morris.

Few prose writers in an age that contained a considerable number of admirable stylists have excelled Newman. He achieved a wonderful ease and clarity in all he wrote, but added to these qualities unconsciously the charm and sweetness of his own personality, and a quiet music which was the reflection of the mildness of his own temperament. His works will be read if only for their high literary value. Of all of them, perhaps because of its nonreligious character, the *Idea of a University* is best known.

The *Idea of a University* was originally a series of nine lectures delivered at Dublin in May and June 1852. Pope Pius IX had agreed to the founding of a new Catholic university in Ireland, but the difficulty in raising the necessary funds among the impoverished Irish seemed insuperable. The Irish bishops themselves were unfriendly to the idea, and did nothing to encourage the formation of the university. On all sides Newman had to deal with spite, jealousy, or, at the best, indifference. He found himself head of a university that did not exist, and that seemed unlikely ever to exist. Despite all this discouragement, Newman made a great success of his lectures. In them he advocated a theory of higher education so enlightened that his ideas are held by some of our best theorists to be the wisest yet advocated. He believed that a university should offer the widest possible range of studies. Even though every subject cannot be studied by a given student, every student can only gain by being in the midst of an atmosphere provided by such a policy. Newman believed that scholars engaged in various pursuits would "learn to respect, to consult, to aid each other." Every student would thus learn to apprehend "the great outlines of knowledge." From this would flow what Newman would call a Liberal Education: "A habit of mind is formed which lasts through life, of which the attributes are freedom, equitableness, calmness, moderation, and wisdom." Above all he was convinced that knowledge was an end in itself, and for that reason he disapproved of any objective in education other than the forming of what he called "the gentleman." It was not the business of an education, he said, to make a man a Christian or a Catholic. A gentleman he defined as a man with "a cultivated intellect, a delicate taste, a candid, equitable, dispassionate mind, a noble and courteous bearing in the conduct of life."

John Ruskin (1819–1900)

John Ruskin was hardly more remarkable for his literary gifts than for the beauty of his character. It is not uncommon for writers to entertain high ideals on the subject of the sufferings of humanity, but not many men have been willing to sacrifice much for their principles. Ruskin, however, inherited a considerable fortune from his father and managed to dispose of most of it in support of various causes and people he believed in. Men like him invite animosity by their very goodness, and some of Ruskin's critics have been ingenious in attempting to "account" for his goodness on grounds that are intended to be discreditable. What is more tragic to record, Ruskin's belief in his ideals seemed more often than not to meet with failure. Nevertheless, many of the reforms he passionately advocated have since been realized. Moreover, the example of his personal unselfishness must continue to provide inspiration to others.

Ruskin began as a critic of the arts. His interest in the arts, however, led him by degrees to an increasing emphasis on social reform until he became almost entirely concerned with the latter. His writing, therefore, falls naturally into two periods. His early work is on matters esthetic; his later work is in political economy.

He was the only child of a prosperous wine merchant, and was born in London on February 8, 1819. From his autobiography, *Praeterita*, we have a vivid notion of Ruskin's childhood and education. In the Ruskin home, sobriety, honorableness, and self-control were the watchwords. Among the studies which his mother (who was his tutor) insisted upon, chief was the mastery of the Bible in its entirety. Perhaps no book is better calculated to impress a boy with a sense of literary style than the King James Bible, and that book young Ruskin came to know from cover to cover. In the garden of their house at Herne Hill, he was also encouraged to study and feel close to plant and animal life. By the age of eight, he was writing verse, and by ten he was already proficient in languages and mathematics. Later he understood that the great defect of his rearing was his dependence upon his parents. When he entered Christ Church College, Oxford, his mother took rooms near him and his father visited him on weekends. The three traveled extensively through the British Isles and on the Continent. While he was in Italy for two years as a boy, he devoted himself to a study of medieval painting. Later at college he read feverishly, did a great deal of drawing, and composed verse. At Oxford, he was awarded the Newdigate Prize for poetry. In short, as a boy and a young man, he was kept from the knowledge of anything but the beautiful and had virtually no contact with the realities of life. It is for this reason that when he became aware of the sordidness of the existence led in metropolitan slums, the shock was violent enough to twist his thinking into a completely new pattern.

Art Criticism: The first great experience of his life was the result of a gift of a volume of a poem called *Italy*, by the minor poet Rogers. The book contained designs by the English painter J. M. W. Turner. The discovery of Turner actually inaugurated Ruskin's career as a writer. As he tells us himself, one day in May 1842 (the year in which he took his degree at Oxford) he realized that all the drawing he had ever done was bad "because no one had ever told me to draw what was really there." This discovery led him to a comprehension of Turner's painting, and his veneration for the painter was so great that he decided to write a book to explain Turner's canvases to the world. In May 1843 appeared the first volume of *Modern Painters*, in which Ruskin in a series of brilliant word pictures reproduced in literary terms some of the finest of Turner's paintings. The result was that Ruskin made both himself and Turner famous. Englishmen were surprised to find that the old painter, whom they had forgotten or believed dead, was very much alive; and Ruskin taught them the true meaning of Turner's contribution to art. *Modern Painters* became a work in four volumes, the last of which did not appear before 1860. During the years between the first and fourth volumes of the series, Ruskin wrote nearly all his most important art criticism.

The prose of *Modern Painters* was something new in the Victorian Age. No writer has managed a complicated style with greater ease than Ruskin. His sentences are often quite long but always easy to follow and heavily laden with rich imagery and color. There is also a splendid music in the cadences of Ruskin's prose.

In addition to Ruskin's becoming recognized as an important stylist, his position as leading art critic was also established. Nevertheless his studies continued. He plunged himself into exhaustive research of the works of the old masters of the fine arts as well as of literature and began a habit of painstaking observation of the details of rock, seascape and landscape. With the second volume of *Modern Painters* (1846), he decided that mere form and color are not enough to achieve the highest reaches in art. The results of his desire to gain greater scope in understanding can be read in his next important book, *The Seven Lamps of Architecture* (1849), a defense of Gothic architecture. In the great cathedrals of the Middle Ages, he found seven qualities more perfectly expressed than in any of the edifices of other periods: sacrifice, truth, power, beauty, life, memory, and obedience. It is to be noted that this is the point in Ruskin's career in which moral values assume importance in the consideration of the arts. The volume itself was rendered more splendid by Ruskin's own drawings, and it is a work that has had considerable influence on the history of subsequent architecture.

But his masterwork is generally conceded to be *The Stones of Venice* (1851–1853), which continues his defense of Gothic architecture by arguing that the architecture of the Renaissance was the product of moral corruption and dishonesty. The superiority of the Gothic is due, he maintains, to the burning faith of the Middle Ages. *The Stones of Venice* contains some of Ruskin's most beautiful prose. Its marvelous descriptions and absorbing history of the beauties of Venice make it still the best guidebook to the Queen of the Adriatic. The description of Saint Mark's Cathedral has been one of the most profoundly admired passages in English prose. All the wealth and splendor of Ruskin's prose style meet in the celebrated chapter in perfect harmony. He begins by taking the reader into the quiet street leading to the close of an English cathedral. After reminding us of the neatness and sobriety and quietness of such a scene, he takes us back to the noisy alley in Venice leading to Saint Mark's, the Calla Lunga San Moisè. The disorder of the houses huddled together, the balconies jutting overhead, the fruit-trees thrusting branches over the walls, the melons heaped like cannon-balls in front of shops, the sights and smells from wineshop and fritter counter are brilliantly recreated for us. Then suddenly all this confusion gives way, the square before the cathedral opens before our eyes, and all the glory of Saint Mark's bursts upon us. Even the birds are different here, for we hear not the black hoarse-throated birds of England, but the soft doves of Italy, nestling amid the marble foliage, and mingling their delicate colors with the delicate colors of the cathedral. The dazzling light of gold, opal, and mother-of-pearl given forth by the sculptured stone shines upon us. But the Venetians themselves, who carry their trade up to the very doorways of their glorious cathedral, and swear, drink, and gamble in its very shadows, are all unaware of the beauty of their possession.

Social Criticism: Carlyle was delighted with *The Stones of Venice* and hailed it as a sermon in stone. Ruskin, on the other hand, whose studies of the relationship between art and morals had been leading him to an awareness of social problems, began to agree more and more with Carlyle's fundamental doctrine that work alone is the salvation for humanity. It was inevitable that the two men should be drawn into intimacy, and Ruskin willingly became a disciple of Carlyle's, though he went far beyond him in penetrating to the roots of social injustice. Through Carlyle he now understood that the factory system was depriving men and women of their natural decency and dignity. But it did not occur to Ruskin to look to great leaders for a cure. Nor did Ruskin, like other English philanthropists, place much stock in the importance of trying to awaken industrialists to a sense of benevolence.

From this time on, Ruskin began rapidly to meet the challenge of social evil. With F. D. Maurice, F. J. Furnivall, Thomas Hughes, and Charles Kingsley, he helped establish the Workingmen's College in London (1854). For the pupils of that institution he wrote *The Elements of Drawing* and *The Elements of Perspective* (1857–1859). In 1858 he delivered a lecture at Manchester on *The Political Economy of Art*. He was now busy studying economics. For the *Cornhill Magazine* (edited by the novelist Thackeray) he began a series of articles in 1860 collected as *Unto This Last*. Here he attacks the materialism of his age, its unenlightened self-interest, and the classical economics that defends things as they are. There is no wealth, Ruskin cries, but life itself. He deplores the philosophy that teaches men to accumulate money. He urges us to remember "that every atom of substance . . . is so much human life spent, which, if it issue in the saving present life or gaining more, is well spent, but if not is either so much life prevented or so much slain." He urges the establishment of trade schools, maintained by the government, and the opening of government factories and shops for every necessity of life; the training, and the subsequent employment in these shops, of the unemployed, and governmental provision for the old and the poverty-stricken.

Though we are familiar now with such demands, when Ruskin issued them the protest of the public was so great that the magazine was forced to terminate the series. Ruskin met with the same opposition when he wrote for *Fraser's Magazine* the articles collected as *Munera Pulveris* (1862–1863)— *Gifts of the Dust*. This time, too, the editor was compelled by his readers to cease printing anything of Ruskin's authorship. In this work, Ruskin proposes a system of economy erected on the foundation that a thing has value only when it is directed "towards the sustaining of life."

The hostility accorded his socialist theories only strengthened Ruskin's determination to develop them. His next important work in economics is *Sesame and Lilies* (1865), a collection of three lectures: *Sesame, Of King's Treasuries; Lilies, Of Queen's Gardens*; and *The Mystery of Life and Its Arts*. The last of these three is perhaps Ruskin's most perfect statement of his social philosophy; in it he exposes the indifference of mankind to the meaning and purpose of life. In the other two lectures he deals with matters connected with education, reading, and the place of women in society. In *A Crown of Wild Olive* (1866) Ruskin collected four lectures on *War, The Future of England, Work*, and *Traffic* (by which he meant the world of commerce).

In 1869 he was appointed Slade Professor of Fine Arts at the University of Oxford—a post he held until 1884. His lectures were greeted with such enthusiasm that numbers of his students joined him in building a road with their own hands as a testimonial to the dignity of labor. From his own income he established the Saint George's Guild, which he intended to serve as a model for a society, industrial and agricultural, and expended vast sums of money upon it. He also financed the establishment of various cooperatives for the making of handicrafts. But Ruskin's great benevolence did not end with his pet experiments. Many artists found him ready to provide them with substantial financial aid so that they might paint free from economic worry. The members of the Pre-Raphaelite Brotherhood were virtually his disciples. They not only received many profitable commissions from him but became the most fashionable painters of their time largely through Ruskin's public enthusiasm over their work. One of the Pre-Raphaelites, J. E. Millais, after achieving recognition chiefly because of Ruskin's endorsement of him, eloped with Ruskin's wife, and later married her.

It is at first puzzling to explain why in an age when so many writers were attacking social injustice and achieving popularity for their efforts, Ruskin should have met with so much indignation. The reason will be found in the violence of his approach. He disclaims any pleasure or hope of reward in the world to come for his goodness. But, as he says in *Fors Clavigera* (1871–1874), a series of letters addressed to the working men of England, "I simply cannot paint, nor read, nor look at minerals, nor do anything else that I like, and the very light of the morning sky . . . has become hateful to me, because of the misery that I know of." He indicts the present order of society for being one in which the rich are generally proud, covetous, unimaginative, insensitive, and ignorant, and the poor are idle, foolish, sensitive, imaginative, impulsively wicked, clumsy, and mercifully just.

The professional economist will have little respect for Ruskin's economics. To them he was too much concerned with moral issues, too much devoted to the arts, and insufficiently objective. But his deep compassion is likely to have a greater hold on the general reader than more scientific writers. Many of his ideas that were once consisidered insane are now part of the laws of Western Europe. And the noble example afforded by his own conduct will always inspire other idealists with hope for the future of humanity.

Autobiography: Ruskin's last work, *Praeterita* (1885–1889), an autobiography that he never finished, is in a class by itself among his writings. In the field of autobiography it has few rivals for its honesty, gentleness, whimsicality, and touching simplicity. As a work of art it is one of his greatest achievements.

The best-known passage deals with a period of his childhood when his father leased a house on Herne Hill. Ruskin's mother, vividly portrayed, took her chief delight in her garden, where she was forever planting something new or weeding out something old. She was his closest friend. From the time he was seven he had no existence apart from hers, partly because his father was too shy to take a hand in his education. Ruskin tells us of his excursions in the world of imagination started by the sights and sounds within the enclosure of the garden—the foliage, the stones, and the shapes of sky. But his father also was dear to him. He used to like to watch the elder Ruskin shave, and listen to stories about the great painters. When his father returned from business, he would give Mrs. Ruskin a full account of the day's happenings as they sat down to dinner in the late afternoon. The novels of Scott were greatly admired in the Ruskin household, although Mr. Ruskin was furious at Scott's having to turn out his books so rapidly in order to liquidate the bankruptcy of his publishing firm. But the elder Ruskin never forgave Scott for having concealed his partnership in the firm. The Bible, of course, was preferred by the Ruskins before all books. Mrs. Ruskin read through the Bible again and again with her son and explained everything that was beyond his immediate understanding.

IMPORTANCE

Ruskin's prose is in the tradition of poetic prose as practiced by De Quincey. He brought to all his writings a rich imagination and a passionate conviction. His devotion to the fine arts was responsible, also, for the unending procession of images and pictures that enliven and make vivid every page he wrote. Indeed, the chief criticism leveled against him has been the superabundance of his figures of speech, which has, in some opinion, brought his prose too near the domain of poetry.

Alfred Tennyson (1809–1892)

The most widely read of Victorian poets was born in Lincolnshire, the fourth son in the large family of the Reverend George Tennyson. Young Tennyson loved the landscape of his native countryside and was very unhappy when he was sent in 1816 to the Grammar School at Louth. He remained there until 1820, when finally he was permitted to return to the rectory at Somersby, his birthplace, to study under his father. The Tennyson children were encouraged to write, and two brothers, Frederick and Charles, were poets. As a boy, Tennyson was busy imitating Pope, Thomson, and Scott in his verse. By fourteen he had discovered Byron and was writing the gloomy rhetoric he admired in his model. Charles and Alfred Tennyson decided to issue a volume together, and this (which also included a few poems by Frederick) appeared in 1827 as *Poems by Two Brothers*. In 1828 the two budding poets entered Trinity College, Cambridge.

Tennyson was an exceedingly handsome boy but unaccountably shy. His first year at Cambridge was a very unhappy one. But in 1829 he won the Newdigate Prize for poetry with *Timbuctoo*, an old poem that his father had insisted he revise for the occasion. In his second year he began to make friends when he joined "The Apostles," a debating society in which he was soon very popular. But the most important of his Cambridge experiences was a friendship he formed with Arthur Henry Hallam, the son of a noted historian. Young Hallam was a spirited boy who knew how to break down Tennyson's reserve; moreover the former's religious convictions were firm and did much to bring the young poet out of the depression into which his agnosticism had plunged him.

Early Poems: A volume entitled *Poems, Chiefly Lyrical,* by Alfred Tennyson alone, appeared in 1830; it contained some excellent pieces and some very inferior ones. During the summer of that year Tennyson and Hallam made a trip to Portugal for the sake of handing over to Portuguese revolutionists funds which had been raised for their cause. Unhappily, the Reverend Tennyson died early in 1831, and thus his son's career at Cambridge was terminated. He now made his residence with his family, and occupied himself in reworking the poems he had already published, and in composing some new ones. The result of these labors was the volume of 1832, which was published as *Poems by Alfred Tennyson*—a collection containing some of his most exquisite pieces: "The Lady of Shalott," "The Palace of Art," "The Lotos-Eaters," and "Œnone."

One can read in Tennyson's lines at this period the profound influence exerted by Spenser and the nineteenth century Romantics; the example of Keats in compressing every line with poetic riches is particularly noticeable. But one also notes that unlike the Romantics Tennyson was an avid student of the Latin and Greek poets. There is more than a casual indebtedness to Homer in "The Lotos-Eaters" and something very close to Theocritus in "Œnone." Despite the high quality of the volume, it was bitterly attacked by the reviewers. Keats's name was still shamefully a subject for derision, and Tennyson was ridiculed as his disciple. Very few copies were sold, but the attacks of the critics made Tennyson well known, even though unfavorably. In fairness it must be admitted that the great poems in the volume had not yet the perfection Tennyson was later to give them, and that the volume did suffer somewhat from excessive decoration and sweetness.

"The Lady of Shalott" is one of the most perfect literary ballads in our language. Tennyson based his story on Malory's account of the love of Elaine for Lancelot. (Later in life Tennyson was to incorporate the Elaine story itself into the long *Idylls of the King.*) Part One sets the scene. Shalott, an island in the river, houses a tower in which lives the Lady of Shalott. On the river heavy barges go by and silken-sailed vessels skim quickly. On the mainland are the fertile fields where the farmers are busy over the soil. Only the reapers have ever heard the Lady of Shalott when she sings in the early morning, as her song echoes over the river that winds down to Camelot. In Part Two we learn that she never leaves her room in the tower. There she is busy weaving a tapestry from the sights that are reflected in her mirror. In it she sometimes catches a glimpse of damsels or a shepherd boy, a page, or a monk astride a horse. But she never looks out her window, for she has heard that a curse will come upon her if she ever looks towards Camelot. But when in the moonlight she sees a reflection of two young lovers, "I am half sick of shadows," she says. In Part Three Lancelot rides into the reflection of her mirror like a bowshot as he passes between the barley sheaves. In the clear weather his brow gleams, and his coal-black curls flow beneath his helmet:

> *She left the web, she left the loom,*
> *She made three paces thro' the room,*
> *She saw the water-lily bloom,*
> *She saw the helmet and the plume,*
>   *She looked down to Camelot.*
> *Out flew the web and floated wide;*
> *The mirror cracked from side to side;*
> *"The curse is come upon me," cried*
>   *The Lady of Shalott.*

Part Four finds the autumn far advanced. The Lady comes down to the river, discovers a boat, and writes her name about the prow. As the day sets, she lies down in the boat, loosens the chain, and allows herself to be borne down the river. Before she reaches the first house in Camelot, she dies. Upon the wharves and on the walls and balconies the people come out to see the strange beautiful sight. Lancelot is among them. He notes her beauty and asks that God in his mercy lend her grace.

"The Palace of Art" has been described as an allegory on the dangers of becoming too proud of the power of one's intellect. The narrator begins by saying that he had built his soul a lordly pleasure-house for merriment and carousal on a lofty crag. There he anticipated that his soul could reign in happy tranquility aloof from the world, and the soul seemed willing. The palace had four courts, each with its own lawn and fountain, cloisters, galleries, beauteous statues. The air was perfumed and the windows set with stained glass. In the palace in a room filled with choicest paintings stood the royal throne for the soul. There could be found Milton, Shakespeare, Dante, Homer, Plato, and Bacon. In the midst of this splendor the soul dwelt for three years. But in the fourth year the soul began to feel desolate and abandoned. In this desperate mood she left her wonderful dwelling and came down into the valley because there she had heard the sound of human footsteps. She threw her royal robes away and went to live in a simple cottage. But she has asked the poet not to destroy the palace, saying, "Perchance I may return with others when I have purged my guilt."

"The Lotos-Eaters" was inspired by the passage in the *Odyssey* describing Odysseus' visit with his men to the land of the Lotos-Eaters. The opening passage is a brilliant example of the use of the Spenserian stanza. As Ulysses (Odysseus) in his ship approaches the shore he sees that he is coming into a place in which it is always afternoon. The stream coming down the mountainside like smoke:

Along the cliff to fall and pause and fall did seem.

It is a land of dreams and quiet, "where all things always seem the same." About the keel of their ship the melancholy lotos-eaters come, bearing branches of the enchanted flower laden with its fruit. They give of these to the mariners. But those who eat the magic plant cease to wish to leave the land, and everything about them takes on the air of a dream. The sea, the oar, the long miles of ocean all seem too wearying to face. And they cry, "We will return no more."

"Œnone." In this exquisite lament the poet brilliantly retells the famous story of the Judgment of Paris. The setting is on the slopes of Mount Ida where lives the nymph Œnone. She sits there looking over the city of Troy. At first the mountain and the valleys are vividly described. Then the lament of Œnone follows. Each stanza begins after this with a variant of the refrain:

> *O mother Ida, many-fountained Ida,*
> *Dear mother Ida, harken ere I die*

It is the quiet of noonday as Œnone sings how her lover the "beautiful Paris, evil-hearted Paris" had come to her leading a black goat, and wearing a leopard skin on his shoulder. He held out to her in his palm a golden fruit with a delicious fragrance. Then he told her how this fruit on whose rind was engraven "for the most fair" ought really to be hers. But, he continued, this fruit had been thrown upon the board of the gods. Immediately a quarrel had arisen as to who deserved the prize. And on this very day Hera (Juno), Pallas Athena (Minerva), and Aphrodite (Venus) were coming to the spot, and Paris was to judge among them. Paris told her that she might hide among the pines and see and hear everything. The goddesses came in the deep mid-noon and stood naked before Paris. Hera offered him power if he awarded the prize to her. Then Pallas Athena offered wisdom and self-control if the prize were hers:

> *Self-reverence, self-knowledge, self-control,*
> *These three alone lead life to sovereign power.*

Œnone, hearing this, cried out to him to give the fruit to Pallas. But then Aphrodite stepped forth in all the glory of her beauty. With a subtle smile she simply said, "I promise thee the fairest and most loving wife in Greece." Œnone shut her eyes for fear, and when she looked again, Paris was giving the prize to Aphrodite. They all left, and Œnone has now been abandoned by Paris. She remembers with pain their hours of love, and knows that she must die now. But she wishes that first she might meet the hated Goddess of Discord, Eris, and tell her how she is abominated and remind her of all the mischief she has caused with her prank. Œnone knows that she will not die alone. She will go down into Troy and talk to the mad Cassandra, who hears always the sound of armed men in her ears.

Middle Poems: The hostile reception of this volume of Tennyson's in 1832 resulted in his refraining from publishing anything for ten years. It is thought that there may have been other reasons, too, for his long silence. He fell in love with Emily Sellwood, much to her parents' disapproval. His small income made marriage impossible in his own eyes, and he was in his forties before he felt justified in asking her to marry him. But during these years there was a greater shock than even this disappointment. In September 1833 Hallam, his beloved friend, died. It was many years before Tennyson recovered from this loss—if he ever did. The testimony of his long anguish can be read in the series of elegies he wrote upon Hallam, and which he arranged in 1850 as the poem *In Memoriam*.

That the public did not hear from him did not mean that he was not working. He was immersed in his private studies and writing all the time. Carlyle, who became his close friend, has told us of the great spiritual struggle through which he was fighting at this time of his life. At last in 1842 he appeared in print with two volumes entitled *Poems*, containing, besides remarkable revisions of earlier poems, many new important ones including "Morte d'Arthur," "Ulysses," "Locksley Hall," and "Break, Break, Break." With this publication Tennyson was at last accorded the recognition due him. He was recognized as one of the most masterful technicians in the whole history of English literature. Certainly in 1842 Tennyson proved equal to any demands of the poetic art, and demonstrated beyond question that he could write in any medium he chose, and place himself with ease in any land or time or historical setting. From this year on, his public grew larger and larger in the English-speaking world. The great Wordsworth proclaimed him as the greatest of living poets.

"Morte d'Arthur," later incorporated as part of the *Idylls of the King* under the title of "The Passing of Arthur," tells of the deathwound of King Arthur and the manner in which he departed from earth. Sir Bedivere takes the mortally wounded King from the battlefield to the nearby chapel. Arthur knows that his end has come even though the magician Merlin has prophesied that Arthur will come again. He bids his faithful knight, the last of his Round Table to survive on his side, throw the sword Excalibur into the lake. But the sword is so beautiful that Sir Bedivere cannot find it in himself to discard it as has been commanded. Twice he conceals it, pretending to the dying King that it has been hurled into the lake; and twice the King recognizes that Sir Bedivere is not telling the truth. The third time, however, the remorseful knight does as he has been bidden. Whereat an arm rises out of the water and catches the sword by the hilt, brandishes it three times, and disappears with it in the lake. Sir Bedivere gives a full account to Arthur of what has happened. Now the King asks Sir Bedivere to bear him on his shoulders to the margin of the lake. Arrived there, they find a dusky barge "dark as a funeral scarf from stem to stern." Among the dark forms on the decks stand three queens with golden crowns. Arthur asks Sir Bedivere to place him in the barge. The three queens now tend to the King's wound.

Bedivere asks what is to become of himself, now that the Round Table is no more. Arthur replies:

> The old order changeth, yielding place to new,
> And God fulfils himself in many ways,
> Lest one good custom should corrupt the world.

The King bids Sir Bedivere pray for his soul. The barge now departs with Arthur to the island of Avilion. Sir Bedivere stands on the shore until the boat disappears on the horizon, "revolving many memories." When this poem was enlarged as "The Passing of Arthur," it contained among its new lines a wonderful passage:

> I found Him in the shining of the stars,
> I marked Him in the flowering of His fields,
> But in His ways with men I find Him not . . .
> . . . For why is all around us here
> As if some lesser god had made the world,
> But had not force to shape it as he would?

The poem shows how perfectly Tennyson has mastered blank verse.

"Ulysses," based upon a passage in Dante's *Divine Comedy*, is also in blank verse and is one of Tennyson's most admired poems. Dante pictures Ulysses as discontented after retiring to private life on his return to Ithaca, and it is this idea that inspired the English poet. The poem is a soliloquy in which the hero reflects on how little it profits him to be idle, sitting with his aged wife by a quiet hearth, and meting out laws to a savage race unable to understand their purpose. He remembers the great enjoyment of his adventures, the exhilarating hazards of his travel. He cries in lines that are justly famous:

> I am a part of all that I have met.
> Yet all experience is an arch wherethrough
> Gleams that untraveled world, whose margin fades
> Forever and forever when I move.

He decides to start out once more, therefore, and leave to his son Telemachus the task of ruling his people. His own must be forever the life of adventure. Even though he and his mariners are old, "Some work of noble note may yet be done." His purpose now is:

> To sail beyond the sunset, and the baths
> Of all the western stars . . .
> It may be we shall touch the Happy Isles,
> And see the great Achilles, whom we knew.

Until death overtakes them they will strive to seek, and not to yield.

"Locksley Hall" is one of the most difficult of Tennyson's important poems to evaluate, it alternates passages of great beauty with passages of low poetic quality. It is written in swinging trochaic octameter couplets. The speaker in the poem is a soldier, who takes leave of his comrades, until he shall hear their bugle, to gaze upon Locksley Hall where so many happy hours of his adolescence were spent. There, as a boy, he nourished his youth "with the fairy tales of science" and clung to the hope that science offered the world:

> *When I dipt into the future far as human eye could see,*
> *Saw the vision of the world and all the wonder that would be.*

But:

> *In the spring a fuller crimson comes upon the robin's breast;*
> *In the spring the wanton lap-wing gets himself another crest;*
>
> *In the spring a livelier Iris changes on the burnished dove;*
> *In the spring a young man's fancy lightly turns to thoughts of love.*

So he fell in love with his beautiful "cousin," Amy. "Love took up the glass of Time," and the moments ran lightly; "Love took up the harp of life," and smote it until the chord of self passed in music out of sight. But Amy was not able to withstand the commands of her parents, and agreed to marry a wealthy clownish man who will hold her, after his passion is spent, "something better than his dog, a little dearer than his horse." The young soldier now curses the social customs that sin against youth. He asks where comfort for him now can lie, realizing:

> *this is truth the poet sings,*
> *That a sorrow's crown of sorrow is remembering happier things.*

He tortures himself by imagining Amy lying sleepless beside her drunken husband while the rain is on the roof. But in the end, even her sorrowful memories will pass because of her baby. When she grows old she will try to stamp out of her daughter's heart all the best instincts, just as her parents had done to her. Where then can the disappointed lover turn? He had enlisted in the Army, hoping to die in battle. But alas! the nations snarl at each other but do not fight. Had he not better go back to his earlier love, Science? In his youth he used to dream of the wonderful airplanes that would be invented, "pilots of the purple twilight." He even foresaw battles in the air, and a World War, after which there would be formed a World Federation to maintain perpetual peace. But all this is too far in the distant future. What can it mean to him in his sorrow now? He tries to remember that though "the individual withers, . . . the world is more and more." His comrades now are calling him. What is he to do? Should he leave civilization and fly away to savage shores, somewhere in the "summer isles of Eden lying in dark purple spheres of sea?" Should he not go there and raise a healthy race of savages? What folly! For the savage is lower than a Christian child:

> *Better fifty years of Europe than a cycle of Cathay.*

And so he decides to cling to the hopes of the future and to the gallant promises of science. Thus he leaves Locksley Hall forever. A storm is arising. He goes with a wish that a thunderbolt may fall on this symbol of his past.

"Break, Break, Break." This song is addressed to the sea. The fisherman's boy "shouts with his sister at play," the sailor lad "sings in his boat," the stately ships pass by, but the poet is haunted by the memory of a vanished hand and a stilled voice. The tender grace of a past time will never return.

Financial reverses, due to unwise investments, now plunged the poet into serious illness. In 1845, however, he was saved by a pension from the government of £200 a year. With some security thus assured him, he began to compose again. *The Princess,* a "medley" on the education of women, was published in 1847. The story, though charming, illustrates the inability of women to compete in the field of the intellect with men—an unenlightened view that has been thoroughly disproved in the twentieth century. This work is perhaps the first in which Tennyson exhibits his chief shortcoming: his thinking is essentially on a mediocre plane. It is only as an artist that Tennyson is superb, and that portion of his poetry in which he did not set himself up as a thinker is the portion (and that is large) which is bound to survive. Characteristically, it is not the bulk of *The Princess* that is read any longer, but seven songs which interpolate the action of the story. These songs, indeed, are among the most amazing in the literature of lyrics. "Sweet and Low" is a wonderful lullaby. "The Splendor Falls" is a brilliant bugle-song, with the refrain:

Blow, bugle; answer, echoes, dying, dying, dying.

Just as the echoes bound from cliff and scar, so:

Our echoes roll from soul to soul,
And grow for ever and for ever.

The third song, "Tears, Idle Tears," is a wonderful achievement—a song without rhyme. It will strike a chord in every human heart:

Tears, idle tears, I know not what they mean,
Tears from the depth of some divine despair
Rise in the heart, and gather to the eyes,
In looking on the happy autumn-fields,
And thinking of the days that are no more.

Such tears are fresh, sad, and strange, and as dear as "remembered kisses after death," and deep as first love, "and wild with all regret"; they are a death in life. The fourth song, "Home They Brought Her Warrior Dead," is a rather sentimental narrative. The widow cannot weep at the sight of her dead husband, and if she does not weep she will die; at last his child is placed upon her knee, and then "like summer tempest came her tears." The fifth song, "Ask Me No More," is the song of the woman in love to the man she loves. She would not yield herself to him, but

> *I strove against the stream and all in vain;*
> *Let the great river take me to the main.*
> *No more, dear love, for at a touch I yield;*
> *Ask me no more.*

The sixth song, "Now Sleeps the Crimson Petal," is another song of love. Now in the evening when the lily slips into the bosom of the lake:

> *So fold thyself my dearest, thou, and slip*
> *Into my bosom and be lost in me.*

The last song, "Come Down, O Maid, From Yonder Mountain Height," is a love song full of beautiful description of the countryside.

In 1850 appeared Tennyson's *In Memoriam*, which the Victorians chose to consider his greatest work. Actually it is a series of poems, as has been said, written in the depths of depression from time to time ever since Hallam had died in 1833. As they were published, they were not arranged in order of their composition. Of necessity there is a lack of unity in the volume, and the judgment which has placed *In Memoriam* by the side of "Lycidas" and "Adonais" as the greatest of English elegies is more enthusiastic than discriminating. The verse is uneven in quality; indeed *In Memoriam* is made up of some of Tennyson's best and worst writing. The leading idea, throughout the stanzas, is a reflection on the relation of mortal man to the destiny of death. It is a poetical argument to sustain the poet's belief in the immortality of the soul. Though upholding no dogma, Tennyson feels that without such a belief mankind can have no hopes. It is a long work, and is studded with many passages which are now well known. Of these we quote some of the best:

> *'Tis better to have loved and lost*
> *Than never to have loved at all.*
>
> *How fares it with the happy dead?*
>
> *Short swallow-flights of song, that dip*
> *Their wing in tears, and skim away.*
>
> *Ring out, wild bells, to the wild sky!*
>
> *Ring out the old, ring in the new,*
> *Ring, happy bells, across the snow . . .*
> *Ring out old shapes of foul disease,*
> *Ring out the narrowing lust of gold;*
> *Ring out the thousand wars of old,*
> *Ring in the thousand years of peace!*

Later Poems: Tennyson's worries were now over, and the many years remaining to him were rich in achievement, happiness, and honors. Oxford University gave him the degree of D.C.L. in 1885. By that time he had already been elevated to the peerage by Victoria as Lord Tennyson (1883). His fame was so widespread that Tennyson, always a shy man, was forced to escape the hosts of his admirers who were forever visiting him by building himself a home at Blackdown in Surrey. Among his good friends, in addition to Carlyle, were Browning, Prince Albert, Gladstone, Huxley, and Ruskin.

His later poetry includes the following volumes: *Maud* (1855), *Idylls of the King* (1850, 1860, 1872, 1885), *Enoch Arden* (1864), *Ballads and Poems* (1880), *Tiresias* (1885), *Locksley Hall Sixty Years After* (1886), *Demeter* (1889), and *The Death of Œnone* (1892). Besides these he wrote a number of closet dramas that had for a time success upon the stage because of the great actors who participated in their performance: a trilogy, *Queen Mary* (1875), *Harold* (1877), and *Beckett* (1884); and *The Cup* (1881); *The Promise of May* (1882); and *The Foresters* (1892). These plays as literature are all worthy of the great poet who wrote them, whatever their inadequacy on the modern stage.

In the volumes, listed above, a certain number of individual poems deserve special notice. "The Charge of the Light Brigade," the quality of which may be obscured because so many schoolboys had to memorize it, is a spirited, manly song on the bravery of six hundred gallant soldiers during the Crimean War. "Milton" is a tribute to the "mighty-mouthed inventor of harmonies," the "organ-voice of England." "The Higher Pantheism" is a confession of faith in the supremacy of God; "the eye of man cannot see," nor can the ear of man hear; but if men could see and hear, they would know that the sun, moon, stars, seas, hills, and plains are only manifestations of Him. *Maud* contains some celebrated lyrics, particularly the one beginning "Come into the garden, Maud." "The *Revenge*," "a Ballad of the Fleet," is a lively narrative taken from Sir Walter Ralegh's account of the last fight of the *Revenge* when it sailed under the command of Sir Richard Grenville; the English ship attacks alone the whole Spanish fleet, and so well that the Spaniards for a while are forced to withdraw and wait, encircling her; Grenville would sink the ship but his men plead that he do not; Grenville surrenders, for the sake of their wives and children but dies aboard the Spanish ship; after he is buried, a storm at night sinks the *Revenge*. "The Throstle" is a poem on the bird that announces the coming of summer. "By an Evolutionist" is a statement of Tennyson's reaction to the Darwinian theories; he accepts the doctrine of evolution, but is convinced that there is a higher being than man; in his old age the poet stands on the heights of his life "with a glimpse of a height which is higher." "The Flower in the Crannied Wall" also affirms the poet's belief in God and his conviction that the mystery of Divinity cannot be solved by reason; as for the flower:

> *. . . if I could understand*
> *What you are, root and all, and all in all,*
> *I should know what God and man is.*

"St. Agnes' Eve" is another religious poem, in which the poet waits like a bride on Saint Agnes' Eve for the bridegroom to appear; the bridegroom, of course, is the Lord. The *Idylls of the King* is one of Tennyson's longest works, a series of tales about King Arthur and the adventures of various of his knights; the main thread holding the poem together is the sinful love of Lancelot for Queen Guinivere, the attempt of Lancelot to fight against that love, and the destruction and corruption which overtake the entire court because of Lancelot's betrayal of his King. *Rizpah* is an attempt on Tennyson's part to write in colloquial English the plea of the mother of a criminal for the life of her son who is about to be hanged.

At the end of the volume of the complete works of Tennyson one always finds one of his last poems, "Crossing the Bar," placed there at his request. It is his view of what death will be like. The thought of death evokes the feeling of sunset and evening star and a quiet sea. He asks that there be no sadness when he embarks on his final journey:

> *For though from out our bourne of Time and Place*
> *The flood may bear me far,*
> *I hope to see my Pilot face to face*
> *When I have crost the bar.*

IMPORTANCE

A fair evaluation of Tennyson will insist that English poetry never had a finer artist than he, when he was satisfied to be only an artist. However profound his intellectual expression may have seemed to the Victorians, it is not so to us. Nevertheless if all of his inferior writing is discounted, there remains in the great work of Tennyson an imposing bulk of fine poetry such as few of our best poets can equal. He is at his greatest as a musician with the language, and as an incomparable painter of scene.

Robert Browning (1812–1889)

The opinion of Robert Browning's work has been as immoderate as his own good health of spirit. Some people have been violent in insisting that he is the best of the Victorian poets; others have been no less so in asserting that he is no poet at all. But it might well be asked, as Samuel Johnson once asked concerning the greatest of the Neoclassical poets, if Browning is not a poet, who is? The difficulty that the Victorian public professed in understanding Browning was due as much to the originality of his style as to the unconventional quality of his thinking. With the passage of time, however, both these obstacles to understanding him have been removed. Once the reader apprehends that Browning's appeal is exclusively to the ear—never to the eye surveying the printed page—the difficulty in following him is dissipated. Not that Browning used the language of the street. No poet, perhaps, could succeed in writing great poetry by faithfully imitating the actual speech of men and women; great poetry requires far too much compression for that. But Browning did catch, in all their varying moods, the rhythms in which men and women actually speak.

A great deal of nonsense has been written about Browning. The most common untruth which criticism has repeated concerning him is that one must admire him for the power of his message rather than for his technical ability. Browning wrote a great deal of poetry—and the level he maintained is perhaps consistently higher than that of any other nineteenth century poet—and it is to be feared that many critics are familiar only with the few songs and monologues reprinted in all anthologies. But the reader of Browning's complete works will come to realize that, when he chose, Browning was as superb and as delicate a technician in English verse as Tennyson could be at his best. Yet critics have not ceased to compare him unfavorably with Tennyson in this respect. It would be fair to say that Browning often chose, because his subject required it, to avoid delicacy. No poet has been more convincingly harsh, dramatic, or grotesque when the occasion demands it. It is also true that to a much greater degree than Tennyson, Browning preferred to create the "art that conceals art."

Browning was born May 7, 1812, in Camberwell, at that time a suburb of London, the son of a clerk in the Bank of England. Robert lived for twenty-eight years in his father's home there. The elder Browning was a gifted amateur of fine arts and literature, and both of the poet's parents were Nonconformists. The latter fact accounts for Browning's not attending Oxford or Cambridge. But he did not, in consequence, miss any great educational opportunities. His parents' library was rich in wonderful books—curious, erudite, and out-of-the-way books, such as he might not have readily met in a university. Most of all was Browning fortunate in his father. The elder Browning, who lived until Robert was sixty-five, remained an active and valuable friend to his son's career, and financed it for many years until some twenty years after he began to issue his volumes Browning was able to find a publisher who would risk publishing him. It was Browning's father who awoke a passion in the boy for medieval legend, Renaissance story, and the curiosa of the Talmud. On the other hand, Browning's mother was a skilled musician, and it is owing to her that love of music played an important part in his life. He was still a boy when he was already haunting the art galleries. He did attend London University for a few months (1829–1830), but his education in art, history, music, philosophy, and the classics, as well as his taste for scholarship, can be attributed almost entirely to the environment of his home. The marvelous sanity and balance in Browning's nature which have made him the most virile of nineteenth century poets, were maintained through his zest for exercise and horsemanship.

Keats and Shelley, whom he discovered when he was a boy, were responsible for his determination to become a poet. His first volume, *Pauline*, was issued in 1833, and did not find one purchaser. It is a remarkable poem for a boy of twenty-one, but is even more remarkable for being so characteristic of its author. To a certain extent the direction of Browning's career as a poet is already indicated by his first work. *Pauline* shows Browning as the historian of the human soul, and such he was to remain for the rest of his career. The style as well as the ideas shows how much he was at this time under the influence of Shelley. But this study of the growth and disintegration of a human spirit also demonstrates Browning's conviction that poetry should aim at a naturalness of idiom.

In 1833 he made a trip to Russia, and for a time was still undecided as to whether he should make a career in diplomacy, the fine arts, music, or poetry. But his next volume, although it was completely ignored by the critics, was recognized for its quality by a small but discriminating circle of literary men, and his future in poetry seemed thereby settled.

No man ever lived who was more social than Browning, and eventually he came to know everyone. Among his good friends he counted first Carlyle (who thought Browning looked more like a poet than anyone he had ever met), Leigh Hunt, Walter Savage Landor, and later, Wordsworth and Dickens. This second volume, which won him his first public, was *Paracelsus* (1835). It is the first of Browning's great works. One of the poet's favorite ideas is the theme for this dramatic poem: that the test of spiritual worth is the extent to which the soul strives for good, not the extent to which it achieves it. *Paracelsus* was based on the biography of a sixteenth century physician about whom Browning had read in various recondite books. It follows its hero's progress to fame, his struggle against charlatans, his weakness in compromising with his principles, and his eventual spiritual triumph in the very midst of worldly failure. The impress of Shelley's muse is even stronger in passages of this work, but the whole could not have been written by anybody but Browning.

Among the readers who were deeply moved by Browning's second volume was Macready, the greatest living interpreter of Shakespeare on the Victorian stage. He was convinced that the poet possessed talents for the drama of a high order, and urged Browning to write for the stage. As a result Browning's *Strafford* was presented at Covent Garden in May of 1837. After that Browning wrote a number of other plays: *King Victor and King Charles* (1842), *The Return of the Druses* (1843), *A Blot on the 'Scutcheon* (1843), *Colombe's Birthday* (1844), *Luria* (1846), and *A Soul's Tragedy* (1846). In the midst of writing these, Browning had a misunderstanding with Macready over the details in the presentation of *A Blot on the 'Scutcheon*, and by degrees he grew less and less interested in writing for the stage. He had had only the most moderate success with his plays, and it is just as well for posterity that he decided to turn away from the theater. As interesting as all of these works are, only *A Blot on the 'Scutcheon* has acting possibilities. Macready was not entirely correct in imagining that Browning possessed the qualifications for being a successful man of the theater. It is true that Browning is not only the most dramatic of English poets and one of the subtlest of psychologists as well as a fascinating storyteller throughout his career, but his genius is for compression and the dramatic moment. He had not the interest or the ability to deal with the problems of a full-length play. As a matter of fact, the best of his plays was written when he had given up the theater for some ten years, and is cast in a single act—*In a Balcony* (1855).

Bells and Pomegranates: In the meantime, his father was making possible the publication of his poems. From 1841 to 1846 Browning issued a series of volumes, which he entitled *Bells and Pomegranates*. This name was intended to indicate an attempt in alternating "music with discoursing, sound with sense, poetry with thought." Number One of the series contained *Pippa Passes* (1841), a poem in dramatic form and demonstrating already that love of Italy which was to be paramount in Browning's life. (He had made a visit there in 1838.) *Pippa Passes* is Browning's first completely achieved masterpiece. The idea on which the work is held together is charming. Pippa is a guileless factory girl of Asolo, who, at the opening of the work rises from her bed with the determination that on this, her one holiday in the year, she is going to make the most of her free time by pretending herself to be in the situation of the four happiest people in town. As the day proceeds, she passes by the window of each place, singing the while an innocent song out of the fullness of happiness in her heart. She is completely oblivious to the truth that none of these beings is happy as she imagines them all to be, and that as she passes each, an intense struggle of the soul is going on indoors. Nor does she know that it is her song that decides the outcome of that soul-struggle. Actually it is she who wields an influence over the fate of people she imagines so far above her in the security of happiness. At the day's close, ignorant that she has saved the souls of these people, she sighs to think how her day has been wasted.

The four episodes that are strung together on the thread of Pippa's singing are dramatic in the extreme. The first deals with the sinful adulterous love of Ottima and Sebald, who have just murdered Ottima's old husband; it is Pippa's song that saves them from being drawn into the quicksand of self-justification. In the second episode, Jules, a disillusioned sculptor, is about to cast off the daughter of a prostitute who has been foisted upon him as an innocent high-born lady, when Pippa's lyric makes him understand that his wife's salvation lies in his hands. In the third episode, the flaming revolutionary patriot, Luigi, to please his mother, is about to give up his high but dangerous exploit of assassinating a tryant, but the words of Pippa's song recall him to his ideal. In the last scene, an old ecclesiast is saved from crime and compromise with the world's villainy by Pippa's innocence. One of the best known songs in our poetry is Pippa's first song:

> *The year's at the spring,*
> *And day's at the morn;*
> *Morning's at seven;*
> *The hillside's dew-pearled;*
> *The lark's on the wing;*
> *The snail's on the thorn;*
> *God's in his heaven—*
> *All's right with the world!*

The third series of *Bells and Pomegranates* (1842) included among its "Dramatic Lyrics" some of Browning's most admired poems: "Cavalier Tunes," "My Last Duchess," and "Soliloquy of the Spanish Cloister." The two last named are cast in a form that Browning in this volume had finally hit upon, the form that was to prove the most perfect medium of expression for his ideas and interests—the *dramatic monologue.*

In these dramatic monologues, there is always some individual speaking (a character historical or imagined) who, in relating some incident in his life, reveals to the reader the inmost secrets of his soul. Sometimes the speaker is a saint, sometimes he is a villain, often he is an admixture of wickedness and godliness. But always the revelation of his inner character is made (as in life it is always made to those who have understanding) without the awareness of the speaker himself. The self-deceived hypocrite exposes his ugliness in the very midst of his self-esteem; the humble, self-depreciating man or woman does not succeed in concealing the spark of divinity shining in his bosom. In Browning's hands the dramatic monologue forms one of the most exciting chapters in the history of English poetry.

"Cavalier Tunes" is a series of three brisk lyrics, "Marching Along," "Give a Rouse," and "Boot and Saddle" (originally called "My Wife Gertrude"). All three convey magnificently the strong-hearted dash of the Cavaliers who were loyal to the cause of King Charles I. "Marching Along" has as its refrain:

> *Marching along, fifty-score strong,*
> *Great-hearted gentlemen, singing this song.*

and cordially sends the churlish leaders of the Puritans to the Devil—Pym, Hampden, and Cromwell's men; the chorus is the cry, "God for King Charles!" "Give a Rouse" is a song in praise of King Charles for all his kindness bestowed on his followers. "Boot and Saddle" is an exciting song in which the horseman spurs on his steed to reach his castle while there is time to save it; his wife Gertrude laughs in his absence at all talk of surrendering their home to the enemy.

"My Last Duchess" is perhaps the most celebrated of Browning's dramatic monologues. It is almost incredible that Browning succeeds in telling so much of his story and revealing so much of two human characters as he does in these fifty-six lines of rhymed couplets. The Duke of Ferrara is escorting around his castle the envoy from a count, his prospective father-in-law, and at the moment is exhibiting with pride his collection of paintings. They have paused before a portrait of the Duke's late wife. The Duke has every appreciation for the painting as a work of art, and having drawn the curtain before it, begins to explain the look on his former Duchess' face. Such an expression of joy was common to her. Perhaps the painter, Fra Pandolf, paid her some pretty compliments while she was sitting for him. Knowing it but courtesy, she yet could feel pleasure at it. She had a heart, says the Duke, "too soon made glad." Everything seemed to please her. And what was intolerable was that she seemed to feel no greater worth attached to being married to the Duke than the pleasure she experienced when some servant brought her a bough of cherries or when she enjoyed a ride around the terrace on her little white mule. The Duke did not mind so much her thanking people as that she seemed not to value any more than such trivial kindnesses his gift of a nine-hundred-years-old name. It was beneath the Duke's dignity to blame her, for in that there would be some stooping, and he chooses never to stoop. At last he "gave commands" and then all her smiles stopped. The two men now leave the portrait, and the Duke expresses his confidence that the Count is not going to prove miserly in awarding a dowry with his daughter, though, of course, it is the girl herself that the Duke is interested in. In the last lines he calls attention to another work of art in his collection, a rare bronze showing Neptune taming a sea-horse.

Browning deliberately was indefinite as to whether the Duke's "commands" were an order for the Duchess' execution or his arrangements to have her immured in a convent. What was important to Browning was the self-revelation of the speaker, a man of refined, artistic taste, but thoroughly inhuman, and coldly materialistic. We are able to see the Duchess as a gracious, charming woman, too exquisite to be understood and appreciated by her arrogant husband.

"Soliloquy of the Spanish Cloister," written in stanzaic form, also has a contemptible man as the speaker. The scene is a cloister of a monastery. Here, as often in Browning, the setting is sketched in so unobtrusively that one cannot point to a descriptive passage in the entire poem, even though the picture could not be clearer if it were painted. The speaker, a monk whose name we never learn, is standing in the late afternoon in a shadow of the cloister looking over the garden where Brother Lawrence is busy with his flowers. At the end of the garden is a low wall beyond which the speaker can see the town fountain beside which two Spanish girls, Dolores and Sanchicha, sit gossiping. There is no one in the world whom the speaker hates so much as Brother Lawrence:

> *If hate killed men, Brother Lawrence,*
> *God's blood, would not mine kill you!*

Everything Brother Lawrence does irritates this monk. He is furious with him for being so busy with his flowers and plants. He is annoyed at the greeting Brother Lawrence gives him at table, and the latter's talk of the weather and crops. He is angered at the cleanliness of Brother Lawrence as the latter cleans his spoon and goblets and shines them until they look as though they were new. The speaker interrupts this pouring-out of his hatred to laugh with delight because one of the lilies has just snapped from its stem. Besides, he is sure, if he could be seeing Brother Lawrence's face just now, it would turn out that he's not the saintly gardener he pretends to be, but is actually watching with carnal desire the two girls by the fountain. Yet, despite his irritating godliness, Brother Lawrence overlooks many pious formalities which the speaker indulges in, such as laying the knife and fork crosswise before dining. The speaker has done what he can against his fellow monk. He has nipped on the sly all the fruit flowers that he could. He even dreams of being able to prove to Brother Lawrence on his deathbed that for all his goodness he is a heretic. He thinks also of tempting Brother Lawrence's soul by inserting an indecently illustrated French novel of his own possession among the fruit where Brother Lawrence will be compelled to see it. As a last resort, the speaker considers even making an agreement with Satan that would enable him to blast Brother Lawrence's plants. But now the vesper bell is ringing, and the speaker automatically breaks into evening prayer, muttering under his breath the while, "Gr-r-r- you swine!"

Only Browning would dare to open and close a poem with "Gr-r-r-." In this poem again we perceive that the object of the speaker's disapproval has a beautiful character, and that the speaker, for all his self-justification and good opinion of himself, is a thoroughly corrupted and debased person. The fact that Brother Lawrence emerges as a beautiful soul should free Browning from any foolish charge that he was prejudiced against ecclesiasts. Browning did not especially like any institution that stunted the soul of the individual, but no man ever wrote in prose or poetry who was so completely free from every kind of prejudice as Browning. In the enormous gallery of portraits he has painted in his poetry, we find as many exquisite beings as lost souls. The poet had the uncanny ability to penetrate to the psychology of every kind of human being.

The seventh series of *Bells and Pomegranates* (1845) was entitled *Dramatic Romances and Lyrics*. Among the celebrated poems it contained were "The Lost Leader," "The Bishop Orders his Tomb," "Home Thoughts from Abroad," and "How They Brought the Good News from Ghent to Aix."

"The Lost Leader" was inspired by the example of men like Wordsworth who give up the idealism of their youth in middle age to become bulwarks of respectability and conservatism, the poem is written in a striking virile rhythm, beginning:

> *Just for a handful of silver he left us,*
> *Just for a riband to stick in his coat—*

a reference to such honors as the Laureateship and the income therefrom, with which former idealists have been bought up by the government. Browning reflects on all that such a man loses for the little silver given him. We would have followed the great leader anywhere. We learned his language and made him our pattern. Shakespeare, Milton, Burns, and Shelley were with us, while this man alone breaks from the freemen. We shall march on to our victory and freedom, but no longer to his music. Let us blot out his name and record his soul as lost. Let him never try to come back to us, for we would suspect him. Let him rather fight on in his new way until he receives the new knowledge. And may heaven pardon him, first of all sinners against the human soul!

"The Bishop Orders his Tomb" is a brilliant monologue in blank verse, giving us, as Ruskin said, the quintessence of the "Renaissance spirit—its worldliness, inconsistency, pride, hypocrisy, ignorance of itself, love of art, of luxury, and of good Latin." The speaker is a very worldly bishop lying on his deathbed and surrounded by his illegitimate offspring. His only thoughts are for the magnificent tomb he wishes raised for him in St. Praxed's Church. He has left plenty of money to insure the purchase of the finest marble, "Peach blossom." It would be torture to him even after death to think that his stone should not be in every respect more magnificent than that of Gandolf, his hated rival, who is buried in the Church. He attempts to force an oath from his children to carry out his wishes, and bribes them with the thought of the fortune he is leaving them. But he does not believe their word after all, and is sure they will try to swindle him by buying the cheapest of stones. Exhausted with the strain of his pleading, he gives them his blessing and bids them go. His last thought is his anticipation of watching in death Gandolf from his tomb to see whether his enemy will not envy him his fine marble and perfect Latin inscriptions, just as Gandolf in life envied the Bishop his mistress.

"Home Thoughts from Abroad" is an exquisite lyric in praise of the English spring. Its opening is already classic:

> *Oh to be in England*
> *Now that April's there . . .*

"How They Brought the Good News from Ghent to Aix" captures in its rhythms more wonderfully, perhaps, than any other poem in English the sense of galloping horses. There seems to be no historical basis for the events recorded in this poem, but it is an incident that could easily have occurred during the War of the Netherlands. Three men set off on horseback as the moon sets, riding hard out of Ghent to save their town. They ride through Boom, Düffeld, Mecheln, Aershot, Hasselt, Loos, Tongres, and Dalhelm to the ancient city of Aix. The true hero is the horse Roland. The other two horses do their best but drop dead on the road. But Roland sustains the rigors of the wild ride, and arrives in Aix with blind distended eyes and nostrils as he falls exhausted in the marketplace. His reward is to be voted the last measure of wine the city had left.

In this year, 1845, Browning began his correspondence with Elizabeth Barrett, a well-established poet, who was an invalid. By the time he met her, five months later, he was deeply in love with her. For many years she had been confined to her room through the excessive concern of her father. Elizabeth Barrett fell in love with Browning too, but she was very reluctant to accept his affection out of dread of burdening him with a wife whose days were numbered. The doctors did not extend any hope for their patient, who was plainly dying of tuberculosis. But Browning was too virile a human being to be deterred by her illness. He swept her off her feet during his brief courtship, gave her a new interest in life, and insisted that she marry him. She dreaded her father's objections, but Browning urged her to elope with him.

In September 1846 they were secretly married and then ran off to Italy. They made their home in Florence at Casa Guidi, famous as the title of one of Mrs. Browning's volumes. She seemed to have a new lease on life and for fifteen years they knew supreme happiness with each other. Their love has been immortalized for us in her *Sonnets from the Portuguese.*

They made a number of trips over Italy, and even visited London again. Their days together were filled with contentment and creativeness. Each venerated the gifts of the other. Browning indeed seems honestly to have imagined (quite without reason) that her gifts were superior to his own.

Men and Women: In 1855 he published his two volumes of *Men and Women*. This great collection was the first of Browning's volumes to achieve anything like an audience. He had been publishing for more than twenty years, but this was the first time that a publisher found it expedient to undertake the expense of a volume of his. The collection contains many wonderful poems—to mention only a few of them: "Love Among the Ruins," "Evelyn Hope," "Up at a Villa—Down at a City," "Fra Lippo Lippi," "A Toccata of Galuppi's," "Childe Roland to the Dark Tower Came," "The Statue and the Bust," "The Last Ride Together," "Andrea del Sarto," "In a Balcony," "Saul," "Two in the Campagna," "A Grammarian's Funeral," "Memorabilia," "Misconceptions," and "One Word More."

"Love Among the Ruins" is a very original poem in which the rhyming of alternating long and short lines creates the effect of tinkling sheep bells. The quiet of the landscape emphasizes the passion of the emotion described. Browning's artistry here is at its most mellifluous. The scene is the Roman Campagna, which is studded with the ruins of famous cities. In the evening air the soul is touched by the melancholy thought that all things are transient. Here a vast city has diminished to a mere memory. A few blocks of marble, a few half-buried columns overrun by vines, are all that is left of the handiwork of a forgotten people. Here the soul is forced to remember how glory and fame alike must decay. Suddenly to the speaker comes a golden-haired girl, her eyes eager with love. And as she passes among the ruins he remembers that centuries of sin and folly after all have no meaning in the moment when love comes—for love is the best of all things.

"Evelyn Hope" is one of Browning's simplest and most pathetic lyrics. It is the lament of a man who loved a girl, Evelyn Hope, whose death occurred at the age of sixteen before she was even able to understand his love for her. Twice her age, he contemplates her as she lies beautiful in death. He wonders whether it be too late for their souls to meet. But God, he knows, creates love to reward love. And Evelyn Hope will be his in the next world and in all the lives to come. No atom in the Universe is lost; how can any good be lost? So he shuts in her cold hand a leaf as a secret reminder to her of his love when she shall awake from the sleep of death.

"Up at a Villa—Down in the City" is a spirited reflection by "an Italian person of quality." He likes the life of the city. It is expensive, but you get your money's worth. For all day long life is a perfect feast in town. But when you are forced to live up at your villa in the mountains, your life is no better than a beast's. There is nothing to see in the country but the oxen dragging the plow. Even in the summer heat the city is better, especially in the square where the fountain plays. Despite all the fuss poets have made about insect-life it is really disgusting. In town you are stirred by wonderful sights and sounds—the church bells, the rattle of the diligence, the buzz of news, the quack doctor, the comedy at the post office, the new plays, the execution of an occasional liberal, new sonnets, new laws, church processions, the bang of the drum, the toot of the fife. "It's the greatest pleasure in life." But it's dear. You must pay for pleasures. And taxes in the city are always mounting. And that's why the speaker is forced to live in the country—the more's the pity. "Beggars can scarcely be choosers."

"Fra Lippo Lippi": Like "Andrea del Sarto," it is a powerful dramatic monologue drawn from the account of the lives of famous painters by the Renaissance painter-historian Vasari. In this poem the monk Fra Lippo has been virtually a prisoner in the palace of the Medici painting saints for Cosimo. His confinement has proved intolerable, so he has tied his sheets together and let himself out the window—just for a night's enjoyment with the girl whom he heard singing and dancing in the street below. But he has been arrested by the nightwatch, who are offended that a man in the garb of a monk should be cutting capers. The monologue is his defense, and his attempt at persuading them to let him go. He tells his history. His parents died when he was only a baby and left him dying in the streets to live on whatever rubbish he could pick up. One day, when he was only eight, he was taken into the monastery and given his first decent meal. This was the first time he had eaten bread in a month—small wonder that the boy agreed to become a monk. They tried to educate him, to teach him Latin. But his hard life in the streets had made him adept at reading people's faces. He found he could draw, and began to draw everywhere. The Prior thought he detected genius in the boy and decided that Lippo was to decorate the church. Thus he began to draw the monks and the people who attend church. But he was too realistic, too true to the facts of nature. The Prior, angered, insisted that he must learn to draw people's souls, not their flesh—a crazy notion in Lippo's opinion. For beauty is God's best creation:

> *If you get simple beauty and naught else,*
> *You get about the best thing God invents.*

Obligingly, Lippo erases his pictures and paints what he is ordered to paint, but his teeth the while grind with rage. Sometimes on a warm evening his saints are more than he can bear, and he plays just such pranks as the one he's been caught in tonight. He knows he is not much more than a beast, but nevertheless he understands the wonder of God's world. The beauties of the world are not to be ignored but are to be painted in thankfulness. It is a crime not to catch the truth when you know how to. We come to love things when we see them well-painted, even when we have passed them over a hundred times before. The Prior complains that Lippo's paintings do not make people pray. But why put art to such use, when a skull and crossbones will do as well? The monologue concludes with a plea to the guard not to report him. He swears that he will make amends for this night's folly. In six months time he promises he will have painted a magnificent saint for the convent. The poem is written in a sturdy natural blank verse alternating with little rhymed songs, *stornelli,* little stanza of three lines such as are still sung in the streets of Italy.

"A Toccata of Galuppi's" demonstrates how intimately Browning knew music. Galuppi was a composer who flourished in Venice in the mid-eighteenth century. A toccata is a kind of overture intended to exhibit the technical accomplishments of the performing musician. This poem is written in Browning's daintiest manner; the music of his lines manages to recreate the feeling of the decaying society in Venice before which Galuppi once performed. The Venetians, Browning reflects, seemed born merely to bloom and droop—to live empty lives in which the chief game was making love. All their gaiety came to nothing. They listened to music which told them that they must die, but they continued their kissing and their dancing until death overtook them. There are other kinds of people too, those with a passion for knowledge; but these also have dissipated their energies, knowing nothing higher to live for than mere accumulation of learning.

> *Dear dead women, with such hair, too—what's become of all the gold*
> *Used to hang and brush their bosoms? I feel chilly and grown old.*

"Childe Roland to the Dark Tower Came" is a triumph of an imagination that could also command the weird and the fantastic. There is a vividness of detail that succeeds in almost depressing us with a feeling of the bleak. The style is hard and distinct in outline. The poem was inspired by the fragment of song sung by Edgar in *King Lear.* The Dark Tower in the poem has been explained by critics as standing for unfaith, or truth, or love, or life, or death—and naturally the poem has been distorted in its meaning according to each conception. But there is no reason to believe the poem allegorical, except in the sense that the hero is plainly setting forth in pursuit of an ideal. It doesn't really matter what the Tower signifies; the central idea is clear enough. Childe Roland has lived a life pledged to his ideal. After a series of overwhelming discouragements, and in the midst of conviction that his destiny is failure, and when the spirits of those who have failed before him seem waiting for his own destruction, he yet can face his great issue when he comes upon it. With foreknowledge that he must fail, he can feel nonetheless that the battle for his ideal is a justifiable end in itself.

The story is simple. The speaker is Roland himself. He tells of all that he met and saw on the way to the great adventure, and how all that he encountered was calculated to kill hope and courage—the hoary cripple, who directed him on the road with gleeful anticipation of Roland's defeat; the dreary plain where nothing grows; the starved blind horse he passes by; the frothing black stream Roland crosses; the depressing hills he comes upon; finally, the round squat Tower itself. Every step of the way has convinced him that he and his cause are lost. Nevertheless, undaunted, he sets his horn to his lips and blows out the challenge to combat.

"The Statue and the Bust" is written in *terza rima* (in three-line stanzas, rhyming *aba, bcb, cdc, etc.*). The poem was inspired by the equestrian statue of Grand Duke Ferdinand the First, which stands in a square of Florence. The Duke is represented in effigy as riding away from the church facing the square, and turning his head in the direction of the old Riccardi Palace, which is situated on the corner. According to tradition, this Duke loved a lady whom the jealousy of her husband kept a prisoner in the Palace; the Duke could see her only at her window. For that reason he had a statue placed where his glance would always be upon her. In Browning's poem, the love is mutual, and the lovers are prepared to fly away together. Nevertheless, each day they find new reasons for postponing their happiness. They take comfort in the thought that on the morrow they will flee. In the meantime, each day they exchange glances as she stands by the window. The days follow one another, and their passion cools. By degrees they become content with mere expectation. In the end they understand that their love has been a dream and their lives wasted. To continue the dream his statue is placed in the square and her bust is set by the window on the Palace. They take a certain satisfaction from the irony that their images can do as much as reality could do for them. The poet blames them for not carrying out their intentions:

> And the sin I impute to each frustrate ghost
> Is—the unlit lamp and the ungirt loin.

"The Last Ride Together" is stirringly lyrical, and yet very dramatic too. The motion of the ride on horseback is in the rhythm of the lines. This is one of the poet's noblest poems. The speaker owns an unrequited love for a woman. But for her he has neither anger nor injured pride. His ideal of her is in his heart, and will transform all that is merely human in him until his soul becomes almost divine. The one great objective in his life has failed, and he therefore has asked for only one more last ride together with her. She has consented. For a moment she lies on his breast, and then the ride begins. He will not ask what he might have done to have won her love. After all, he has been spared evoking her hatred. All the men in the world strive for something and only a few succeed in attaining their object. The meaning of the struggle only a poet could tell, because only a poet can say what we feel. But even the poet never achieves the sublimity he seeks. Earth could not afford perfect happiness or what need would there be of heaven:

Earth being so good, would heaven seem best?

And so they ride on together, and while they ride the instant becomes his eternity. What if heaven should prove:

that I and she
Ride, ride together, for ever ride?

This poem, like "The Statue and the Bust" (and "In a Gondola"), contains one of Browning's favorite ideas: the importance to human beings of seizing the moment of perfection when it comes, whatever the cost thereafter to pay. The rider in this poem has seized his moment in the last ride with his sweetheart.

"Andrea del Sarto" is one of the most wonderful of Browning's dramatic monologues. It is impossible to read it without being profoundly moved by this tragic self-revelation of Florence's "faultless painter." The material for this poem, as in the case of "Fra Lippo Lippi," was taken from Vasari's *Lives of the Painters*. Andrea del Sarto, the painter, is sitting by the window in his home with his beautiful wife Lucrezia, looking over the streets of Florence as evening falls. He asks her not to quarrel with him any longer; he will paint the pictures the commission for which she has urged him to accept, and will give the money to her. He begs that for just one half-hour they will sit quietly there, gazing up at the little town of Fiesole. He is so tired! She will have to pose as a model for the five pictures to be painted, and that delights him. For never has he known such beauty as hers. As he looks on her face he sees his picture already made. They hear the clinking of the bell in the chapel behind the convent wall across the way. Autumn is coming on, and he knows that he is in the autumn of his creation. He looks back into the room at the pictures that she doesn't understand or care about. These paintings are all done with technical perfection. He has so much mastered his craft that he does not need to make sketches before he paints. What other painters dream of doing all their lives, he does easily. The others dream and fail; he succeeds. Nevertheless, in their failure there burns "a truer light of God," than in his perfect craftsmanship. Their works are chained to the ground but they themselves attain Heaven in their dreams. His works are nearer Heaven, but his soul is of the earth. What should the Mountain Morello care if someone criticizes its outline as in bad taste?

> *Ah, but a man's reach should exceed his grasp,*
> *Or what's a heaven for?*

In his work all is perfection of technique without soul. In the room there's a drawing by Raphael, who died so young recently. The arm in the drawing is out of perspective. But its soul is right. Ah, if Lucrezia, with all her perfect features had only brought a mind, as some women do, to their marriage! If she had only urged him not to worry about financial success, but to strive to reach God in his work, as did Michelangelo and Raphael! But after all, those two had no wives to urge them. That divine striving must lie in the man himself. Luckily for him, he is now somewhat underrated and neglected these days. He is afraid to leave home lest by chance he meet the ambassadors from Paris who would perhaps speak to him of the money he has misappropriated, the money King Francis entrusted to him for expenditure on works of art, and which he has spent building a house for Lucrezia. Ah, that time in France when he was painting under the eye of the good King! Those were kingly days when no enterprise seemed too difficult. But they ended when she called to him and he came back to Italy to her. Well, in the end, men will say that whatever Raphael painted, Andrea had a beautiful woman as his wife. Yet once Michelangelo himself prophesied great things of Andrea—a future greater than Raphael's! And still the arm on Raphael's drawing is wrong. Quickly Andrea takes a piece of chalk to draw the arm correctly, but at once erases it, for the soul of the picture is still Raphael's! Realizing that Lucrezia is hardly listening to him, and understands nothing of what he is saying, he nevertheless continues. If she would only sit by him every night in this way he might be able to paint better. The dark has fallen, and they must go in now. But suddenly her "cousin's" whistle is heard below, and Lucrezia insists she must leave. The money she needs is plainly for her gambling cousin. It was for that money that Lucrezia was willing to smile at her husband. He pleads with her not to go but to sit with him a while longer, and he will give her all the money she will desire for her cousin, and in addition some extra coin for a ruff for herself. His own parents lived and died poor, and he may have been a bad son. But behold how one gets rich! Moreover, let some good son paint those two hundred pictures Andrea has completed. But Lucrezia is anxious to go, and he sadly agrees. The half-life he is living must suffice him. What more would one have:

> *In heaven, perhaps, new chances, one more chance—*
> *Four great walls in the New Jerusalem,*
> *Meted on each side by the angel's reed,*
> *For Leonard, Rafael, Agnolo, and me*
> *To cover!*

The blank verse of this dramatic monologue has the muted coloring and music of the twilight which is the setting of the incident.

"In a Balcony," a one-act play, is the most effective of Browning's compositions in the dramatic form. It is said to have been acted with considerable success. The work is replete with passionate utterance, and the three characters of the drama are drawn to the life. Here again we have the crisis of a lifetime in the drama of an hour in this tragedy enacted on the balcony of a palace. The Queen is fifty years of age, wasted in body by frustration, but still craving the love which is her due. Constance, a lady of the court, is a young cousin of hers, and is loved by Norbert. He has been in the Queen's service and served the state so well and faithfully, that, though half in fear, the Queen has fallen in love with him. This evening there is a festival in his honor to commemorate the successful completion of his great work for the state. What Norbert has done has been done in the hope that he may ask for Constance as his reward. But she, with the intuitive cunning of a real woman, advises him to be diplomatic, to pretend that he has served the Queen for the Queen's sake alone. He is amazed that Constance can thus ask him to act against the interests of their mutual love, but she does this in the conviction that in the long run her tactics will prove wiser. If the Queen perceives his love for Constance, she is bound to feel that she has been used, and will never forgive the slight. He goes within and the Queen steps out. In a tense interview with Constance the Queen admits that although she is legally tied in marriage, she is prepared to divorce her husband and marry Norbert. She confesses her violent attachment for him, and pleads with Constance to be reassured that her love will not be in vain. Cowardly, Constance tells the Queen that Norbert does love her. Constance tries to excuse her position to herself, that her own giving up of Norbert will bring happiness to the Queen and him. But she is also a woman, and telling the state of affairs to her lover, when he returns, inevitably throws the responsibility upon him. In a burst of passion, Norbert is prepared to risk all in telling the truth. As he embraces her while violently declaring his love, they are overheard by the Queen. The Queen sees all her hopes collapsing at once and leaves without a word. The music in the hall ceases, the guards approach, and the lovers know that doom is upon them. But, as they are about to be led away to death, they cling together in one passionate moment of union which unites their souls forever.

Nowhere in Browning's work is there a subtler understanding of the involutions, the oversubtlety, the resourcefulness of the female character. Constance is very true, very tender, but is seized up in a whirl of emotions which she cannot direct. She is unable to see how her self-sacrifice is the worst of burdens for a man to bear. The Queen is simple, tragic, pathetic, and terrible in her frustrated love. Norbert is less subtle than the women, but more honest, strong and noble. "In a Balcony" was one of Browning's favorites among his poems.

"Saul" is one of Browning's most beautiful works. It is based upon the account of the shepherd David's playing before King Saul, as related in I Samuel, xvi:14–23. The young David speaks in this dramatic monologue like the youth he is and the great poet he was to become. He took his harp, entwined with lilies against the burning heat of the desert, and went, as bidden, to King Saul's tent. For three days Saul had been oppressed by an evil spirit and had maintained the silence of death within his tent. At first David played the music that would appeal to Saul's animal nature, to remind him of mankind's bond with the animals. He played the tune the sheep knew, the song the quails loved, the song of the crickets. Then he sang the music of man's sympathy with man—the song of the reapers, the song of the friendship of toilers. Then he went higher. He sang the march of the honored dead, and of how the faults of the dead man are forgotten in the praise. After that came the joyful chant of marriage, and the march of men working as comrades to aid the progress of the race. Then he sang the exalted notes of the sacrifice before Jehovah's altar. By slow degrees the music had done its work. Saul began to tremble and thus gave token that the forces of life were awakening in him. David's song proceeded to celebrate the wild joys of living, the importance of man's life, the never-failing providence of God, Saul's kingship, the manifold gifts God had showered on Saul, Saul's high ambitions, his great deeds and his fame. Saul suddenly became released from his torpor, and aware. His despair was gone. Pale, and exhaused, he was recalled to life, yet did not desire to live. Seizing the moment, David pushed on in his song to sing of the future, the glorious prospect of Saul's race, and the reward God must have in store for Saul's successors. Now Saul began to live again. He put out his hand and touched the brow of the harpist. At that gesture, David's soul went out in love to Saul, and he longed to be able to give Saul more than knowledge of the past and present. He longed to give Saul a new life altogether. If he could only have saved and redeemed Saul from failure and ruin, and bid him win the bliss of a reward in the next world! David would gladly have starved his own soul to make up Saul's lot. But then David realized that God must exceed all that he himself could wish to do, just as the Infinite must transcend the finite. In a sudden magnificent outburst, the singer found himself singing a new prophetic strain, in which he told Saul of the Christ who would love him and be loved by him, and open for him the gates to a new life. David left the tent and went home in the night. But he was not alone. Clouds of witnesses hovered over him, the angels who had come to listen to his prophecy. The very earth seemed to waken, and the stars seemed to beat with emotion in their courses. And now that he is back among his sheep, thinking over the remarkable events of the night before, wondering whether all this could have really happened, the very trees, the very brooks murmur:

> *With their obstinate, all but hushed voices—*
> *'E'en so, it is so!'*

"Two in the Campagna" is a lyric written in an undertone of weariness, the lament of a man to the woman at his side on the imperfection of the love they had. The two can never grow to be one, as love requires. He is oppressed by the sense of their imperfect understanding of each other. He seems forever to be seeking, to be achieving, and to be losing again their union of spirit which he so much desires:

> *Just when I seemed about to learn!*
>   *Where is the thread now? Off again!*
> *The old trick! Only I discern—*
>   *Infinite passion, and the pain*
> *Of finite hearts that yearn.*

"A Grammarian's Funeral" is described by the poet as taking place "shortly after the revival of learning in Europe." It contains a wonderful union of extreme seriousness and humor, of the dignified and the grotesque. The very lines seem to be climbing to the steady beat of this song of the pallbearers. They are bearing the Grammarian's corpse up the mountainside to bury him in the cleaner atmosphere of the mountain:

> *Our low life was the levers and the night's;*
>   *He's for the morning.*

He lived long without fame. He never seemed to notice how old age was encroaching on his years. He stuck to his hard task of unearthing the secrets of Greek grammar so that the world would have the key to its rich stores of literature. It never occurred to him to regret all the excitement and the gaiety he was missing in life. For him there was no end to learning. He had to know all. While fools urged him to live now or never,

> *He said, "What's time? Leave Now for dogs and apes!*
>   *Man has Forever!"*

So, although his body began to be wracked by disease he went on with his work, even when he was paralyzed from the waist down. The pallbearers reach the top of the mountain and leave him in the lofty place so suiting his thirst for knowledge.

"Memorabilia" is an exquisite tribute to Shelley. The poet is addressing someone who was a contemporary of Shelley's, someone who lived before Shelley was born, and is still living now:

> *Ah, did you once see Shelley plain,*
>   *And did he stop and speak to you?*
> *And did you speak to him again?*
>   *How strange it seems and new!*

The poet is moved at his meeting. It is like the time he crossed a deserted moor and found a molted eagle feather.

"Misconceptions" is a beautiful lyric, the product of exquisite fancy.

> *This is a spray the bird clung to,*
> *Making it blossom with pleasure.*

In pride at being so honored, the branch has burst into bloom. It is like the heart that has been thrilled for a moment by the smiles of a queen before she went on to the throne of her true love.

"One Word More" is Browning's answer to his wife's tribute to their love in her sonnets. In it Browning has enshrined his deepest and most sacred feelings. As the opening lines show, it was intended as an epilogue to the volume of *Men and Women*:

> *There they are, my fifty men and women*
> *Naming me the fifty poems finished!*
> *Take them, Love, the book and me together:*
> *Where the heart lies, let the brain lie also.*

He considers what other artists and poets have striven to communicate in their love for a woman. For this reason Raphael was prompted to try poetry and Dante to paint. Every artist longs once "to find his love a language fit and fair." Browning will never paint his love a picture or carve her statues. He must be content to stand on his poems. Yet for once he would like to speak to her not as a poet but as himself. His greatest joy is, perhaps, to know that while the world praises his wife for her poetry ("my moon of poets"), he alone is the one that knows her in all her wonder:

> *Oh, their Raphael of the dear Madonnas,*
> *Oh, their Dante of the dread Inferno,*
> *Wrote one song—and in my brain I sing it,*
> *Drew one angel—borne, see, on my bosom!*

Mrs. Browning died in June 1861. After so much happiness with her, Browning naturally felt as though his entire life had been disrupted. What she had meant to him can be read in "Prospice," a poem written after her death. He could not bear to live in Italy, the scene of his best life with her, and so left it—he thought, forever. Back in London, Browning by degrees began once more to shape a life for himself. He was far too healthy a man to live a secluded life of memories. After a year of avoiding people, he decided that Mrs. Browning would never have approved of his being a recluse. Before long he had a wide circle of friends. Thereafter he turned to his work for peace, and he began to exercise his gifts with greater application than ever before.

Dramatis Personae: Thus far he had been recognized as a great poet only by the comparatively few. The less virile art of Tennyson was much more sympathetic to Victorian tastes. Browning's next volume, *Dramatis Personae* (1864), was his first volume to achieve a good sale. From this time on his public increased rapidly. Yet, even in 1871, the 2,500 copies that *Balaustion's Adventure* managed to sell in five months, he estimated as a considerable sale. (The year before Tennyson had disposed of 40,000 copies of the *Idylls of the King.*)

Dramatis Personae contains among its important poems: "Abt Vogler," "Rabbi Ben Ezra," "Caliban upon Setebos," and "Prospice."

"Abt Vogler" is another one of Browning's marvelous poems upon music. It is the words of the musician "after he has been extemporizing upon the musical instrument of his invention." (This instrument was the orchestrion.) Vogler was a musician who flourished in the late eighteenth century. His performance on this adaptation of the organ now over, the musician wishes that all the beauty and completeness he had achieved in that music could be permanent. He has unfolded a great mystery and now it has vanished. It was a palace of sweet sounds, such as the spirits once raised in actuality for Solomon. This composition, improvised under the impulse of an inspiration, was too perfect to be lost. Only evil can perish, only good can last. And this music, Vogler knows, was good. But, after all, he was only an extemporizer, for it was God who was the composer. Where would he find this perfection again? In heaven we are to find the perfect circles of the broken arcs that we are allowed to see here:

> *On the earth the broken arcs; in the heaven, a*
> *perfect round*

The harmonies of a few bars of music played by a mortal on earth give a hint of the eternal harmonies of God. What is failure but a pause in the music? Thus it is better for us to bear the tasks of this life and acquiesce. It is enough that at moments we are allowed to participate in the concerns of Eternity. This poem is Browning's most profound attempt to set forth the secret of artistic inspiration. The lines reveal the poet's profound knowledge of the science of music.

"Rabbi Ben Ezra" states most completely the philosophy everywhere implicit in Browning's poetry. In the mouth of the medieval Jewish sage he has put his own deepest convictions—though it is true that the old Talmudist did teach a philosophy not too dissimilar from Browning's. The poem has been called the noblest of modern religious lyrics. It is one of the most restrained of Browning's poems. Here old age is depicted as not a period of decay in a man's life, as the Romantic poets had felt, but a pinnacle of experience. The Rabbi is speaking:

> *Grow old along with me!*
> *The best is yet to be,*
> *The last of life, for which the first was made:*
> *Our times are in His hand*
> *Who saith "A whole I planned,*
> *Youth shows but half; trust God: see all*
> *nor be afraid!"*

Ben Ezra does not object because youth was a period of such uncertainty, full of fears and hopes. Rather, he prizes the doubt that a young man may nourish, for it is that which is divine in him. Let us indeed welcome life's reverses, let "our joys" be "three parts pain." For the measure of a man is what he aspired to be and could not achieve. In youth a man stores up experience; in old age he begins to see God's design. That youth is tempted by earthly concerns is no cause for complaint. Flesh helps soul and soul helps flesh. But just as it was the business of youth to struggle and experiment, it is the business of old age to pause and take stock before the soul wages its next battle—with death.

> *Youth ended, I shall try*
> *My gain or loss thereby;*
> *Leave the fire ashes, what survives is gold.*

It is fitting for old age to judge now of past acts and be able to say with certainty that this anger was right, that submission wrong. It is enough if we can catch the hint of God's intent. As it was better for youth never to rest, so it is better for age no longer to struggle, but to reflect and know—to know the Right and the Good and the Infinite. In estimating his acts a man now will be able to understand that the measure of his worth has been all that was too vast for a mortal to accomplish:

> *Thoughts hardly to be packed*
> *Into a narrow act . . .*
> *All I could never be,*
> *All men ignored in me,*
> *This I was worth to God*

We are as clay in the hands of God, the Potter. The image of the Potter's wheel explains why in youth, at the beginning of our shaping, everything spins dizzily—why, too, it is impossible to stop the flight of time, for we are being whirled in a dance of "plastic circumstance." What if at the base of the cup which God makes of us, there is much laughter, while at the rim there are skull things? Look not down but up. The cup was intended for the new wine that must be poured into it in the Hereafter. And we are fashioned so only to slake God's thirst.

"Caliban upon Setebos" is another masterpiece of the grotesque—and has been called the finest piece of grotesque art in English poetry. The scientist Huxley deeply admired it for its accurate representation of the development of religious ideas in primitive man. Setebos is the God of Caliban (the monster in Shakespeare's *Tempest.*) Here Caliban is talking to himself in the third person while pretending to Prospero and Miranda that he is working. As he lies sprawled in the mud, he decides that Setebos must live in the moon, though He made the sun too—but not the stars. His God created the world only because Setebos was ill at ease. He hated the cold, which having made He could not change. In pure spite He made the birds, beasts and trees. Since it was not in His power to make Himself a mate, He sports with His creations. Just so Caliban can, if he wishes, make a bird of clay and then proceed to break its leg. Such an act is neither cruel nor kind, but is merely a manifestation of Divine Power. Watching the crabs walking over the sand, Caliban, for instance, could choose to stone the twenty-first of them. God, of course, is good on the whole. But He has made things better than Himself, and occasionally envies some of His creations. But His creations can do nothing without God. Therefore, it behooves Caliban to be humble. If Setebos is ill at ease, it must mean that there is a something beyond Setebos. Sycorax, Caliban's mother, thought it was the great Quiet beyond the stars that made all things. But God is terrible, especially in the hurricanes and storms He raises. There is no telling what will please Him. It would be better therefore, to fear Setebos until the great Quiet conquers Him. Suddenly a storm rises up, and Caliban realizes what a fool he has been to gibe at Setebos. He lies flat in his mud and promises to love Setebos and do penance. The poem is a brilliant criticism of the orthodox view of an anthropomorphic God.

"Prospice," like Tennyson's "Crossing the Bar," is Browning's reflection on death. The title means, "look ahead." To Browning death is no quiet sea of peace and calm, as it was to Tennyson. He cries:

> *Fear death?—to feel the fog in my throat,*
> *The mist in my face,*
> *When the snows begin, and the blasts denote*
> *I am nearing the place,*
> *The power of the night, the press of the storm,*
> *The post of the foe*

There lies ahead one last great grapple. The poet would not want his eyes bandaged, and is only too happy to pay with a few minutes of pain for all the joy life has given him. And then the storm shall dwindle and shall pass by degrees into peace and light. And at the end he will clasp the soul of his soul (his wife).

The Ring and the Book: One day, in June 1860, about a year before Elizabeth Barrett Browning's death, Browning had come upon an ancient yellow vellum-bound book in a bookstall on a street of Florence. It contained an uninspired account of an old trial for murder. The outlines of the story made a profound impression upon him, although for a while he did nothing about it. After his wife's death, however, he began to work on what became his most ambitious poem, *The Ring and the Book*, which he finished in 1869. In its composition he found his chief relief from his great sorrow. The poem was received with great enthusiasm, and established Browning's position beside that of Tennyson as a major poet of the age.

The Ring and the Book is the crowning achievement of Browning's experiment with the dramatic monologue. The plot of the story is simple enough. Guido Franceschini, a cruel aristocrat of Arezzo, marries an innocent girl, Pompilia, the daughter, by adoption, of an elderly middle-class couple. Guido tortures Pompilia until she escapes with the aid of Caponsacchi, a young carefree monk. Caponsacchi, whose frivolous life suddenly seems shameful to him because of Pompilia's trusting purity, undertakes at great personal danger to conduct her to the home of her foster parents in Rome. Count Guido catches up with the pair just before they reach their destination and has them both taken into custody with the accusation of adultery. Because she is about to bear Guido's child, Pompilia is allowed by the convent, where she has been confined, to visit her parents. Her husband watches his opportunity, forces his way into her parents' home, and murders her and the old people. In the end, Guido is condemned to death for the murder.

What is remarkable about *The Ring and the Book* is the method. In a series of dramatic monologues, Browning examines the narrative from every point of view. Each person speaking throws new light upon the truth. At the beginning we are not so sure about the characters of the principals. At the end Pompilia emerges as an exquisitely innocent and saintly girl, the victim of a cruel and crafty villain. Caponsacchi is seen to be a man who is saved from a wasted life by the dangerous and noble deed he was at first loath to undertake. Experience has made of him a fine courageous man of exalted soul. Guido is a saturnine, complicated, self-deceiving devil.

In Book I, entitled "The Ring and the Book" itself, Browning makes us acquainted with the bald facts of the case—how he found the "old yellow book," how the idea for the poem grew in him, and what the inspiration of his wife meant to him. We are given the outline of the story without elaboration, and then a brief summary of each of the books which are to follow. Book I concludes with a wonderful apostrophe to his wife and his love of her:

> *O lyric Love, half angel and half bird*
> *And all a wonder and a wild desire . . .*

Book II is entitled "Half-Rome," wherein the story of the murders is rehearsed by a man inimical to the wife's point of view. This partisan of Guido is lounging in the public square as he delivers his pronouncements to his listener. At the very end of the book we are given to understand the prejudice of the speaker. He himself has reason to be jealous of the attentions being paid his wife by a certain serenader. A well-known passage from "Half-Rome" is:

> *Call in law when a neighbor breaks your fence,*
> *Cribs from your field, tampers with rent or lease,*
> *Touches the purse or pocket,—but woos your wife?*
> *No: take the old way trod when men were men!*

Book III is "The Other Half-Rome," and records the view of those who are sympathetic to the wife. The point of view as well as the poetry is in fine contrast to Book II. Here the speaker is much nearer the truth, as we shall see it to be in the end. He is more scrupulous in his desire to be just, and even tries not to have his judgment influenced by his pity for Pompilia's beauty and suffering. He concludes that Pompilia is a martyr, though he does less than justice to Caponsacchi. Certain details of the story not previously covered are here elaborated. The speaker is a refined sensitive bachelor, whose heart is peculiarly sensitive to woman in distress. An often-quoted passage from this book is:

> *There is but one way to browbeat this world,*
> *Dumb-founder doubt, and repay scorn in kind,—*
> *To go on trusting, namely, till faith move*
> *Mountains.*

It is to be noticed that there is a wonderful symmetry in the planning of *The Ring and the Book*. The first book is the Prologue and the last book is the Epilogue. In between these two the narrative proceeds by threes. Just as we shall have the Pope weighing the evidence after the advocates have present-ed each his side, so now, in Book IV, "Tertium Quid" (the third element), we have the opinions of those who are not committed wholly to one side or the other. The speaker here is an aristocrat, and the people he addresses as well as the things in which he is interested, belong to his class. He is almost, we feel, too objective—as though there were no such thing as truth. He is the kind of person who can be elaborately fair to both sides only because he does not care where justice lies. This book has some wonderful details of contemporary seventeenth century life: the crowd at the puppet play, the shops and mouldering palaces, the powdered wigs of the court circle—a marvelous picture of the age. A well-known passage from Book IV is:

> *"The serpent tempted me and I did eat."*
> *So much of paradisal nature, Eve's!*
> *Her daughters ever since prefer to urge,*
> *"Adam so starved me I was fain accept*
> *The apple any serpent pushed my way."*

Book V begins a new series of three, each presenting the principals of the drama. It is called, "Count Guido Franceschini." The murderer is allotted two books in *The Ring and the Book*, and is often quoted in the other books. Thus, he actually occupies more space in the poem than any other character. Browning was fascinated by him, as he was with all such complicated souls. It is all the more remarkable when we note that the "old yellow book" con-tains no direct remarks of Guido. In Book V we meet him in an antechamber to the court. He has just been put to the torture, and tries his best to win his case by restraining the passionate evil which is part of him, and to stand on his dignity as an aristocrat and an outraged husband. He does this brilliantly.

Book VI, "Giuseppe Caponsacchi," is again almost pure invention on the poet's part. There is no record of Caponsacchi's confronting the judges as he does here. In some respects it is the most wonderful of all the books of this long work. The poem in this book is uttered by a man recently converted to spiritual understanding and still overwhelmed by the insight Pompilia has given him into the beauty of the human heart. Caponsacchi emerges as a man of dignity and passion, who can speak with charm, with beauty, with burning anger or with sharp irony, as the occasion demands. He has a vision of the truth, and he is indifferent to his fate. All that is important is to speak out. As love, loathing, scorn, pity, self-contempt, wild despair against circumstances, and resignation follow one another, we live with him in the intensities of his passions. His attacks on the cynicism and worldliness and empty learning of the churchmen are done with brilliance; his conflict between his old frivolous self and the true Caponsacchi, which Pompilia's need of him dis-covered for him, is dramatically and vividly shown us. The description of their flight is a triumph of artistry in its lyrical speed and breathless excitement. This book abounds in wonderful passages. Well known is:

> 'Twas a thief that said the last kind word to Christ:
> Christ took the kindness and forgave the theft.

In Book VII, "Pompilia," Guido's child-wife speaks from the bed where she is dying from the wounds he gave her. Here the tone shifts to heartbreaking simplicity. The saintliness and innocence of the seventeen-year-old girl are implicit in every line. Her amazing lack of resentment against her persecutor, her sense that death will be a release from the heavy trials that life has thrust upon her, bring one almost to the point of tears. Even with all that she has suffered she valiantly tries to find excuses for Guido, and seems almost unaware of what knowing her has done for Caponsacchi's soul. Him she expects to love with permission of God in the Hereafter. "Let him wait God's instant men call years." Her tribute to him is marvelous:

> Through such souls alone
> God stooping shows sufficient of His light
> For us i' the dark to rise by. And I rise.

Book VIII, "Dominus Hyacinthus De Archangelis, Pauperum Procurator," and Book IX, "Juris Doctor Johannes-Baptista Bottinius," present the opposing lawyers, each with his side of the case. Archangelis, in the bosom of his family, is going over the points he intends making in his address. His heart is wrapped up in the future of his son Giacinto, for whom, as Book VIII proceeds, he has an endless variety of affectionate nicknames. His intended speech and his thoughts are interlarded with ponderous Latin, which he hopes will set a noble precedent for his son in the boy's future studies. His opponent, Bottinius, is a sour bachelor with almost all humanity drained out of him. Neither is the least bit interested in the truth. Both are anxious only to find the loopholes in the law that can help win the case. The fate of his client, the justice of the cause, never occurs to either of these men. They are chiefly interested in winning the contest between each other. It is the irony of life that the lawyer who loves his family so much should be defending Guido, and that the other, who has never understood women, should be called upon to defend Pompilia's memory.

Book X, "The Pope," has usually been called the greatest of the books by critics. Here we meet a very old man, mellowed by experience and thought until he has proved worthy of his great elevation. He has come to understand everything about the tragic issues of life, and when he speaks his references are not only to books but very frequently to nature too. He is plainly Browning's mouthpiece. Through all the hypocrisy of Guido's pretenses, through all the guilty appearances of Pompilia's actions, through all the lightheaded conduct of Caponsacchi, he knows how to pierce. He weighs all the evidence and decides that Guido is not fit to live. If Guido should be allowed his life, the Pope asks, "How should I dare die?"

Book XI, "Guido," introduces the murderer again. He is speaking to his visitors in prison. Now he proves himself for what he is. His diplomacy gone, he shows his fangs. Alternating between defiance and whining, he finds relief for his doom only in laying bare the ugliness of his soul. Browning never drew a more powerfully repulsive picture of depravity. Guido is a master of invective and irony; he has a brilliant mind—but he is a demon. Too late, he understands that:

> You never know what life means till you die:
> Even throughout life, 'tis death that makes life live,
> Gives it whatever the significance.

Book XII, "The Book and the Ring," is the Epilogue, tying together the ends of the story. It concludes with a tribute to the power of art in telling truth and an invocation to Lyric Love.

As a poet, Browning must have taken some satisfaction in his last years. The long overdue recognition of his accomplishments followed the publication of *The Ring and the Book*. All over England and America Browning Societies were instituted for the study and appreciation of his works. Oxford University awarded him an honorary D.C.L. and an honorary Fellowship at Balliol College. In 1871 Browning found that he could return again to Italy, where his heart always had been, and he spent many of his last years there.

Late Works: His later books do not generally equal the incomparably high quality of those we have thus far discussed. But they contain many interesting poems. In 1879 and 1880 appeared *Dramatic Idyls*, in 1883 *Jocoseria*, in 1884 *Ferishtah's Fancies*, in 1887 *Parleyings with Certain People of Importance*, and in 1889 *Asolando*. The Epilogue to *Asolando* is a powerful piece of self-description. Here Browning looks back on his life as he thinks of the world to come, and says of himself that he has been:

> One who never turned his back but marched breast forward,
> > Never doubted clouds would break,
> Never dreamed, though right were worsted, wrong would triumph,
> Held we fall to rise, are baffled to fight better,
> > Sleep to wake.
>
> No, at noonday in the bustle of man's work-time
> > Greet the unseen with a cheer!
> Bid him forward, breast and back as either should be,
> "Strive and thrive!" cry "Speed—fight on, fare ever
> > There as here!"

Browning enjoyed the best of health until the time of his death. He died in Venice, at the home of his son, on December 12, 1889. He is buried at Westminster Abbey.

Elizabeth Barrett Browning (1806–1861)

Elizabeth Barrett, the oldest of eleven children in her family, was born March 6, 1806. Her childhood was happy, and her wealthy loving father indulged her in her passion for poetry. He published for her an "epic poem" which she wrote at the age of thirteen, *The Battle of Marathon*. But when she was fifteen an accident to her spine rendered her an invalid for the rest of her life. Her father presently moved from Devonshire to London. Their residence at 50 Wimpole Street became her prison. She developed tuberculosis, and the accidental drowning of her brother Edward seemed likely to hasten her end. With the best of intentions her father kept the world away from her room under the delusion that he was thus conserving her life.

Her only pleasure was in reading and writing. In 1844 an edition of her poems was issued dedicated to her father. The best known of the poems in this volume is "The Cry of the Children." "The Cry of the Children" is a powerful protest against child labor. Elizabeth Barrett had been deeply stirred by an official report on the situation in the mines and factories.

> *Do ye hear the children weeping, O my brothers,*
> *Ere the sorrow comes with years?*

Why do the children cry? They look up out of their haggard faces and say:

> *Few paces have we taken, yet are weary—*
> *Our grave-rest is very far to seek.*

If only the iron wheels would stop turning for one day in the factories! How can God hear the children crying through the noise? How long will the cruel nation allow this state to continue? These children can never see the sunshine. They are orphans of "earthly love and heavenly."

In a certain poem of her 1844 collection, she paid tribute to Robert Browning as a great poet. Browning, delighted with her notice of him, at a time when very few readers knew he existed, wrote her a letter of thanks. Characteristically, he began, "I love you with all my heart, dear Miss Barrett." He asked to come to see her, but she postponed their meeting till the spring. At last they met. From that time on there was no question of their love for each other. Up to the time of their marriage, a year and a half later, they maintained a dramatic and very moving correspondence—among the most romantic love letters ever written. Full of fear of her father's anger, she met Browning on September 12, 1846 for a secret marriage. The next week they fled England to avoid Barrett's fury.

For all Browning knew, his wife might have died within the year. But love and Italy proved the best doctors. For fifteen years the Brownings lived in perfect happiness with each other. They went first to Pisa and from Pisa to Florence. In Florence they made the Casa Guidi their home.

One day Elizabeth Barrett Browning showed her husband the manuscript of a sequence of forty-five sonnets that she had written since first she knew she loved him. She was prepared to destroy them if he did not approve of them. But he was so deeply impressed with their quality that he insisted, despite the highly personal revelation of feeling in them, that they must be published. It was his idea that by issuing them under the title of *Sonnets from the Portuguese* she might imply that they were translations and thus preserve her modesty before the public. They appeared in 1850.

The Sonnets from the Portuguese have, with scant justice, been placed beside Shakespeare's, Spenser's, and Rossetti's as forming the greatest sonnet sequences in the language. Actually her level is far below that of these men. The worst of her sonnets are stilted and often labored. Nevertheless, about a dozen of them are among the most passionately sincere ever written in English. Indeed, it is the power of the feelings expressed that enables one to overlook her considerable limitations in managing the form and the music of the Italian sonnet. But she has spoken directly to the heart of her readers, and her best sonnets are likely to be better known than the superior works of other poets.

The best of the *Sonnets from the Portuguese* are numbers 1, 3, 4, 7, 14, 22, 26, 28, 35, and 43. In the first, the poet speaks of being saved from death when Love drew her "backward by the hair." The third contrasts the pallor of her sick days with the bright health of her lover. The fourth recognizes that his calling is "to some Palace floor," not to the ruined tower where she dwells. The fourteenth asks to be loved not for pity but for love's sake only. The twenty-sixth rejoices that all the lost hopes and dreams of youth have met in his love for her:

> *with satisfaction of all wants—*
> *Because God's gifts put man s best dreams to shame.*

The forty-third is deservedly the best-known.

> *How do I love thee? Let me count the ways.*
> *I love thee to the depth and breadth and height*
> *My soul can reach, when feeling out of sight*
> *For the ends of Being and ideal Grace.*
> *I love thee to the level of every day's*
> *Most quiet need, by sun and candle-light.*
> *I love thee freely, as men strive for Right;*
> *I love thee purely, as men turn from Praise.*
> *I love thee with the passion put to use*
> *In my old griefs, and with my childhood's faith.*
> *I love thee with a love I seemed to lose*
> *With my lost saints,—I love thee with the breath,*
> *Smiles, tears, of all my life!—and, if God choose,*
> *I shall but love thee better after death.*

Her impressions of Italy are recorded in the volume called *Casa Guidi Windows* (1851). The poem, written in *terza rima*, is on current political events, but is overly didactic. *Aurora Leigh* (1857) is an attempt at writing a novel in verse. Its blank verse tells a story that puts forward the rights of oppressed Victorian women, particularly those trodden down by poverty. Despite an excessive prosiness, Elizabeth Barrett Browning's all-too-frequent limitation, the poem has a certain interest for the autobiographical nature of some of its passages. Her last volume was *Poems Before Congress* (1860), mostly on political matters.

It contained, however, one of her best pieces, "A Musical Instrument." This lighthearted poem tells how the great god Pan took a reed by the river, sat on the shore, hewed at the reed, cut it short, drew out the pith, cut notches, and began to make sweet music. Just so does Pan make out of a man a poet.

Elizabeth Barrett Browning's poetry is too often disturbing by its inaccuracy of rhyme and rhythm. Her diction, too, suffers sometimes from stiltedness, sometimes from dullness. But she was passionately aware of social injustice, and in many passages the beauty of her own spirit shines through. Of course, the *Sonnets from the Portuguese* is her major contribution to poetry. She also made several excellent translations—notably, from Theocritus and Aeschylus.

Edward Fitzgerald (1809–1883)

There is little to record in the biography of the author of *The Rubaiyát of Omar Khayyám*. He was born March 31, 1809, into a very wealthy family of noble connections. Never did he feel the pinch of necessity, for he lived in affluence all his life. At Trinity College, Cambridge, he made many life-long friends. Fitzgerald, indeed, had a genius for friendship, and among his intimates were Carlyle, Tennyson, and Thackeray.

His friendship with E. B. Cowell, the Orientalist, became very significant to his career. Because of it, he learned to read Persian and in 1856 made a translation of Jami's *Salaman and Absal*. Soon after that he began working upon an English version of the *rubaiyát* (quatrains) of the twelfth century Persian poet Omar Khayyám.

As published in 1859, *The Rubaiyát of Omar Khayyám* was as much an original poem as a translation. Fitzgerald freely rearranged lines from the five hundred philosophical quatrains left by the Persian epicurean. He even added ideas from other Persian writers, as well as several of his own.

There must have been a great affinity of temperament between the Persian poet and his English adapter. Actually, the poem expresses a number of philosophies, not all of them consistent with one another. There is an undercurrent of skepticism, of course, throughout; but there are touches also of pantheism, epicureanism, and the doctrine of predestination.

When the volume appeared it was almost completely ignored. But later Rossetti discovered it and introduced it to his fellow Pre-Raphaelites. The exquisite artistry of the quatrains delighted them, and it is owing to the Pre-Raphaelites that the book began to be among the most popular of all English poems. In its highly chiseled lines, the English-speaking world has found the perfect voice for all its own feelings in moments where the human spirit seems to have nothing to hope, nothing to expect.

The poem is so frequently quoted that there is hardly a stanza that is not well known. Among the most celebrated lines are:

> *Come, fill the Cup, and in the fire of Spring*
> *Your Winter garment of Repentance fling*

> *A Book of Verses underneath the Bough,*
> *A Jug of Wine, a Loaf of Bread—and Thou*
> *Beside me singing in the Wilderness—*
> *Oh, Wilderness were Paradise enow!*

> *Ah, take the Cash, and let the Credit go,*
> *Nor heed the rumble of a distant Drum!*

> *I sometimes think that never blows so red*
> *The Rose as where some buried Caesar bled*

> *The flower that once has blown Forever dies*

> *The Moving Finger writes; and, having writ,*
> *Moves on*

Fitzgerald was the author of a number of other works in addition to the two already mentioned. In 1849 he published the poems and letters of his Quaker friend, Bernard Barton, and included a memoir on him. *Euphranor*, a Platonic dialogue, was published in 1851. *Polonius*, a collection of aphorisms, was issued the following year. During the subsequent years he made many translations, including some of the plays of Calderon, the *Agamemnon* of Aeschylus (1865), and the *Oedipus Rex* of Sophocles (1881). His last work was an edition of Crabbe's poems, a tribute to Fitzgerald's friendship with Crabbe's son and grandson.

Only the *Omar Khayyám* of Fitzgerald has proved of literary importance.

NEW SCIENTIFIC THOUGHT

Charles Darwin (1809–1882)

In the 1830s Charles Darwin, the naturalist, made a voyage around the world aboard the *Beagle*. For five years Darwin studied the rock formations, the plant life and animal life of remote parts of the globe. From 1837 he began to collect facts on the selection of breeds in domestic plants and animals. His purpose was to find out whether the inaugurating of new types by deliberate selection of breeders might not have been paralleled by Nature herself. After endless hard work he issued his *Origin of Species* in November 1859.

The controversy that followed was earthshaking. Among the scientists, Darwin encountered staunch disbelief in the mutability of species. Among the clergy and pious laymen the objection was more violent, for Darwin's theories threatened to set at naught many of the bases of orthodoxy. The theory that the human species has evolved from a lower one was certainly at variance with a literal interpretation of the account in *Genesis* of the origin of man.

Overcoming tradition and prejudice was a long and arduous task for the Darwinian theory. No one fought more valiantly in its cause than Thomas Henry Huxley. Darwin had paid little attention to the all-important matter of man's role in the development of species. This was the very question that most engaged the interest of Huxley. One of the most effective speakers of his age, Huxley is largely responsible for the fact that by 1880 the Darwinian theory was accepted by scientific thinkers the world over.

Reactions to Darwinism

Of course, Darwin's work was merely the most sensational instance of the cataclysmic effect which scientific theory was having upon religious opinion. The science of geology had already done much to undermine the literal interpretation of the Bible. Once that process had begun, the whole ground-work of morals and ethics seemed to give way.

A world of new problems was born after the Darwinian theories made their first inroads. Matthew Arnold, for instance, accepting the new science, tried to discover a way of bringing the fundamentals of Christian faith into consonance with new thought. George Eliot, the novelist, and Swinburne, the poet, scorned any compromise with the Church, and subscribed to the new French philosophy of Positivism (the denial of supernaturalism).

Other writers felt free to seek sanction in pagan systems of ethics: stoicism or epicureanism. If there were to be no rewards in the Hereafter, if goodness is not for the sake of God's glory, what should be the good life? A group of writers influenced by the teachings of Walter Pater developed a new aestheticism from the doctrine of epicureanism. The most notorious of these was Oscar Wilde. Still others, like the poets Henley and Housman, found an answer in stoicism.

Naturally a number of writers were totally unaffected by the new scientific skepticism. The temper of the age moved men like Newman and the poet Francis Thompson to fall back on faith and accept the Roman Catholic Church's dogma; the poet Christina Rossetti was similarly led to a life of devotion to Anglicanism.

Thomas Henry Huxley (1825–1895)

Huxley was born at Ealing, a suburb of London, on May 4, 1825, the son of a schoolmaster. His father was his first teacher. While still a boy, Huxley was powerfully impressed by Carlyle's *Sartor Resartus*, and from it developed a curiosity about German literature. He also read widely in the philosophical writers of his day.

He became an apprentice to a physician in 1841 and entered Charing Cross Hospital on a scholarship. Here he received excellent medical training. In 1845 he took his M.B. at the University of London. But he was too young to enter the College of Surgeons, and therefore applied for a position in the Navy. He was granted a post on the *Rattlesnake* as assistant surgeon for a four-year voyage to the South Seas. During this trip he gathered an enormous collection of all kinds, and sent home a series of scientific papers for publication. In Australia, he met the woman who became his wife, and with whom he had an extremely happy life.

He returned to England in 1851. For the next ten years he was extremely busy. He was made a Fellow of the Royal Society, and Lecturer at the Royal Institution. He occupied various teaching positions. But none of his tasks was more important to his future than the lectures he delivered to working men, for in these it was necessary for him to present his scientific principles with the utmost simplicity without being false to the facts. This experience was highly valuable in preparing him for public lecturing. In the meantime he was continuing his researches into several sciences.

When Darwin's *Origin of Species* appeared in 1859, Huxley found stated there many of the convictions that he himself had slowly been coming to. The book became the most important influence in his life. For the next twenty years he devoted himself to popularizing and defending the theory of evolution. In all the bitterness that arose, Huxley was the best fighter of the century for the new science. Although battling under Darwin's banner, he was himself much more interested than Darwin in applying the new theory to man's place in the universe.

After much reflection, he issued his first book, *Evidences as to Man's Place in Nature*, in 1863. Here is stated in no uncertain terms man's kinship with the lower animals. It is the work which has fathered the modern science of anthropology.

To the literary world he is best known for three lectures that he delivered during this decade: *A Liberal Education and Where to Find It; On a Piece of Chalk;* and *On the Physical Basis of Life*. In these he sought to relate the new scientific theories to conduct in the modern world.

A Liberal Education compares education with a game of chess; this game we must master if we are to survive. A true education is an instruction in the laws of Nature, and the laws by which men live. A man has a liberal education who has been trained to make his body the servant of his will, whose intellect is a logical machine in working order, and whose mind is stored with the fundamental truths and laws of Nature. The other two lectures are popularizations of scientific fact, and plead for the advancement of science.

As a stylist, Huxley has no interest in elegance or charm. He speaks with the power and energy of conviction and knowledge. Among his opponents, none was more formidable than Matthew Arnold, who defended against Huxley the survival of the classics in the educational curriculum.

Huxley became so well-known to the public that he had less and less time for research because of his lectures. He gave courses to teachers of science and of laboratory demonstration, and he served on many public boards to further the cause of science.

He fought with conservative scientists, with prime ministers, and with clergymen. When he died on June 29, 1895, he was in the midst of a new collection of polemical writings. By that time, the victory of his cause was assured.

Huxley's prose has served as a model for scientific composition. The clarity and power of his presentation enabled him to deal with complicated ideas as though they were really simple. Even though research in the twentieth century has altered many of Huxley's teachings, the fundamental line he took remains the same in biology today. The leading role natural sciences have played in our educational institutions is largely the product of Huxley's efforts.

Matthew Arnold (1822–1888)

Matthew Arnold takes his place beside Carlyle, Newman, and Ruskin as a great teacher of his age in its revolt against the Utilitarian philosophy; but he did not turn, as they did, to the Middle Ages for his values. Though he could regret the chaos which the new scientific theories had brought into the intellectual horizons of the Victorians, he understood that something positive must be found to take the place that the authority of the Bible had once had as a foundation for ethics.

His solution was essentially a modern one. He felt that the dignity of the human spirit was enough justification for men to lead good lives, without consideration of possible rewards and punishments in the Hereafter. Nor could he agree that the material prosperity of England was enough cause for believing that society had attained perfection, when he considered the horrors of slum life. For those who could no longer turn to religious faith for the moral basis of conduct, Arnold was a shining light in the new darkness of post-Darwinianism. For those who were disgusted with the self-satisfaction of middle-class prosperity, but who were inclined to look to the future for hope rather than back to the Middle Ages, the nobility of Arnold's cultural ideals was a source of confidence.

Arnold's father, Thomas Arnold, was a very famous man, well known all over England as the celebrated headmaster of Rugby—an educator whose views were widely discussed and whose breadth of vision was universally admired. Arnold's *Rugby Chapel*, like his correspondence, reveals the poet's deep attachment to his father. Young Arnold studied at his father's school under his personal tutelage. For vacations the family went to the Lake Country, near Grasmere, so deeply associated with their friend Wordsworth. Unquestionably, the friendship of his elders with the old poet had much to do with the young Arnold's enthusiasm for poetry.

Arnold won a classical scholarship to Balliol College, Oxford. There he was less interested in intense study than wide reading. He developed, moreover, a passionate attachment to the university city, which in his celebrated *Preface* to *Essays in Criticism*, he was to call "Beautiful city! so venerable, so lovely, so unravished by the fierce intellectual life of our century, so serene! . . . Who will deny that Oxford by her ineffable charm keeps ever calling us nearer to the true goal of all of us, to the ideal, to perfection . . . ?" His recollections of Oxford form part of the tissue out of which he made two of his best poems, "The Scholar Gypsy" and "Thyrsis." At the university he developed his deep admiration for the literature of Rome and Greece. During these years he also formed his close friendship with Arthur Hugh Clough.

He was granted his degree in 1845, and after a few months of teaching at Rugby, he was made a Fellow of Oriel College. In 1847 Lord Landsdowne offered him a position as his private secretary, and for the three years in which he held this post he was necessarily deeply immersed in politics. He was granted enough leisure time to read copiously, and to pay a visit to France to see George Sand and Chopin.

Poetry: He also composed most of the poems in his first volume during these three years. The book was called *The Strayed Reveler, and Other Poems* (1849). It contained some remarkable poems, now accepted as classics in our literature; but the volume was hardly noticed. Among the finest of these poems are "The Forsaken Merman," "To a Friend," "Shakespeare," "Quiet Work," and "Resignation."

"The Forsaken Merman" is a very lyrical poem in which the monologue is spoken by the merman of the title. He is addressing his children, bidding them come with him. But before they go, he asks them to call on their mother Margaret once more. But she does not answer. The children are allowed one last look at the little town before they are to go. It was only yesterday that their mother left her "red-gold throne in the heart of the sea," and at the sound of a far-off bell decided that she must go on shore to pray because it is Eastertime, lest she lose her soul. She soared up through the waters, and they followed her. They went up on the beach by the white-walled town to watch and wait. But Margaret never looked back at them. The priest was praying loud, and she could not hear her children calling. And today she seems half-happy, half-sad to be on shore. But she will not return to her lover and her children. They must be content to gaze at the white town hereafter and to sing:

> *There dwells a loved one,*
> *But cruel is she.*
> *She left lonely for ever*
> *The kings of the sea.*

"To a Friend" is a sonnet which answers the question as to what prop one can find in these bad days. He can thank Homer and the philosopher

Epictetus for enlarging his mind. But his special thanks are for Sophocles, who inspired Arnold throughout his life, because the Greek poet "saw life steadily, and saw it whole."

"Shakespeare" is another sonnet. It acknowledges that Shakespeare's greatness is beyond analysis. Shakespeare was self-schooled, and walked among men who probably never guessed his greatness. But that was better so. For all the pains, the weakness, the griefs which the human spirit knows "find their sole speech in that victorious brow."

"Quiet Work" is another sonnet. In it the poet asks nature to teach him the lesson that work need not be accomplished without tranquility. Arnold believes that work performed with a tranquil mind must outlive all that is done with noise and fury.

"Resignation" reminds us that a tranquil mind will do one in good stead when passion and fervent hopes have left us.

The poems in this volume are overcast by a quiet melancholy that is characteristic of Arnold's poetry. The uncertainties current in the intellectual atmosphere of the Victorian Age impelled him to cultivate the sad resignation that his beloved Greek tragic poets taught. Nevertheless, his personal life was very happy. Through Lord Landsdowne's connections, he managed to acquire the position of Inspector of Schools (1851), and in the same year he married Frances Wightman, the daughter of a judge. The marriage was very fortunate, and the chief annoyance to Arnold was the continual traveling his position involved. He resented these enforced absences from his home circle, to which he was deeply attached. Circumstances required his maintaining his post, however, until 1866. But there were compensations during these years too. He was able to travel a great deal on the Continent, which he visited to study the educational systems of other countries. And he came to know very well some of the finest European men of letters of his time, notably Renan and Saint-Beuve, celebrated French critics.

Poetry is very hard to write when a poet is always on the move. Nevertheless, Arnold seized whatever leisure time he had to continue his career. In 1852 *Empedocles on Etna, and Other Poems* appeared, and in the next year a volume entitled *Poems*. To this 1853 collection Arnold wrote a *Preface* that is perhaps the most important piece of literary criticism England had seen for decades. In it Arnold began to turn the tide away from the influence of the Romantics. He urged a study of the Greek writers as an important discipline for the moderns. "Their noble simplicity and their calm pathos" will teach the moderns to achieve moral profundity by classic example. Poetry deserves a spirit superior to the mere desire of satisfying "the passing time." It is not that we do not owe our contemporaries our attention. But "commerce with the ancients" cannot fail to produce a steadying effect upon the judgment. Students of the classics will neither applaud nor revile their own age. But they will wish to know what it actually is, and whether what it has to offer is what they want. Most of all, the study of the noble Greeks will rid the mind of irritation and impatience.

These opinions constitute Arnold's reaction against the prosaic qualities of his age. He had small sympathy for the excesses of the Romantic Movement, and even less for the Romantics' futile abhorrence of life. Of them, Wordsworth was the sole object of his great admiration. But even in Wordsworth he objected to the lack of variety. He could not accept Wordsworth's pantheism, for he felt that man has all that Nature has—and more. It is true that the music of Arnold's poetry is quite close to Wordsworth's best in its quiet reflective tone. Unlike Wordsworth, however, he is concerned not with man's place in nature, but with the future of civilization. It is his inability to find a solution for his time that imparts to his poetry, written (as most of it was) in his earlier career, an air of frustrated hope. His poetry, therefore, is the voice of many of his contemporaries who were dissatisfied with Victorian materialism, but could find no comfort in religious dogma.

The volume of 1852 contains some important poems: "Lines Written in Kensington Gardens," "To Marguerite," "A Summer Night," "Self-Dependence," and "The Buried Life." The 1853 volume contains others of equal importance: "Philomela," "Requiescat," "Sohrab and Rustum," and "The Scholar Gypsy."

"Lines Written in Kensington Gardens" is composed in quatrains of interlocked rhymes (*abab*). The poet describes the lonely glade where he is lying amid the song of birds. Sometimes a child passes with his nurse. Sometimes a thrush flits overhead. In the huge world that is roaring outside the park, there is not this peace. The poem ends with a moving prayer:

> *Calm soul of all things! make it mine*
> *To feel, amid the city's jar,*
> *That there abides a peace of thine,*
> *Man did not make, and cannot mar.*
>
> *The will to neither strive nor cry,*
> *The power to feel with others give!*
> *Calm, calm me more! nor let me die*
> *Before I have begun to live.*

"To Marguerite" is one of a series of "Switzerland love poems," all dealing with a girl living at Thun. This poem is subtitled "in returning a volume of the letters of Ortis." It reflects upon the fact that "we mortal millions live alone," but when the gentle winds of spring blow and the nightingale sings in the moonlight, we have a deep longing to feel union with all others. But God ordered our souls to be severed from one another by unplumbed seas.

"A Summer Night" finds the poet in "the deserted, moon-blanched street." The moonlight asks him whether he can still feel his old unquietness. Alas! "Most men in a brazen prison live," toiling their lives away at some unmeaning task, asking no questions of what may lie beyond their prison walls. Only a few men escape their prison, and embark "on the wide ocean of life," braving the chances of a tossed sea, inevitably engulfed in tempests. The poet asks: Must every man be either "madman or slave"? The heavens, at least, are without stain, are "untroubled and unpassionate." They remind man:

> How boundless might his soul's horizons be,
> How vast, yet of what clear transparency!
> How it were good to abide there, and breathe free;
> How fair a lot to fill
> Is left to each man still!

"Self-Dependence" is another poem in quatrains expressing the poet's search for tranquility. He stands at the vessel's prow, going out to sea, pleading that the stars and the sea calm him as they could in his childhood. In the night the answer comes that he must learn to live, like the sea and the stars, unaffrighted by silence, undistracted, self-poised:

> Resolve to be thyself; and know that he,
> Who finds himself, loses his misery.

"The Buried Life" is one of the most deeply moving of these poems. With his loved one he is holding a light "war of mocking words," and yet his eyes are wet with tears. Despite man's power to jest, there is something in a man's breast to which words can bring no peace. Even love is too weak "to unlock the heart and let it speak." If only for a moment we can free our hearts and speak out, well indeed it is for us! Fate, which knew how frivolous man insists upon being, made "the unregarded river of our life" pursue its way undiscerned. We never see this buried stream. Often in the midst of confusion we have a burning desire to know our buried life, but we almost never succeed in finding it. We may say or do things well, but they are not true of our inner selves. And so, we ask "of all the thousand nothings of the hour" that they benumb us, and make us forget this buried life. Only "when a beloved hand is laid in ours," and we can read in a loved one's eyes his love, "a bolt is shot back somewhere in our breast...":

> The eye sinks inward, and the heart lies plain,
> And what we mean, we say, and what we would we know.
> A man becomes aware of his life's flow,
> And hears its winding murmur; and he sees
> The meadows where it glides, the sun, the breeze.
>
> And there arrives a lull in the hot race
> Wherein he doth for ever chase
> That flying and elusive shadow, rest.
> An air of coolness plays upon his face,
> And an unwonted calm pervades his breast.
> And then he thinks he knows
> The hills where his life rose,
> And the sea where it goes.

"Philomela" is an apostrophe to the nightingale. It reproduces wonderfully the intensity of the bird's song, a song of pain. It makes reference to the old legend of the sisters Philomela and Procne, who were changed into the nightingale and the swallow, respectively, when they escaped from Procne's husband Tereus, king of Thrace. (Tereus had violated Philomela's honor, and cut out her tongue to prevent her revealing his act. But Philomela wove her story into a tapestry. In revenge Procne killed her son Itylus.)

"Requiescat" is an exquisite lyric, beginning:

> *Strew on her roses, roses,*
> *And never a spray of yew!*
> *In quiet she reposes;*
> *Ah, would that I did too!*

Her heart was tired and yearned for peace. Tonight her spirit inherits "the vastly hall of death."

"Sohrab and Rustum" is Arnold's finest long poem. It is a narrative, its story taken from an incident related in the Oriental storyteller Firdawsi's *Book of Kings*. There is a wonderful fusion in Arnold's verse of Oriental color, romantic passion, and classical serenity. Its blank verse ranks among the noblest in English. In deeply moving cadences it tells of the mortal combat between a great warrior and his son on the field of battle, when the latter, who has been raised in another land, is in ignorance of the fact that his opponent is the father he has been seeking everywhere.

"The Scholar Gypsy" is one of Arnold's best known and most perfectly wrought poems. The idea came to him from a passage in a seventeenth century book, Glanvil's *Vanity of Dogmatizing*. This account told of an Oxford student whom poverty forced to quit his studies. He joined a band of gypsies, and quickly won the love of his new comrades; one day, at last, some of his old friends found him among the gypsies, and he informed them that he had learned to profoundly respect gypsy lore and learning. Arnold's poem begins with the poet in the country reading his Glanvil. He recounts the episode of the gypsy scholar. This former Oxford student informed his former schoolmates that the gypsies know how to work on men's brains. He too, the Scholar-Gypsy declared, would learn that art and then write a book to inform the world about it. The poet then speculates on where the gypsy scholar may now be. He thinks of him in many spots dear to the lover of Oxford and its environs. He is sure he has seen him at the Ferry returning home on summer nights, or at the dance around the elm at Fyfield in May,— or above Godstow Bridge in haying time, or in autumn in Bagley Wood. Once he may have passed him on the wooden bridge going toward Hinksey. But what a dream this is! For two hundred years have passed since Glanvil told his story. No, the Scholar Gypsy is timeless, and has not "felt the lapse of hours," for he had "one aim, one business, one desire" in life. He left the world of men, and left "sick fatigue" and "languid doubt." The youth of this scholar is perennial. Let him never come back to the world of men, to "this strange disease of modern life," where he would forever be "clutching the inviolable shade."

Arnold was himself an excellent critic of his own verse. He realized that he lacked Browning's dynamic energy as a poet and Tennyson's exquisite artistry. But he also knew that he maintained a better balance of both qualities than either of his great contemporaries. In consequence, as he wrote to his mother, he felt that he, would have his day just as they were having theirs. Arnold, moreover, brought back a classic sense of polish that the Victorians had forgotten. This love of elegance and symmetry that he nurtured was the very basis of his social beliefs as well as of his literary practice.

Despite the fact that he was not yet widely read, he had made enough impression upon a limited audience to be offered the Professorship of Poetry at Oxford (1857). The first talk he gave in his new position was to prove how modern the Greek classics were. In 1858 he published one of his less successful works, *Merope*, a closet drama, to further his position on the importance of knowing the ancients. In 1867 appeared his last volume of poetry, *New Poems*. This last collection contains a number of important poems: "Thyrsis," "Dover Beach," "Growing Old," "The Austerity of Poetry," "Rugby Chapel," and "The Last Word."

Whether "Thyrsis" deserves to be placed beside "Lycidas" and "Adonais" in a trio of the greatest English elegies, as some critics claim, need not be settled here. It is certainly a poem of high quality, a perfect expression of the sad tranquility and intellectual serenity of which Arnold was master. It is subtitled "A monody to commemorate the author's friend, Arthur Hugh Clough, who died at Florence, 1861." The poem is saturated, like "The Scholar Gypsy," with the atmosphere of Oxford. The poet reflects on how changed everything is near Oxford now. Are the hills changed too? Here in the old days, Thyrsis and he came often, looking down on the "dreaming spires" of Oxford. Too rarely does the poet come here now, though once he knew "each field, each flower, each stick." But Thyrsis left here of his own will because he could not rest. The cuckoo bird sings: "The bloom is gone, and with the bloom go I!" But where will the bird go? For midsummer soon will be here with its sweet williams, snapdragons, carnations, jasmine, and the white evening star. The bird flies away, unheeding. But it does not matter, for the cuckoo will return next year. But never again will Thyrsis return. Never will he sing a strain that the world shall at last heed. So in this place the poet vents his grief in sorrowful reminiscence of remembered scenes. The dusk descends while he sings his sorrow, and now, against the sunset, "bare on its lovely ridge" stands outlined the tree that was dear to both of them. "O Thyrsis, still our tree is there!" But it is not there for Thyrsis, for he is now "in happier air." He is now a companion of the old Sicilian singers, who sing to him their immortal music. Yet though left alone, the poet will not despair while that tree stands, reminding him that the spirit of their favorite, the Scholar Gypsy, still haunts the place. Why should the poet himself not seek, with that old Oxonian, "a fugitive and gracious light." Thyrsis himself wandered abroad on such a quest. What if Thyrsis's music did not retain its happy rustic tone, and lost it all too soon? What if he learned too soon the language of sorrow? Still, always he had before him a vision of light. Too rare, too rare are the poet's visits to this spot. He asks his dead friend to remind him often:

> *I wandered till I died.*
> *Roam on! The light we sought is shining still,*
> *Dost thou ask proof? Our tree yet crowns the hill,*
> *Our Scholar travels yet the loved hillside.*

"Dover Beach" is Arnold's most famous poem, and is a perfect example of the kind of quiet music over which no one had greater mastery. The poet stands by the window looking over the channel from Dover. In the moonlight the French coast gleams for a moment and the cliffs of England stand out glimmering. He bids his loved one come to the window. There, where the spray is on the shore, you can hear the grating roar of pebbles as the waves retreat. It is such a note of eternal sadness as Sophocles heard long ago on the Aegean. The sea of religion was once at the full and lapped the whole world in peace. But now it is retreating down the vast edges of the world. Ah love, the poet cries, let us be true to one another. For the world that seems to lie before us so beautiful and new, has in it no certainty, no peace, no help for pain:

> *And we are here as on a darkling plain*
> *Swept with confused alarms of struggle and flight,*
> *Where ignorant armies clash by night.*

"Growing Old" asks the question, "What is it to grow old?" It is indeed to lose the beauty of youth, to lose our strength. But it is more than this. It is not what youth hoped it would be. It is not to find life mellowed and softened, it is not to see the world from a height with prophetic eyes. It is to spend long days forgetting we were ever young. It is to suffer long days of pain and to but half-feel what we feel. It is to lose the gift of emotion. It is at the very end, when we have become but a phantom of ourselves:

> *To hear the world applaud the hollow ghost*
> *Which blamed the living man.*

This poem is unique among Arnold's works for its extreme pessimism.

"The Austerity of Poetry" is a sonnet built around the experience of the Italian poet, Giacopone Di Todi, who lived in the thirteenth century. Giacopone had led a merry life in his youth and culminated his joys by marrying a beautiful girl. In the midst of the bridal festival, the platform on which all the company was seated gave way. Among the many hurt was the bride, who lay there dying. As they drew her raiment off they found underneath her gorgeous robes a garment of haircloth. (This discovery turned Giacopone to a religious life). Arnold's poem recounts the accident and concludes that the bride of poets, the Muse, is like Giacopone's bride, happy and radiant outside, but "a hidden ground of thought and of austerity within."

"Rugby Chapel" is a tribute to the memory of the poet's father, Thomas Arnold, the celebrated headmaster of Rugby. The poem is dated November 1857. The autumn evening descends, and in the cold the poet looks upon the field strewn with withered leaves, silent but for the shout of a few boys still playing. Here in the chapel the poet's father lies. But one cannot think of gloom when thinking of him. For he was a man of buoyant cheerfulness. It is fifteen years since he trod "the road of death." For fifteen years his family has lacked his protection. On what shore does his spirit now tarry? Wherever he is the poet knows his father will be upraising the humble good from the ground and teaching where the border lies between vice and virtue. This was his life upon earth. Most men eddy about in life, "chatter and love and hate," achieve nothing and die. No one asks where they have gone. But there are some who strive not to die fruitless and these must walk a perilous road. Many are lost in the storm. Those who survive come in the end to a lonely inn among the rocks, where a gaunt host holds his lantern to scan their weather-beaten faces and ask whom in their party they bring. Sadly they answer, "We bring only ourselves. We lost sight of the rest in the storm." But the poet's father will not have come alone to his rest. He never tired of encouraging the trembler or of giving the weary his hand. It is through his father that the poet has come to understand the great souls who have shed their radiance on earth. There were such men. Unlike the vile men of the crowd who live today, they were men who helped the wavering line of humanity. In the hour of need men like the poet's father appear:

> *Radiant with ardor divine!*
> *Beacons of hope, ye appear!*
> *Languor is not in your heart,*
> *Weakness is not in your words,*
> *Weariness not on your brow.*

You recall the stragglers to the line. You fill up the gaps. You strengthen the march on to the City of God.

"The Last Word" is a meditation before death. Let the long contention of life go. Let the greedy have their fill. You have been hissed at, torn at. Better men have fared so, too:

> *Charge once more, then, and be dumb!*
> *Let the victors, when they come,*
> *When the forts of folly fall,*
> *Find thy body by the wall.*

His duties in the field of education gave Arnold less and less time for poetic composition. But he continued to write well, as his fine elegy, "Westminster Abbey," written in 1881, will testify. Though his position as Inspector of Schools was little to his liking, Arnold gave his best abilities to it. His reports were done with care; and the extent of his observation in methods of education can be read in *Popular Education in France* (1861), *A French Eton* (1864), and *Schools and Universities on the Continent* (1868).

Prose and Criticism: Writing prose he found easier to manage during the years of his extensive traveling. At last he embarked upon a career of a prose writer which marks him as one of the most brilliant prose stylists and one of the greatest critics England has ever had. It was in his prose works that he found the answers to the dilemma recorded in his poetry. In consequence, while his poetry is prevailingly sad, his prose is cheerful.

He began with the publication of three lectures delivered at Oxford, *On Translating Homer* (1861). These pieces, which examine the various translations of Homer made in English as well as discuss the Homeric poems themselves, constitute the most important body of Homeric criticism of the Victorian Age. The next year he appended to these thoughts his *Translating Homer: Last Words*. But his first great piece of prose was actually his *Essays in Criticism, First Series* (1865). It has been said of this book that it is the work that taught Englishmen how to write criticism. It was certainly the first book to deal with criticism as an art containing "laws and methods of its own," and certain standards of good taste.

Here Arnold began his long battle against Philistinism—a term he borrowed from the German poet Heine, and which he used to designate the appalling taste of the English middle class. The word *Philistine* came to mean for him narrowmindedness, chauvinism, provincialism, and the vulgarity of middle-class culture. In Arnold's day the average Englishman considered art either as a profitless waste of time or as an exercise bordering on the indecent. It is to Arnold's credit that to a certain degree the general public no longer maintains such a view. Few periods in the history of ideas show such an incredibly low level of public taste as Arnold's age. If public taste has improved, it is somewhat owing to the fact that Arnold never tired of insisting on the importance to life of literature and art.

The first series of the *Essays in Criticism* contains a memorable *Preface*, and an all-important essay on "The Function of Criticism at the Present Time." The *Preface* contains the beautiful tribute to Oxford that we have already quoted in this piece. Arnold says of his alma mater that she is an:

> Adorable dreamer, whose heart has been so romantic! Who hast given thyself so prodigally, given thyself to sides and to heroes not mine, only never to the Philistines! Home of lost causes, and forsaken beliefs, and unpopular names, and impossible loyalties! What example could ever so inspire us to keep down the Philistine in ourselves . . . ?

> . . . Apparitions of a day, what is our puny warfare against the Philistines, compared with the warfare which this queen of romance has been waging against them for centuries, and will wage after we are gone?

"The Function of Criticism at the Present Time" opens with a consideration of an earlier observation of his. He had said that Continental literature and the Continental intellect have for some time been largely critical; English literature and English thought, on the other hand, have been largely indifferent to critical effort. Wordsworth found the level of criticism very low in his time. But is it true, as Wordsworth implies, that criticism itself is necessarily injurious? Would it have been better for Samuel Johnson to have written more works like his boring *Irene* instead of his brilliant *Lives of the Poets?* Indeed, are Wordsworth's Ecclesiastical Sonnets equal to his important *Preface* to *The Lyrical Ballads?* It is true that the critical power is lower than the creative but the writing of good criticism can be the exercise of the creative faculty. Moreover, pure creativeness is not possible in all periods. There must be materials at hand for a great poet. In some ages, like our own, they may not be available because of contradicting currents of belief and thought. The function of criticism is to provide these materials, to sift through doctrines, to provide the atmosphere in which creative literature can flourish. Goethe "was nourished by" a greater critical effort sifting the materials of life than was available to Byron. That is why Goethe is a greater poet. Had Wordsworth read more, he would have been greater than he is. But books are not enough to nourish a poet, as the cases of Coleridge and Shelley would prove (to Arnold). Sophocles and Shakespeare, both of whom are beyond praise, read very little. But in their times the atmosphere was charged with nourishing ideas and beliefs. They lived in a world shot through with alert and intelligent thought. If it be asked why the French Revolution produced no great works of genius in France, the answer is that the French Revolution was concerned with purely political and practical issues. If Burke is a great writer it is because, even when dealing with politics, his writings are permeated with profound philosophical truth. In England there has been recently great advance in material comforts. When England has had enough of material advancement, Englishmen will remember that they have minds. Then the question will be: What should one do to make a good life? It is to supply this need that English criticism will have to step forth. English criticism can make a contribution only by remaining disinterested, by keeping aloof from a practical view of things, by steadily refusing to lend itself to any ulterior practical considerations. English criticism has kept so little to the realm of pure intellect, has so much meddled with political considerations, that it has failed in its best work—which should be to keep men from smugness and self-satisfaction, which vulgarize and retard. The function of criticism is to lead men toward perfection by teaching the mind to dwell on excellence, by urging the mind to consider beauty and symmetry in life. There are too many people like Roebuck, Member of Parliament, who are convinced that England is achieving perfection because property is safe. According to such men England has an unrivaled happiness. But then one may read in the newspapers such shocking accounts as that of a girl named Wragg who was recently taken into custody for the murder of her illegitimate child. How do such events fit in with the notion that England has achieved the height of social progress? What can be the meaning of Roebuck's phrase, "our unrivalled happiness," in the face of such ugliness? And such ugliness is the product of the crass materialism in English life. Indeed, the much vaunted British Constitution is, from some points of view, a perfect manufactory of Philistines. Criticism, as the author understands it, is:

> A distinterested endeavor to learn and propagate the best that is known and thought in the world. . . . There is so much inviting us!—What are we to take? what will furnish us in growth towards perfection? That is the question which, with the immense field of life and literature lying before him, the critic has to answer.

In essence, Arnold argues in this important critical essay that great literary art is both gnostic and inspiriting—that is, that literature has the power to communicate important knowledge about the nature of existence and, simultaneously, to move us emotionally and spiritually to seek the good in our conduct and relationships. This grand claim for literature has not been heard in such a cogent and extended argument since the days of the Greek philosphers and rhetoricians, including Aristotle.

The fundamental philosophy advanced in this essay was continued, expanded, and applied to the less theoretical aspects of life itself in Arnold's next work, *Culture and Anarchy* (1869), which had appeared as a series of articles in the *Cornhill Magazine*. The first essay in this book, "Sweetness and Light," is the most celebrated, though hardly less so is the one on "Hebraism and Hellenism." The entire volume is a strong argument for the exercise of an unrestricted critical intelligence. English society, in Arnold's opinion, is divided into three classes: the Barbarians (the aristocracy), the Philistines (the middle class), and the Populace. There can be little hope for improvement, he feels, until critical understanding will view society as a whole.

Society, he says in "Sweetness and Light," must learn to take up the pursuit of perfection, which is what he means by the pursuit of sweetness and light. This "Hellenistic" cult of beauty ("sweetness") and reason ("light") is the only hope Arnold sees for a future that can no longer turn to the Bible for guidance. He admits that the larger importance in life belongs to conduct. The mistake of the Puritans was to imagine that conduct is all of life. Unnourished by the grace of beauty and the sanity of reason, conduct is bound to be distorted and warped. We can learn from the Greeks the value of making our religion and our search for beauty identical.

> He who works for sweetness and light, works to make reason and the will of God prevail. He who works for machinery, he who works for hatred, works only for confusion. . . . Culture has one great passion, the passion for sweetness and light. . . . It is not satisfied till we all come to a perfect man; it knows that the sweetness and light of the few must be imperfect until the raw and unkindled masses of humanity are touched with sweetness and light.

Culture he defines as a pursuit of "total perfection" through a knowledge of "the best which has been thought and said in the world." Such a conviction makes it plain that Arnold was hardly less religious in his faith that the propagation of ideas would save the world than Carlyle had been in his conviction that work would regenerate humanity.

In the thrust of his essay, Arnold allies himself with a quite traditional British argument about the place and force of "right ideas" (or, in Arnold's phrase, "the best") in human affairs. Arnold thus stands as the nineteenth century father of what in the twentieth century would become known as the "cultural literacy" movement. Although Arnold was no ideologue for his position, he would generally agree that a canon of superior ideas and art, including literacy art, could be broadly defined and culturally perpetuated by right-thinking men and women. Arnold, in other words, would have little intellectual or emotional interest in more dialectical approaches to culture, including versions of multiculturalism that present competing values as equally valid.

"Hebraism and Hellenism" contrasts this Hellenistic pursuit of sweetness and light with the Biblical insistence on rewards and punishments in the Hereafter. Under "Hebraism" Arnold included both the traditional Hebrew and Christian religions. He was convinced that it was a nobler and more fitting idea for human beings to lead ethical lives for the sake of the dignity of the human spirit than for considerations of their eventual fate in Heaven or Hell.

These speculations led him to an examination of what claims traditional religion might have for one's respect. In *Saint Paul and Protestantism* (1870), he began a series of writings that embroiled him in theological controversy. In this work was none too successful in attempting a study of the Bible on scientific principles. *Friendship's Garland* (1871), one of his wittiest works, continued the arguments of *Culture and Anarchy*. *Literature and Dogma* (1873) evoked a fury of rage from orthodox Christians. In an avowed desire to return the Bible to plain people, he attacked the literal interpretation of the Bible and those theologians who stressed the letter of the Scriptures instead of its spirit. He felt the Bible was an important guide to ethics, but he refused to agree that human nature must be made to conform to the dicta of the Bible. A sequel to this work, *God and the Bible* (1875), though less well-known, is far more scholarly.

Arnold, as we have said, was an inveterate traveler, and in 1883 he came to the United States for a series of lectures on "Democracy," on "Emerson," and on "Literature and Science." These were collected eventually as *Discourses in America* (1885).

The lecture on "Literature and Science," in which Arnold debated the views of Huxley, is one of the most important statements of the claims of classical education and literature to an important role in modern education. Under Huxley's powerful onslaught in behalf of the natural sciences, the study of *belles-lettres* suddenly was put upon the defensive. (It has been there ever since.) A movement was already beginning to evaluate studies only in terms of social or pragmatic usefulness. Arnold's lecture came brilliantly to the defense of the humanities. Never a fanatic, he willingly admits the value of including science among necessary studies. But he reminds us that the sciences teach nothing about *conduct* in life. The literature of ancient Greece and Rome is important to know, not for the languages in which it is written but for its profound understanding of man's place in the scheme of things. A knowledge of classical literature will help us find a way of life. All knowledge is interesting. But if there must be a separation between literature and science, "The great majority of mankind, all who have not exceptional and overpowering aptitudes for the study of nature, would do well . . . to be educated in humane letters [literature] rather than in the natural sciences. Letters . . . will make them live more."

Arnold thus argues that such important human traits as creativity, compassion, ethics, and love itself are engendered more by literature than by scientific experimentation or reflection. Through literature, for Arnold, we not only come to know the good but are moved to do it.

Arnold's last works include *Last Essays on Church and Religion* (1877), *Mixed Essays* (1879), *Irish Essays and Others* (1882), and *Essays in Criticism, Second Series*, (1888). Of these, the last is the most important. It contains a brilliant essay on Wordsworth, which has been largely responsible for Wordsworth's being accepted as the leading poet of the century. With characteristic sanity, Arnold realizes that the bulk of Wordsworth's poetry had better be discarded. It is on the basis of the quality of a small quantity of Wordsworth's poetry that Arnold believes him the best poet England has had after Shakespeare and Milton. The volume also contains an essay on "The Study of Poetry," which advances the claim of poetry to a major place in our life and our education, which itself should be a preparation for life. This essay also contains some brilliant studies of English poetry through the ages; here Arnold indicates precisely how intelligent criticism should function in evaluating the worth of any piece of writing.

After a full and rewarding life, Arnold died in 1888 from a heart attack in Liverpool, on his return from America.

IMPORTANCE

Arnold emerges as the most modern as well as the most cultivated writer of his generation. He had the intelligence to be aware of the new order of life which the scientific era was ushering in. But, unlike some less wise, he did not hesitate to treasure what was valuable in the past. It was characteristic of him that he should have believed no work of literature worth preserving from the past unless it had something to say to our own times. And it was on that basis that he fought to conserve the best of what had been said and thought in the world as a contribution to a better life in the future.

MINOR VICTORIAN POETS

Emily Brontë (1818–1848)

Emily Brontë is best known as the author of a remarkable novel, *Wuthering Heights*, which will be discussed later. Her two sisters, Charlotte and Anne, both gifted, lived with her a retired lonely life in a remote corner of Yorkshire. Their father was a clergyman, and they kept house for him. The only excitement in their household was provided by the unpredictable conduct of their talented but wayward brother. The sisters spent a little time together in Belgium (1842) while Charlotte did some tutoring. With a great deal of trepidation they published a volume of poems by all of them; but they did not dare issue the book under their own names, and took the pseudonyms of Currer Bell, Ellis Bell, and Acton Bell. Nobody purchased the volume. Nevertheless, the work is much esteemed today because of Emily's poems.

Although Charlotte Brontë had at first a much larger reputation, it is now clear that Emily was the genius in the family. Her *Wuthering Heights* has been unrivaled among English novels for its distinctive qualities. And her poetry, which has been rediscovered only in our own century, has won much admiration from the discriminating. Hers was a very intense nature. Despite the apparent uneventfulness of her life, Emily Brontë must have known a torrential existence within her bosom. Her poems give ample testimony of that.

Among her best poems are "Remembrance," "The Visionary," "The Old Stoic," and "Last Lines." "Remembrance" opens with an apostrophe to her only love, lying cold in the earth beneath the deep snow; do her thoughts not linger over that heath?

> *Cold in the earth—and fifteen wild Decembers*
> *From those brown hills, have melted into spring:*
> *Faithful, indeed, is the spirit that remembers*
> *After such years of change and suffering!*

There can never be for her another light of happiness or another morn of hope. She has learned to exist without joy. Nor does she dare to indulge "in memory's rapturous pain" or how could she face the world again?

"Last Lines" has an opening that has often been quoted:

> *No coward soul is mine,*
> *No trembler in the world's storm-troubled sphere:*
> *I see Heaven's glories shine,*
> *And faith shines equal, arming me from fear.*

There are no creeds that could waken doubt in her faith. She knows that God's spirit pervades all things eternally. Even if the universe ceased to exist, God would still be:

There is not room for Death,
Nor atom that his might could render void:
Thou—Thou art Being and Breath,
And what Thou art may never be destroyed.

Arthur Hugh Clough (1819–1861)

Arthur Hugh Clough was one of the talented Victorians the fabric of whose mind was destroyed by the new onslaught on orthodox religion. His mind was not strong enough to bring him to port in the tempests then raging on the sea of faith. He remained skeptical but undecided. For a while he tried to accept Carlyle's recipe for relief in doing work at hand, but found little help in that. In the end he gave the question up in despair. Of course, whatever the judgment of posterity may be on his poetry, he will always be interesting as the man whose death inspired his friend Arnold to write a great elegy.

He was born in Liverpool January 1, 1819, and spent some of his boyhood in South Carolina. When he was nine he was sent to school at Rugby, and came under the influence of Matthew Arnold's famous father, Dr. Arnold, the headmaster. He formed there some lasting friendships. Winning a scholarship to Balliol College, Oxford, he entered in 1837, and became friendly with Benjamin Jowett, the great translator of Plato, and with Matthew Arnold.

At that time, all of Oxford was agitated by the movement being led by Newman. Clough found its return to medievalism repugnant. Although he accepted a fellowship at Oriel College, his doubts on religion became stronger and stronger. Finally, his religious skepticism decided him to resign in 1848. This step for a time gave him a sense of release.

He began to publish some of his poetry. His first volume contained his longest work, the poem of the title, *The Bothie of Tober-na-Vuolich*. This long narrative in hexameters reflects Clough's momentary high spirits after his break with Oxford. The tone of gaiety is generally foreign to his later works. The story is a graceful one of an Oxford student who falls in love with a Highland lassie. At first they cannot marry because of differences in their rank. But an elopement to the Southern Hemisphere makes a happy ending possible.

Clough then traveled to Paris and to Rome (1848), where he witnessed the events of the revolutions in that year. His buoyancy was soon ended, for his religious doubts overwhelmed him again. It is true that he had a great capacity for evoking friendship, and during his next restless years he became close to Carlyle and Emerson. Indeed, it was because of the latter that he visited Harvard (1852), where he lectured and began a translation of Plutarch. But despite the quality of his friendships, he knew little peace of mind.

In 1853 he was back in England, married a girl with whom he was much in love, and took a position as Examiner in the Education Office. In 1860 his health began to fail, and he sought to better it in Italy. He died in Florence, November 13, 1861.

Clough had been writing poetry for eight years before he published his first book. His other volumes are: *Amours de Voyage* (1849), *Ambarvalia* (in collaboration with a friend, Thomas Burbridge, 1849), *Dipsychus* (1850), and the posthumous *Poems* (1862) and *Poems* and *Prose Remains* (1869).

The level of Clough's poetry is very uneven. Some of his pieces read like hastily composed memoranda of his travels. But his best poetry is an excellent reflection of his temperamental melancholy, and the dilemma of an essentially conservative man whom conviction has forced to surrender past modes of belief. The most admirable quality of Clough's poetry is its honesty. His best poems are "*Qua Cursum Ventus*," "Say Not the Struggle Nought Availeth," "*Qui Laborat Orat*," "All Is Well," and "Life Is Struggle."

"*Qua Cursum Ventus*" ("As the Wind Blows") is a record of a debate with a friend over religion. It opens:

> *As ships, becalmed at eve, that lay*
> *With canvas drooping, side by side,*
> *Two towers of sail at dawn of day*
> *Are scarce long leagues apart descried.*

These ships may plough, unknown to each other, long seas apart. But in the end they meet in the same port. So, too, he hopes his friend and he will find union with each other at the end of their search.

"Say Not the Struggle Nought Availeth" expresses a conviction that life is worth the struggle. One procures light from the sun not only in the dawn of life, but even more brilliantly in the late afternoon of experience.

"*Qui Laborat Orat*" ("He Who Labors Prays") is an address to God, the source of life and light. If the heart cannot pray, God will forgive it as long as it can make of its work its prayer.

"All Is Well" expresses the conviction that though our destiny is uncertain, all is well with humanity. Even if no one knows whither the ship is bound, yet it travels on.

"Life Is Struggle" is a record of the poet's experience that it is pain and endless disillusion which keep us alive—the imperious struggle itself, not joy.

6
THE VICTORIAN NOVEL

The novel became by degrees, in Victorian times, increasingly important as a literary medium. Though regarded a century earlier as appealing only to light-headed girls who might have spent their time in better occupations, it now won a position as the most respected of prose forms. Among the Victorians there is, for the first time, an imposing number of novelists, and an equal impressive variety in style and subject-matter.

Many novels continue the tradition of the historical novel as established by Scott; others deal with contemporary life, as did the works of Jane Austen. But few novelists confined themselves to either of these approaches. Moreover, there is a great widening in the tone of the various writers. Some novelists write tragically of life, some satirically; some are realists, some are romanticists; some write to reform, others only to amuse. And in the careers of certain individual Victorian novelists, all these purposes can be found.

FREDERICK MARRYATT (1792–1848)

Frederick Marryatt continued the tradition of the sea story begun by Smollett and later flowering magnificently in the twentieth century in the words of Joseph Conrad. Marryatt knew the sea well; his novels are lively, running over with good health, and admired by men of the sea for the accuracy of their details. The best known are *Peter Simple* (1834), *Jacob Faithful* (1834), and, best-liked of all, *Midshipman Easy* (1836).

THOMAS LOVE PEACOCK (1785–1866)

For a while Thomas Love Peacock tried his hand none too successfully at poetry. *Palmyra* (1806), *The Genius of the Thames* (1810), or *Rhododaphne* (1818) is not likely to be read any more by others than scholars. No wonder he concluded in his prose treatise, *The Four Ages of Poetry* (1820), that it would no longer be possible for poets to write great poetry. (It was this piece that evoked Shelley's noble *Defense of Poetry*.) But Peacock's novels, *Headlong Hall* (1816), *Melincourt* (1817), *Nightmare Abbey* (1818), *Maid Marian* (1822), *The Misfortunes of Elphin* (1829), *Crotchet Castle* (1831), and *Gryll Grange* (1860) have been something of a cult with certain modern readers.

There is a surprisingly modern quality in his willingness to sacrifice plot interest to the exposition of ideas during the elaborate conversations that take place in his fanciful novels. Peacock was staunchly unsympathetic to new ideas, and leveled the shafts of his engaging wit at radicalism, medievalism, romanticists, transcendentalists, and every kind of fanatic. Though a friend of Shelley and his circle, he did not hesitate to draw recognizable satirical portraits of Shelley, Byron, Southey, Coleridge, and Wordsworth. His satire is too delicate ever to degenerate into burlesque. He makes these great men sound just like themselves—and yet manages to make them look quite ridiculous.

WILLIAM HARRISON AINSWORTH (1805–1882)

William Harrison Ainsworth continued the tradition of the historical novel as established by Scott. To it he joined his addiction to the horror effects of the Gothic novel. He was a solid antiquarian—perhaps a little too obviously so—but wrote far too much to write well. He is, nonetheless, a spirited novelist, and his novels read better today than most of the historical stories of his contemporaries. The best of his books are: *Rookwood* (1834), *Jack Sheppard* (1839), *The Tower of London* (1840), *Old Saint Paul's* (1841), *Windsor Castle* (1843), and *The Lancashire Witches* (1848).

EDWARD BULWER-LYTTON (1803–1873)

Edward Bulwer-Lytton illustrates very well the tendency of the Victorian novelist to interest himself in many kinds of novel writing. Two early novels, *Falkland* (1827) and *Pelham, or the Adventures of a Gentleman* (1832), inspired by the success of the witty Byronic hero, have each a dandy for a hero; *Pelham* illustrates how impudence and a ready tongue can bring the world to adore one. *Paul Clifford* (1830), *Eugene Aram* (1832), and *Lucretia, or Children of the Night* (1846) are somewhat in the tradition of the Gothic novel, deal with criminals, and are frankly terror novels. Another book, *Zanoni* (1842), akin to these, deals with the supernatural and is outfitted with quasi-scientific trappings; theosophists are very fond of this work, and it was a kind of classic to their movement.

Occasionally, Bulwer-Lytton claimed a social purpose for his books by making his criminals the victims of social institutions. But it was as a disciple of Scott that he achieved his greatest successes. *The Last Days of Pompeii* (1834), *Rienzi* (1835), *The Last of the Barons* (1843), and *Harold* (1848) were all widely read and admired; and as an historian he is more painstaking than Scott.

Later he turned to the domestic novel, when public taste had veered in that direction, with *The Caxtons* (1850), *My Novel* (1853), and *What Will He Do With It?* (1858). Bulwer-Lytton is the author of a number of other novels. Like Scott, he wrote far too much, and like him usually wrote well enough without achieving great heights or falling to abysmal levels. For modern tastes his style is marred by theatricality and swollen rhetoric; but he was very clever at carrying his story along with interest and a certain verve.

BENJAMIN DISRAELI (1804–1881)

Benjamin Disraeli, who later became the Earl of Beaconsfield, not only played a decisive role as a political leader of his country but was also a highly successful novelist. Most of his books reflect his great interest in contemporary political events, and were frankly written in order to demonstrate a thesis. The Victorian Age is one of contradictions, and although Disraeli was a leader of the Tories, his principles were essentially democratic, and he was a sincere friend of the demands of the workingmen of England. He disliked ultra-Toryism as much as he detested the Utilitarian philosophy of the Whigs, as may be seen in his novel, *Coningsby* (1844).

His earlier novels deal with life in high society, and are written with admirable grace: *Vivian Grey* (1826), *The Young Duke* (1831), *Contarini Fleming* (1832), *Alroy* (1833), and *Venetia* (1837). In this group belongs the most delightful of them all, a satire-fantasy, *Ixion in Heaven* (1828); here, as elsewhere, Disraeli enjoyed portraying easily recognized contemporaries.

After he had entered upon his political career in Parliament, Disraeli's novels became more and more immersed in political issues. *Coningsby* has been called the finest political novel ever written; in addition to satirizing current events, it is also a spirited defense of Disraeli's own people, the Jews. By the time he wrote *Sybil* (1845), Disraeli had come under the influence of Carlyle; it is an attack on Chartism as the product of worship for gold and for the machine; the author sees as the only hope for England a return to disinterested patriotism on the part of rich and poor alike. *Tancred* (1847), written in its author's most satirical vein, deals with religious matters; *Lothair* (1870) and *Endymion* (1880) are both political novels, plainly written by a man who knows the world of fashion and politics inside and out, are replete with wit, but, like many of Disraeli's novels, are more brilliant than profound.

Despite the cleverness and skill of his books, Disraeli's novels have inevitably lost much of their appeal because of the very contemporaneousness of their topics. Perhaps, too, had he been as able in solving the problems he dealt with as he was in presenting them, his work would have been less ephemeral.

ELIZABETH CLEGHORN GASKELL (1810–1865)

Elizabeth Cleghorn Gaskell, the wife of a clergyman in Manchester, was well acquainted with the appalling conditions prevailing in industrial England. Her *Mary Barton* (1848), laid in Manchester, was inspired by the same kind of disgust that called forth Carlyle's fury against the machine. There are powerful pictures in it of the wretchedness and starvation which were epidemic among mill workers and factory employees, as well as generous indignation against the callousness of their employers. *North and South* (1855) is written in the same strain. Both books were looked upon as seditious by her contemporaries. *Ruth* (1853) is a surprisingly courageous defense of women as victims of the "double standard," and shocked many of its readers.

Her first novel having attracted the attention of Dickens, he invited her contribution to his magazine, *Household Words*. As a result, she wrote serially the best-known of her books, *Cranford* (1851–1853). It is less a novel than a series of highly realistic pictures of village life. The material for it she drew from her memories of her childhood in Cheshire. The quiet narrative of the daily occurrences common to simple villagers is replete with sweetness and charm. The slender thread of story which holds the various incidents together is the distress of Miss Jenkyns upon her sudden loss of her little property until her rescue at the hands of her brother when he returns from India.

Sylvia's Lovers (1863) is a tragedy, and *Cousin Phyllis* (1864) a well-wrought pastoral story. What promised to be the best of her novels, *Wives and Daughters* (1864–1866), was never completed; it contains some fine satire at the expense of two daughters of opposing natures and their inept mother.

Gaskell's *Life of Charlotte Brontë* (1857) is one of the great classics of English biography.

CHARLES KINGSLEY (1819–1875)

Charles Kingsley led a varied and active life. He was a minister, a leader in the Protestant movement opposing Newman, a professor of history at Cambridge University, a good poet, a lover of sports, and an amateur naturalist. *The Saint's Tragedy* (1848) is a drama in verse on St. Teresa; *Andromeda* (1858) is a narrative poem in hexameters; but of all Kingsley's poetry *The Sands of Dee* is the only one now generally known. When he did turn to the novel, it was as a disciple of Carlyle and an active participant in the new Christian Socialist Movement. It is not surprising, therefore, to find him a vigorous propounder of social reform. His first novel, *Yeast*, appeared in 1848, a year of social revolutions. His second, *Alton Locke, Tailor and Poet* (1850), was published two years later. In both novels plot is subordinated to discussion. Kingsley tried to prove that the Chartist Movement had failed because it had employed force. He is no friend of trade unions, but he is a bitter foe of slums, illiteracy, and the oppression of the masses. His solution is progress through Christian ethics, to be accomplished by the examples set by practicing Christians.

Kingsley now turned to the historical novel to give his ideas a more imaginative setting. In *Hypatia* (1853) he mirrors Victorian social issues as merely a recapitulation of similar issues in old Alexandria when Christian, Jew, and pagan—not to speak of heretics—were at one another's throats. *Westward Ho!* (1855) is the most interesting of these historical novels; in a breezy tale of Elizabethan adventure on the sea Kingsley here defends the principles of the nineteenth century Broad Church Movement. *Hereward the Wake* (1866) is fervidly patriotic in its vaunting of sturdy Anglo-Saxon courage in the fight against the conquering Normans.

Kingsley also wrote *Two Years Ago* (1857) to show the purifying effect, during the Crimean War, of the endurance and self-sacrifice that war makes possible to men. His *The Water Babies* (1863), a fantasy, is one of the best-loved of children's books.

THE BRONTËS

In recent years there have been a great many books and plays written about the Brontë sisters. Charlotte Brontë (1816–1855), Emily Brontë (1818–1848) and Anne Brontë (1820–1849) were the youngest of five daughters of a Yorkshire clergyman. The two oldest daughters died in youth from a combination of tuberculosis and malnutrition while at school. Charlotte and Emily were tutored by their father at their home in Haworth. They had one brother, Branwell, a youth of great gifts, who was completely undisciplined, but who encouraged the girls in their furtive literary attempts. Charlotte, as the eldest surviving sister, went out first into the world as a governess. In 1843–1844 she was employed as a teacher in Brussels at a school where she and Emily had once briefly been sent to learn French and where she fell in love vainly with a married pedagogue. Back at Haworth, Charlotte and Emily intended to open a school, but they could find no students. These years were embittered by the spectacle of their talented brother developing into an alcoholic and drug addict until in 1848 he drank himself into the grave.

One day Charlotte discovered by accident a manuscript in Emily's hand that proved that the latter had secretly been writing poetry. Since she and Anne had also been composing verse they decided to issue a joint volume (1846) under the pen names of Currer, Ellis, and Acton Bell. Although their book made no impression, all three turned busily to novel writing. Charlotte's first attempt, *The Professor* (1857), was not published until after her death. No publisher was interested in it, though one firm indicated that it might be interested in seeing other examples of the author's work.

She submitted *Jane Eyre* (1847), which was accepted, and proved an enormous success. Another publisher in the meantime had accepted Emily's *Wuthering Heights* (1848) and Anne's *Agnes Grey*, both of which were published together in one volume. Anne's *The Tenant of Wildfell Hall* (1848) was accepted soon after in an attempt to capitalize on the sensation that the name "Bell" was causing in literary circles. Story has it that the publishers were considerably shocked when three retiring maidens appeared in London and proved to be the much-talked-about Messrs. Bell. On their return from the city, they found their brother near his end. He died soon afterward. At his funeral Emily caught her death-cold, and in December of the same year she died. In May of the following year Anne followed her sister to the grave, and Charlotte was left alone to take care of her father in his growing blindness.

In the midst of these anxieties Charlotte now finished *Shirley* (1849). Her desire to bring some happiness into her own mind caused her to twist the story from an inevitable tragic conclusion to an unacceptable happy ending. After its publication, her reputation was greater than ever, and she found herself drawn to London, where she met and was admired by many famous people—including Thackeray, Arnold, and Gaskell. In 1854 she accepted the proposal of the Reverend Mr. Nichols, her father's curate. In March of the next year she died. In the meantime, *Villette* (1853) had appeared.

Charlotte Brontë

Charlotte Brontë's novels are subjective in the sense that they capitalize on her own experience, and that is perhaps their importance in the history of the novel. The personal equation is so strong in her novels that even in her best books there is an almost pathetic ignorance of the ways of the world. Her dialogue, too, when the speakers belong to the higher ranks in society, is unconvincing and stilted. Her attempts at humor are even sadder. Nevertheless, *Jane Eyre* is conceived in a vein of authentic passion. Its story of a girl (Jane) in love with a married man (Rochester) was drawn from her own abortive love for the schoolmaster in Brussels under whom she had studied and taught. She is at her best in humble scenes, and the atmosphere of gloomy foreboding was the very air she breathed in her little corner of Yorkshire. The emotional tension of *Jane Eyre* is so well-managed that the book is still exciting to read.

Shirley deals with materials foreign to her own observations. Like Gaskell, she chose as her setting the bitter contention between the mill workers and their employers. The book attempts modernity in its excessively long discussion of women's rights. But the love interest, which again reflects her unhappy experience in Brussels, is interesting. Best of all is the fine portrait of the clear-headed heroine, for which her sister Emily sat. *Villette* is of all Charlotte Brontë's novels the most completely autobiographical. Again, the blighted love affair with the schoolmaster furnished the idea for the central theme. It is the least successful of her novels.

Emily Brontë

Though Charlotte Brontë had the reputation, it was Emily Brontë who had the genius among the sisters. There is nothing to record in her biography. From childhood till her seventeenth year she never left Haworth, and in the few years allotted her after that nothing external in the way of important experience can be recorded of her. But she led a fierce and torrential inner life, as her poetry shows—but that we have already discussed. Nevertheless, it is in her only novel, *Wuthering Heights*, that she completely expresses what her poetry less perfectly attempts to say. The moors about her home had held her imagination and plunged her into reveries of dark but exalted thoughts. The violence of her novel is itself the best index of all her inner turbulence during her apparently uneventful life. Scholars have been too ready to describe the book as a continuation of the Gothic school of novel. Actually, Emily Brontë's own temperament is responsible for the darkness, the wildness, the intensity, and the transcending of moral standards which the novel exhibits. For her poetry shows that she was a girl who lived entirely in her own imagination, and that her values nowhere impinged upon the world's notions of right and wrong. Fundamentally her nature was deeply mystical, and she was no less tied closely to the gloomy land she knew so well than ecstatically fervent in her search for God.

The story of *Wuthering Heights* deals with the havoc caused by the frustrated love of Catherine Earnshaw and Heathcliff. An orphan brought from the slums of the city to be raised with Catherine and her brother, Heathcliff exhibits an almost mad pride, which is only augmented by the arrogance of Catherine's brother. Catherine comes to love Heathcliff deeply, but she is too much like him, too proud to accept his proposal of marriage. He leaves Wuthering Heights in a fury. When he returns later with a fortune, he finds her already married to Edgar Linton, a neighbor. Motivated purely by revenge, Heathcliff marries Linton's sister and maltreats her. Before he is through, he causes Catherine's death. Still unremitting in his revenge, he forces his weakling son to marry Catherine's beautiful daughter. But Catherine, even in death, belongs to Heathcliff. She calls to him from beyond the grave, and in an access of madness, he destroys himself to join her. This story of violent, elemental love and hate is told with unremitting intensity and dark power. As Charlotte Brontë said of it, one seems to breathe lightning in its pages. *Wuthering Heights* is perhaps the first novel in English to dare depict the clash of souls with such power, passion, and beauty. It is a unique accomplishment, and time has singled it out as one of the best novels ever written.

Anne Brontë

Agnes Grey, Anne Brontë's first novel, is based upon her own experiences as governess. *The Tenant of Wildfell Hall*, although uneven, is one of the earliest attempts in the novel to protest the subordinate position of women in marriage.

CHARLES DICKENS (1812–1870)

IMPORTANCE

Charles Dickens was certainly the most popular and best-loved of Victorian novelists. For that reason, certain of his critics were too quick to disparage his value to posterity. They have been proved quite wrong. It is true that he wrote too rapidly, that he could be flagrantly sentimental, that a few of his novels are now too dated to be interesting. Nevertheless, countless of his pages are written with the imaginative power and sweep of a great poet; he has never been surpassed as a delineator of character; and everything he wrote was animated by a noble humanitarianism that makes it easy to be charitable even with his sentimental excesses. Among the characters he created are a host who have already passed into the common heritage of the English-speaking world. Mr. Micawber, Scrooge, Mrs. Gamp, Pecksniff, Joe Gargery, Chadband, Uriah Heep, Fagin—to mention only a few—are part of our language. Despite Dickens' many faults, it would be hard to find another novelist who has left an equal number of works that are so rewarding to read as his.

Dickens knew the pinch of poverty as a boy. His education was fragmentary, and while his father was in a London debtor's prison, he worked hard, though only a lad, in a warehouse. For a time he was apprenticed to a solicitor, and then tried reporting for newspapers. He never forgot the misery he knew in his youth, and Carlyle's teachings never fell on more fertile ground. To the end of his days Dickens chose to be a champion of society's victims in slums, poorhouses, prisons, stuffy London offices and cluttered London streets. There is an exhilarating fusion, in his temperament of idealism, sturdy realism and stubborn optimism which makes him the most typical English writer of his day. Some novelists (like Thackeray) are more consistently artists in their handling of the language; some (like Meredith) are subtler psychologists; some (like Thackeray and Eliot) are more thorough-going realists; and many knew more about weaving a closely knit plot. But none possessed all these qualities to the extent that Dickens did, none seems so *English* a writer—and none seems gifted with so large a soul. And it may be that he is therefore the greatest of them all.

Dickens, for all the dark characters who cross his pages, never lost his basic belief in human goodness. He strove valiantly for reform in the prison system, orphanages, and slum areas without ever suggesting that a new order of society is necessary. He did not like the industrial system, but he counted upon the common humanity of men and women to alleviate its ills.

He became, in these matters, the voice of England's conscience, and beyond question is responsible for the improvement of conditions in those social injustices he exposed.

The chief weakness of his novels, the structure of their plots, can be directly traced to the fact that the stories were written for serial publication. Each installment had to end in a dramatic complication. Sometimes the author had as little idea as his readers as to what was to follow next. For a time his energies seemed inexhaustible, and he had several novels running (and hence, being composed) concurrently. His death in his late fifties was owing chiefly to the strain of overwork. His last years found him not only writing feverishly, but lecturing, reading in public from his books, participating in theatricals, and editing periodicals. He loved his public as much as it loved him.

Early Novels

His career as a novelist began by accident. In 1833 he started publishing in magazines a series of impressions of contemporary life. These were collected as *Sketches by Boz* (1836). The next year (1837) a second series appeared. The popularity of these was responsible for Dickens' being asked to write prose pieces to accompany the merry sporting prints of the artist Robert Seymour. The series had not gone far when Seymour committed suicide. His successor, H. K. Browne, allowed Dickens to lead the way, and before he knew it the latter was embarked upon his first novel, *The Posthumous Papers of the Pickwick Club* (1836–1837). The history of the genesis of this, his first novel, will explain the length of pages consumed before the story gets down to its business. Its hilarity and romantic touches have kept it a favorite.

Dickens' second novel, *Oliver Twist* (1838), though in some respects a novel of terror, deals with its criminals realistically, with no romantic varnish in their depiction. Already the author had begun his plea for social improvement with this attack upon the Poor Law. *Nicholas Nickleby* (1839) is his first exposé of the shocking conditions in English schools. *The Old Curiosity Shop* (1840–1841) and *Barnaby Rudge* (1840–1841) were originally planned as one book to be called *Master Humphrey's Clock*, but the two stories involved could not be fitted into the original design. *The Old Curiosity Shop* contains Dickens' most sentimental figure, Little Nell, but also his most remarkable portrait of the grotesque, the dwarf Quilp. *Barnaby Rudge* was its author's first attempt to follow in Scott's footsteps as an historical novelist; but historical re-creation was not one of Dickens' talents, and the eighteenth century does not come to life in these melodramatic pages. *A Christmas Carol* (1843), too familiar to the English-speaking world to require comment, for all its sentimentality, seems to have found a permanent place in the heart of the world.

A trip to America resulted in the none-too-complimentary collection of *American Notes* (1842). It was followed by a merciless attack on American vulgarity in *Martin Chuzzlewit* (1844); this novel is an instance of the difficulty in appraising Dickens, for its attack on the ethics of the business world (which is concerned largely with the scenes in America) is often dull, while the scenes in England contain some of Dickens' most memorable pages. Mrs. Gamp in this novel is one of the greatest comic creations in our literature; hardly less immortal is her friend, Mrs. Harris, who never appears; in Tom Pinch, Dickens drew one of his most moving figures; Todgers is the quintessence of lower-class London; the hypocrisy of Pecksniff is part of English mythology. *Martin Chuzzlewit* is hence a book that everyone owes it to himself to read.

A visit to Italy was responsible for Dickens' *Pictures from Italy* (1846). *Dombey and Son* (1848), an indictment of the inhumanity of capitalists, marks a departure for its author in dealing with people higher in the social sphere; the novel is more painstakingly designed, and has little of Dickens' usual grotesquerie.

Major Novels

David Copperfield: (1850) This was not only the author's own favorite, but has been his readers' as well. The earlier sections draw heavily on Dickens' own childhood for material. The character and trials of Mr. Micawber were based upon Dickens' recollections of his own father. Despite its looseness of structure this novel has an almost endless gallery of unforgettable characters—Dora Copperfield, Uriah Heep, Mr. and Mrs. Micawber, Mr. and Mrs. Murdstone, Peggotty and Dan, Mr. Dick, and Aunt Betsey Trotwood. Here, although the story of Little Em'ly's seduction is too sentimental, there is a fine air of reality maintained throughout.

The hero of *David Copperfield* is born six months after his father's death. His widowed mother, left with a tiny income and the services of Peggotty, a maid, is visited the night of her confinement by Betsey Trotwood, the maiden aunt of the deceased Mr. Copperfield. Miss Betsey leaves in anger when she learns that the baby is a boy. After a few happy years with his mother and Peggotty in Suffolk, David is taken to Yarmouth to Peggotty's brother Dan, a fisherman. There he meets Dan's nephew and niece (Ham and Em'ly) and Mrs. Gummidge ("a lone lorn creetur"). On his return home he finds his mother married to Edward Murdstone. David is treated cruelly by his stepfather, while his mother stands by helpless. The boy is sent to the school of Mr. Creakle, a bully, where he makes the friendship of handsome James Steerforth. Mrs. Murdstone's death puts an end to David's schooling. Peggotty, now dismissed, marries the town coachman, Barkis (who up to this point has indicated his matrimonial views by the phrase, "Barkis is willin'"). David is ten when he is put to work in the firm of Murdstone and Grinby, wine merchants of London. He is sent to lodge with Mr. and Mrs. Micawber, who have four children of their own. The Micawbers, though devoted to each other, live in a state of perpetual financial embarrassment that requires frequent trips to the pawnbroker. Mr. Micawber is always expecting something to turn up. But the creditors can no longer be silenced, and Mr. Micawber is thrown (like Dickens' own father) into debtors' prison. David decides to leave London. Penniless and starved, he arrives at his Aunt Betsey Trotwood's at Dover. Although the old lady is very gruff with him, she keeps him with her, and refuses to surrender him to Mr. Murdstone. His aunt now sends David to school at Canterbury, where he lodges with her lawyer Wickfield. The lawyer's clerk is carrot-haired Uriah Heep, whose slimy humbleness and damp hands revolt David's sensibilities. David is happy at Canterbury, and does his aunt credit in his studies. On graduation, he goes back for a visit to Yarmouth, comes across Steerforth en route, and takes him along to meet Peggotty and her brother, and Barkis. Steerforth is attracted to Em'ly, now a lovely young woman. David enters the law offices of Spenlow and Jorkins. From Mr. Wickfield's daughter Agnes he hears that her father has taken Uriah Heep into partnership. When David meets Mr. Spenlow's daughter Dora, he falls madly in love with her. David is summoned to Yarmouth because Barkis is dying. During his stay, Em'ly elopes with Steerforth a few days before she is to marry her cousin Ham. Dan sets out to find her. Back in London David discovers that his Aunt Betsey has lost all her money. David tries vainly to get back for her the money she had paid for his apprenticeship at Spenlow and Jorkins. He procures a secretarial position and begins to learn shorthand. Mr. Spenlow has forbidden his daughter Dora to marry David. But Spenlow dies, and Dora is left almost a pauper. Looking forward to their marriage, David begs Dora to master the art of running a home. She is temperamentally a child, hopelessly impractical, and cannot manage any household affairs. On a trip to Canterbury, David discovers Uriah in complete control of Wickfield, planning to marry Wickfield's daughter, and ruling Micawber (who is now a clerk in the office) with an iron hand. David, now making money as a reporter and writer for periodicals, is able to marry Dora when he is twenty-one. But Dora is hopelessly inefficient. Even with the help of a servant she cannot live within her budget or provide a comfortable home. David is forced to resign himself to the fact that the price he must pay for his enchanting wife is to live in a disordered house. Dora becomes ill. He is tenderly concerned for her, but his problems only increase. A mysterious letter from Mr. Micawber results in David's meeting his old friend in London. Mr. Micawber can bear no more of Uriah Heep's villainy, and wishes the world to know him for the scoundrel he is. Em'ly appears again upon the scene after being abandoned by Steerforth. Her Uncle Dan is only too happy to take her home again. The exposure of Heep follows. At the home of Mr. Wickfield, Mr. Micawber has as his audience Aunt Betsey, David, Uriah Heep, and Mr. Wickfield's daughter Agnes. Micawber reveals all the thefts, forgeries and speculations that Heep has indulged in to win ascendency over Wickfield. These revelations result, among other things, in Aunt Betsey's recovering her fortune, a part of which she invests in giving the Micawbers a new chance in life as they embark for Australia. On the same ship Em'ly and her uncle sail to leave behind them the scenes associated with her shame. In the midst of this good news David's happiness is ruined by the death of

Dora. He goes abroad to escape his memories. He stops off at Yarmouth in time to witness a shipwreck near the coast. Ham loses his life in vainly trying to rescue a man, whose body, when it is washed on shore, turns out to be Steerforth's. After a few years on the continent, David comes to England. He now understands that the sisterly love that he imagined he has been entertaining most of his life for Agnes Wickfield has a deeper meaning. But he probably would have done nothing about his discovery had not Aunt Betsey privately arranged a meeting between the two. Agnes admits that she has always loved David. They are married, and Agnes proves a perfect wife and companion for David Copperfield.

Bleak House: Some critics would insist that Dickens' next novel is his masterpiece. *Bleak House* (1853), the story of a tragedy caused by the endless red-tape and delay of legal processes, contains an amazing number of brilliantly portrayed characters. Lady Dedlock is perhaps his most majestic tragic personage; and poor Joe, child of the slums, is perhaps his most heartbreaking waif. The novel has height as well as breadth, and somehow conveys, of all Dickens' novels, the most vivid sense of reality of London streets: its dark alleys, its evil-looking houses, its tinsel and its misery.

Hard Times and Little Dorrit: *Bleak House* was followed by one of Dickens' major failures, *Hard Times* (1854). In this book Dickens makes no attempt to disguise the fact that he is writing as a propagandist. There is no question of the integrity of his intention; he was always the champion of society's victims. But this attack on the conditions prevailing in cities such as industrial Manchester, is written with too much anger. A novel in which the employers are demons and the workingmen saints loses all pretense to reality, and fails of its own purpose. Moreover, Dickens has no solution for the problems he so heatedly discusses, other than an appeal to Christian kindness. *Little Dorrit* (1857) is even more discouraging to read. It is another exposé of debtors' prisons. The satire somehow misses fire and the passages which take place on the Continent convey no sense of actuality.

One of Dickens' less-popular novels, and a product of his middle period before his great success, *Little Dorrit* explores the cruelties inflicted on people by one of England's most-reviled institutions: the debtors' prison. The heroine, Amy Dorrit, is born in prison as her mother cares for her incarcerated father and waits for his release. Although the mother dies, Dorrit continues to live in the prison, as was customary for children of the prisoners. Little Dorrit sews for a number of families, one of which, the Clennams, takes interest in her. Arthur Clennam, a disillusioned businessman, returns to his infirm mother after his father's death. Having suffered great injustices at the hands of the prison system, Mr. Dorrit is discovered to be the sole surviving heir to a large fortune. He and his family immediately leave for the European continent. Arthur, originally attracted to Dorrit's sweet and feminine manner, eventually falls in love with her. But in the meantime, he too has fallen into debt and is imprisoned. As the novel resolves, Little Dorrit returns to England, and Mrs. Clennam reveals to her son that she is not his real mother, and that he too has a large inheritance. He and Little Dorrit are married, and begin what promises to be a comfortable and peaceful life.

Although this novel lacks the fire of Dickens' later work, the theme of social injustice is strikingly clear. Dickens' own father was imprisoned for debt, and this undoubtedly had a devastating effect on the author's already troubled childhood. But Dickens also portrays another side to the debtor question, and many of his characters are self-indulgent; in some sense they bring themselves down. Survival in an inhuman world often requires them to be self-interested, but this means alienation, a prison-like existence. Thus the author, while expressing sympathy for characters trapped in the industrial age, still views the individual as acting upon his or her own destiny.

A Tale of Two Cities: (1859) Like *Hard Times* (which Dickens had dedicated to him), it is a result of Dickens' admiration for Carlyle. A reading of Carlyle's *French Revolution* inspired Dickens to try his hand for the second time at a historical novel—but this time with great success. Despite a certain pretentiousness of style quite foreign to his genius, this powerful picture of events in France leading inevitably to the Reign of Terror, has made the novel one of his most popular. The figures of Mme. Defarge, the bloodthirsty Revolutionist, and Sidney Carton, the wastrel who rises to heroic self-sacrifice, have been indelibly stamped on the imagination of the English-reading world.

The novel opens in 1775 with England and France quite convinced that everything in the world is about as perfect as it could be. Mr. Jarvis Lorry, representing the banking firm of Tellson's in London, is en route on a cold night to Dover. There he meets Lucie Manette, a lovely golden-haired girl. Lorry informs Lucie that her father, Dr. Manette, is not, as she supposes, dead, but that he had been incarcerated by the French government before she was born. Lucie's tiny fortune is invested at Tellson's. Her father has just been released, and Lucie accompanies Lorry to Paris to meet the aged physician for the first time. The scene shifts to the St. Antoine section of Paris where Dr. Manette is living in an attic of the Defarges, wine merchants. There Dr. Manette sits at a shoemaker's bench with blank look. His daughter and Lorry convey him back to London. Five years later we find a young French aristocrat, Charles Darney, being tried in Old Bailey on the charge of spying for the French. Dr. and Lucie Manette are called upon as witnesses against him. When everything seems to be going fatally for Darney, Sidney Carton comes to the rescue. Carton is being employed as assistant by the lawyer Stryver. Capitalizing upon Darney's great resemblance to himself, Carton establishes in Court the possibility of confusion of identity. Darney is released. Darney himself has preferred living in England by teaching and translating French to living in France in luxury rightfully as an Evremonde, a family hated by the peasantry for its oppression. Carton is a highly gifted man who seems deliberately to have ruined the makings of a great career, by dissipation; he manages to scrape along by doing Stryver's thinking in difficult cases. Darney and Carton now become intimates at the Manette home, where the doctor has recovered his mind through Lucie's tender care. He is again practicing his medicine, although any undue excitement can send him back to his shoemaker's bench. Both men fall in love with Lucie, but it is Darney's affection that she returns. Carton asks to be allowed merely to visit them on occasion. The storm is rising in France. No one is waiting for the day of reckoning more tenaciously than Mme. Defarge. Into her knitting she has entered an account (through use of symbols of her own), of all those guilty of cruel arrogance towards and oppression of the people. In England, Darney and Lucie, now married, rejoice in a little copy of Lucie, a daughter born to them. When the day of the Fall of the Bastille comes, Mme. Defarge is among the leaders. For three years, expiating blood flows freely in France. Then Lorry is sent again to Paris by Tellson's on business for the bank. Darney goes there too to help save the life of an old servant who has been unjustly arrested in the mass seizures by the populace of everyone connected with the Old Régime. As an Englishman, Lorry is safe enough. But Charles Darney is arrested as an aristocrat. When they discover that he is an Evremonde, he is kept in solitary confinement. Dr. Manette with Lucie and the little girl hasten to Paris, and find the city in the hands of men and women crying for more and more blood. Manette, as an old prisoner of the Bastille, is respected, but can do nothing for Darney—not even so much as procuring permission for Lucie to see her husband. After a year in jail, Darney stands before the tribunal. The Reign of Terror is on. Darney is able to show that his leaving and returning to France were both voluntary, and that he had given up his connections with the Evremonde fortunes long ago. Manette's plea for him proves decisive and he is voted his freedom. But Mme. Defarge, present at his trial, has not forgotten that the Evremonde family had ruined hers. She wishes to see everyone connected with the Evremondes wiped out. Charles is arrested again. Next day in court, Mme. Defarge gives as evidence a letter which Manette had written in the old days telling the story of injustices suffered by him at the hands of the Evremondes. The jury now votes the death sentence for Darney. Carton, in Paris too, and hearing of Darney's danger, recognizes a criminal now serving as a spy in the prisons. Carton blackmails this rogue into taking him to Darney's cell. Carton visits him, drugs him, effects a change in clothes, and has Darney carried out. As Carton, pretending to be Darney is on his way to the guillotine, Lorry, Darney, Lucie, the child and Dr. Manette make their way out of Paris. Mme. Defarge, still in search of revenge, tries to wring out of Lucie's servant in Paris the information as to where Lucie has gone. In the struggle Mme. Defarge is killed with her own pistol. When Carton mounts the steps to the guillotine, Mme. Defarge is not in the audience, after all. As Carton takes Darney's place in death, he feels that this act of self-sacrifice is the best thing that he has ever done in his life.

Great Expectations (1861) is one of Dickens' most perfectly written novels, and takes its place beside *Bleak House* as one of his triumphs in literary excellence. The opening in the dark moors of Kent is painted with unforgettable power. From there on the story moves with a kind of dignity and (for Dickens) an almost quiet certainty of power that make one wish Dickens had exploited this vein more. There are many exciting events in this novel, but despite the Gothic quality of Miss Havisham's home, there is a steady air of actuality in all the events. Joe Gargery and the old convict are among the most realistic of Dickens' portraits. The rise of the hero from privation to the dangerous borderland of snobbery, from which he is rescued just in time by his basic soundness, makes one of the most dramatic as well as the most romantic stories Dickens ever told.

Our Mutual Friend: This 1865 novel is Dickens' last completed novel. Though somewhat underprized by critics, it contains some marvelous scenes on the dark water-front of the Thames; and Headstone's mad obsession for Lizzie is one of the most gripping themes Dickens employed anywhere. There is an air of unpenetrated darkness overhanging the novel that imparts to it considerable fascination and power.

The Mystery of Edwin Drood: Dickens died in 1870 at a point halfway through the writing of his final and potentially his darkest novel, *The Mystery of Edwin Drood* (1879). In its cynicism about the unethical exercise of power and the deep roots of hatred in the political and commercial world, this novel stands thematically alongside Hardy's *Jude the Obscure* and *Tess of the D'Urbervilles.*

Edwin Drood, from his earliest years, has been betrothed by his parents to Rosa Bud. As an engineering student, he finally visits her in Cloisterham (Dickens' version of Rochester) where he falls into a strange and ultimately fatal love rectangle. It comes to light that John Jasper, his opium-addicted uncle, and the hot-tempered Nevill Landless also have romantic interests in Rosa Bud. Shortly after Edwin meets with Rosa to break off their engagement, he falls mysteriously out of sight. Jasper is quick to point the finger at Landless as the possible murderer. The river is dragged for Drood's body, without result.

Who killed Drood? Dickens never lived to complete his tale. He did, however, weave together in this final, incomplete novel the main threads of his deepest anxieties about the contemporary world: its selfishness, moral depravity, faithlessness, and deception. As in virtually all Dickens' novels, there are a sprinkling of "salt-of-the-earth" characters. But these are minor characters in *Edwin Drood*—a dying breed, as it were, powerless and impoverished in a world of increasing violence, racism, and treachery.

The charge has often been brought against Dickens that in delineating character it was his tendency to exaggerate the outlines and heighten the coloring of life. It is true that he is constantly near the borderline of caricature when he is characterizing. He often seems to be taking the easy way out of his task by giving certain characters tag lines or actions. Thus Jerry (in the *Tale of Two Cities*) is always the "honest tradesman," always objecting to his wife's "floppin'"; Mrs. Gamp is always quoting her friend Mrs. 'Arris; Uriah Heep is always wringing his hands and protesting that he is "'umble"; Mr. Micawber is always waiting for something to turn up. But the important thing to remember is that Dickens so manages these matters that he creates his own world of reality even in these exaggerations—and that accomplishment is what we mean by art. They are part of the chiaroscuro in which he chooses to paint—part of the air of fantasy and the grotesque which lend his fundamental realism so strong an appeal to the imagination.

WILLIAM MAKEPEACE THACKERAY (1811–1863)

IMPORTANCE

William Makepeace Thackeray eventually shared with Dickens the position of being one of the two leading Victorian novelists, but it took him some time to find himself. His approach to the world could not be more at variance with Dickens' than it is. His point of view was essentially clear-eyed and level-headed, and largely urbane. He observed the world with disenchantment, though without cynicism. Most of all he hated hypocrites and pretenders, and on every level he saw civilization crowded with them. He always maintained a deep respect and veneration for genuine goodness and kindliness, but he was under no illusion that good people are necessarily clever. The mischief-makers in his books are often far cleverer and more brilliant than the kindly people who are their victims. But his sympathy was always with the latter. His figures are drawn chiefly from the upper classes, which he knew well. Their cruelty and shallowness, their self-deception and greed, form his chief theme. Although he sometimes wrote satirically, he was not fundamentally a satirist, but rather an artist who without either hoping or despairing too much could view with a certain detachment the spectacle of human conduct.

As a stylist, he is never chargeable with the lapses of carelessness to which Dickens was subject. It has been said of him that he never wrote a dull page in his life. The clarity of his perceptions is mirrored in the lucid and racy prose over which he was at all times master. Some of this same quality has made him not only the finest artist among his contemporary novelists, but also the best essayist of his age. He was also far subtler a psychologist than Dickens. He had no interest in the grotesque, and his characters are all recognizably human.

Thackeray came from a family that had done much to help build England's empire in India. He was born July 11, 1811, at Calcutta, but lost his father early. When sent to school in England he found his studies far less absorbing than his enthusiasm for drawing. His mother remarried; Thackeray's stepfather was a very good man who won the boy's affection quickly. He attended Charterhouse School, and in 1829 he entered Trinity College, Cambridge. Among the friends of his youth were Fitzgerald and Tennyson. For a while he studied law, but dropped that as much too dull. His chief interest in life was still art. To study it he went to Paris (1834), and while there contributed articles to *Fraser's Magazine*. His first book, *Flore et Zéphyr* (1836), appeared two years later with his own illustrations. For some time after this Thackeray continued to illustrate his writings. His drawings are always interesting, but it seems just as well that he eventually abandoned his ambitions to be an artist.

In 1836 he married Isabella Shawe, who only a few years later became insane after the birth of their third daughter. This catastrophe, which blighted the rest of Thackeray's life, may have done much to deepen his native skepticism, but he was never a bitter man. Deeply attached to his family, he concentrated his affection on his daughters. During this period his stepfather had failed in business, and Thackeray took upon himself the task of paying all the debts—an undertaking that kept him turning out his writings without rest for ten years.

The Yellowplush Papers (1837–1838) and *Barry Lyndon* (1844) were written for *Fraser's Magazine*; for *Punch* he wrote, among other pieces, *Tickletoby's Lectures on English History*, and *Snobs of England* (1846–1847)—the last-named better known as *The Book of Snobs*. *The Yellowplush Papers* is a view of high society from the point of view of the servants' quarters, its author being supposedly a footman with his own ideas of spelling; *Barry Lyndon* is a satirical account of the adventures of a scoundrel, and was modelled on Fielding's *Jonathan Wild; The Book of Snobs* is an attack on social climbers and toadies. In the same vein he later wrote *Punch's Prize Novelists* (1847), a series of burlesques on the novels of Bulwer-Lytton, Disraeli, and other popular novelists whose view of the world Thackeray believed fundamentally dishonest.

Vanity Fair

His great success came with the publication of *Vanity Fair* (1848). This, which some critics would call the greatest novel in English, originally appeared serially. It is described by its author as a "novel without a hero." But it has a new kind of heroine, the incomparable, wicked, brilliant, half-tragic Becky Sharp, through whose meteoric career to the heights of social success we view the crass stupidity and vulgarity of English aristocracy.

The novel is conceived on a large scale. It has a host of characters, all brilliantly managed, set against the exciting background of the Napoleonic Wars. Though the modern reader has little taste for the Victorian convention of the novelist's stepping forth to comment on his characters and the progress of events in the story, Thackeray exhibits his wonderful powers as an essayist in those passages. Throughout the wit is of the best, but pathos and grandeur are not absent either.

The story of *Vanity Fair* opens with the departure of two girls from Miss Pinkerton's School: Amelia Sedley and Becky Sharp. The school was very sorry to see Amelia go but felt less concerned about Becky. Becky is on her way to pay a visit at Amelia's home before starting out to earn a living as a governess. Miss Sharp, the orphan of an impoverished artist and a French mother who had been in opera, never seemed sufficiently grateful for the education she had received in exchange for having helped with the pupils' conversational French. Amelia is fair, gentle and kind. Becky is small, tawny-haired, intelligent, with strange, large eyes. Ever since her childhood Becky has known what it is to shift for one's self. At the Sedleys, Becky decides to capture Amelia's fat brother Joseph. She is succeeding in turning his head when George Osborne, in love with Amelia, awakens a sense of shame in Joseph for making a fool of himself after drinking too much punch. In consequence Joseph Sedley stays away from the girls. Becky now goes to the home of Sir Pitt Crawley in Hampshire at Queen's Crawley, to undertake her duties as governess. Sir Pitt is slovenly and miserly, and Becky is almost dying from boredom when her employer's maiden sister and Sir Pitt's younger son, Rawdon, appear. The old lady and Rawdon both take a fancy to Becky—the former because of Becky's cleverness, and the latter because of her charm. Rawdon is a captain without too much intelligence, a wastrel, but his aunt's favorite. In the meantime, despite the objection of his sisters, George Osborne proposes to Amelia Sedley and is accepted. Despite their engagement George is not the most attentive of suitors, and frequently absents himself for his own pleasures. He becomes quite annoyed with his friend, the generous-hearted but clumsy Captain William Dobbin, when the latter lets it be known in the Horseguards that George is engaged to Amelia. At Queen's Crawley, old Miss Crawley, during a temporary illness, receives the careful attention of Becky. When she returns to London, she brings Becky along as a companion, and thus gives her favorite nephew an opportunity to visit Miss Sharp. Sir Pitt, suddenly a widower, comes to London and knowing that he cannot procure Becky on any other terms, expresses his willingness to marry her and make her Lady Crawley. Becky is overwhelmed with genuine sorrow on this occasion. She weeps out the information that she is already married, inwardly regretting her haste. Her husband is Rawdon. Sir Pitt is outraged and Miss Crawley has a fit. But Rawdon, head-over-heels in love with his wife, is unconcerned. By this time Amelia's father has lost his fortune and gone into bankruptcy. George's father tries to break off the match with Amelia, but Dobbin is at George's elbow to urge him not to abandon his fiancée. George and Amelia marry and go to Brighton for their honeymoon. At the seashore they meet Becky and Rawdon, who are managing to live on nothing a year in great style, by paying no bills. At this point news comes that Napoleon has escaped from Elba. Rawdon and George are called away to Brussels for the great battle. George has already dissipated his little allowance, and though still a newlywed, finds himself attracted to Becky. The Battle of Waterloo takes place, and George falls in the combat. Amelia is now a widow treasuring the memory of her hero-husband. Rawdon, on the other hand, has been advanced to the rank of colonel for bravery, and on the basis of this new glory Becky and he go for a whirl to Paris. Rawdon proves so successful at cards and dice, that he begins to discover it hard to find people to play with him. All this time Becky and Rawdon have been hoping that old Miss Crawley will relent and reinstate her old favorite in her good graces. But the birth of an heir to Rawdon, instead of propitiating the maiden lady, so much incenses her that she selects Rawdon's elder brother, Pitt, whom she has always detested, as her heir. Amelia also becomes the mother of a son whom she names after his father. She is living all this while with her impoverished father and mother. After a few years in Paris, Becky is able to buy off Rawdon's debts in England at a discount, and they go back to the English capital to live in style again without any money. Becky, who makes no attempt to mother her son, has a winning way with all men, and it is owing to her talents only that she and Rawdon manage to swim above the tide. Indeed, Becky never ceases to plot for Rawdon's advancement. She even undertakes winning the good will of Rawdon's brother Pitt, though she finds it difficult to make him part with any money. At last, through the personal interest of the powerful Lord Steyne, she not only is invited to the most exclusive homes, where she finds to her satisfaction no one equal to her in readiness of wit, but also is actually presented at court. Lord Steyne becomes more and more attentive. While Becky is thus on the dizzy summits, poor Amelia is forced to part with her son, whom she sorrowfully agrees to send to George's parents. Rawdon is finding it harder and harder to keep up with his wife. Now that their son is at school, Becky makes no pretense of being a wife. One night, Rawdon, who has been escaping creditors for some time, is seized and put in jail. Becky expects to have him released the next day, but by accident he is freed sooner than she has counted upon. He returns home and is shocked to find Lord Steyne and his wife in a situation that is clearly compromising. Knowing no other way, he knocks Lord Steyne down, and leaves his wife in a fury. Lord Steyne, on the other hand, convinced that Becky has arranged all this to blackmail him, picks up all the gifts that he has given her and departs too. In one stroke Becky is hurled from her eminence.

Some time elapses now. Joseph Sedley and William Dobbin have been in India for ten years after the Battle of Waterloo. On their return to England, they find Amelia's mother dead. Dobbin has never ceased to love Amelia, even though she has given him no encouragement. Dobbin, now a Major in rank, discovers that Amelia has chosen to remain a widow devoutly treasuring memories of George. Joseph Sedley is now wealthy and goes with Dobbin, Amelia, and little George for a trip to the Continent. In Germany they met Becky. Though far down again in society, the energy of her character has prevented her from being extinguished. She has wandered from place to place in Europe, squeezing what she can out of admirers, piling up debts for as long as that can be done, and trying to keep up with a new taste she has developed for gambling. Becky appeals to Amelia's old friendship so successfully that the latter wishes to bring Becky home with them. Dobbin tries to warn Amelia against Becky in vain. Once again Joseph finds Becky irresistible. But Becky now endangers her chances for security by the one good deed of her life. Seeing how Amelia fails to appreciate the devotion of Dobbin, even though the Major is her own enemy, she shows Amelia a letter George had written her, just before Waterloo, asking Becky for a private meeting. Amelia's idol tumbles, Dobbin comes back, and Amelia and Dobbin marry and go to live in the country. Joseph is now Becky's devoted admirer. They begin to travel extensively, and she persuades him to insure his life heavily, naming her as beneficiary. After that, he dies (no one knows how) in the tropics, and Becky goes to live at fashionable resorts like Bath, where she becomes well known for her charities. Her son is now Sir Rawdon Crawley, since his father's death. He makes her a competent allowance but steadily refuses to see her. The puppet show is over.

Henry Esmond

The great success of *Vanity Fair* made Thackeray's reputation secure. He began to lecture on *The English Humorists of the 18th Century* (1853) in England, Scotland and America. It is probably the material he collected for these critical pieces that inspired him to write *Henry Esmond* (1853). This is an historical novel that departs from the Scott tradition. Discarding the romantic extravagance thus far associated with that kind of work, Thackeray proved in *Henry Esmond* that an historical novel can be written realistically. Laid in the times of Sir Richard Steele, who is one of the characters of the story, this novel has been called by some critics Thackeray's finest piece of artistry. He deliberately employed a style reminiscent of the Neoclassical age, both in sentence structure and vocabulary. There are scenes of intense dramatic power, and the character of Beatrix is one of the most memorable in all fiction.

Henry Esmond opens at the time that James II, the last of the Stuarts to hold the throne, was rapidly losing his prestige. The boy Henry Esmond, generally supposed to be the illegitimate son of Viscount Castlewood, is during these days growing up at Castlewood House. Lady Castlewood, once a great beauty and favorite at the Court, is now desperately trying to repair the ravages of time with cosmetics. One of her constant attendants is Father Holt, a Jesuit, who tutors little Henry in Latin and the use of the sword. James II flees England and Viscount Castlewood dies in the services of the Stuarts. Lady Castlewood is taken prisoner by the soldiers of the new king. Thus Henry Esmond finds himself suddenly amidst many soldiers, now occupying Castlewood House. Among these, his favorite quickly becomes Dick, the scholar, otherwise known as Corporal Steele. Francis Esmond, the new Viscount Castlewood, arrives with his wife Rachel, now Lady Castlewood, a lovely girl many years younger than the new Viscount. So begins a lifetime of devotion on Henry's part to this family, particularly to Rachel, and her children Frank and Beatrix. Rachel is a good wife, but her husband seems bored with her devotion. She is put through the humiliation of observing her beauty disappearing for a time as a result of an attack of small-pox. Viscount Francis, once insanely jealous when the objectionable Lord Mohun was forcing his attentions upon Rachel, deserts his wife in her trouble, and goes off to London to court the beauties there. But the Viscount has already challenged Mohun to a duel. The duel comes off, and the Viscount is killed. While he is dying, he reveals that Henry Esmond should have been the rightful heir. Henry is actually the legitimate son of the former Viscount by an early marriage, and as such should now be bearing the title. But Henry destroys the document substantiating his claims in order to avoid bringing disaster upon his beloved Lady Rachel, who has been living in expectation of her son's succession. In her grief, at her husband's death, Rachel upbraids Henry for not having prevented the duel. She does not know that he has even tried to fight in the Viscount's stead, and is badly wounded. She forbids him to ever visit them again and renounces all connection with him. Luckily for Henry, the former Lady Castlewood, his father's second wife, asks him to visit her in Chelsea. She suspects that he knows what his true position ought to be. She tries to treat him like a son, and exerts her influence to procure him a commission as ensign. Esmond serves under Marlborough, and is wounded at the Battle of Blenheim. He advances to the rank of Colonel. Once more he meets Father Holt in the Netherlands, and learns that his mother was the daughter of a weaver, and died long ago. In the Cathedral of Winchester, Henry meets Rachel again. Without a word they know their misunderstanding is over. Though she is his elder, he loves her dearly. But now he sees Beatrix, incomparably beautiful at sixteen, and a maid of honor at court. His heart becomes enslaved to Beatrix, and for years he begs her love in vain. She greets his suit with disdain. A born flirt, she does not hesitate to enchant him deliberately, and then chide him for his seriousness. Young Frank, now Viscount, has grown up, too, into a handsome, graceful young man. He marries an aristocrat of the Dutch nobility, and through her becomes converted to Roman Catholicism. In England, Henry begins a literary career by assisting Addison with his poem on the Battle of Blenheim. Beatrix, in the meantime, has had numerous suitors, has encouraged many, but remains unwed. At last, the Duke of Hamilton, a widower of powerful position, is accepted by her, although he is old enough to be her father. Henry, still loving her, gives Beatrix as a wedding present a beautiful diamond necklace that he had inherited from the now deceased second wife of his father. When Beatrix's fiancé protests the gift from an illegitimate man, Rachel angrily replies that Henry is the rightful heir to whom her family owes everything. Before her death, the old Viscountess has revealed the truth to her. Beatrix apologizes to Henry for her long injustice. But before Beatrix can be married, the Duke of Hamilton is killed in a duel by the same savage Lord Mohun. In France, young Frank has been serving the cause of the exiled Stuart, Pretender to the throne of England. The Pretender and Frank come in disguise to London, the Pretender passing as Viscount Frank. In an endeavor to please Rachel and Beatrix, Henry is prepared to throw in his fortune with the Stuart claims. The Pretender hopes that Queen Anne, his sister, will name him as her successor. The Pretender, like all his Stuart forebears, is a philanderer. He pursues Beatrix with his attentions and she does not discourage them. As a measure of protection, Beatrix is sent off to Castlewood House. The Queen dies and the Pretender has apparently disappeared. Henry and Frank ride out to Castlewood House. There they discover Beatrix with the Pretender. The proud girl's ambition has proved her undoing. Henry now understands that he has been loving someone unworthy of him. In a brilliantly dramatic scene, Henry showing the Pretender his family's papers, and recounting all the sacrifices of the Castlewoods in the Stuart cause, burns the document in the Pretender's presence, breaks his sword, and renounces all connection hereafter with the claims of the Stuarts. As Henry and Frank are returning to London, the Elector of Hanover is being proclaimed George I of England. Beatrix follows the Pretender to France. In the end Henry realizes that Rachel has been the woman he has loved all his life. They marry, and migrate to Virginia, where they live out the rest of their happy life.

The Virginians (1859) is a sequel to *Henry Esmond* in the sense that it deals with the grandsons of Henry, the Warringtons. The chief flaw in this entertaining novel is that there is too much movement back and forth between England and America. The career of George Washington and the American Revolution form the background, and Beatrix reappears as old blasé Madame Bernstein. Though admirers of Thackeray laud the book, it is rather loose-jointed.

Minor Works

The Newcomes (1855) is considered by some critics the most beautiful novel Thackeray ever wrote. The character of Ethel Newcome is an expression of the author's warm appreciation for the best in womanly qualities; Colonel Newcome, too, is one of Thackeray's most endearing men, with all his simplicity and folly. The novel also contains some of Thackeray's most merciless realism.

With some readers *Pendennis* (1850) is the favorite. This is the most autobiographical of Thackeray's works, and though it is more of a biography of a hero than a well-plotted novel, it has a vitality which carries the reader along. The sketches of life at the university and in London are vividly done. Major Pendennis is one of the author's finest portraits. But the canvas is broadly rather than intensely painted. *Pendennis* is one of Thackeray's raciest novels, but not his most profound.

In 1859 Thackeray accepted for a while the duties of editing the *Cornhill Magazine*. The fruits of these labors can be read in his *Roundabout Papers* (1860), a collection of essays he wrote for the magazine. His reputation as a great novelist has somewhat obscured the fact that Thackeray was the finest familiar essayist of his generation, as this book proves. Some of the essays are among the best in our language.

It is to be regretted that Thackeray did not learn to exploit this vein of his genius earlier. His powers were already on the decline as *Lovel the Widower* (1860) and *The Adventures of Philip* (1862) prove. He died a completely exhausted man at the age of fifty-two. It is ironic that his insane wife survived him by thirty years.

CHARLES READE (1814–1884)

Charles Reade began his career as a dramatist with considerable success. His addiction to the stage can be seen not only in the subject matter of some of his novels but also in the fact that they lean heavily upon dialogue for their effect. *Peg Woffington* (1853), his first novel, was a rewriting of his comedy already presented on the stage as *Masks and Faces*. Its central characters are actors, and its story deals with life on and about the stage. In the same year appeared his *Christine Johnstone* (1853). Reade was a great admirer of Dickens, and in *Put Yourself in His Place* (1870) we find him employing the novel for a social message. His subject is the injustices of trade unions upon the worker. *A Terrible Temptation* (1871) has as its hero a novelist concerned with social problems, whose only interest is to champion the cause of the underdog. *Drink* (1879), Reade's dramatization of Zola's novel *L'Assommoir*, shows his continued interest in social questions. The only one of his novels, however, that is still read is of another kind entirely: *The Cloister and the Hearth* (1861), a picaresque novel laid in the early English Renaissance with Erasmus' father as its hero. Reade did a great deal of painstaking research for his historical background, but managed it so well that the book is certainly one of the finest historical novels. Reade's other novels include *It Is Never Too Late to Mend* (1856), an attack on the conditions in English prisons; *Hard Cash* (1863), an exposé of the appalling conditions prevailing in insane asylums; and *Griffith Gaunt* (1866), a powerful character study.

GEORGE ELIOT (MARY ANNE EVANS) (1819–1880)

Although it dipped significantly in the mid-1900s, the reputation of George Eliot (Mary Anne Evans) has again risen, so that she is now viewed as among the greatest of the Victorian novelists. As a woman she exhibited an enormous amount of courage in leading an independent life according to her own highly developed moral values. But it is perhaps this same quality of intense moral purposefulness that has made the reading of her novels for some a fairly dull experience. There can be no question of her integrity or earnestness. To her the subject of greatest interest is the nature of the moral choices which human beings must make. The recurring theme in her novels is precisely that, man or woman choosing between two members of the opposite sex. Her favorite background is the countryside and small towns of Warwickshire. There is some humor in her novels, but it is exceedingly quiet. There are, happily, some less mediocre characters in her books, but they are never in a central position.

She tried to look at life steadily; her philosophy was not one of easy optimism, and her novels generally end on a gloomy note. On one occasion, when she wrote *Romola* (1863), she tried to escape from contemporary England into the Italian Renaissance. But despite her scholarliness, her persistent moral purposefulness makes her Italian fifteenth century men and women no more than Victorian Englishmen dressed up for a masquerade. She, however, can be said to have furthered the growth of the novel by the sincerity of her psychological analysis. Indeed, sometimes the conscientiousness of her psychological investigations is ruinous. *Middlemarch* (1872) lacks a hero or heroine, the emphasis being apportioned to various groups of people; but the reader is forced to wade through an analysis of the characters of fifty-odd people.

Her first book of fiction was *Scenes from Clerical Life* (1858), a collection of three short stories originally published in *Blackwood's Magazine*. *Adam Bede* (1859) is her first novel. *The Mill on the Floss* (1860) followed the next year.

The Mill on the Floss centers about Dorlcote Mill which for five generations has been operated by the Tulliver family. The present Tulliver is Edward, a kind but rash-tempered man, with a passion for going to the law. His affections are centered on his two children, Maggie, aged nine, and Tom, aged twelve. The children live mostly out of doors. But Tom must be educated. Edward Tulliver is very anxious that his son be taught to be cleverer than any lawyers he is bound to have to deal with later on. Tom is sent to King's Lorton, fifteen miles away, to study at the Reverend Mr. Stelling's school. Tom was never meant to be a scholar and is very unhappy because of his yearning for his old carefree life outdoors at the Mill with his sister Maggie. Despite the boy's pleas, Tulliver will not allow him to quit school. A new pupil arrives at Mr. Stelling's, Philip Wakem, the son of an old enemy of Tulliver's, the lawyer John Wakem. Tom has been conditioned in advance to dislike any of the Wakems and does not change his opinion even though Philip is a bright student and highly sensitive. But Philip falls in love with Maggie, on a visit she makes to her brother's school. The little girl kisses him before she leaves with the kind remark that she wishes he were her brother too. Maggie is soon sent to school herself. Time passes and Tom is now sixteen. Edward Tulliver is in a bad way, having lost a long suit over the rights to the water on the River Floss. The shock of his financial ruin causes an apoplectic fit during which he falls from his horse; for two months he lies in his bed insensate. The Wakems take over the mill. Though they allow the Tullivers to keep their house, they sell some of the Tulliver household effects at auction. Wakem is willing to employ Edward Tulliver as manager at the mill, but Tom wishes his father to refuse. Tulliver believes it wise, however, to accept. He intends to be a faithful employee of Wakem's, but asks his son Tom to inscribe the family Bible with the promise that Tom will never rest until he has repaid the Wakems for the injustice done to his father. Maggie does what she can to prevent such an oath from being made, but Tom fully agrees with his father. During her walk to an old quarry, Maggie, now seventeen, meets Philip again. She feels herself strongly drawn to him. Philip begs her to believe that his father had no desire to ruin hers. Soon after that Philip tells her that he loves her, and Maggie believes that she returns his love. Philip goes abroad, but he and Maggie meet again in the spring. Tom, hearing of their meeting, gives her the alternative of giving Philip up completely or having to face her father. For the sake of her father, Maggie renounces Philip. The elder Tulliver and Tom have been working steadily to pay off the family debt. They plan a gala dinner to celebrate the payment of the last sum due their creditors. On that day old Tulliver meets Wakem outside the mill. His excitable nature gets the best of him, and the old man attacks Wakem without injuring him. But he himself suffers another stroke, which proves mortal. On his deathbed he charges Tom to look after his sister. Maggie now goes away to teach at a boarding school. She receives an invitation from her cousin Lucy Deane, the daughter of well-to-do people, to visit their home at St. Ogg's. This is Maggie's first experience of the pleasures of human society. Stephen Guest, a handsome and wealthy young man who is paying court to Lucy, is attracted to Maggie, and she falls in love with him. One day, when they are out in a little boat on the Floss, they are carried downstream by the current. Stephen begs her to elope with him. But Maggie will not marry him in spite of the fact that she loves him. When she returns to her home, she finds that Tom has heard that she had run off with Stephen, and to her sorrow she is not admitted into the house. Guest and Company, Tom's employers, purchase the Mill, and appoint Tom manager. Maggie is now living with her Aunt Jane. In September the tide swells and the land begins to be flooded. Out of concern for Tom, Maggie takes a boat and rows for the Mill. When she gets there Tom climbs through the window into her boat. But the current is too much for them and they are swept along into the wreckage piled into the river. Knowing that they cannot be helped, they cling to each other and so, their quarrel appeased, go to meet their death together.

George Eliot's other novels include *Silas Marner* (1861), *Felix Holt* (1866), and *Daniel Deronda* (1876). Her verse is quite inferior, but one of her poems, *O May I Join the Choir Invisible*, is well known.

WILKIE COLLINS (1824–1889)

Wilkie Collins worked under Dickens on his magazines. His stories are a mixture of complicated plot, extravagant humor, and love interest. His best books are *The Woman in White* (1860), the story of a crime due to mistaken identity; *Armadale* (1866), a story of "Gothic" atmosphere; and *The Moonstone* (1868), about a jewel stolen from a Hindu idol and elaborating the efforts of certain Hindus to retrieve it. The characterization in the Collins' novels is poor, but he is very skillful in telling a story with speed and dramatic suspense.

GEORGE BORROW (1803–1881)

George Borrow traveled extensively all over Europe, and his books are in many cases the products of his wanderings. He is one of the most picturesque writers of his period, as well as an interesting philologist. *Lavengro* (1851) and *The Romany Rye* (1857) are exotic and highly flavored accounts of gypsy life in the British Isles. *The Bible in Spain* (1843) was written as a result of his adventures as salesman for the Bible Society in trying to sell copies of the Gospels in Spain. *Wild Wales* (1862) is the last of his picaresque narratives. It is an open question whether he can be considered a writer of fiction at all. There is such a confusion of autobiography and play of imagination in his works that they are hard to categorize. But they are a delight to read for their wonderful feeling for the outdoors and the racy tales he intersperses throughout his books.

ANTHONY TROLLOPE (1815–1882)

Anthony Trollope was the author of some fifty novels, the reading of which requires a special taste. He was a master of quiet, unexciting realism. He has no message to expound, no vices to correct, no criticism to level— except for a certain good-humored amusement at petty human foibles. Less of an artist, less of a humorist, and less of a stylist than Thackeray, he is yet to a degree a novelist of the same school in that he pictured human beings as they are. His best novels are the "Barsetshire" series, including *The Warden* (1855), *Barchester Towers* (1857), *Doctor Thorne* (1858), *Framley Parsonage* (1861), *The Small House at Allington* (1864) and *The Last Chronicle of Barset* (1867). These are faithfully reproduced scenes of the life in a small English cathedral town. Trollope's greatest talent is his ability to create lifelike characters. His most famous portrait is that of Mrs. Proudie, the bishop's wife, who will be found in several of the Barsetshire novels.

REVIEW QUESTIONS

THE VICTORIAN AGE

Multiple Choice

1. _____ Queen Victoria's reign can best be described as
   a. short and tumultuous
   b. short and calm
   c. filled with social change
   d. spanning two decades

2. _____ The First Reform Bill of 1832
   a. placed political power in the hands of the middle class
   b. changed English immigration law
   c. solidified the power of the Tories
   d. was repealed one year after its passage

3. _____ John Henry Newman was famous in his era as
   a. a noted poet and novelist
   b. a Catholic convert and, eventually, Cardinal
   c. a Methodist reformer
   d. a Church of England bishop

4. _____ The prose style of Thomas Carlyle can best be described as
   a. shocking in its sudden changes
   b. dull and lifeless
   c. legalistic in tone and pace
   d. simple in structure and diction

5. _____ Like that of many of Browning's poems, the form of "The Bishop Orders His Tomb" is
   a. four-line stanzas rhyming *abab*
   b. blank verse monologue
   c. prose paragraphs
   d. linked sonnets

6. _____ Like Malory before him, Tennyson wrote several poems concerned with
   a. the matter of Britain
   b. religious pilgrims
   c. sculptors
   d. Protestant reformers

7. _____ In "The Function of Criticism at the Present Time," Matthew Arnold argues that
   a. the creativity of critics is no less than that of poets
   b. criticism inhibits art of all kinds
   c. criticism provides needed cultural materials for the fashioning of art
   d. negative criticism serves no useful function

8. _____ Elizabeth Gaskell's novels contain frequent descriptions of
   a. wretched working conditions in factories
   b. American landscapes
   c. native Indian villages
   d. European urban scenes
9. _____ In his day, Charles Dickens was
   a. little known as a novelist
   b. both popular and respected
   c. known primarily as a statesman
   d. known primarily as a poet
10. _____ George Eliot was
   a. the grandfather of T. S. Eliot
   b. a pseudonym for Mary Anne Evans
   c. Prime Minister of England
   d. the protagonist in *Hard Times*

True or False

11. _____ Thomas Carlyle involved himself in an intense study of German.
12. _____ Macaulay is best known as a satiric poet.
13. _____ John Henry Newman was deeply interested in the nature and structure of the university.
14. _____ With regard to the beliefs and politics of his age, John Ruskin can best be said to be in quiet agreement with the majority of the middle class.
15. _____ In "In Memoriam" Tennyson pays tribute to his deceased brother.
16. _____ *The Ring and the Book* is an extended prose essay on literacy by Robert Browning.
17. _____ Elizabeth Barrett Browning was the sister of Robert Browning.
18. _____ The tone of Matthew Arnold's poetry is usually giddy and high-spirited.
19. _____ Clough was the subject of a famous elegy by Arnold.
20. _____ Emily Brontë wrote many more novels than her sister, Charlotte.

Fill-in

21. In the Victorian age, the prime proponents of the theory of evolution were _____.
22. In evaluating world history, Carlyle focused primarily upon _____ rather than movements or parties.
23. The Oxford Movement involved an interest in _____ on the part of many English scholars and artists.
24. In *The Stones of Venice* Ruskin praises _____ architecture over Renaissance architecture.

25. *The Sonnets from the Portuguese* records Elizabeth Barrett Browning's feelings of love for _____.
26. *The Rubaiyát of Omar Khayyám* was technically a _____, though in many ways also an original poem.
27. Darwin's staunchest intellectual defender was _____.
28. Benjamin Disraeli, a prominent English political leader, was also a _____.
29. The dark, brooding lover of Catherine Earnshaw in *Wuthering Heights* is _____.
30. The most autobiographical of Dickens' novels is _____.

Matching

31. _____ Reform Bill	a.	*Apologia Pro Vita Sua*
32. _____ Ruskin	b.	"Fra Lippo Lippi"
33. _____ Carlyle	c.	*Past and Present*
34. _____ Arnold	d.	*Origin of Species*
35. _____ Browning	e.	*Little Dorrit*
36. _____ Dickens	f.	*Jane Eyre*
37. _____ Charlotte Brontë	g.	*Praeterita*
38. _____ Elizabeth Barrett Browning	h.	Friend of Clough
39. _____ Darwin	i.	Extended voting rights
40. _____ Newman	j.	*Aurora Leigh*

Answers

1. c	15. f	28. novelist
2. a	16. f	29. Heathcliff
3. b	17. f	30. *David Copperfield*
4. a	18. f	31. i
5. b	19. t	32. g
6. a	20. f	33. c
7. c	21. Darwin and	34. h
8. a	Huxley	35. b
9. b	22. individuals	36. e
10. b	23. Catholicism	37. f
11. t	24. Gothic	38. j
12. f	25. Robert Browning	39. d
13. t	26. translation	40. a
14. f	27. Huxley	

Part 3

LATE CENTURY
EXPERIMENTATION

WORKS AT A GLANCE*

Dante Gabriel Rossetti

1850	"The Blessed Damozel"	1870	*The House of Life*
1861	*The Early Italian Poets* (translation)		"Sister Helen"

Christina Rossetti

1850	"Dreamland"	1866	*The Prince's Progress*
1861	"A Birthday"	1872	*Sing-Song*
	"Uphill"	1881	*A Pageant*
1862	*Goblin Market*		"Monna Innominata"
	"When I Am Dead, My Dearest"	1893	*Verses*
	"After Death"	1896	*New Poems*

William Morris

1858	*The Defense of Guenevere and Other Poems*	1890	*The Roots of the Mountains*
	"The Haystack in the Flood"		*The Story of the Glittering Plain*
	"The Eve of Crecy"	1891	*Poems by the Way*
1867	*The Life and Death of Jason*	1894	*The Wood Beyond the World*
1868–1870	*The Earthly Paradise*	1895	*Child Christopher and Goldilund the Fair*
1872	*Love Is Enough*	1897	*The Water of the Wondrous Isles*
1876	*Sigurd the Volsung*	1898	*The Sundering Flood*
1889	*The House of the Wolfings*		

Algernon Charles Swinburne

1860	*The Queen Mother*	1876	*Erectheus*
	Rosamund	1878	*Poems and Ballads, Second Series*
1865	*Atalanta in Calydon*		
	Chastelard	1880	*Study of Shakespeare*
1866	*Poems and Ballads*		*Songs of the Springtides*
	"The Garden of Prosperpine"		*Studies in Song*
1867	*"Ave Atque Vale"*		*Heptalogia*
1871	*Songs Before Sunrise*	1881	*Mary Stuart*
1874	*Bothwell*	1882	*Tristram of Lyonesse*
1875	*Songs of Two Nations*	1883	*A Century of Roundels*
	Essays and Studies		

*Dates refer to date of publication unless otherwise noted.

Algernon Charles Swinburne (continued)

1884	*A Midsummer Holiday*	1896	*The Tale of Balen*
	Astrophel	1899	*Rosamund, Queen of*
1885	*Marino Faliero*		*the Lombards*
1886	*Miscellenies*	1904	*Channel Passage*
	A Study of Victor Hugo		*Collected Poems*
1887	*Locrine*	1908	*The Age of Shakespeare*
1889	*A Study of Ben Jonson*	1909	*Shakespeare*
1892	*The Sisters*	1919	*Contemporaries of*
1894	*Studies in Prose and Poetry*		*Shakespeare*

George Meredith

1851	*Poems*	1883	"The Woods of Westermain"
	"Love in the Valley"		"Earth and Man"
	(first version)		"The Lark Ascending"
1855	*The Shaving of Shagpat*		"The Day of the Daughter
1859	*The Ordeal of*		of Hades"
	Richard Feverel		"Phoebus with Admetus"
1861	*Evan Harrington*		"Melampus"
1862	*Modern Love*		"Lucifer in Starlight"
1864	*Sandra Belloni*	1885	*Diana of the Crossways*
1865	*Rhoda Fleming*	1888	*A Reading of Earth*
1866	*Vittoria*		"The Appeasement
1871	*The Adventures of*		of Demeter"
	Henry Richmond	1891	*One of Our Conquerors*
1875	*Beauchamp's Career*	1894	*Lord Ormont and*
1879	*The Egoist*		*His Aminta*
1880	*The Tragic Comedians*	1895	*The Amazing Marriage*
1883	*Poems and Lyrics of the*	1897	*The Idea of Comedy and the*
	Joy of Earth		*Uses of the Comic Spirit*
	"Love in the Valley"	1910	*Celt and Saxon* (unfinished)
	(enlarged version)		

Robert Louis Stevenson

1878	*An Island Voyage*	1886	*The Strange Case of*
1879	*Travels with a Donkey*		*Dr. Jekyll and Mr. Hyde*
1881	*Virginibus Puerisque*		*Kidnapped*
1882	*Familiar Studies of*		*The Merry Men*
	Men and Books	1887	*Underwoods*
	The New Arabian Nights		*Memories and Portraits*
1883	*Treasure Island*	1888	*The Black Arrow*
	Silverado Squatters	1889	*The Master of Ballantrae*
1885	*The Dynamiter*	1892	*Across the Plains*
	Prince Otto	1893	*Catriona*
	More New Arabian Nights		*Island Nights' Entertainment*
	A Child's Garden of Verses	1894	*The Ebb Tide*

*Dates refer to date of publication unless otherwise noted.

Robert Louis Stevenson *(continued)*

1895	*Vailima Letters*	1897	*St. Ives*
1896	*Songs of Travel*	1899	*Letters to Family*
	Weir of Hermiston		*and Friends*
	(unfinished)		

Walter Pater

1873	*Studies in the History of*	1893	*Plato and Platonism*
	the Renaissance	1895	*Greek Studies*
1885	*Marius the Epicurean*		*Miscellaneous Studies*
1887	*Imaginary Portraits*	1901	*Essays from the Guardian*
1889	*Appreciations*		

Oscar Wilde

1881	*Poems*	1893	*A Woman of No Importance*
1888	*The Happy Prince*	1895	*An Ideal Husband*
1890	*Intentions*		*The Importance of*
1891	*Picture of Dorian Gray*		*Being Earnest*
1892	*Lady Windermere's Fan*	1898	*The Ballad of Reading Gaol*
	Salomé	1905	*De Profundis*
	The House of Pomegranates		

Thomas Hardy

1871	*Desperate Remedies*	1897	*The Well-Beloved*
1872	*Under the Greenwood Tree*		*A Changed Man*
1873	*A Pair of Blue Eyes*	1898	*Wessex Poems*
1874	*Far from the Madding Crowd*	1901	*Poems of the Past and*
1876	*The Hand of Ethelberta*		*the Present*
1878	*The Return of the Native*	1903–1908	*The Dynasts*
1879	*The Trumpet-Major*	1909	*Time's Laughing*
1881	*A Laodicean*		*Stocks*
1882	*Two on a Tower*	1911	*Satires of*
1885	*The Mayor of Casterbridge*		*Circumstance*
1887	*The Woodlanders*	1914	*Lyrics and Reveries*
1888	*Wessex Tales*		"Ah, Are You Digging
1891	*Tess of the D'Urbervilles*		on My Grave?"
	A Group of Noble Dames	1917	*Moments of Vision*
1894	*Life's Little Ironies*	1922	*Late Lyrics*
1895	*Jude the Obscure*		

Alfred Edward Housman

1896	*A Shropshire Lad*	1922	*Last Poems*
	"When I Was One and Twenty"	1936	*More Poems*
	"To an Athlete Dying Young"		
	"Think No More, Lad"		

---

*Dates refer to date of publication unless otherwise noted.

James Thomson

1880	*The City of Dreadful Night*	1884	*A Voice from the Nile*
1881	*Vane's Story*		*Satires and Profanities*
	Essays and Phantasies	1885	*Shelley, a Poem*

William Ernest Henley

1888	*A Book of Verses*	1900	*For England's Sake*
	"*Invictus*"	1901	*Hawthorn and Lavendar*
1890	*Views and Reviews*	1903	*A Song of Speed*
1893	*London Voluntaries*		"*To W. A.*"
1898	*Poems*		

Francis Thompson

1893	*Poems*	1897	*New Poems*
	"The Hound of Heaven"	1909	*Essay on Shelley*
1895	*Sister Songs*		

Ernest Dowson

1895	*Dilemmas*	1897	*The Pierrot of the Minute*
1896	*Verses*	1899	*Decorations*
	"*Non Sum Qualis Eram Bonae Sub Regno Cynarae*"		

Gerard Manley Hopkins

1918	*Poems*
	"The Windhover"
	"The Wreck of the *Deutschland*"

Lewis Carroll (Charles Dodgson)

1895	*Alice in Wonderland*	1876	*The Hunting of the Snark*
1871	*Through the Looking Glass*		
1876	*Phantasmagoria*	1889–1893	*Sylvie and Bruno*

Sir William Schwenk Gilbert

1869, 1873	*Bab Ballads*	1884	*Iolanthe*
1875	*Trial by Jury*	1885	*The Mikado*
1878	*H.M.S. Pinafore*	1887	*Ruddigore*
1879	*The Pirates of Penzance*	1888	*The Yeoman of the Guard*
1881	*Patience*	1899	*The Gondoliers*

---

*Dates refer to date of publication unless otherwise noted.

George Robert Gissing

1884	*The Unclassed*	1892	*Born in Exile*
1887	*Thyrza*	1893	*The Odd Women*
1889	*The Nether World*	1903	*The Private Papers of*
1891	*The New Grub Street*		*Henry Ryecroft*

Samuel Butler

1872	*Erewhon*	1901	*Erewhon Revisited*
1877	*Life and Habit*	1902	*The Notebooks of*
1879	*Evolution, Old and New*		*Samuel Butler*
1880	*Unconscious Memory*	1903	*The Way of All Flesh*
1897	*The Authoress of the Odyssey*		

George Moore

1883	*A Modern Lover*	1901	*Sister Teresa*
1884	*A Mummer's Wife*	1906	*Memoirs of My Dead*
	Esther Waters		*Life*
1888	*Confessions of a Young Man*	1911–1914	*Hail and Farewell*
1890	*Impressions and Opinions*	1916	*The Brook Kerith*
1895	*Celibates*	1921	*Heloise and Abelard*
1898	*Evelyn Innes*		

---

*Dates refer to date of publication unless otherwise noted.

7
THE LATER VICTORIANS

The enormous success in international trade, over which England had exercised almost a monopoly, began to dwindle as the century approached its close, with the emergence of the United States and Germany as competitors. Bankruptcies became epidemic, and workers in the cities went through prolonged stretches of unemployment. In 1886 more than twenty thousand Englishmen emigrated to the New World or Australia, and within the next two years there were an additional thirty thousand emigrants. The vague radicalism that had been slowly growing in England began to be crystalized in the development of various socialistic theories. The experience of the short-lived Paris commune of 1871 did much to fan revolutionary sentiment all over Europe. In 1880 three Labour candidates won seats in Parliament for the first time. In 1881 the historic Social Democratic Federation was founded by H. M. Hyndman. Three years later the Fabian Society was formed to prepare the way for a socialist state, and included later among its leaders George Bernard Shaw, Beatrice and Sidney Webb, and H. G. Wells.

But the middle classes were not suffering, as the increase in their numbers proves. In 1880 the fierce struggle for colonies began all over Europe. That year found Britain with few possessions in Africa. By 1914 the British Empire included millions of square miles in Africa. To justify English penetration into a new continent, there developed the hypocritical moral theory of "the white man's burden," best known as exhibited in the writings of Kipling. The Conservative Party came into power again, and chauvinism was rampant. The extension and maintenance of the British Empire was represented as a responsibility to the uncivilized who, perforce, must be civilized with or without their will, wherever British commerce penetrated.

In the meantime, reaction on the part of writers against middle-class prosperity continued. The first movement to attract wide attention after the mid-century was the so-called Pre-Raphaelite Brotherhood, of which the leading writers were Dante Gabriel Rossetti, his sister Christina Rossetti, and his friend William Morris. This movement formed the basis for a new aestheticism, which by degrees sought to draw the province of art further and further away from life, until the doctrine of "art for art's sake" took form in the works of Oscar Wilde and some of his lesser contemporaries of the 1890s. The poetry of Algernon Swinburne and the prose of Walter Pater, although of greater literary importance, tended to increase the vogue of this new aestheticism.

DANTE GABRIEL ROSSETTI (1828–1882)

Rossetti was born in London on May 12, 1828, the son of a scholarly Italian, who was a political refugee, and an English mother of Italian parentage. Thus, in his home he became familiar with the cultural heritage of Italy, its warmth and heavily sensuous appeal. It is not strange, therefore, that he was able to bring a voluptuousness and richness to his writing that are not common in English literature. The Rossetti household was a lively and interesting one, for it was a gathering place of political exiles. But Rossetti was essentially an artist, with little taste for politics. His earliest ambition was to be a great painter. For a long time, indeed, he looked upon painting as his profession and the writing of poetry as a hobby. Time, however, has established his poetry on a far higher plane than his painting. His paintings will always be interesting, not only as characteristic of the movement he inaugurated, but as showing a highly poetic vision. But criticism has not accorded them the importance of his poems.

When he entered the Royal Academy to study art at the age of eighteen, he was already an eager student of poetry. Browning, whose works had been published only a few years, was Rossetti's first passion—at a time when only a handful of Englishmen knew Browning existed. Led by his reading in Browning, young Rossetti began to immerse himself in the Middle Ages, and to start a translation of Dante's *Vita Nuova*.

When he was twenty Rossetti formed, with the help of two fellow art students—John Everett Millais and Holman Hunt—the Pre-Raphaelite Brotherhood. The name of their movement, with which they intended to revolutionize the world of art, was the result of their agreeing with Ruskin that the best painting had been done in Italy before the corruption of the worldly values of the Renaissance set in. The days of Raphael had been the turning point. Their declaration of war on contemporary art included a protest against current "intellectual emptiness." It was necessary to bring back sincerity to art and truthfulness to artistic representation. "We must be Early Christian—Pre-Raphaelite!" they exclaimed. They drew up a list of "Immortals" and the highly selected index included Christ, Shakespeare, Keats, Shelley, Joan of Arc, Browning, and Elizabeth Barrett Browning. In their own paintings the young Pre-Raphaelites had the impudence to use primary colors as a revolt against the subdued tones of the accepted painting of the academy.

Disciples flocked to them. William Michael, Rossetti's brother, became the official critic of the group, and his sister, Christina, although she never actually joined, became their poet. Among the gifted men who were in one way or other associated with them during the following years were the versatile William Morris, the poets Swinburne and Coventry Patmore, the painter Burne-Jones, and the sculptor Woolner.

In 1850 the Pre-Raphaelite Brotherhood published a magazine to exhibit their principles in literature, *The Germ*, William Michael being editor. Its contents were to prove the advantages of "a rigid adherence to the simplicity of nature." That such was their theory must seem incredible to the modern reader of *The Germ* when he realizes that nothing could sound less like an imitation of the simplicity of nature than the contents of this magazine. What the Pre-Raphaelites actually meant was that they were determined to be faithful in representing the details of natural and human life.

"The Blessed Damozel," which is the best poem ever published in *The Germ*, is one of Rossetti's finest, an achievement of great brilliance and shining sweetness. Rossetti is said to have been inspired with the idea after reading Poe's *The Raven*. Poe had written about the grief of a lover for his dead love. Rossetti wrote about the yearning of the loved one in Heaven for the lover still on earth. (As was so often the case with his poems, he painted a picture on the same subject.)

"The Blessed Damozel" is presented as the reverie of the lover in the forest as he sits looking up through the trees while the autumn leaves are falling about him. He dreams that the blessed damozel is leaning out from the gold bar of Heaven:

> *Her eyes were deeper than the depth*
> *Of waters stilled at even;*
> *She had three lilies in her hand*
> *And the stars in her hair were seven.*

Although she has been in Heaven ten years, to her it seems scarce a day. (In the forest her lover feels as though the falling leaves are the folds of her hair falling about his face.) She tries with her glance to penetrate the depths of space. Around her, newly met lovers are rehearsing their old loves, and the souls ascending to God go by her "like thin flames." At last, her gaze traces the moon looking like a little feather down in the gulf of space, and then the earth. And she begins to speak. (Her lover thinks he hears her voice in the bird's song overhead.) She wishes that he would come to her. When he comes she will take his hand and teach him the ways of Heaven and its songs. If he should fear the new wonders he will see, she will lean her cheek on his and tell him of their love, speaking out at last as she had never done before. And she will ask of Christ only that they may both love forever as they did on earth. But "all this is when he comes." Suddenly she throws her arms along the gold bar, and begins to weep.

It was in this eventful year of 1850 that Rossetti fell in love with Elizabeth Siddal. He felt from the moment he met her that his destiny was settled. Her face appears again and again in his paintings and drawings and haunted him for years after her death. Rossetti was temperamentally the director of the movement, so that his worship of Siddal made her the idol and favorite model of the whole Brotherhood. She suffered from very poor health and put off marriage for ten years. This was the period in which Rossetti became a confirmed Bohemian in his way of life.

It was his good fortune to become a close friend of John Ruskin's, whose generosity in financing talented artists became a godsend to Rossetti and his fellow painters. Ruskin began to champion the Pre-Raphaelite cause in his lectures, offered to buy every water color Rossetti produced, and did his best to bring about the marriage with Siddal. In 1860, although Rossetti knew her days were numbered, they were married.

Their brief life together was tragic. There were endless quarrels over his infidelities—some real, many imagined. On February 10, 1862, he left their home presumably to teach at Ruskin's Workingmen's College. When he returned about midnight he found her unconscious from an overdose of laudanum. She died without ever recovering consciousness. Rossetti never knew thereafter whether her death was an accident or suicide, for she had often taken the drug to help her sleep. The rest of his life is the story of a man who sought in vain to escape his sense of guilt.

When she was buried, he took the only manuscript of his poems, most of which had been written to her or for her, and laid it between her cheek and her hair in the coffin.

Soon after this he went to live in a large house in Chelsea, which he shared with his brother. For a time Swinburne and Meredith lived there too. The clash of temperament among these geniuses was too much, and presently Rossetti had the house to himself.

Up to this time he had published only a few poems in *The Germ* (which had ceased publication after the fourth issue) and in the *Oxford and Cambridge Magazine* (1856). He had also issued a volume of translations, *The Early Italian Poets* (1861). Now he began to write once more, although he lived in a perpetual torture of remorse and superstition. Many of his friends who were winning literary recognition, pleaded with him to publish his poems, the quality of which they remembered as extraordinary. But he could not reconstruct the contents of the buried manuscript. At length, terrified at the undertaking, he consented to allow his friends to exhume the poems in his absence. The texts were in a sad state, but complete enough to enable him to prepare a volume. In 1870 his *Poems* was published.

For a brief while the volume was a great success, and was frequently reprinted. But there appeared suddenly *The Fleshly School of Poetry*, one of the most vicious attacks ever aimed at a poet. This article was published anonymously by Robert Buchanan, himself a good poet, because of his fury against William Michael and Swinburne for their savage reviews of a friend's book. Rossetti was here accused of moral corruption in his poetry. He took it as a sign from Heaven—retribution for his past deeds and his lack of faith in not allowing the poems to remain under the earth. Rapidly he sank deeper and deeper into despair, began to use drugs, and made himself a prisoner in his home for weeks at a time. His last years were an increasing nightmare of suspicion. He even believed, without cause, that Browning and Lewis Carroll had been ridiculing him in their verse. He found some relief in writing, and in 1881 published a two-volume edition of his poetry. He died a complete wreck in April 1882.

IMPORTANCE

The artistic sincerity for which the Pre-Raphaelites stipulated is exhibited in Rossetti's best poems. Keats was a kind of god to the Movement, and they followed him in attempting to enrich every phrase of their writings with sensuous appeal. Thus, through their elaborate use of symbols in their figures of speech, they became the parents of the Symbolist Movement in France at the very end of the century. Rossetti desired above everything else that his poetry should be at white heat of emotion from beginning to end. He worked hard at it to achieve this effect. His best poems are, in addition to "The Blessed Damozel," a long ballad, "Sister Helen," and a sonnet sequence, *The House of Life*.

The ballad of "Sister Helen" is based on the ancient superstition connected with witchcraft, that if a wax figure representing one's enemy is melted slowly over fire, as the figure melts so the enemy will die by slow degrees. The two speakers in this poem are a little boy standing on a balcony in the moonlight, and his sister, Helen, who is busy melting her waxen man over the flame. She bids her brother tell everything he sees. There come three men on horseback, one in advance of the other two. He is Keith of Eastholm, who comes to say that Keith of Ewern is dying. Three days ago he suddenly sickened on his wedding day, and has been lying in a bed of agony ever since. He cries that Helen must take her curse away from him. Helen answers through her little brother that since her prayers have been heard, let Keith of Ewern pray too. In vain the dying man calls on her name and cries that he is melting as in a fire. Helen answers that her heart fared the same for his pleasure. Now Keith of Westholm comes riding up, bearing a ring and a broken coin, and begging Helen to remember "the banks of Boyne." Last comes Keith of Keith with his white hair streaming in the wind. The old man pleads that Helen at least forgive his son so that the dying man's soul may not be forfeited. Helen is still remorseless. A lady has arrived now. And as her hood falls back in the moonlight, the golden-haired Lady of Ewern is revealed. She clasps her hands and prays, but is too full of despair to speak. Helen's comment is to hope that the gold hair of the new bride will turn whiter than snow. A bell is heard chiming in the air, and the three men turn around hastily homewards, leaving the Lady to go back alone. The bell is the funeral-bell of false Keith of Ewern. The waxen man is melted. At the end Keith's ghost appears in the doorway:

> *A soul that's lost as mine is lost,*
> *Little brother!*
> *(O Mother, Mary Mother,*
> *Lost, lost, all lost, between Hell and Heaven!)*

The House of Life is considered by some one of the greatest of English sonnet sequences. Many of these sonnets were inspired by the poet's love for his wife; but some of the later ones are an expression of the war within his bosom between his intention to remain faithful to her memory and his desire for another woman. These sonnets, written in an adaptation of the Italian form, possess a marvellous fusion of intellectuality and furious passion, which make them quite unique in English literature. The title is taken from the first of the twelve "Houses" of astrology. The best of the sonnets are the introductory sonnet on the sonnet, the fourth, the nineteenth, the fifty-fifth, the sixty-third, the sixty-fifth, the seventy-first, the seventy-second and the seventy-third, the eighty-fifth, the eighty-sixth, the ninety-seventh and the one hundred first.

The introductory sonnet, "The Sonnet," describes that form as a monument "to one dead deathless hour." "Love-Sight" (number 4) wonders when the poet sees his loved one most—at day or night; but if he should see her no more there would be an end of hope and only death would be. "Silent Noon" (number 19) is a wonderful painting of the two lovers lying amid the long grasses in the silent noon, when "two-fold silence was the song of love." "Lost Days" (number 86) asks what has happened to the lost days in the poet's life; but after death he knows the faces that he must meet, each one another murdered self. "A Superscription" (number 97) is a poem on all that might have been; for him there never can be peace because memory ever awaits in ambush to remind him of what could have been and no more shall be.

CHRISTINA ROSSETTI (1830–1894)

Christina Rossetti, Dante Gabriel's sister, led an apparently uneventful life, but within her heart mighty dramas were enacted. As a girl she was very womanly, giving little hint of the intensity of her spirit. For a time a timid youth, James Collinson, attached to the Pre-Raphelite Brotherhood, won her heart, and it was expected that they would marry. But he suddenly decided to become a priest in the Roman Catholic Church. She never forgot her love for him, even when he again changed his mind and married another woman. When she was twenty-seven there came another suitor, the pedantic Charles Cayley. She fell in love with him. But he was slow and unimaginative, and by the time he actually proposed to her, she had successfully smothered all her affections.

She continued to live a quiet life as a devoted daughter and sister. Few guessed the violence that lived behind her tranquil exterior. She worshipped her poet-brother so much that, despite her battles with herself, she was envious of his wife. In her later years she found an outlet for her intense feeling by turning to the Anglican Church, in the service of which she became a mystical devotee. She had, however, one advantage over most intelligent Victorian women: the conversation and friendship of many men of talent, her brother's friends, all of whom profoundly admired her poetic gifts.

IMPORTANCE

It is likely that Christina Rossetti's genius has not yet been sufficiently appreciated. Here and there a critic has suggested that it was she who was the genius of the Pre-Raphaelite group. Others, bold souls, have even hinted that the poetry of this woman, whose life somewhat resembles in its frustration that of Emily Dickinson, is at least as good as the poetry of that now highly esteemed New England spinster.

Christina Rossetti composed more than nine hundred English poems and sixty poems in Italian—most of them very brief. Her first writings appeared in *The Athenaeum* (1848) and *The Germ* (1850). Her first volume was *Goblin Market* (1862). There followed *The Prince's Progress* (1866), *Sing-Song* (1872), *A Pageant* (1881), and *Verses* (1893). After her death *New Poems* appeared in 1896.

Her poetry is of three classes, poems of fancy, poems of religious exaltation, and poems of passion. In the first category, *Goblin Market* stands as a masterpiece of technical cleverness and fantasy. Most of her poetry is religious, and is written almost as though she were a disciple of the seventeenth century poet George Herbert.

Her art is intense and metrically precise, like her brother's. But he is much more elaborate than she; indeed, some of her songs are among the most movingly simple in our literature. Nor is there any hint of that sensuality which colors his work; her own ascetic nature rises to exaltation and religious piety in her lines. Her constant inspiration is obviously the King James Bible.

In her personal poems expressing her frustration in love, the austerity of her mind only intensifies the throb of passion. Of these last, some of the best are to be found in the fourteen sonnets which make up the sequence, *"Monna Innominata"* ("Lady Nameless"). Her most frequent subject is the contemplation of death and the everlasting peace which it must bring. Her simplicity robs death of any terror. If the Brotherhood was indeed devoted to artistic simplicity, they could have found it nowhere better expressed than in her poetry.

Among her lyrics the most celebrated are: "When I Am Dead, My Dearest;" "A Birthday;" "Mirage;" "Dreamland;" "Uphill;" and "The Lowest Place." The opening lines of the first-mentioned carry its message:

> *When I am dead, my dearest,*
> *Sing no sad songs for me.*

"A Birthday" begins: "My heart is like a singing bird"; the last line explains: "My love is come to me." "Mirage" is an address to her broken heart bidding it lie still, for the world and herself have been changed because of a dream. "Dreamland" is an obituary poem on one who sleeps "where sunless rivers weep"; do not awake her for she is resting until time shall cease. "Uphill" describes life as a long journey up the mountain towards death, the resting place; the traveller will meet many other wayfarers; and all shall find beds at the end where their journeys end. "The Lowest Place" asks for the most humble spot by God's side—only a place where the poet may sit and see God and love Him.

Her best sonnets include "After Death," "The First Day," and "In an Artist's Studio." In "After Death" the speaker is lying dead while her lover bends over her form weeping; he did not love her while she lived, but now that she is dead he can pity her. "The First Day" expresses the wish that she could still remember the moment of their first meeting; at the time it seemed to mean so little; she now knows that it meant so much. "In An Artist's Studio" is an acknowledgment of the fact that only one face is to be found in her brother's pictures (his wife's); sometimes she is a queen, sometimes a girl, sometimes a saint, sometimes an angel; he has painted this face not as it ever was but as it "fills his dream."

WILLIAM MORRIS (1834–1896)

William Morris had the most fabulous array of talents of any of the members of the Pre-Raphaelite Brotherhood. Luckily his inexhaustible energy and his delight in work could keep pace with his gifts. He was lucky, too, in being the son of a wealthy man and in enjoying boundless good health. At Oxford he met Edward Burne-Jones, with whom he embarked on a study of medieval art. Both young men came to study painting under Rossetti. Morris was six years younger than his teacher, and soon became one of his closest friends. He was soon a willing disciple of the Pre-Raphaelite credo, and accomplished a great deal more than all the other members put together in making their influence felt generally in Victorian life. He established a firm that dealt in furniture, woodcarving, stained glass, tapestries, and hammered metals. Through his handmade furnishings, Morris enabled the new aestheticism to invade the English home—where some standard of beauty was badly needed. Soon his services were much in demand for decorating the interiors of Victorian houses. As a disciple of Ruskin he began a revival of handicrafts. In protest against the drab sameness of furnishings turned out by machines, he promoted appreciation of the finer qualities which the work of skilled hands could impart. From the designing of rugs and furniture, he carried his influence further. At no time in the history of bookmaking were volumes printed with such complete indifference to their physical appearance as when Morris began his good work. He opened the Kelmscott Press, where on his own printing press he began to turn out beautiful books designed by himself and his friends, printed on fine paper and handsomely bound. This was the beginning of the modern limited fine editions idea.

It might well be thought that such a career could have kept a number of men busy. But in addition to all this work, Morris was also the author of many poems, prose works and translations. one of these is perhaps truly great, but all of of them maintain an astonishing level of excellence. His devotion to the Medieval setting, held in common with his fellow Pre-Raphaelites, can be seen everywhere in his work.

The Defense of Guenevere and Other Poems (1858) is his first volume and his best. Here he can be found successfully achieving a realistic representation of the Middle Ages, such as his associates all aimed at. *The Life and Death of Jason* (1867), *The Earthly Paradise* (1868–1870), *Love Is Enough* (1872), *Sigurd the Volsung* (1876), and *Poems by the Way* (1891) are his other volumes of poetry. Of these, *The Earthly Paradise* is the most admired; in a framework similar to that of *The Decameron* and *The Canterbury Tales* he presents a series of stories in verse as recounted at meetings twice a month by a group of Norsemen and a group of descenclants of the ancient Greeks, who have met each other. The "Apology" and "L'Envoi" of this work are well known, particularly for the phrase which occurs in both, describing the poet as "the idle singer of an empty day."

But it is a handful of poems from *The Defense of Guenevere* that constitutes the poetry of Morris which is best known. In these Morris views the Middle Ages realistically as hard, brutal, and unpolished. The title poem presents Guenevere speaking in defense of herself in answer to the charge of adultery with Lancelot. In the same volume "The Haystack in the Floods" recounts the story of Sir Robert encountering Godmar, who tries to prevent the former's rescue of Jehane; betrayed by his men, Sir Robert is threatened with death unless Jehane yields herself to Godmar. When she refuses, Robert is slain. Another poem, "The Eve of Crecy," is the dream of Lambert of his sweetheart Margaret just before he goes to battle where he is doomed to die; every stanza has the refrain: "Ah! Qu'elle est belle La Marguerite."

His prose tales include *The House of the Wolfings* (1889), *The Roots of the Mountains* (1890), *The Story of the Glittering Plain* (1890), *The Wood Beyond the World* (1894), *Child Christopher and Goldilind the Fair* (1895), *The Well at the World's End* (1896), and two posthumously published books, *The Water of the Wondrous Isles* (1897) and *The Sundering Flood* (1898). These do not include his many volumes of translations.

In his poetry and his prose romances, Morris is the typical Pre-Raphaelite in his avoidance of the contemporary scene. But his work in interior decoration shows a concern for life about him. In his later years he became a Socialist, and joined the Social Democratic Federation. *A Dream of John Ball* (1888) and *News From Nowhere* (1891) are concerned with his Socialistic dreams, and present his picture of an ideal society.

ALGERNON CHARLES SWINBURNE (1837–1909)

There has been so much dissension on the subject of Swinburne's place in the history of English poetry that it is still impossible to evaluate him accurately. His angriest detractors would not deny that no English poet—not even Shelley—has been his equal in making elaborate and enchanting music out of the English language. His mastery over the melody and rhythms of our language is not only remarkable, but also fresh and novel. A volume to include all of his technically perfect works would make a book of enormous size.

The charge against him has been that his poems are intellectually thin. He did not pretend to a philosophical mind, although it cannot honestly be said that there are no ideas in his poems. Anyone with his restless and wide imagination is bound to have enough to say. Nevertheless, it is true that one comes away from Swinburne's poetry enchanted, but unenriched with any important ideas. Perhaps if his music were less dazzling, less might have been expected of him in the way of thought. But even his most enthusiastic admirers must recognize the fact that he seems to be at his very best as a music maker when he has least to say. His love poetry and descriptive poetry are, for that reason, his most characteristic. There is a feeling of sheer profligacy of talent in the luxuriance of his verses. He adored the Greeks, but he had none of their veneration for sharp outline. And only too often one is forced to concede that Swinburne seems drunk with the sound of his own beautiful voice.

Swinburne came from an honored family, and was the grandson of a baron on his father's side, the grandson of an earl on his mother's. His father was an Admiral in the Navy, but Swinburne, despite his passion for the sea, had not the temperament to continue the family tradition in that profession. He was born in London, April 5, 1837, and educated in foreign languages from his earliest years. He attended Eton, and later Balliol College, Oxford. At school he distinguished himself for his brilliance in the classical languages. Nevertheless, he was far too nervous a boy to adapt himself to college routine, and he managed to be something of a minor scandal on the campus. Just as he was about to take his degree he left Oxford, to his mother's great anguish.

However he was to disparage his years spent in school as wasted, he actually was preparing himself very well at the time for the profession of letters. He composed many imitations of the world's great writers, Sappho, Boccaccio, the Elizabethan dramatists, the folk-ballad writers, among others. When he met Rossetti, Morris and Burne-Jones in 1857, he became a disciple of the Pre-Raphaelite Brotherhood for a time. Even after he had declared his independence from the movement, he supported its ideal of art for art's sake, its distaste for Victorian modes of living, its love of the Middle Ages, and its stipulation for ecstasy in art.

But Swinburne's interests were too many and too curious to allow him permanently to give allegiance to any one cult. His was the genius of a true eclectic. One will find in his works the coloring of his enthusiasm for every kind of art in every kind of period. The Bible, the Greek lyrical poets, the Greek dramatists, the Pre-Raphaelites, Walter Savage Landor, François Villon, Baudelaire, Victor Hugo—to mention some—all influence his work at one time or another. It has been said of Swinburne that he was a man given to "isms." Certainly, one can find in his poems republicanism, paganism, medievalism, nihilism, anticlericalism, and radicalism of all sorts.

He lived in London on a family allowance after leaving Oxford, and was an intimate of the Rossetti circle. His first works, *The Queen Mother* and *Rosamond*, were published in 1860; these poetic dramas attracted no attention at all. Following their failure he spent several years writing reviews. Swinburne loved literature passionately, and no critic has every expressed his enthusiasm more rhapsodically or his dislikes with such venom. Among his accomplishments during these years were two spirited appreciations of George Meredith and the contemporary French poet Baudelaire. With the latter he felt a particularly deep kinship because of the Frenchman's untiring praise of the joys of the flesh—a point of view that Swinburne himself tended to make into a religion. He visited various countries on the Continent in 1864, and in Florence met Walter Savage Landor, whom he humbly acknowledged as his master. It was on his return to London the next year that he took lodgings for a while in the same house with Rossetti and Meredith.

He now issued his masterpiece, *Atalanta in Calydon* (1865), a poetic tragedy in the Greek style in the manner of Aeschylus. Had Swinburne been able to proceed from the level he established with this work, there could be no question of his title to be considered one of the truly great English poets. For *Atalanta in Calydon* is the only classic tragedy in English that one would dare mention along with *Samson Agonistes*, although no art could be more dissimilar from Milton's than Swinburne's. Unfortunately, it is with this early work that he achieved his highest literary triumph.

It was so well received that he started immediately on a trilogy of plays dealing with the fortunes of Mary, Queen of Scots: *Chastelard* (1865), *Bothwell* (1874), and *Mary Stuart* (1881). But the flagrant eroticism of the poetry that appeared in *Poems and Ballads* (1866) and the perversions hinted at in them raised a storm of anger; *Chastelard*, on much less obvious grounds, had commenced a wave of indignation against him; his volume of poems fomented it into a tempest. Swinburne was only delighted, and began at once a novel with the express purpose of shocking "Mrs. Grundy out of her remaining wits." Judging from the description of what it was like, we may conclude that it is fortunate that Swinburne never published it.

At about this time Swinburne made the friendship of the great Italian exile, Mazzini. Ever ready to accept a hero, he began to worship him and the cause of republicanism. This new interest in politics became all the easier because he was already a devout admirer of Victor Hugo, whose life was dedicated to the republican ideal. His *Songs Before Sunrise* (1871) therefore finds Swinburne free of his erotic concerns, and singing the cause of liberty. The mood is continued in *Songs of Two Nations* (1875), which contains more hymns to liberty. He was now writing almost feverishly. *Erectheus* (1876) is another tragedy in the Greek style written with considerable austerity. The year 1878 saw publication of *Poems and Ballads, Second Series.* (A third series appeared in 1889.) In the meantime, he had published a critical essay on Blake (1868), one on the Elizabethan dramatist Chapman (1874) and a volume of *Essays and Studies* (1875). Now he issued his well-known *Study of Shakespeare* (1880).

At this juncture occurred the crisis of his life. He had, like Baudelaire, been feeding his senses with experiences that brought them to the point of collapse. Not yet forty years of age, he suddenly fell into a prostration that brought him near to death. During his convalescence, his worried mother arranged with his pedantic friend, Theodore Watts-Dunton, that both men go to live at Putney, a quiet suburb of London. From then on, Swinburne was practically a prisoner of his friend. With almost childlike obedience he submitted himself to a regular routine of daily living that Watts-Dunton arranged for him. He was not allowed to leave Putney without his friend, and was permitted to see only such people as Watts-Dunton agreed might be admitted. There is no record of any protest on Swinburne's part for the last thirty years of virtual enslavement to the rules and regulations of his guardian. His escape was to bury himself deeper and deeper in his books.

Although on occasion he could still write beautifully, Swinburne's imagination gradually died in the respectable atmosphere provided for him. He was well aware that his powers were waning, and admitted that he wrote only because he was bored. This acknowledgement in no way interfered with his issuing a steady flow of volumes: *Songs of the Springtides* (1880), *Studies in Song* (1880), *Heptalogia* (1880)—a book of parodies on English poets, *Tristram of Lyonesse* (1882), *A Century of Roundels* (1883), *A Midsummer Holiday* (1884), *Astrophel* (1894), *The Tale of Balen* (1896), *A Channel Passage* (1904), *Collected Poems* (1904); a series of plays—*Marino Faliero* (1885), *Locrine* (1887), *The Sisters* (1892) and *Rosamund, Queen of the Lombards* (1899); and a series of enthusiastic critical works—*Miscellanies* (1886), *A Study of Victor Hugo* (1886), *A Study of Ben Jonson* (1889), *Studies in Prose and Poetry* (1894), *The Age of Shakespeare* (1908), *Shakespeare* (1909), and the posthumous collection, *Contemporaries of Shakespeare* (1919). As a critic

Swinburne manifests a delicate and warm appreciation of everything he wrote about. His poetic imagination equipped him to touch the quintessence of what was best in every writer that he examined. The one objection that can be raised against these criticisms is that one gets the impression that every author as Swinburne appraises him in turn is the greatest who ever wrote.

As a poet, with the exception of his first play, *Atalanta in Calydon*, Swinburne is inevitably best when he is most lyrical. Even in that case the choruses are particularly remarkable; the coming of spring is hailed in wonderful stanzas beginning:

> *When the hounds of spring are on winter's traces*
> *The mother of months in meadow or plain*
> *Fills the shadows and windy places*
> *With lisp of leaves and ripple of rain*

and the passage commencing "Before the beginning of years . . . " tells of the gift of tears which time brought to man as an essential to his spirit.

"Itylus" is the song of the nightingale to her sister, the swallow:

> *Swallow, my sister, o sister swallow,*
> *How can thy heart be full of the spring?*
> *A thousand summers are over and dead.*

"A Match" is a love song beginning:

> *If love were what the rose is,*
> *And I were like the leaf,*
> *Our lives would grow together*
> *In sad or singing weather.*

"The Garden of Proserpine" is a picture of the morphean garden of the goddess of the nether world; only sleep seems good to the poet now, and he yearns for its release from mortal care when he shall taste of it in Proserpine's garden:

> *From too much love of living,*
> *From hope and fear set free,*
> *We thank with brief thanksgiving*
> *Whatever gods may be*
> *That no life lives forever;*
> *That dead men rise up never;*
> *That even the weariest river*
> *Winds somewhere safe to sea.*

"Ave Atque Vale" ("Hail and Farewell") may yet be numbered among the greatest of English elegies. It was written by the poet upon hearing a false rumor that Baudelaire had died; but that misunderstanding in no way interferes with the depth of feeling, sincerity of tribute, and poetic wealth of the poem. "A Ballad of Burdens," a variation of the *ballade* form common to

French poetry, has characteristically a refrain as the last line of each stanza; this poem celebrates the burdens that we must bear: the burden of fair women, of bought kisses, of sweet speeches, of long living, of bright colors, of sad sayings, of the four seasons, of dead faces, and of much gladness; the envoy of this ballad cries:

> *For life is sweet, but after life is death.*
> *This is the end of every man's desire.*

"Hertha" is a song of the earth in which the goddess of the earth explains to us man's relation to her; it is laden with republican sentiment. "To Walt Whitman in America" is a tribute to the American poet, the great singer of freedom, whose singing in a free land has a message that he must send to enslaved Europe; to love God is, like Whitman, to love freedom.

Swinburne has exerted a considerable influence on his successors, not only because of his defiant emphasis on sensual experience, but also for his insistence on the music of his language. A logical extension of his practice is the twentieth century notion of one group of poets that the intellectual connotation of words is only a bar to true poetry. These men would drain words of all appeal but the aural. That way, perhaps, madness lies.

GEORGE MEREDITH (1828–1909)

It will still be some time before Meredith's place in English letters can be accurately judged. Like all writers whose philosophy is far in advance of their contemporaries', Meredith had a small but very important circle of admirers in his own day, and his readers are still only the discriminating few. It is astonishing now to consider that his first novel, *The Ordeal of Richard Feverel* should have been published in 1859, the year of *Adam Bede* and *A Tale of Two Cities,* and two years before *Silas Marner* ! Its modernity of view and its subtlety of psychology seem decades ahead of Dickens and Eliot. There is little that is Victorian about Meredith. His belief in the complete equality of women, his understanding of their modes of thinking, his clear-eyed understanding of male vanity—all seem to belong to the twentieth century.

Even his admirers tend to concentrate on his novels and overlook his poetry. Yet it is possible that Meredith may eventually be counted as one of the four or five major poets of his century. Again, it is surprising to find that his first publication of poetry antedates the first poetry which Rossetti, Christina Rossetti, Morris, Swinburne, Henley, Francis Thompson or James ("B. V.") Thomson issued—strange, because his poetry is so much more modern than any of theirs.

The greatest drawback to his attracting a wide audience has been the compression of his style. In verse and prose he crams so much meaning into every line, records such subtle nuances of ideas, and sparkles with such brilliant intelligence, that the hasty reader will have little patience with him. The much-discussed "difficulty" of his style can be seen as meaning only that he requires too much intelligence of his reader. It is significant that towards Meredith there has never been indifference: He has been either disliked or adored.

His father was a tailor at Portsmouth, and he was born over his father's shop on February 12, 1828. Meredith was always proud of his Celtic heritage—Welsh on his father's side, and Irish on his mother's. When George was only five, his mother died. His father, remarrying soon after, went off to South Africa, leaving his son at school to live on a small inheritance from the first Mrs. Meredith. All his life George Meredith was extraordinarily handsome, and he was rather aloof as a boy. At fourteen he was sent to school in Germany. Two years later he was apprenticed to a London solicitor with literary interests. Through his employer he met the youthful editors of the *Monthly Observer*. His first poem, *Chillianwallah*, appeared in its pages.

His friends included Edward Peacock, son of the novelist. Meredith fell madly in love with Peacock's sister, a widow nine years his senior. She married him when he was twenty-one. But the marriage was catastrophic. Both high-strung and clever though ill-mated, they made each other miserable. After some years of increasing incompatibility, she ran off with another man. Abandoned by her lover, the unhappy woman later committed suicide. This tragic experience forms the root of Meredith's startlingly original sonnet sequence, *Modern Love*.

By this time Meredith had done some important writing. In 1851 he published his first volume of *Poems*. The most important work in that collection was his first version of "Love in the Valley," a new kind of love poem—and in the opinion of some critics, the finest love poem of the century. Tennyson was among its earliest admirers, although the general public paid little attention to the volume. Against the background of the shifting seasons and changing hours of the day the lover in "Love in the Valley" paints a series of wonderful pictures of his sweetheart; his point of view is subtly modern:

> *Love that so desires would fain keep her changeless;*
> *Fain would fling the net, and fain have her free.*

In this poem Meredith employs the four-accent line of "Christabel."

The failure of his volume of poems made Meredith turn to prose for his next, *The Shaving of Shagpat* (1855), a thoroughly contemporary extravaganza modeled on the *Arabian Nights*, and running over with healthy good spirits. In 1858 he came with his abandoned little son to live in London, and began work on his first novel, *The Ordeal of Richard Feverel* (1859), one of his best. His objectivity here is admirable, for he drew upon his own unhappy experience to create the first truly modern study of the evil which well-meaning parents can work upon their children. Although Meredith was to concentrate more and more on the novel, he never lost his poetic vision. There are passages in this book that, if split up into lines, would make some beautiful free verse poems. The thesis of the story, that the best-thought-out systems of education can never succeed in thwarting nature, is presented with wit and brilliant portraiture. *Evan Harrington* (1861) followed—a study of social snobbery.

Modern Love (1862) was his next publication. The title poem consists of fifty sixteen-line sonnets (a form not uncommon in the Renaissance, the rhyme-scheme being *abbacddceffeghhg*). No poet has ever described so accurately the alternation of sympathy and hostility between mismated husband and wife as does Meredith in these sonnets. "Juggling Jerry," in this volume, is a reminiscence of a juggler at the end of his career. "Ode to the Spirit of Earth in Autumn" is the earliest of many nature poems by Meredith celebrating the doctrine of evolution.

In 1863 he met Marie Vulliamy, a fine musician, whom he married in 1864, and with whom he knew great happiness until her death (1885). In 1868 they went to live in the country at Box Hill, and there Meredith spent the rest of his days. He was not a man to cultivate a tragic life, and his life was not shattered by the tragedy of his first marriage, once he had written it out of his system. He lived a very active life, took long walks with his friends, filling their ears with his invigorating talk, and ever drawing on his endless resources of wit, gaiety, and profound knowledge.

Wholesomeness and sanity were basic traits in his character and thinking. The Darwinian Theory had not at all the disturbing effect on him that other leading Victorians suffered. He welcomed the idea that man had developed from lower forms of life. If man is the apex of the evolutionary process, he reasoned, that made Intelligence the flowering of all of Nature's labors. He had none of Rossetti's inclination towards Bohemianism, none of Swinburne's towards paganism. He chose to believe that men, "not forfeiting the beast with which they are crossed," are destined to move on and upwards toward godhead.

Meredith's other volumes of poems are: *Poems and Lyrics of the Joy of Earth* (1883), containing an enlarged version of "Love in the Valley," some wonderful nature-poems ("The Woods of Westermain," "Earth and Man," "The Lark Ascending"), several beautiful re-workings of classical myths ("The Day of the Daughter of Hades," "Phoebus with Admetus," "Melampus"), and the powerful sonnet, "Lucifer in Starlight;" *Ballads and Poems of Tragic Life* (1887); and *A Reading of Earth* (1888), which contains the wonderful "The Appeasement of Demeter."

"In Lucifer in Starlight" Meredith brilliantly states the immutability of Nature; Satan, remembering his old cause for hate, appears once more to wreak evil on humanity, but as his huge form threatens the peace of men, he looks up at the stars

> *Which are the brain of heaven, . . . and sank.*
> *Around the ancient track marched, rank on rank,*
> *The army of unalterable law.*

In the last lines of the forty-third sonnet of *Modern Love* he states the point of view from which in his novels he later leveled his satire at humanity:

> *In tragic life, God wot,*
> *No villain need be! Passions spin the plot:*
> *We are betrayed by what is false within.*

To expose "what is false within" Meredith believed only in the medicine of laughter. Good laughter to him was holy. In "The Appeasement of Demeter" he shows a sterile world reborn to life by laughter, "wine and bread . . . reviver of sick Earth!"

The Idea of Comedy and the Uses of the Comic Spirit, given as a lecture in 1877 and printed in 1897, explains his preference for comedy in the representation of life. After a brilliant review of leading writers of comedy, he propounds his theory of comedy as "the sword of common sense" which slays egotism, vanity, and false sentiment.

Meredith detested the current mode of realism in the novel. The conscientious piling up of detail, he understood, is the antithesis of art, the business of which is to present the *quintessential* realities of life. And that can be achieved only through selection and compression. The dialogue in Meredith's novels is far too witty and intelligent to be naturalistic; but it compresses, while it delights us, the important truths of character within mere phrases.

The level of his novels is high. The others are: *Sandra Belloni* (1864), originally called *Emilia in England*, a study of a sentimental egotist in the character of Wilfrid Pole; *Rhoda Fleming* (1865), a new interpretation of a "fallen woman," who, in this case, rises in dignity after her misfortune; *Vittoria* (1866), an historical novel set in the exciting background of the 1848 revolutionary movement in Milan; *The Adventures of Harry Richmond* (1871), containing some of his most enchanting women; *Beauchamp's Career* (1875), a love story against the background of contemporary British politics; *The Egoist* (1879), Meredith's masterpiece, a study of the boundless vanity of every man in his dealings with women; *The Tragic Comedians* (1880), a novelizing of the love affair of the celebrated Socialist Ferdinand Lassalle and Helen von Dönniges; *Diana of the Crossways* (1885), a study of the dilemma faced by a modern intellectual woman; *One of Our Conquerors* (1891), a study of "illicit love"; *Lord Ormont and His Aminta* (1894), another study of a love triangle; *The Amazing Marriage* (1895), a story of matrimonial tragedy; and the unfinished *Celt and Saxon* (1910).

ROBERT LOUIS STEVENSON (1850–1894)

"R. L. S." was born in Edinburgh, November 13, 1850, the son and grandson of engineers. He was of very delicate health even as a boy, and his schooling was therefore necessarily constantly interrupted. Very early in life he was determined to be a writer. He deliberately schooled himself by consciously imitating the style of countless great writers whom he admired. Eventually he forged a style entirely his own, but the influence of his admirations can be read in it.

First, to please his family, he took up engineering, and even wrote articles on the subject. Then he tried law. He took his degree and was admitted to the bar before he gave that up too. By that time he was a victim of tuberculosis. The rest of his life is the story of a long fight to live and hold off the ravages of the disease.

He made the friendship of several distinguished literary men. Through Sir Leslie Stephen, editor of the *Cornhill Magazine,* he met the poet Henley, with whom he later collaborated on three plays. In time he had won the affection and friendship of many men of letters. Stevenson was a gentle, lovable man, and cultivated the art of friendship with rare wisdom.

In his twenty-fifth year Stevenson began his habit of traveling, a habit he maintained for the rest of his life. *An Inland Voyage* (1878) and *Travels with a Donkey* (1879) are amusing collections of essays, the fruit of his observations while wandering on the Continent. Although he was to make a considerable reputation as a novelist, it is likely that posterity will look upon his later essays as the crowning achievements of his career. His hand was kept very busy writing stories and essays for the periodicals.

He had met Mrs. Osborne in 1876 and became engaged to her before her return to California. Two years later, hearing she was in ill health, he crossed the ocean and the American continent to be with her. His impoverished state required his traveling with the worst of accommodations, and he was very ill when he reached the West. In serious financial straits, he spent some time at Monterey, and then married his fiancée. All these experiences he later used in his writings, particularly in *Silverado Squatters* (1883), a record of his honeymoon spent at an abandoned mining camp near San Francisco.

The Stevensons came back from Scotland for a visit, and spent the ensuing years seeking his health in various places on the Continent. It was during this period that some of his most significant works were appearing: his *Virginibus Puerisque* (1881), containing his celebrated "An Apology for Idlers;" and *Familiar Studies of Men and Books* (1882). Now began a steady stream of stories and novels: *The New Arabian Nights* (1882), *Treasure Island* (1883), *The Dynamiter* (1885), *Prince Otto* (1885), *More New Arabian Nights* (1885), *The Strange Case of Dr. Jekyll and Mr. Hyde* (1886), *Kidnapped* (1886), *The Merry Men* (1886), *The Black Arrow* (1888), *The Master of Ballentrae* (1889). His incomparable collection of children's poetry, *A Child's Garden of Verses* (1885) was followed by a collection of his poetry, *Underwoods* (1887), and the volume of *Memories and Portraits* (1887), the last named containing his popular essay, "A Gossip on Romance."

In the meantime Stevenson had left Europe forever. He was convinced by 1887 that he must find a place to live across the ocean. He spent an encouraging winter at Saranac Lake, New York, where he regained enough energy to write some very important essays, notably *"Pulvis et Umbra."* He found himself very much liked by the American public, but he nevertheless decided upon the South Seas as the last resort for prolonging his life. To make the voyage, he chartered a yacht on the west coast, and spent more than a year, chiefly at various ports in Polynesia, before he made his home at Samoa. His choice proved wise. Despite the development of his disease, he was able to win back a considerable amount of stamina, and for four years he worked well. He became very popular with the natives, and participated in their life. His last books are *Across the Plains* (1892), a volume of essays; *Catriona, Island Nights' Entertainments* (1898), *The Ebb Tide,* (1894), and the uncompleted *Weir of Hermiston* (1896) and *St. Ives* (1897)—all fiction; and a volume of poems, *Songs of Travel* (1896). The *Vailima Letters* (1895) and *Letters to his Family and Friends* (1899) are a fascinating record of his life in the South Seas.

IMPORTANCE

As a novelist Stevenson belongs in the school established by Scott, for he was strictly a romanticist. But he is interested in the psychology of action to a degree that never engaged the attention of Scott. Eclectic as he was, we see in some of the novels however, more than a hint of Meredith's influence. His style sometimes reminds one of Lamb's, sometimes of DeQuincey's, sometimes of Sir Thomas Browne's—but it is always his own.

WALTER PATER (1839–1894)

The new aestheticism to which the Pre-Raphaelite movement had given considerable impetus had as its philosopher Walter Pater. His point of view, succinctly stated, is that one should learn to make out of life itself an art.

He was born the son of a physician in the slums of London's East End on August 4, 1839. After his father's death, the family moved to Enfield, a suburb of London, where he lived under the guidance of his mother, aunt, and grandmother. These exclusively feminine surroundings in youth may be responsible for a certain want of virility in Pater's writing, for his dislike of practical affairs, but also for the extraordinary refinement of his understanding. These early years have been recorded in his beautiful essay, *The Child in the House* (1894).

He was sent to King's College, Canterbury, to prepare for the ministry when he was fourteen. He entered Queen's College at Oxford in 1858, and rarely left the University town for the rest of his life. By the time he was twenty-one he gave up all belief in Christianity, and was busying himself with the study of philosophy. The works of Plato and the German Transcendentalists (augmented by several trips to Germany during vacations) were the chief influences brought to bear on his thought. In 1864 he was given a classical fellowship at Brasenose College, Oxford; for the remainder of his life he lived the unexciting existence of a college don. Nothing could have been more to his taste.

The German aestheticians led him to studies in the arts of the Renaissance. In order to establish personal contact with the art of antiquity and the Renaissance, he spent some time in Italy in 1865. He was also much interested in the work of the English Romantic poets, and his first published work was on Coleridge, an essay which appeared in the *Westminster Review* (1866). But his greatest discovery was Winckelmann, the famous German critic of Greek art. Pater's essay, "Winckelmann" (1867), was the first of a series of studies he made of the Renaissance, later collected into his first book, *Studies in the History of the Renaissance* (1873). The celebrated "Conclusion" to this book contains an eloquent statement of Pater's philosophy:

> We are all under sentence of death but with a sort of indefinite reprieve. . . . We have an interval, and then our place knows us no more. Some spend this interval in listlessness, some in high passions, the wisest . . . in art and song. For our one chance lies in expanding that interval, in getting as many pulsations as possible into the given time. Great passions may give us this quickened sense of life, ecstasy and sorrow of love, the various forms of enthusiastic activity. . . . Only be sure it is passion—that it does yield you this fruit of quickened, multiplied consciousness. Of this wisdom, the poetic passion, the desire of beauty, the love of art for art's sake, has most; for art comes to you professing frankly to give nothing but the highest quality to your moments as they pass, and simply for those moments' sake.

Pater took no interest in social problems. Self-consciously a follower of the teachings of Epicurus, he felt that all a man can know of the destiny of his soul is what the experiences of this life can teach. Consequently, he reasoned, one should deliberately seek out and carefully select one's experiences in terms of their maximum reward of refined sensation. Nothing could have been further than this from English middle-class morality.

In 1885 appeared Pater's only novel, a beautiful book, *Marius the Epicurean*. It contains one of the most amazing pieces of historical reconstruction to be found in the field of the novel. His setting is Rome in the days of the Emperor Marcus Aurelius. His hero, a man of the most refined and exquisite tastes, leads the perfect Epicurean life, the culmination of which is his sacrificing his life for his friend. But he does that, not as a Christian might do it, for the sake of a Christian ideal, but as an expression of the highest good he can seize at that moment.

IMPORTANCE

A natural consequence of Pater's philosophy was that he should lay great importance upon style. In the perfectly turned phrase one had the equivalent of a perfectly selected experience, to afford the best pleasure of the moment. In France the great novelist Flaubert was insisting that a writer must be satisfied with nothing less than the "precise word" in every part of his writing. Pater's "Essay on Style," which appeared in his volume of *Appreciations* (1889), accepts this criterion, and develops Pater's theories on writing as a fine art. His own style was worked over with endless care. Pater is so scrupulous about the shade of meaning and emphasis of every phrase that his writing, for all its perfection, has an air of emasculation. Nevertheless, no English stylist has a prose of more unostentatious grace.

His other essays will be found in *Plato and Platonism* (1893), *Greek Studies* (1895), *Miscellaneous Studies* (1895), and *Essays from The Guardian* (1901). His collection of *Imaginary Portraits* (1887) contains some very interesting and sensitive portraiture.

OSCAR WILDE (1854–1900)

The scandal attaching to Wilde's name has occasioned so much opprobrium on the one hand, and such sentimentality on the other, that his achievement is often obscured as a truly important writer.

He was born in Dublin, October 15, 1854, and christened Oscar O'Flahertie Fingal Wills Wilde. His names are a result of his mother's absorption in Celtic lore. Lady Wilde was a clever but highly artificial and unbalanced woman who, disappointed at not having a girl, dressed her son up as one for many years. His father, a brilliant physician, led a dissolute life.

Oscar attended Trinity College in Dublin for a while and then entered Magdalen College, Oxford in 1874. He distinguished himself in the classics and won the Newdigate Prize for poetry with *Ravenna* (1878). But his great enthusiasm was for the teachings of Walter Pater, whose disciple he announced himself to be. He decided to popularize, personally illustrate, and develop Pater's doctrine of making of life an art, and of art a life. While at Oxford the general trend of his talents was already clear. He loved to be popular, at any cost, and discovered that affectation has the reward of always attracting attention. His association with the American painter Whistler was also an invaluable preparation for developing the art of epigram and impudent repartee.

When he had taken his B.A., he came to London with the self-bestowed title of "Professor of Aesthetics." Very soon the public was thinking of him as the leader of the "art for art's sake" movement. In 1881 he issued a volume of *Poems*, exquisitely bound, but containing little more than imitations of various poets. But he had an extraordinary talent for self-advertising, and although his pen had accomplished little, he was well enough known to make it profitable for a lecture manager to arrange a tour in the United States in 1882. The tour was an enormous success. He did not disappoint his audiences: his dress was properly extravagantly aesthetic, his locks were appropriately long, the word Beauty was ever on his lip, and he insulted the American audience for American vulgarity in the manner in which Americans adore being insulted by visiting Englishmen. On his return to England he was reputed the best wit of his day.

In 1884 he married a very fine woman. His next book was a charming though artificial collection of fairy tales, *The Happy Prince* (1888). In 1890 appeared one of his best books, a brilliantly witty series of critical essays elaborating the new aestheticism, *Intentions*. His best known book, the novel *The Picture of Dorian Gray* (1891), though heavily imitative of the French novelist Huysmans, is written with extraordinary wit and hints just enough at mysterious wickedness to have insured its enthralling the public.

His first attempts at playwriting were all unsuccessful. But in 1892 he achieved his greatest success with his problem comedy, *Lady Windermere's Fan*. In the same year he wrote in French (a language he was by no means master of) *Salomé*, an exotic one-act play, which Lord Alfred Douglas later translated into English. *A Woman of No Importance* (1893) and *An Ideal Husband* (1895) were his next plays.

The Importance of Being Earnest

The top of Wilde's dramatic achievement, and probably his most important literary contribution, is his scintillating comedy *The Importance of Being Earnest* (1895). *The Importance of Being Earnest* is perhaps the first play written for the stage during the whole extent of the nineteenth century worthy of being preserved as a classic. It follows in the tradition of Congreve, and can well hold its own as a comedy of manners when measured beside *The Way of the World* and *The School for Scandal*. Nothing could be more artificial than the plot and characterization of this play, but nothing could be more delightful. The dialogue sparkles from beginning to end. The play is as delicate and heady as champagne.

A comedy of manners set in the late nineteenth century, it was intended as an attack on Victorian false piety, which created an atmosphere of hypocrisy. Wilde used his wit to exaggerate the absurdity of the Victorian concept of earnestness.

The two main characters are Algernon Moncrieff (Algy) and Jack Worthing. The play's main commentary is played out through these men's need to escape the strictness of Victorian society. The irony is that the men can only be earnest outside of the society that values earnestness. Both men invent alter egos to escape the discomforts of their lives. Algy creates an ill friend named Bunbury in order to avoid his Aunt Augusta's dull dinner parties. Jack finds his life in the country with his young ward Cecily and her stern governess too restraining because of the high moral tone he must adopt. He invents an unprincipled brother named Ernest whose identity and conduct he adopts on his frequent visits to London. There, as Ernest, he falls in love with Algy's Aunt's daughter, Gwendolyn Fairfax. She loves him too, but coyly claims she is attracted to the name Ernest. Lady Bracknell, Algy's Aunt Augusta, is interested in Jack-as-Ernest's qualifications as a suitor for her daughter and rejects him when he cannot produce a pedigree. In fact, Jack reveals that he had been found in a leather bag at Victoria Railway Station.

Jack responds to his rejection by having Ernest die and returns to the country to mourn for him. There he finds Algy on a "Bunburying" foray posing as Ernest. Cecily and Algy grow fond of each other and Algy refuses to leave despite Jack's pointed suggestions. Because of Cecily and Gwendolyn's attraction to the name Ernest, both men make appointments to be rechristened. Meanwhile Gwendolyn has arrived at the manor house. She and Cecily are confused by so many Ernests and think that they are in love with the same man. Finally the two men appear together, admit their real identities, and are rejected by the girls. When they explain that their ruses were schemes to get closer to the girls, they are forgiven. Lady Bracknell arrives and interrupts the engagements to investigate Cecily and Jack's qualifications to marry her relatives. She finds Cecily suitably rich, but Jack, as Cecily's ward, will not allow her to marry unless he has consent to marry Gwendolyn. The governess steps forward to confess that she had left Jack in the railway station in the leather bag. She declares that he is truly the son of Lady Bracknell's sister, and his real name is Ernest. The play is resolved with the engagements of the two couples.

Late Work

Tragically, the year of Wilde's greatest triumph was also the year of his fall. His friendship with Lord Alfred Douglas proved in the end his undoing. In 1895 Wilde was convicted of what was termed in the day homosexual immorality and sent for two years to Reading Gaol. For a man of his temperament, prison turned out worse than a death sentence. He left Reading Gaol with every intention of leading a decent life. But he was a broken man, and everywhere he went he was shunned by the self-righteous. He escaped to Paris, but the bitterness of his memories was too much for him, and he began to drink himself to death. He died there in a third-class hotel in November 1900, and lies buried in Père Lachaise Cemetery.

Wilde's later volumes include *A House of Pomegranates* (1892), another collection of fairy tales; *The Ballad of Reading Gaol* (1898), a long poem written in a masculine, almost popular rhythm on the fate of a criminal who is hanged for murdering his sweetheart; and *De Profundis* (1905), a very moving and sincerely intended autobiographical account, which as it stands is only a portion of the document Wilde actually wrote in self-examination while he was in prison.

IMPORTANCE

For such varied achievements in drama, children's literature, poetry, and autobiographical prose, Wilde's reputation continues to be revalued, usually positively so, by each generation of critics since his death. In Wilde is glimpsed the traits of wit, commitment to one's beliefs, mastery of literary forms, and thematic experimentation so evident in the later drama of George Bernard Shaw, the poetry of Eliot and Pound, and the novels of Woolf and Lawrence.

THOMAS HARDY (1840–1928)

The last of the great Victorians began and ended his career as a poet, although he did not publish poetry until many years later. His novels and stories occupy many volumes: *Desperate Remedies* (1871), *Under the Greenwood Tree* (1872), *A Pair of Blue Eyes* (1873), *Far from the Madding Crowd* (1874), *The Hand of Ethelberta* (1876), *The Return of the Native* (1878), *The Trumpet-Major* (1879), *A Laodicean* (1881), *Two on a Tower* (1882), *The Mayor of Casterbridge,* (1885), *The Woodlanders* (1887), *Wessex Tales* (1888), *A Group of Noble Dames* (1891), *Tess of the D'Urbervilles* (1891), *Life's Little Ironies* (1894), and *Jude the Obscure* (1895). The hostility and sanctimonious charges of indecency brought against *Jude the Obscure,* which many critics believe to be his greatest novel, determined Hardy to write no more novels and turn again to the writing of poetry. (Two works of fiction, nevertheless, were published after this decision: *The Well-Beloved* (1897) and *A Changed Man* (1897).) Hardy's volumes of poems are *Wessex Poems* (1898); *Poems of the Past and the Present* (1901); the poetic drama, *The Dynasts* (1903–1908); *Time's Laughing Stocks* (1909); *Satires of Circumstance* (1911); *Lyrics and Reveries* (1914); *Moments of Vision* (1917); and *Late Lyrics* (1922).

Novels

It was George Meredith who discovered Hardy and urged the publication of his novels. Yet nothing could be more dissimilar from Meredith's art than Hardy's. Hardy was actually an uncompromising realist and a man with little interest in comedy. His view of the world was profoundly pessimistic. He saw humanity as inevitably defeated in its hopes by the irony of circumstance. In

Hardy's novels no matter how valiantly his characters strive for a good life, the Immutable Will of fate strikes them down.

Tess, the heroine of *Tess of the D'Urbervilles*, is essentially a pure woman, but unlucky accident after accident twists her life into endless patterns of disaster. At the beginning, in order to help her father, she seeks the help of the D'Urbervilles, a family that has bought the estate and assumed the name anciently belonging to Tess's ancestors. The son of the D'Urbervilles, Alec, first rescues her from an annoying situation and later violates her honor when she is helpless to defend herself. She only despises him and runs away. Her illegitimate child dies and is refused Christian burial. Tess goes from employment to employment through the countryside, willing to undertake any hard task. At Talbothays Dairy, a more decent life opens for her. There she meets Angel Clare, son of a minister, a youth of high ideals, who falls in love with her. Though returning his love, she is afraid to marry him because of her experience. But her love for him is too strong to be put by, and, since she can never manage to tell him the truth, she writes it in a long letter to him the night before their wedding. Unhappily, when she slips the message under his door, it also goes under the carpet and is never received. After the wedding ceremony, finding to her dismay that he has not read it, she blurts out the facts and shatters his illusion of her. He finds he cannot live with her, since she is not what he believed her to be, and sets out for Brazil to think things over. Tess now seeks employment again, but is hounded from place to place by Alec D'Urberville. Finally, believing Alec to be the evil demon in her life, she stabs him to death. Angel, seeing the light at last, returns, but finds Tess too late. He tries to escape with her, but the police catch up with them, and Tess pays the supreme penalty.

This story illustrates the thesis exhibited in all of Hardy's novels, notably in *The Return of the Native*, *The Mayor of Casterbridge*, and *Jude the Obscure*, that we are all victims of circumstance.

In *The Mayor of Casterbridge* (1885) we see an early indication of Hardy's later interpretations of Immanent Will, as it worked itself out in human affairs.

In a moment of drunkenness, Michael Henchard sells his baby daughter and his wife to Newsom, a sailor. Once sober, Henchard realizes what he has done and begins a fruitless search for the three. He eventually settles in Casterbridge and joins the gentry as a successful grain merchant and, in time, as the mayor. Working under him as a manager is Farfrae, a young grain expert. One day Henchard's wife returns with her daughter by Newsom, Elizabeth-Jane. Her previous child by Henchard has died. Farfrae courts Elizabeth-Jane, but ends up marrying a former lover of Henchards, Lucetta Le Sueur. As Henchard's business falls off, Farfrae prospers in his own enterprises. Henchard is revealed as a wife-seller and is stigmatized for his involvement with Lucetta (who dies in miscarriage). Henchard has only Elizabeth-Jane to cling to, but that support, too, is removed when her father, Newsom, returns. Henchard dies bitter and alone.

Jude exhibits Hardy's philosophy more remorselessly than any of the others. It is the story of a man born in obscurity and poverty, with an unquenchable thirst for knowledge. His one dream is to achieve an education. But try as he will, Jude cannot get within the walls of the college whose spires have for years been a symbol of all that he desires in life. Instead, he manages to entangle his life, without meaning to, in hopeless tragedy. He falls an easy victim to the wiles of an older, coarse-grained woman, who will have a husband at any cost. When he meets the girl he can love, he can be united with her only by defying the conventions of society because she is already married. And her own high-strung sensibilities cooperate as much to destroy him as the selfish machinations of his first wife. In the end, she, his children, and he himself all come to catastrophe one by one.

The title of *The Return of the Native* points out what Hardy means to make the basis of his novel. The ill-starred heroine, Eustacia, might have managed to accommodate herself to the distasteful aspects of her life were it not that Clym Yeobright returns to his native village at a time that proves catastrophic to them both.

It must be said, however, that despite Hardy's intention of making the Immutable Will responsible for the catastrophe that befalls the heroes and heroines of his novels, he is so fine an artist that he manages to make his readers feel that the men and women themselves are the authors of their own doom. Hardy's descriptions of the countryside he knew so well are written in a richly poetic vein, and the shapes of land and sky almost always are present in the reader's consciousness. It is as though the very lives of his characters were predetermined by the moody landscape in the midst of which they dwell.

Poetry

In 1904, after Hardy's official retirement from novel writing, he issued the first part of his huge drama of the Napoleonic Wars, *The Dynasts*. This monumental work eventually extended to three volumes, nineteen acts, and one hundred thirty scenes. The play alternates passages in verse with others in prose, and the *dramatis personae* vary from leading figures, like Wellington and Napoleon, to simple peasants and city folk. There is an impressive mythology, in which the various fortunes of humanity are personified as spirits—all conducing to the proposition that it is the Immutable Will which destroys the life of every man and woman.

The Dynasts was the beginning of Hardy's prolific period as a publisher of verse. His poems show considerable variety, from verses of pure lyricism to others of sober realism. Some critics would say that in the latter category Hardy too often approaches the prosaic in language and style. Nevertheless, some of the short narrative poems compress the grim irony of an entire novel within the compass of a few stanzas.

Characteristically, the poem "To Life" finds the author tired of life but prepared to go along with it until the game is over. "New Year's Eve" describes

God as amazed at Man's concern over good and evil, since the Creator works in his own inscrutable ways. "Nature's Questioning" has the poet asking nature whether some Vast Imbecility has built the structure of the world as a joke; there are no answers, only the eternality of death and short-lived joy.

Hardy's occasional extreme pessimism can be seen in poems like "Ah, Are You Digging on My Grave?" In this poem the buried woman finds that the form digging on her grave is not her lover, for he has just married someone else; is not a relative, for her relatives see no point in wasting flowers on the dead; is not her enemy, for her enemy has forgotten her; is only her little dog, who digs not out of affection—but because he has buried a bone there.

A. E. HOUSMAN (1859–1936)

Alfred Edward Housman was born March 26, 1859, took his Master's degree at Oxford, worked in the British Patent Office until 1892, then became Professor of Latin at University College, London, and later at Cambridge University. His life was uneventful, and he was careful to discourage any prying into it. He was widely known among Latin scholars for his careful and sometimes irascible scholarship, and probably thought of himself not as a poet but as an authority on the Latin classics.

It was the publication of a single volume of poetry, *A Shropshire Lad* (1896), that established him in the popular mind as one of the leading poets of his day. It was twenty-six years before he published his next volume, *Last Poems* (1922), which had nothing new to say. His explanation concerning the origin of *A Shropshire Lad* was that all his poems were a product of "the continuous excitement under which in the early months of 1895" he lived. He also said that he expected never again to live through such an emotion, "nor indeed could well sustain it if it came." After Housman's death, his brother Laurence published a volume of final poems, *More Poems* (1936). Housman's contribution to English literature also includes his sardonic lecture, *The Name and Nature of Poetry* (1933).

Housman, like Hardy, was a pessimist interested only in the tragic aspects of life. Everywhere he looked in life he saw cause for disillusionment and a sense of the vanity of men's efforts. He lacks the overtone of pity that is in Hardy's work, but, on the other hand, his best poems have a kind of classic perfection and simplicity of outline.

No recent poetry is more eloquently simple than his. The celebrated "When I Was One and Twenty" tells of old age's advice to youth to keep the fancy free; and how, in a year's span, the lad learn the truth that one must pay with endless sufferings for giving away one's heart. "To an Athlete Dying Young" congratulates a dead athlete for his wisdom in leaving life while he is still a champion. "Think No More, Lad" urges youth to dance, to jest, to drink, and to avoid thinking, for thinking brings men to their death.

8
Late Century Poets, Humorists, and Novelists

POETS

James ("B. V.") Thomson (1834–1882)

James Thomson, who wrote under the initials "B. V.," was one of the most pessimistic poets of his time. As a child, he lived in an orphan asylum, and later in a military asylum. When he fell in love with a beautiful and gifted girl, her sudden death struck him down. Thereafter, his life was one of unbroken gloom. He was unsuccessful in business and a failure as a newspaper correspondent. A great part of his life was spent in a wretched London room, where he became more and more a confirmed alcoholic.

The City of Dreadful Night (1880) is his most important poem. It was followed by *Vane's Story* (1881) and *Essays and Phantasies* (1881). After his death *A Voice from the Nile* (1884), *Satires and Profanities* (1884), and *Shelley, a Poem* (1885) appeared.

Thomson's pessimism is as dark as any to be found in English literature, and seems part of the poet's very nature. But it has imaginative power and intensity. And there is a sonority in his verses, though they tend to a certain monotony. The phrase that occurs so often in *The City of Dreadful Night* is peculiarly effective:

> *As I came through the desert thus it was,*
> *As I came through the desert.*

William Ernest Henley (1849–1903)

William Ernest Heney was born in Gloucester and was educated at the Grammar School there. He was largely a self-taught man. While still a boy, he was afflicted with tuberculosis. In an attempt to halt the progress of the disease, his foot was amputated at the Edinburgh Hospital. While at the hospital he wrote some of his best-known poems (1873–1875), which were published in Sir Leslie Stephen's *Cornhill Magazine*. It was through this connection that Stevenson's friendship with Henley began.

In 1877 Henley commenced a long career as editor in London, and eventually established himself in a position of high critical regard.

A Book of Verses (1888) was followed by *London Voluntaries* (1893), *Poems* (1898), *For England's Sake* (1900), *Hawthorn and Lavendar* (1901), and *A Song of Speed* (1903). A collection of his criticisms was published as *Views and Reviews* (1890).

Henley's poetry is aggressively masculine. It is not surprising that it should have been Henley that discovered Kipling. His own most celebrated poem, *"Invictus"* (1888) cries, "My head is bloody but unbowed," and avers that the poet is master of his fate and captain of his soul.

Henley was an avowed enemy of the new aestheticism, which he considered effeminate. But in his own assertion of virility, he may affect some modern readers with the suspicion that he protests too much. He sought a vocabulary plain and "unpoetical." In this objective, it must be admitted, he succeeded. One of his best-known poems is the ballad "To W.A.," with its well-known conclusion:

> *When I was King in Babylon*
> *And you were a virgin Slave.*

Francis Thompson (1859–1907)

Francis Thompson was the son of a doctor and was intended originally for the priesthood. But his father desired him to become a physician, so he went to Owen's College at Manchester. Thompson was a man of hopeless impracticality, failed his examinations thrice, and, for a long time, drifted. He lived in the completest poverty for three years, where he was supplied by an old bootmaker with scraps of paper which the young man used as stationery. It was on such manuscript materials that he wrote two poems and an essay, which he sent to the editor Meynell.

Characteristically, he had omitted sending his address, and Meynell had considerable difficulty locating the author, who he was convinced was a genius. When the editor finally caught up with him, Thompson was already the victim of the opium habit. Meynell and his accomplished wife became Thompson's guardians, helped him fight his slavery to the drug, and encouraged him to write, although at best irregularly. The result was three volumes of poems: *Poems* (1893), *Sister Songs* (1895), and *New Poems* (1897). In addition Thompson is the author of an inspired piece of prose on his favorite poet, *Essay on Shelley* (1909). Thompson died of tuberculosis in 1907.

He has been recognized as a rightful heir of the traditions of the seventeenth century metaphysical poets, and his kinship to the mystical ecstasy of Crashaw has been noted. As a technician he owes most to Shelley, whom he loved despite the Romantic poet's irreligion. Thompson is one of the greatest of English Catholic poets, and in the ritual of the Catholic Church he found some of his greatest inspiration.

"The Hound of Heaven" is his best poem, and one of the finest of his generation. Its opening lines establish its exalted mood:

> *I fled Him, down the nights and down the days;*
> *I fled Him, down the arches of the years;*
> *I fled Him, down the labyrinthine ways*
> *Of my own mind; and in the mist of tears*

The poet finds that no matter where he flees, Love follows. In the end, he knows that it is God, whom he seeks, that he has been fleeing.

Ernest Dowson (1867–1900)

Ernest Dowson was one of a group of young men associated with the publication of *The Yellow Book*, a magazine devoted to the new aestheticism, and edited by Henry Harland and the artist Aubrey Beardsley. *The Yellow Book* was intended to complete the victory of "art for art's sake." The poets connected with this movement were expert technicians who had very little to write about.

Dowson left Oxford without a degree, and came to London where his company was the literary Bohemia of the day. He acknowledged France to be his intellectual home, and often paid visits to the Latin Quarter of Paris or the French countryside. His associates in London were often people of very low habits, and he drank excessively. The one event of importance in his life is his falling madly in love with the daughter of a man who ran a restaurant. (He has immortalized her in his poetry as "Cynara.") She allowed him to worship her for several years, and then she married one of her father's waiters. His unfulfilled love drove Dowson into deeper depravities, and he died of disease while still a young man.

He had made a point of throwing his life away, and his poetry is a record of that experiment. His tone varies between self-conscious eroticism and religious exaltation. His volumes include *Dilemmas* (1895), a collection of stories; *Verses* (1896); *The Pierrot of the Minute* (1897), a fanciful play in verse; and *Decorations* (1899), a collection of verse and prose.

There is an admirable finish and a melancholy music in Dowson's best poetry. The best-known is *"Non Sum Qualis Eram Bonae Sub Regno Cynarae,"* the title taken from an ode of Horace, and meaning "I am not what I used to be in the days of the good Cynara." It opens with the well-known lines:

> *Last night, ah, yesternight, betwixt her lips and mine*
> *There fell thy shadow, Cynara!*

The poet sought forgetfulness in the arms of purchased love. He has forgotten much that is "gone with the wind," flung roses with the throng, and danced, to forget his old passion. But when the feast is over and the lamps are dead, her shadow falls and takes possession of his heart. Each stanza concludes:

> *I have been faithful to thee, Cynara! in my fashion.*

Gerard Manley Hopkins (1844–1889)

Gerard Manley Hopkins was the most "modern" of his contemporaries, and has exerted an enormous influence upon the writings of certain twentieth century poets. He studied at Balliol College, Oxford, and for a while was a disciple of Walter Pater. Just as he was about to take his degree, he wrote to Newman confessing his intention of becoming a Roman Catholic. His parents violently objected, but nevertheless Hopkins became a Jesuit.

When he entered the Society of Jesus, he burned his early poetry and determined never to write again. For seven years he wrote very little. After some time spent with Newman, he was given a church at Oxford. A fellowship in the Catholic University at Dublin, 1884, resulted in his going to Ireland, where he spent his last years.

When Father Hopkins found it in himself to write again, he soon discovered that no periodical was interested in publishing his poetry. He was prepared never to see his poems in print. Luckily, the poet Robert Bridges became eagerly interested in the work of Hopkins and did all he could to have a few poems published in anthologies. Nevertheless, it was only after Hopkin's death that his poetry was at last printed. He left it to Bridges' discretion as to how much should be published. It was with loving care that Bridges at last saw justice done to his friend when Hopkins' *Poems* (1918) were issued by Bridges, who was then Poet Laureate, with a preface and notes.

Hopkins also belongs in the metaphysical tradition. His poetry, too, is an account of his intense spiritual experiences. But it is in his technique that he is a modern. He gave the utmost attention to rhythmic effects in his poetry, and was so original that even in 1918 his poetry struck some as strained and obscure. Admiration and understanding of his work have increased with the years, however. Hopkins uses what he calls "running rhythm" (syllabic verse), "sprung rhythm" (stressed verse), and combinations of the two. His "sprung rhythms" were an attempt to bring back the old accentual basis of Anglo-Saxon poetry. Hopkins was also a bold innovator in assonance and alliteration.

Hopkins' poetry, for all its verbal pyrotechnics, is equally interesting for the profundity and complexity of its themes. In "The Windhover," for example, Hopkins casts himself (the observing, reflecting poet) as a "heart in hiding" that watches the aerobatics of the falcon, representing Christ. Just as the falcon swoops down to catch a mouse, so Hopkins describes the heroic "fall" of Christ from heaven to earth to catch and redeem souls. That fall, Hopkins suggests, should not be sentimentalized or pitied. Though Christ fell to earth and crucifixion, His divine form shone all the more brightly, just as blackened embers begin to glow as they fall through the air, or a plow is polished bright by being driven through the ground.

In his longer work, "The Wreck of the *Deutschland*," Hopkins memorializes the death of several nuns by drowning as they returned from assignment abroad. Hopkins treats their heroic deaths on several levels: the historical and literal level, in which we hear the nuns praying throughout the last hours as the ship sinks; the personal level, as we glimpse Hopkins' own struggles of faith occasioned by this disaster; the theological level, as we understand God's larger design; and the mythic level, in which the nuns rise to the proportions of archetypal heroines.

WRITERS OF HUMOROUS VERSE

English literature has always been remarkable for the large share which humor has played in its history. In the late Victorian period the vogue of humor became particularly important.

Lewis Carroll (Charles Dodgson) (1832–1898)

Charles Lutwidge Dodgson, who as a humorist wrote under the name of Lewis Carroll, was a lecturer at Oxford on Mathematics, and the author of textbooks on that subject. On the surface he led a dry and, in many respects, a narrow-minded life. He did not particularly like company— except that of children. This self that loved children he called Lewis Carroll. When Carroll decided to write a story based on a young girl whom he admired, he created one of the most popular children's books of all time. As with most great children's literature, such as the Grimm's Fairy Tales or Dr. Seuss's charming and poetic texts, *Alice's Adventures* are as readable for adults as they are for children. The fantastic world of men and beasts that the child finds in this book appears to the adult reader as a light and witty satire of Victorian life. Carroll's style is colloquial, incessantly surprising, and remarkably creative.

Alice's Adventures in Wonderland: (1865) Alice's adventures begin when she chases a white rabbit and finds herself falling down a rabbit hole. When she reaches the bottom she sees the rabbit dash off, mumbling that he'll surely be late. Left standing in front of several locked doors, Alice soon finds a tiny key, which unlocks the smallest door, revealing a miniature garden. Unable to fit through the door, Alice drinks a potion that causes her to shrink so small that she cannot reach the key. When she then eats a piece of cake, she grows until she fills the whole room, weeping huge tears of despair. Meanwhile the White Rabbit reappears, and Alice picks up his fan and gloves. This causes her to shrink, so small in fact that she falls into her own pool of tears. In the pool she meets a mouse, whom she taunts unknowingly with stories of her cat Dinah. Soon a Dodo bird and all sorts of other animals appear in the pool, and they have a race to dry themselves off. While the mouse is telling his "Tail," Alice again mentions her cat and frightens all of the animals away. The White Rabbit then invites Alice to his house to get a new pair of gloves and a fan. When she gets there, she drinks yet another potion, growing to enormous size so that her leg sticks up the chimney. She again nibbles on the cake and leaves the house, whereupon she enters a wood and meets a pipe-smoking caterpillar sitting on a mushroom. After taunting her with nonsense, and her own poor memory for poems, the caterpillar tells her that by eating the mushroom she can change her size as she wishes. Finally the right size for her environment, Alice meets two footman, a fish and a frog, the former presenting an invitation to the latter for the Duchess to play croquet with the Queen. Alice then enters the chaotic house of the Duchess, where she finds a screaming child and a very violent cook. Everyone is sneezing because of the pepper which the cook puts in the soup, except for the grinning Cheshire Cat on the hearth. Alice, pitying the child, steals him away, only to find that he is a pig, and he waddles off into the forest.

Alice again meets the Cheshire Cat, who sits smiling on the tree, and he tells Alice to go to the Mad Hatter's tea party. Soon the cat has vanished, all except his smile. At the tea party, Alice meets the Hatter, the March Hare, and the sleepy Dormouse. The game at this party is to ask senseless riddles that have no answer, which soon frustrates Alice. Leaving the party, Alice meets two hapless gardeners trying to paint white roses red, following a request by the Queen for red roses. But they are too slow, and the Queen arrives, exclaiming "Off with their heads!" The reader soon discovers that this is all the Queen ever says, and in the end no one is executed. The Duchess arrives for croquet, but disappears when threatened by the Queen. Alice then meets the Mock Turtle and the Gryphon. Engaged in a Lobster Quadrille (a dance), they hear of the trial of a thief, the Knave of Hearts who attempted to steal some tarts. Alice rushes to the courtrom, and is called upon to testify as a witness to the crime before the King and Queen of Hearts. Alice angers the Queen when she is unable to say anything of the crime, and the Queen orders that her head be cut off. But Alice gathers her strength and cries that they are nothing but a pack of cards, at which point she awakens from her dream.

Through the Looking-Glass and What Alice Found There: (1871)
Alice's adventures continue in this second volume, published six years after Wonderland. In this sequel and complement to his first fantastic story, Carroll explores many of the themes hinted at in Wonderland in much more explicit terms, especially the theme of cruelty. Both more complex and darker than *Alice's Adventures in Wonderland*, the world inside the Looking-Glass is highly sructured and symbolic, leaving literary critics with several paths to interpreting the work. The story centers around moves in a chess game, in which the pieces of the game are alive. Alice enters into this game, where she encounters talking flowers and insects, a host of chess pieces, including the Red and the White King and Queen, and famous Looking-Glass characters such as Humpty Dumpty and Tweedledum and Tweedledee. Carroll's art seems more subtle and refined here, and much of the silly wordplay of Wonderland appears more clearly as questioning the true meaning of words in the Looking-Glass world. Again, Carroll presents the adult reader with a satirical representation of Victorian life and its class hierarchies.

His next two volumes of comic verse, *Phantasmagoria* (1876) and *The Hunting of the Snark* (1876), are full of priceless verses. *Sylvie and Bruno* (1889–1893), though far below in quality, has some delightful stanzas.

Lewis Carroll is the king of humorists for children of all ages. Nonsense, which would seem to be an almost exclusively English kind of humor, is a department in which he has no equal. But he also is a master of literary satire. "Father William" and "The White Knight's Song" are delicious parodies of originals by Southey and Wordsworth, respectively—the latter, of "Resolution and Independence."

Charles Stuart Calverley (1831–1884)

Charles Stuart Calverley is a brilliant parodist and writer of light verse. These pieces are likely to be remembered longer than his serious Latin poetry. They will be found in his *Verses and Translations* (1862), *Fly-Leaves* (1872) and *Literary Remains* (1885). His best-known burlesque is that of the Pre-Raphaelite ballads, which has as a refrain "butter and eggs and a pound of cheese."

Edward Lear (1812–1888)

Edward Lear wrote "purer" nonsense than any of these men, and is responsible for the vogue of the limerick. His poetry is addressed almost entirely to the ear, and his purposes are never satirical. Everyone knows "The Owl and the Pussycat." His volumes are: *The Book of Nonsense* (1846), *Nonsense Songs and Stories* (1871), *More Nonsense Songs* (1871), *Laughable Lyrics* (1877), and *Nonsense Botany* (1877).

W. S. Gilbert (1836–1911)

Sir William Schwenk Gilbert is best-known to the world as the author of the texts for the perennial Gilbert and Sullivan operas. But he is also the author of an earlier work, two volumes of brilliant nonsense poetry, *Bab Ballads* (1869; 1873). He later said that for his highly original ideas in the operas, he was indebted "to the author of the *Bab Ballads*." Gilbert was a very able caricaturist and his fantastic drawings decorate many a page of his poems.

His highly successful collaboration with the popular composer Sir Arthur Sullivan began with *Trial by Jury* (1875), and was followed by *H.M.S. Pinafore* (1878), *The Pirates of Penzance* (1879), *Patience* (1881), *Iolanthe* (1884), *The Mikado* (1885), *Ruddigore* (1887), *The Yeoman of the Guard* (1888), and *The Gondoliers* (1899). These "Savoy Operas"—as they are called after the theater where they were performed—have proved an inexhaustible storehouse of fun, nonsense and satire, and seem unlikely to stale.

Gilbert was thoroughly English and thoroughly middle class in temperament, and had a middle-class aversion for the nobility, politicians, doctors, snobs, aesthetes, sentimentalists, and lovers of foreign opera. Against all these he lashed out. His most celebrated exploit in literature is his attack on the new aestheticism in *Patience*, where Swinburne's name is thinly disguised as Bunthorne, and Oscar Wilde is pilloried for his affectations in dress and speech. It was a healthy, if somewhat Philistine, blast of fresh air upon an atmosphere that was becoming fetid with preciosity.

NOVELISTS

George Robert Gissing (1857–1903)

George Robert Gissing followed in Dickens' footsteps as a novelist of social problems. He lived in great poverty in the slums, and his daily surroundings became the topic of his novels. There is considerable integrity of purpose and faithfulness to the facts of life in Gissing's works. Unhappily, he was not much of an artist, and the connoisseur of style will find few rewards in him. *The Private Papers of Henry Ryecroft* (1903), the most popular of his novels, is also the least depressing. It is the product of his pleasure at being able to escape briefly from London slums to the country. *The New Grub Street* (1891) is the record of his experiences in the poverty-ridden districts of London. His other novels include: *The Unclassed* (1884), *Thyrza* (1887), *The Nether World* (1889), *Born in Exile* (1892), and *The Odd Women* (1893).

Samuel Butler (1835–1902)

Samuel Butler was a very influential writer. George Bernard Shaw, for instance, acknowledges a life-long indebtedness to Butler's writings. He was only by accident a novelist, for his interest was even greater in scientific, musical, and critical matters.

The ruling passion in his life was an unqualified detestation for everything Victorian. *The Way of All Flesh* (1903), his most important novel, is heavily autobiographical. Like its hero, Butler was the son of a clergyman, and like him reacted violently against his religious environment. Butler went off to New South Wales when he was twenty-two and returned years later with something of a fortune. He then gave himself up to painting, music, scientific research, and some writing. His first interesting work is *Erewhon* (1872), one of the more challenging Utopias of fiction, the name being an anagram of "nowhere." Some critics have called it the most brilliant satire on civilization since Swift, but that praise is possibly too high. The author leveled his attack against economic and social injustice. *Erewhon Revisited* (1901) is a sequel.

Butler was fond of dissension, and spent much energy trying to prove the superiority of Handel to Beethoven, and of Lamarck's theory of evolution over Darwin's. The latter point he argued in *Life and Habit* (1877), *Evolution, Old and New* (1879) and *Unconscious Memory* (1880). Among Butler's other efforts was an attempt to identify a non-Homeric author of the *Odyssey* in *The Authoress of the Odyssey* (1897).

The Way of All Flesh, however, seems his only permanent contribution. Its hero, Ernest Pontifex, mirrors perfectly the kind of struggle against home environment that is so common to young men all over the world. Butler worked on this book for more than two decades, and it was published only after his death.

The Notebooks of Samuel Butler (1902) are full of interesting observations and reflections.

George Moore (1852–1933)

George Moore set himself up first as a disciple of Zola, the French natural-istic writer. An Irishman who had studied art in London and Paris, George Moore was a belated member of the aesthetic group of the closing years of the century. He took a particular delight in shocking the moral sensibilities of the respectable middle class, and succeeded in doing so especially in *A Mod-ern Lover* (1883), *A Mummer's Wife* (1884), and *Esther Waters* (1894). The last-named, the best of these, is a realistic study of the life of a servantgirl.

Thus far in Moore's career his style was sober and simple. His next works deal with neurotics and untypical experiences: *Celibates* (1895), *Evelyn Innes* (1898), and *Sister Teresa* (1901). After this, Moore identified himself for a while with the new Irish literary movement, and went to live in Dublin, where he became an inspiring force in the founding of the Abbey Theatre.

Continuing his interest in religious subjects, he wrote the much-discussed *The Brook Kerith* (1916), a bold and heretical novel of Jesus. Here his new richly associative style can be seen, full of mannerisms and an effective but somewhat artificial simplicity. In the same manner, he wrote *Heloïse and Abelard* (1921).

Actually Moore is most interesting in a series of autobiographical books: *Confessions of a Young Man* (1888), *Impressions and Opinions* (1890), *Mem-oirs of My Dead Life* (1906), and *Hail and Farewell* (1911–1914).

LITERARY CRITICISM IN THE NINETEENTH CENTURY

The foundations of literary criticism, including the several roles of the pro-fessional literary critic, were established well before the nineteenth century. Pope, Dryden, Swift, and Johnson all wrote voluminous literary commentary on the works (and characters) of their predecessors and contemporaries. But by general agreement the "father" of modern literary criticism is Samuel Tay-lor Coleridge. In such works as "On the Principles of Genial Criticism," *Biographia Literaria*, "On Poesy or Art," "Shakespearean Criticism," "The Statesman's Manual," and "*Animae Poetae*," Coleridge defined many of the key terms of modern criticism (idea, symbol, allegory, theme, imagination, fancy, literary architecture, organic form, and even the word "psychology" itself) as well as the process of criticism itself.

For Coleridge, a work of literary art is to be appraised primarily by refer-ences to the internal balance, arrangement, and working of its parts, as eval-uated by their contributions to the effect achieved by the work as a whole. This approach differs substantially from eighteenth century Neoclassicism, in which the excellence of a work of art is determined by comparing it to clas-sical models. In Coleridge's process of criticism, all things are possible, no matter how unusual or even grotesque (witness portions of "Christabel" or "Rime of the Ancient Mariner") so long as they "belong" in the overall design and *raison d'etre* of the work itself.

Nor must a literary work pass the test of external moral or aesthetic standards in Coleridge's system. Instead, a literary work functions (in Coleridge's analogy) much like a solar system. Each part influences and, in turn, is influenced by all other parts of the system. The question is not whether any individual part is "moral" or "attractive," as measured by some external standard, but instead whether it is meaningful and proportionate within the literary system of the work itself.

During his lifetime, Coleridge applied his critical insights to the works of many previous authors, including Shakespeare, as well as to the poetry and prose of his contemporaries, especially Wordsworth. Those examples of literary criticism, some of which have come down to us only through the notes of listeners to Coleridge's public lectures, proved of crucial importance to the establishment of so-called "New Criticism" in the twentieth century (as practiced by Robert Penn Warren, Cleanth Brooks, Elder Olsen, John Crowe Ransom, W. K. Wimsath, and others).

Distinct from, though contemporary with, Coleridge was a more common approach to nineteenth century literary criticism—critical expressionism. Thomas DeQuincey, in *Confessions of an English Opium Eater* and other works, provides many examples of such expressive criticism. The reader/critic takes the role of emotional and intellectual "expresser" of the thoughts and feelings aroused by the literary work. Obviously, the "criticism" that results depends directly upon the sensitivity and awareness of the critic. In expressive criticism, the critic demonstrates to other readers the kind of insights and emotions that are possible (and, for some critics, appropriate) with regard to particular works of art. The critic thus functions as a barometer of public taste, indicating what works are or are not worthy of attention. In our own day, most movie reviewers follow the nineteenth century model of expressive criticism, especially when their reviews are little more than the expression of their personal feelings about the movie at hand.

In the later half of the nineteenth century, Matthew Arnold returned to Neoclassic assumptions in his many works of literary and social criticism— *The Modern Element in Literature* (1857), *Essays in Criticism* (1865), *Culture and Anarchy* (1869), *Literature and Sciences* (1883), and others. Arnold proposed that the purpose of literary art—or art of any kind, for that matter— was to capture and communicate the "best" of mankind's insights and feelings. Art is thus viewed by Arnold not only as the emblem of humanity at its finest moments but also the spur to moral and aesthetic growth.

The question often posed to Arnold, of course, concerned the nature of the "best" and how it was to be known. Arnold answered with his famous "touchstone" theory: Certain works of the past (for example, the plays of Shakespeare) are universally acknowledged for their excellence. They are useful, therefore, not as rigid forms for imitation, but instead as general standards against which the excellence of contemporary works can be appraised. A contemporary sonnet, for example, can be evaluated by the degree to which it achieves or even surpasses the high-water mark of excellence already established in the sonnets of Shakespeare, Sidney, Milton, or others.

Arnold was also deeply interested in the social and political role of literature. Like Shelley (who called poets "the unacknowledged legislators of the world"), Arnold believed that literature was more than a mirror of individual and societal beliefs, preferences, habits, and actions. Viewed correctly, literature could also function as a lamp—an active, guiding principle that called society to moral, responsible behavior. Unlike Coleridge, Arnold saw no problem in establishing the aesthetic worth of a particular work of literature according to its social effects and utility. For Arnold, art of all kinds could be assessed by what it *does*; for Coleridge, art could be evaluated only by what it *is*.

REVIEW QUESTIONS

LATE CENTURY EXPERIMENTATION

Multiple Choice

1. _____ The Fabian Society favored
   a. pure capitalism
   b. absolute monarchy
   c. socialism
   d. communism

2. _____ The Pre-Raphaelite Brotherhood included all of the following members except
   a. Charles Dickens
   b. Dante Rossetti
   c. Christina Rossetti
   d. William Morris

3. _____ *The House of Life* is a
   a. sonnet cycle
   b. novel about alternative lifestyles
   c. play about parents and children
   d. prose biography of Dante Rossetti

4. _____ William Morris brought new aesthetic standards particularly to
   a. elder Romantic writers
   b. the English home
   c. America
   d. India

5. _____ The predominant criticism against Swinburne is that his poems are
   a. too Romantic
   b. too obscure
   c. too dull
   d. too intellectually thin

6. _____ Meredith's beliefs were
   a. typically Victorian
   b. more liberal than those of most of his peers
   c. more conservative than those of most of his peers
   d. hidden from all but a few close friends

7. _____ Robert Louis Stevenson spent his adult life in
   a. frequent travel
   b. hermit-like withdrawal from society
   c. prison
   d. Ireland

8. _____ In *Marius the Epicurean* Walter Pater carefully
   a. reconstructs history
   b. avoids references to actual places and events
   c. follows the Spenserian stanza form
   d. avoids controversial themes

9. _____ Oscar Wilde was best known in his day for his
   a. somber philosophy
   b. sharp wit
   c. many novels
   d. sonnets

10. _____ At the turn of the century, Thomas Hardy
    a. turned from the writing of novels to the writing of verse
    b. turned from the writing of verse to the writing of novels
    c. ended his literary career
    d. began his literary career

True or False

11. _____ The late Victorian decades saw the struggle for colonies among major trading nations.

12. _____ William Morris mocked those who endeavored to bring artistic design into the manufacture of such common items as furniture and wallpaper.

13. _____ Meredith's *Modern Love* is a novel in imitation of the style of George Eliot.

14. _____ Edward Dowson was one of a group of young men associated with the publication of *The Yellow Book*.

15. _____ Gerard Manley Hopkins, although quite famous in his own day, exerted little influence upon later poets in the twentieth century.

16. _____ Lewis Carroll intended almost every line of his children's stories to be a satire upon specific English political figures and events.

17. _____ Gilbert wrote the music for the famous Gilbert and Sullivan operettas.

18. _____ Samuel Butler avoided all references or allusions to his personal life in his novel *The Way of All Flesh*.

19. _____ Like Dickens, Gissing was a novelist concerned with social problems.

20. _____ Virtually all important literary critics throughout the nineteenth century thought the purpose of literature to be essentially moral rather than aesthetic in nature.

Fill-in

21. The "white man's burden" was a political rationale popularized in the writings of _____.

22. Most of Christina Rossetti's poetry is _____ in nature and theme.

23. Swinburne's *Atalanta in Calydon*, like Milton's *Samson Agonistes*, is a classic _____.

24. George Meredith demonstrated his literary talent in both poetry and _____.

25. "The Wreck of the *Deutschland*" is Hopkins' tribute memorializing the death of several _____.

26. At the end of *Tess of the D'Urbervilles*, Tess _____ her tormentor, Alec.

27. James ("B. V.") Thomson was notable in his period for his extreme _____.

28. Kipling was discovered by the editor, _____.

29. "The Hound of Heaven" is the most famous poem written by _____.

30. Edward Lear is memorable primarily for his _____ verse.

Matching

31.	_____ Dante Rossetti	a.	*Goblin Market*
32.	_____ Oscar Wilde	b.	*The Garden of Proserpine*
33.	_____ Meredith	c.	*Modern Love*
34.	_____ Hardy	d.	*The Blessed Damozel*
35.	_____ Hopkins	e.	*Jude the Obscure*
36.	_____ Swinburne	f.	*Alice's Adventures* . . .
37.	_____ Carroll	g.	*De Profundis*
38.	_____ Morris	h.	"The Windhover"
39.	_____ Christina Rossetti	i.	*Marius the Epicurean*
40.	_____ Pater	j.	*The Earthly Paradise*

Answers

1.	c	15.	f	29.	Francis Thompson
2.	a	16.	f	30.	nonsense
3.	a	17.	f	31.	d
4.	b	18.	f	32.	g
5.	d	19.	t	33.	c
6.	b	20.	t	34.	e
7.	a	21.	Kipling	35.	h
8.	a	22.	religious	36.	b
9.	b	23.	tragedy	37.	f
10.	a	24.	prose	38.	j
11.	t	25.	nuns	39.	a
12.	f	26.	kills	40.	i
13.	f	27.	pessimism		
14.	t	28.	Hensley		

GLOSSARY

Allegory: A literary device, in prose or poetry, in which a literal character, event, or object also possesses a symbolic meaning. Thus an allegory may illustrate a philosophical idea, or a moral or religious principle. A work of literature is said to be allegorical if it has more than one level of meaning. (Examples: the *Romance of the Rose*, La Fontaine's *Fables*, Kafka's *The Penal Colony*, Orwell's *Animal Farm*)

Alliteration: The repetition of a sound, especially an initial consonant, in a line of poetry or prose. (Example: "Five miles meandering with a mazy motion")

Allusion: An indirect or explicit reference to a well-known place, event or person. Allusion in literature often takes the form of a figure of speech. (Example: Keats' "Ode to a Nightingale": "and Lethe-wards [I] had sunk." The poet alludes to Hades, the underworld).

Anapest: A foot consisting of two unaccented syllables and one accented syllable (the first three syllables of "unreliable").

Archetype: In literature, archetypal criticism examines types of narrative, character and image that occur in a large variety of texts. Literary archetypes, like the Jungian archetypes of the collective unconscious, are said to reflect a group of elemental and universal patterns that trigger an immediate and profound response from the reader.

Assonance: The repetition, in a line of prose or poetry, of similar or identical vowel sounds.

Ballad: A narrative song, originally danced by the folk. (Example: *Edward*) An "art ballad" (or "literary ballad") is a ballad written by a known poet according to the model of the folk ballads. (Example: Keats's *La Belle Dame Sans Merci*)

Ballade: A lyrical form borrowed from the French, consisting of three stanzas and an envoi. Each stanza and the envoi conclude with the same line as a refrain. (Example: Swinburne's *A Ballad of François Villon*)

Blank verse: Iambic pentameter unrhymed. (Example: Wordsworth's *The Prelude*)

Caesura: A break in a line of verse. (Example: the versification of *Beowulf*)

Catharsis: An Aristotlelian term referring to the purgation (the literal meaning of *catharsis*) of such emotions as pity and fear achieved by tragedy. For Aristotle, the diffuse and unfocussed anxieties and fears of audience members could, in witnessing tragic drama, be imaginatively placed upon the central characters. As these characters go inevitably but knowingly to their doom, the now localized fears of the audience are vicariously brought to a climax and, in the resolution of the climax, inevitably purged.

Conceit: An involved figure of speech. (Example: Shakespeare's sonnet No. 30)

Consonance: The repetition of consonant sounds, with a change in the vowel that follows the consonant. (Example: give-gave)

Couplet: Two consecutive lines of verse, often rhymed.

Dactyl: A foot consisting of one accented syllable and two unaccented syllables. (Dóminant)

Dimeter: A line containing two feet. ("And nó birds síng.")

Elegy: A lyrical poem in memory of someone dead. (Example: Shelley's *Adonais*)

Enjambment: Verse the meaning of which runs on into the next line. (Example: most of Shakespeare's plays)

Epic: A long narrative poem. A folk epic celebrates the exploits of a national hero or national heroes. An art epic also follows the principles laid down by the classical epic tradition beginning with Homer. (Examples: folk epic—*Beowulf*; art epic—*Paradise Lost*)

Epigram: A brief pointed observation.

Euphuism: An artificial style invented by Lyly, and characterized by the use of balanced and antithetical clauses, alliteration, and farfetched conceits.

Foot: The fundamental unit of verse.

Free verse: Verse without any regular meter or foot.

Genre: A French word meaning type, kind or form; in literature the term is used to designate different literary forms, such as *tragedy, satire, epic*, and more recently *novel, biography*, and *short story*.

Heroic couplet: Two lines of iambic pentameter, rhyming and containing a complete unit of thought. (Example: Pope's *Rape of the Lock*)

Hexameter: A line containing six feet. ("Fáir hárbor thát them seéms, so ín they éntered áre.")

Hyperbole: Overstatement or exaggeration, usually for dramatic or comic effect. (Example: In *Don Juan*, Byron uses hyperbole to inflate and gently deride young Juan's infatuation with Donna Julia: "He thought about himself, and the whole earth, / Of man the wonderful, and of the stars, / . . . Of air-balloons, and of the many bars / To perfect knowledge of the boundless skies;— / And then he thought of Donna Julia's eyes.")

Iamb: A foot consisting of one unaccented syllable and one accented syllable. (prefér.)

Imagery: Literary language suggesting visual (and sometimes auditory) pictures and sensations. Imagery can depict actual scenery or suggest qualities of abstract concepts and ideas. (Example: in Keats's "To Autumn," the abstract idea of Autumn is captured through imagery of Autumn represented as a woman: "Thy hair soft-lifted by the winnowing wind.")

Intentional fallacy: The critical error of evaluating a literary work according to the author's success or failure in achieving his or her intention or expectation for the work. For such critics as W. K. Wimsatt and Cleanth Brooks, the completed work of literary art should stand apart, for purposes of evaluation, from the author's intentions in creating the work.

Invocation: An appeal for inspiration.

Irony: A figure in which the implicit meaning of a statement or action differs drastically from its implicit meaning. Types of irony include dramatic irony, verbal irony, and structural irony.

Lyric: A short poem, usually nonnarrative, in which the text expresses the speaker's emotional or mental state. A lyric is usually written in the first person, and is often associated with songs and other musical forms. (Example: Shelley's "Stanzas" [1814])

Lyrical poetry: Poetry expressing the personal feelings of the author. (Example: Shelley's *The Indian Serenade*)

Metaphor: A figure of speech identifying an object or person with another object or person. ("It is the star to every wandering bark.")

Meter: Designates the recognizable and repeated rhythms and stresses created by verse form. Iambic pentameter is the most common meter of English poetry.

Metonomy: A figure of speech in which a literal term or attribute of one thing comes to represent another to which it has a contiguous relation. (Example: the use of "crown" to mean king)

Mimesis: A Greek word meaning imitation, mimesis is the active or dynamic representation of a literal (sensual) or metaphysical (spiritual) reality in a work of art or literature.

Motif: A thematic or structural element used and repeated in a single text, or in the whole of literature. A motif may be a literary device, an incident, a formula, or a reference. (Also "leitmotif" or guiding motif)

Monometer: A line containing only one foot.

Octave (also called **Octet**): The first part of an Italian or Petrarchan sonnet, consisting of eight lines. (Example: Rossetti's *Sonnet on a Sonnet*)

Ode: A lyrical poem of high and formal style, usually rhymed, which often addresses itself to a praised person, object, or quality. (Example: Wordsworth's "Ode: Intimations of Immortality")

Onomatopoeia: Sound imitative of sense ("*clanking* chains.")

Ottava rima: A stanza of eight lines in iambic pentameter rhyming *abababcc*. (Example: Byron's *Don Juan*)

Pastoral: A poem in which the characters are shepherds and the setting is in the country. (Example: Shelley's *Adonais*)

Pathetic fallacy: The literary technique (and, for some critics, the literary mistake) of attributing human actions or characteristics to inanimate objects. (Example: In Kingsley's phrase, "the cruel, crawling foam," the foam cannot be literally cruel, nor does it actually crawl.) Many critics, beginning with John Ruskin, condemn the use of the pathetic fallacy as a mark of the author's inability to describe and understand objects in themselves, without immediate resort to human attributes.

Pentameter: A line containing five feet. ("Nine tímes the spáce that meásures dáy and níght")

Persona: Originally the Latin word for the mask worn by an actor in classical theater, the term now denotes the character or set of identifying traits adopted by the speaker or narrator in a work of literature. (Example: The persona of a frustrated, timid, middle-aged figure is adopted as a persona by T. S. Eliot in "The Love Song of J. Alfred Prufrock.")

Personification: A figure of speech or rhetoric in which inanimate objects or abstractions are given human qualities, or represented as having human form. (Example: "that lazy old sun")

Petrarchan or **Italian sonnet:** A sonnet consisting of two sections, an octave and a sestet. The octave rhymes *abbaabba*; the sestet rhymes *cdecde*, or *cdeedc*, or *cdcdcd*. (Example: Rossetti's *Sonnet on a Sonnet*)

Pindaric ode: A lyrical poem of lofty mood written in groups of three stanzas: a strophe, an antistrophe, and an epode. The strophe and antistrophe are in the same meter and follow the same rhyme scheme. The epode is free. (Example: Gray's *The Bard*)

Psychoanalytic Criticism: Analysis and evaluation of literary art using principles of mental and emotional functions, based first on speculations by Samuel Taylor Coleridge (originator of the term "psychology") and, in the twentieth century, primarily on the theories of Jung and Freud. In psychoanalytic criticism, a literary work is valued primarily for its power to reveal to and even create within the reader psychological states important to self-awareness and personal fulfillment.

Quatrain: A stanza of four lines.

Rime royal: A stanza consisting of seven lines in iambic pentameter rhyming *ababbcc* (Example: Chaucer's *Troilus and Criseyde*)

Satire: A work of literature that attacks society's vice and folly through irony and wit.

Scansion: The analysis of verse or poetry to uncover its meter and rhythmic patterns.

Sestet: The second part of a Petrarchan or Italian sonnet, consisting of six lines.

Shakespearean or **English sonnet:** A sonnet consisting of two sections, twelve lines and a couplet. The twelve lines rhyme *ababcdcdefef.* The couplet rhymes *gg.* (Example: Shakespeare's sonnets)

Sonnet: A lyrical poem in 14 lines of iambic pentameter, written according to the Petrarchan or Shakespearean scheme, or some variation of either.

Spenserian stanza: A stanza consisting of nine lines, the first eight in iambic pentameter, the last in iambic hexameter, and rhyming *ababbcbcc*. (Example: Keats's *Eve of St. Agnes*)

Synecdoche: A figure in which a part of something is taken to represent the whole. (Example: "ten sails on the horizon" for ten ships)

Tension: A term of literary criticism popularized by the New Critic Allen Tate, tension denotes the simultaneous presence of two often conflicting forms of meaning (literal meaning and metaphorical meaning) in a literary work. (Example: In *Moby Dick*, literary tension exists between the literal tale of whale hunting and the metaphorical or spiritual story of the quest for the nature of the eternal or divine.)

Terza rima: Verse arranged to rhyme *aba bcb cdc* etc. (Example: Shelley's *The Triumph of Life*)

Tetrameter: A line containing four feet. (Ah, whát can áil thee, wrétched wíght")

Theme: An idea presented and expanded upon in a literary work. A theme can be explicit or implicit and is usually suggested by the narrative action.

Trimeter: A line containing three feet ("And yét is hére todáy")

Trochee: A foot consisting of one accented syllable and one unaccented syllable. (Lísten)

SUGGESTED READINGS

Pre-Romanticism in the Eighteenth Century

Brown, F. K., *Fathers of the Victorians*, Cambridge, 1961.

Deane, P., *The First Industrial Revolution*, Cambridge, 1979.

Lessenich, R. P., *Aspects of English Pre-Romanticism*, Koln, 1989.

Marcus, G. J., *The Age of Nelson*, New York, 1971.

James Thomson

McKillop, A. D., *The Background of Thomson's Seasons*, Ann Arbor, 1942.

Sambrook, J., *James Thomson*, Oxford, 1991.

White, S., *James Thomson*, London, 1986.

Thomas Gray

Golden, M., *Thomas Gray*, Boston, 1988.

Kaul, S., *Thomas Gray and Literary Authority*, Stanford, 1992.

Weinbrot, H. D., *Context, Influence, and Mid-Eighteenth Century Poetry*, Los Angeles, 1990.

William Collins

Wensdorf, R., *William Collins and Eighteenth Century Poetry*, Minneapolis, 1981.

William Cowper

Hutchings, B., *The Poetry of William Cowper*, London, 1983.

King, J., *William Cowper*, Durham, 1986.

Newey, V., *Cowper's Poetry*, Liverpool, 1983.

Thomas Chatterton

Haywood, I., *The Making of History*, Rutherford, 1986.

Thomas Chatterton *(cont'd.)*

Kaplan, L., *The Family Romance of the Imposter-Poet Thomas Chatterton*, New York, 1988.

James Macpherson

DeGategno, P. J., *James Macpherson*, Boston, 1989.

Haywood, I., *The Making of History*, Rutherford, 1986.

Edward Young

Andrews, D. R., *A Vindication of Providence*, Los Angeles, 1984.

Thomas Percy

Davis, B. H., *Thomas Percy*, Philadelphia, 1989.

Mark Akenside

Houpt, C. T., *Mark Akenside, a Biographical and Critical Study*, Philadelphia, 1944.

The Wartons

Vance, J. A., *Joseph and Thomas Warton*, Boston, 1983.

Weinsheimer, J., *Imitation*, London, 1984.

Wellek, R., *The Rise of English Literary History*, Chapel Hill, 1941.

George Crabbe

Edgecombe, R. S., *Theme, Embodiment and Structure in the Poetry of George Crabbe*, Salzburg, 1983.

Edwards, G., *George Crabbe's Poetry on Border Land*, New York, 1990.

Robert Burns

Bentman, R., *Robert Burns*, Boston, 1987.

Grant, R. J., *The Laughter of Love*, Calgary, 1986.

Robert Burns *(cont'd.)*

Low, D. A., *Robert Burns*, Edinburgh, 1986.

McGuirk, C., *Robert Burns and the Sentimental Era*, Athens, 1985.

William Blake

Eaves, M., *The Counter-Arts Conspiracy*, Ithaca, 1992.

Essick, R. N., *William Blake's Commercial Book Illustrations*, Oxford, 1991.

Fuller, D., *Blake's Heroic Argument*, London, 1988.

Norvig, G. S., *Dark Figures in the Desired Country*, Berkeley, 1992.

Otto, P., *Constructive Vision and Visionary Deconstruction*, Oxford, 1991.

Schorer, M., *William Blake: the Politics of Vision*, New York, 1946.

Vine, S., *Spectral Visions in Blake's Poetry*, New York, 1992.

Werner, B. C., *Blake's Vision of the Poetry of Milton*, New York, 1986.

The Romantic Movement

Burwick, F., *The Haunted Eve*, Heidelberg, 1987.

Clubb, J., *English Romanticism*, London, 1983.

Gaull, M., *English Romanticism*, New York, 1988.

Martin, R. G., *English Romanticism and Modern Fiction*, New York, 1993.

Robert Southey

Butler, M., *Literature as Heritage*, Cambridge, 1988.

Curry, K., *Robert Southey*, Boston, 1977.

William Wordsworth

Claridge, L. P., *Romantic Potency*, Ithaca, 1992.

Hewitt, R., *Wordsworth and the Empirical Dilemma*, New York, 1990.

Manning, P. J., *Reading Romantics*, New York, 1990.

McFarland, T., *William Wordsworth*, Oxford, 1992.

Noyes, R., *William Wordsworth*, Boston, 1991.

Sharpe, W., *Unreal Cities*, Baltimore, 1990.

Samuel Taylor Coleridge

Beer, J., *Tennyson, Coleridge, and the Cambridge Apostles*, New York, 1992.

Ellison, J., *Delicate Subjects: Romanticism, Gender, and the Ethics of Understanding*, Ithaca, 1990.

Fulford, T., *Coleridge's Figurative Language*, New York, 1990.

Haven, R., *Samuel Taylor Coleridge*, Boston, 1976.

Sir Walter Scott

Duncan, I., *Modern Romance and Transformations of the Novel*, Cambridge, 1992.

Kerr, J., *Fiction Against History*, Cambridge, 1989.

Lauber, J., *Sir Walter Scott*, Boston, 1989.

George Gordon, Lord Byron

Christensen, J., *Lord Byron's Strength*, Baltimore, 1992.

Claridge, L. P., *Romantic Potency*, Ithaca, 1992.

Coote, S., *Byron*, London, 1988.

Percy Bysshe Shelley

Gelpi, B. C., *Shelley's Goddess*, New York, 1992.

Reiman, D. H., *Percy Bysshe Shelley*, Boston, 1990.

Trory, E., *Cradled into Poetry*, London, 1991.

Ulmer, W. A., *Shelleyan Eros*, Princeton, 1990.

John Keats

Bullett, G., *The Poems of John Keats*, London, 1974.

DeAlmeida, H., *Critical Essays on John Keats*, Boston, 1990.

Wasserman, E. R., *The Finer Tone: Keats' Major Poems*, Baltimore, 1953.

Yost, G., *Keats's Apprenticeship*, New York, 1989.

Walter Savage Landor

Dilworth, E., *Walter Savage Landor*, New York, 1971.

Pinsky, R., *The Poetry of Walter Savage Landor*, New York, 1966.

Thomas Moore

Legge, S., *Affectionate Cousins*, Oxford, 1980.

Tessier, T., *The Lyric Poetry of Thomas Moore*, Paris, 1976.

Leigh Hunt

Blainey, A., *Immortal Boy*, New York, 1985.

Thompson, J. R., *Leigh Hunt*, Boston, 1977.

Thomas Hood

Jeffrey, L. N., *Thomas Hood*, New York, 1972.

Charles Lamb

Aaron, J., *A Double Singleness*, Oxford, 1991.

McFarland, T., *Romantic Cruxes*, Oxford, 1987.

Monsman, G. C., *Confessions of a Prosaic Dreamer*, Durham, 1984.

William Hazlitt

McFarland, T., *Romantic Cruxes*, Oxford, 1987.

Uphaus, R. W., *William Hazlitt*, Boston, 1985.

Thomas De Quincey

McFarland, T., *Romantic Cruxes*, Oxford, 1987.

The Romantic Novel

Clayton, J., *Romantic Vision and the Novel*, Cambridge, 1987.

William Godwin

Clemit, P., *The Godwinian Novel*, Oxford, 1993.

Roberts, M., *Gothic Immortals*, London, 1990.

William Beckford

Gemett, R. J., *William Beckford*, Boston, 1977.

Maria Edgeworth

Harden, O., *Maria Edgeworth*, Boston, 1984.

Maria Edgeworth *(cont'd.)*

Kowaleski-Wallace, E., *Their Fathers' Daughters*, New York, 1991.

Jane Austen

Dussinger, J. A., *In the Pride of the Moment*, Columbus, 1990.

Gard, R., *Jane Austen's Novels*, New Haven, 1992.

Mukherjee, M., *Jane Austen*, New York, 1991.

Stout, J. P., *Strategies of Reticence*, Charlottesville, 1990.

The Victorian Age

Eldrige, C. C., *Victorian Imperialism*, London, 1978.

Hughes, L. K., *The Victorian Serial*, Charlottesville, 1991.

Marcus, S., *The Other Victorians*, New York, 1964.

Michalson, K., *Victorian Fantasy Literature*, New York, 1990.

Perkin, H., *The Origins of Modern English Society*, London, 1969.

Roberts, D., *Paternalism in Early Victorian England*, New Brunswick, 1979.

Ryals, C., *A World of Possibilities*, Columbus, 1990.

Thompson, F. M., *English Landed Society in the Nineteenth Century*, London, 1963.

Thomas Carlyle

Timko, M., *Carlyle and Tennyson*, New York, 1988.

Vanden Bossche, C., *Carlyle and the Search for Authority*, Columbus, 1991.

Thomas Macaulay

Edwards, O. D., *Macaulay*, London, 1988.

John Henry Newman

Biemer, G., *John Henry Newman*, Mainz, 1989.

Foister, S., *Cardinal Newman*, London, 1990.

Gilley, S., *Newman and His Age*, London, 1990.

Ker, I. T., *Newman on Being a Christian*, Notre Dame, 1990.

John Ruskin

Finley, C. S., *Nature's Covenant*,
Philadelphia, 1992.
Gerard, D. E., *John Ruskin and William
Morris*, London, 1988.

Alfred Lord Tennyson

Goslee, D., *Tennyson's Characters*,
Iowa City, 1989.
Shaw, M., *Alfred Lord Tennyson*,
London, 1988.
Thorn, M., *Tennyson*, London, 1992.

Robert Browning

Bloom, H., *Caliban*, New York, 1992.
Bristow, J., *Robert Browning*,
New York, 1991.
Woolford, J., *Browning the Revisionary*,
New York, 1988.

Elizabeth Barrett Browning

Cooper, H., *Elizabeth Barrett Browning:
Woman and Artist*, Chapel Hill, 1988.
Stephenson, G., *Elizabeth Barrett
Browning and the Poetry of Love*, Ann
Arbor, 1989.

Edward Fitzgerald

Jewett, I. B., *Edward Fitzgerald*, Boston,
1977.
Martin, R. B., *With Friends Possessed*,
New York, 1985.

Thomas Henry Huxley

Di Gregorio, M. A., *T. H. Huxley's Place
in Natural Science*, New Haven, 1984.
Jensen, J., *Thomas Henry Huxley*,
Newark, 1991.

Matthew Arnold

Buckler, W. E., *On the Poetry of
Matthew Arnold*, New York, 1982.
Collini, S., *Arnold*, Oxford, 1988.
Osborne, D. G., *Matthew Arnold*, New
York, 1963.
Riede, D. G., *Matthew Arnold and the
Betrayal of Language*, Charlottesville,
1988.

Arthur Hugh Clough

Barish, E., *Arthur Hugh Clough*,
Cambridge, 1970.

Arthur Hugh Clough *(cont'd.)*

Biswas, R. K., *Arthur Hugh Clough*,
Oxford, 1972.
Kenny, A., *God and Two Poets*, London,
1988.

The Victorian Novel

Blake, A., *Reading Victorian Fiction*,
New York, 1989.
Horsman, E. A., *The Victorian Novel*,
Oxford, 1990.

Frederick Marryat

Gautier, M. P., *Captain Frederick
Marryat*, Montreal, 1973.

Thomas Love Peacock

Burns, B., *The Novels of Thomas Love
Peacock*, London, 1985.
Butler, M., *Peacock Displayed*, London,
1979.
Kiernan, R. F., *Frivolity Unbound*,
New York, 1990.
Mulvihill, J., *Thomas Love Peacock*,
Boston, 1987.

Edward Bulwer-Litton

Engel, E., *The Victorian Novel Before
Victoria*, New York, 1984.

Benjamin Disraeli

Engel, E., *The Victorian Novel Before
Victoria*, New York, 1984.

Elizabeth Gaskell

Duthie, E. L., *The Themes of Elizabeth
Gaskell*, New York, 1980.
Fryckstedt, M. C., *The Early Industrial
Novel*, Manchester, 1980.
Lucas, J., *The Literature of Change*,
London, 1980.

Charles Kingsley

Chitty, S., *The Beast and the Monk*,
London, 1974.
Colloms, B., *Charles Kingsley*, London,
1975.
Hartley, A. J., *The Novels of Charles
Kingsley*, London, 1977.

The Brontës

Case, K. S., *Romance, Realism and the Psychological Aspect of the Mid-Victorian Novel*, New York, 1980.

Homans, M., *Women Writers and Poetic Identity*, Princeton, 1980.

Sedgwick, E. K., *The Coherence of Gothic Conventions*, New York, 1980.

Visick, M., *The Genesis of Wuthering Heights*, London, 1980.

Charles Dickens

Ackroyd, P., *Introduction to Dickens*, London, 1990.

Ganz, M., *Human, Irony and the Realm of Madness*, New York, 1990.

Jaffe, A., *Vanishing Points*, Berkeley, 1991.

Lettis, R., *The Dickens Aesthetic*, New York, 1989.

Lynch, T., *Dickens's England*, London, 1986.

Tomalin, C., *The Invisible Woman*, London, 1991.

William Makepeace Thackeray

Goldfarb, S., *William Makepeace Thackeray*, New York, 1989.

Lund, M., *Reading Thackeray*, Detroit, 1988.

Prawer, S. S., *Israel at Vanity Fair*, London, 1992.

Ritchie, A. T., *The Two Thackerays*, New York, 1988.

Charles Reade

Smith, E. E., *Charles Reade*, Boston, 1976.

George Eliot

Booth, A., *Greatness Engendered*, Ithaca, 1992.

Brady, K., *George Eliot*, New York, 1992.

Carroll, D., *George Eliot and the Conflict of Interpretations*, Cambridge, 1992.

Tush, S. R., *George Eliot and the Conventions of Popular Women's Fiction*, New York, 1993.

Wilkie Collins

Heller, T., *Dead Secrets*, New Haven, 1992.

O'Neill, P., *Wilkie Collins*, London, 1988.

Rance, N., *Wilkie Collins and Other Sensation Novelists*, London, 1991.

George Borrow

Collie, M., *George Borrow, Eccentric*, Cambridge, 1982.

Williams, D., *A World of His Own*, Oxford, 1982.

Anthony Trollope

Miller, D. A., *The Novel and the Police*, Berkeley, 1988.

Nardin, J., *He Knew She Was Right*, Carbondale, 1989.

Swingle, L. J., *Romanticism and Anthony Trollope*, Ann Arbor, 1990.

Wall, S., *Trollope and Character*, London, 1988.

The Later Victorians

Arnstein, W. L., *The Bradlaugh Case*, Columbia, 1983.

Himmelfarb, G., *Poverty and Compassion*, New York, 1991.

Dante Gabriel Rossetti

Bass, E. E., *Dante Gabriel Rossetti, Poet and Painter*, New York, 1990.

Faxon, A. C., *Dante Gabriel Rossetti*, New York, 1989.

Richardson, J., *Vanishing Lives*, Charlottesville, 1988.

Riede, D. G., *Dante Gabriel Rossetti*, Boston, 1992.

Christina Rossetti

Harrison, A. H., *Christina Rossetti in Context*, Chapel Hill, 1988.

Jones, K., *Learning Not to Be First*, New York, 1992.

Mayberry, K. J., *Christina Rossetti and the Poetry of Discovery*, Baton Rouge, 1989.

William Morris

Gerard, D. E., *John Ruskin and William Morris*, London, 1988.

Hodgson, A., *The Romances of William Morris*, Cambridge, 1987.

Kirchhoff, F., *William Morris*, Athens, 1990.

Tompkins, J. M., *William Morris*, London, 1988.

Algernon Charles Swinburne

Harrison, A. H., *Swinburne's Medievalism*, Baton Rouge, 1988.

Louis, M. K., *Swinburne and His Gods*, Toronto, 1990.

Richardson, J., *Vanishing Lives*, Charlottesville, 1988.

George Meredith

Miller, J. H., *Ariadne's Thread*, New Haven, 1992.

Robert Louis Stevenson

Hammond, J. R., *A Robert Louis Stevenson Companion*, London, 1984.

Naugrett, J. P., *Robert Louis Stevenson*, Paris, 1987.

Walter Pater

Barolsky, P., *Walter Pater's Renaissance*, Philadelphia, 1987.

Borghi, L., *Pater's Flowers and Gentlemen Are Forever*, London, 1985.

Bucker, W. E., *Walter Pater*, New York, 1987.

Fellows, J., *Tombs, Despoiled and Haunted*, Stanford, 1991.

Oscar Wilde

Behrendt, P. F., *Oscar Wilde*, New York, 1991.

Gagnier, R., *Idylls of the Marketplace*, Stanford, 1986.

Raby, P., *Oscar Wilde*, Cambridge, 1988.

Roditi, E., *Oscar Wilde*, New York, 1986.

Sedgwick, E. K., *Epistemology of the Closet*, Berkeley, 1990.

Thomas Hardy

DiBattista, M., *First Love*, Chicago, 1991.

Gatrell, S., *Hardy, the Creator*, Oxford, 1988.

Thomas Hardy *(cont'd.)*

Morgan, R., *Cancelled Words*, London, 1992.

Widdowson, P., *Hardy in History*, London, 1989.

A. E. Housman

Bayley, J., *Housman's Poems*, Oxford, 1992.

Graves, R. P., *A. E. Housman*, Oxford, 1981.

Naiditch, P. G., *A. E. Housman at University College*, London, 1988.

James Thomson (B. V.)

Dobell, B., *The Laureate of Pessimism*, New York, 1970.

Kenshur, O. S., *Open Form and the Shape of Ideas*, New York, 1977.

Salt, H. S., *The Life of James Thomson*, New York, 1972.

William Ernest Henley

Connell, J., *W. E. Henley*, New York, 1972.

Cornford, L. C., *William Ernest Henley*, New York, 1972.

Flora, J. M., *William Ernest Henley*, New York, 1970.

Ross, J. D., *Henley and Burns*, New York, 1970.

Francis Thompson

Boardman, B. M., *Between Heaven and Charing Cross*, New Haven, 1988.

Taylor, B., *Francis Thompson*, Boston, 1987.

Ernest Dowson

Longaker, J. M., *Ernest Dowson*, Philadelphia, 1967.

Plarr, V. G., *Ernest Dowson*, Philadelphia, 1976.

Swann, T. B., *Ernest Dowson*, New York, 1965.

Gerard Manley Hopkins

Conti, Camaiora, L., *Gray, Keats, Hopkins*, London, 1985.

Downes, D. A., *Hopkins' Sanctifying Imagination*, Baltimore, 1985.

Gerard Manley Hopkins
(cont'd.)
Gardner, W. H., *Gerard Manley Hopkins*, New Haven, 1975.
Milward, P., *A Commentary on the Sonnets of G. M. Hopkins*, Chicago, 1985.

Lewis Carroll
Clark, B. L., *Reflections of Fantasy*, New York, 1986.
Johnson, C. W., *Philosophy in Literature*, San Francisco, 1992.
Kelly, R. M., *Lewis Carroll*, Boston, 1992.

Charles Stuart Calverley
Scott, P., "From Bon Gaultier to Fly Leaves: Context and Canon in Victorian Parody," *Victorian Poetry*, Autumn, 1988, pp. 249–266.

Edward Lear
Byrom, Thomas, *Nonsense and Wonder*, New York, 1977.
Hark, I. R., *Edward Lear*, Boston, 1982.
Kelen, E., *Mr. Nonsense*, Nashville, 1973.
Noakes, V., *Edward Lear*, London, 1985.

W. S. Gilbert
Fischler, A., *Modified Rapture*, Charlottesville, 1991.
Hayter, C., *Gilbert and Sullivan*, New York, 1987.

George Gissing
Collie, M., *George Gissing*, London, 1985.
Coustillas, P., *Brief Interlude*, Edinburgh, 1987.

Samuel Butler
Holt, L. E., *Samuel Butler*, Boston, 1989.
Jeffers, T. L., *Samuel Butler Revalued*, Philadelphia, 1981.
Norman, R., *Samuel Butler and the Meaning of Chiasmus*, London, 1986.

George Moore
Baldwin, T., *G. E. Moore*, London, 1990.
Levy, P., *Moore*, London, 1989.
Regan, T., *Bloomsbury's Prophet*, Philadelphia, 1986.
Sorensen, R. A., *Blindspots*, Oxford, 1988.

INDEX

325